Preface

前言

This second, bilingual edition of *International Financial Management* with Peking University Press provides a working knowledge of international business finance with applications to real world problems. It is designed not only to introduce the Chinese student to modern finance and new financial instruments, but also to provide a solid foundation for the English reader. This edition has case studies, concept boxes, and exercises. The solutions are provided at the back of the text.

Corporate aspects of international finance are analyzed, especially hedging techniques. The book also aims to help readers understand how managers of international corporations do or should behave. We also examine the mechanics of the foreign exchange market, reviewing spot, forwards, futures, and options—the main tools used to hedge exchange rate risk. The book constructs the building blocks of international finance: (1) interest rate parity, (2) purchasing power parity, and (3) the international Fisher equation. It then turns to international management issues and international financial scams, including Ponzi games. We then lay out the optimal portfolio model in an international setting based upon an investor's degree of risk aversion and the reward—risk ratio. It specifically highlights the role of the exchange rate in portfolio decisions.

My students in international finance at Duke University kindly provided suggestions on the final version of the manuscript. I would specifically like to acknowledge Luyuan Fan, now at JPMorgan, New York, and Yi-wen Zhu, at Goldman Sachs, New York for their valuable contributions.

In recent years, I have been teaching international finance at Hunan University, China, as well as doing joint research with colleagues there. It is exciting to witness China's movement toward free markets and the development of new financial markets and instruments. Futures markets in petroleum were only launched in March 2005, and new options markets in the yuan were hampered by prohibitions on investors selling calls and puts, which are more exposed to loss than buying calls or puts. Since 2006, foreign banks and companies may have full ownership of local operations. Capital transfers still require approval of SAFE, the State Administered Foreign Exchange System. SAFE approved the withdrawn offer of $18.5 billion by CNOOC Ltd. for UNOCAL. The Chinese government is encouraging direct foreign investment and acquisitions, making available the foreign exchange necessary for this and other investments. These investments are often to secure sure supplies of raw materials for production by state enterprises involving petroleum, copper, or other items. The offshore use of the yuan as a settlement currency is increasing, especially for cross border transactions with China.

I owe thanks to Robert Z. Aliber of the Graduate School of Business, University of Chicago, and to Ed Tower, Duke University, who made significant, detailed suggestions on the content and focus of the volume. Robert Langham, Taylor and Francis Books plc, London, made helpful editorial suggestions in the earlier stages of this project. I owe a debt of gratitude is to my thesis advisor at the University of Chicago, Robert A. Mundell, Columbia University, who taught me economics and the fun of learning. Cheng Li, a doctoral student at the University of Miami, translated key concepts, explanations, the table of contents and the index into simplified Chinese. Yi Pan, Duke University, proofread and edited the final manuscript for both substance and style.

I am especially indebted to Yan Zhang, Economics and Finance Editor, Peking University Press for her steadfast encouragement and professional editing. This second edition could not have been accomplished without her able and constant guidance.

The plan of the book is as follows:

• Chapter 1 introduces the topic of international finance by highlighting its main characteristics, in particular currency risk and conversion.

• Chapter 2 begins with the history of international finance and monies, stressing the importance of money as a medium of exchange, a store of value, and a unit of account. Bills of exchange are identified as the source of the first financial securities in foreign currency and the origin of the stock exchanges. The concept of seigniorage, i.e. the printing press, to finance fiscal deficits is highlighted as the source of inflation in several countries.

• Chapter 3 deals with the exchange rate. The foreign exchange market is analyzed, including spot, future, forward, options, and swap markets in foreign exchange. The basic building block for forecasting future exchange rates—interest rate parity—is illustrated as a no-profit arbitrage condition. The bid-ask spread—the difference between the ask and the bid price of foreign exchange dealers—represents the currency dealers' profits, in addition to any commission paid, and as a transaction cost in currency conversion for the firm. Unanticipated foreign exchange risk involves the risk that a subsequent spot rate will deviate from its current forward level. Forwards and foreign exchange swaps are analyzed and laid out as a particularly useful way of hedging long-term and operational exposure in foreign exchange.

- Chapter 4 covers the hedging of foreign exchange risk by the firm. To hedge or not is the first issue addressed, then hedging techniques. If a firm or an individual has a "long" position in say euros, foreign exchange risk is said to be hedged or guarded against by acquiring an opposite, offsetting "short" position in euros. A simple hedge of a million euros of accounts receivable in 90 days could involve the sale of one million euros forward for delivery in 90 days. The firm would no longer be subject to foreign exchange risk: neither unanticipated gains if the euro rises relative to the forward price in dollars or pounds, nor unanticipated losses if the euro declines relative to the forward rate. Chapter 4 also covers contractual hedges: futures, forwards, money market hedges, and options, as well as operational, accounting, and transactional hedging by offsetting cash flows, such as foreign exchange swaps, by the international firm.

- Chapter 5 deals with international financial management issues that confront the multinational firm: transfer pricing, working capital management, international taxation, offshore banking, and international mergers and acquisitions. In addition, the currency conversion of free-cash flows in an international business plan is covered in detail.

- Chapter 6 covers financial scams and swindles, including pyramid schemes, insider trading, accounting malfeasance, and other scams that have surged worldwide in recent years. Partly, the problem seems to be old-fashioned greed, but another culprit seems to be the linking of bonus and options compensation with reported earnings, not necessarily actual earnings.

- Chapter 7 reviews the financial crisis of 2007—2009, stressing the importance of financial leverage, securitization, and moral hazard in precipitating the rapid near-collapse of the US financial system. The US government played a role in triggering the collapse, through Fannie Mae and Freddie Mac promoting, bundling, and guaranteeing low quality, subprime mortgages. The Troubled Asset Relief Program (TARP) rescued the investment banks of Wall Street, but firmly established a moral hazard — "too big to fail."

- An appendix on the time value of money follows with several applications.

Problem sets are also provided at the end of every chapter to give the reader confidence in problem-solving with numerical and conceptual analysis.

Answers to these problems and an index close the book.

I hope you enjoy this volume. My students do and I had fun writing it.

Michael Connolly
Department of Economics
School of Business Administration
University of Miami, Florida, USA

Department of Finance
College of Finance and Statistics
Hunan University
Changsha, People's Republic of China

Contents

Figures   ix

Tables   xiii

Abbreviations   xv

Chapter 1

Features of International

   Finance   1

   Currencies   1

   Accounting rules   2

   Stakeholders   3

   Legal framework   3

   Institutional framework   4

   Language   5

   Taxation   6

   Regulatory framework   7

   Political risk   10

   Intellectual property rights   11

   Conclusion   12

Chapter 2

The History of Money, Finance, and Sei-

   gniorage   14

   Prerequisites of good money   15

   Money and exchange rates   16

   History of monies   17

   Foreign exchange history   23

   Banks and banking   25

   The Federal Reserve System   26

   The international monetary

     institutions   27

   History of the stock exchanges   29

   Conclusion   37

Chapter 3

The Foreign Exchange Market   41

   A floating exchange rate system   42

   A fixed exchange rate system   45

   The Euro—"irrevocably fixed" exchange

     rates   53

   The Chinese yuan   57

   The SWIFT international clearing

     system   60

   Theories of the long-run movement

     of exchange rates   61

   Purchasing power parity   61

   The monetary approach to

     the exchange rate   66

   The IMF's real effective exchange rate   70

   Foreign currency futures

     versus forward contracts   71

   Forwards and futures in commodities   74

   Arbitrage determination of the spot

     and future rates   78

   Exchange rate forecasting   87

   Random investing   89

   Conclusion   103

Chapter 4

Hedging Foreign Exchange Risk   113

   Hedging defined   113

   Credit ratings   116

   Default risk premium   121

   Hedging foreign exchange

     transactions exposure   123

   Related techniques for hedging

     foreign exchange risk   133

Hedging operating exposure   135
Foreign currency swaps   140
Back-to-back (parallel) loans   141
Accounting exposure   142
Financial Accounting Standards Board
    —FASB 52   142
Hedge accounting   143
Trade finance   144
Hedging interest rate exposure   145
Reference rates   146
Forecasting forward interest rates   147
The yield curve   147
A strip of the yield curve   148
Conclusion   154
Appendix: Risk and Insurance   155

Chapter 5
International Financial
Management   167

Capital structure   167
Cross-listing on foreign stock
    exchanges   170
International liquidity and
    market integration   171
Transfer pricing   171
International taxation   175
Working capital management   178
International mergers and
    acquisitions   180
Offshore banking   187
An international business plan:
    the Azteca Café   194
Optimal investment analysis   196
Conclusion   209

Chapter 6
International Financial Scams
and Swindles   221

Pyramids: an international
    perspective   221
Corporate governance failures   231
The Sarbanes-Oxley Act of 2002   237
Lessons learned   256
Conclusion   257

Chapter 7
Financial Leverage, Moral Hazard and
Counterparty Risk: The Financial Crisis
of 2007—2009   261

Financial leverage   262
Securitization   265
Leveraged households   267
The role of the government: Fannie Mae
    and Freddie Mac   268
Rising and falling home equity   269
Strategic default   274
Counter-party risk   280
Leveraged financial
    institutions   281
The bankruptcy of Lehman
    Brothers   283
The macro-economic impact of the
    financial crisis   288
The Volcker Rule   292
The Dodd-Frank Regulatory Bill   295
Conclusion   295

Appendix: The Time Value of Money   300

Solutions to Problems   316

Index   332

中文目录

图形列表　ix

表格列表　xiii

重要缩写词　xv

第1章　国际金融的特征　1
　货币　1
　会计准则　2
　利益相关者　3
　法律框架　3
　制度框架　4
　语言　5
　税收　6
　监管体系　7
　政治风险　10
　知识产权　11
　小结　12

第2章　货币和金融历史　14
　良币的必要条件　15
　货币和汇率　16
　货币的历史　17
　外汇交易的历史　23
　银行和银行业　25
　联邦储备体系　26
　国际货币组织　27
　股票交易的历史　29
　小结　37

第3章　外汇交易市场　41
　浮动汇率制度　42
　固定汇率制度　45
　欧元:不可撤销的固定汇率　53
　中国人民币　57

SWIFT 国际清算系统　60
长期汇率变动理论　61
购买力平价　61
汇率的货币方法　66
IMF 真实有效汇率　70
外汇期货与远期合约　71
商品期货与远期合约　74
即期汇率与远期汇率的无套利决定
　方法　78
汇率预测　87
随机投资　89
小结　103

第4章　外汇风险的套期保值　113
套期保值的定义　113
信用评级　116
违约风险溢价　121
外汇交易风险的套期保值　123
外汇交易风险套期保值的相关
　技术　133
经营风险的套期保值　135
外汇互换　140
背对背(平行)贷款　141
会计风险　142
FASB 52　142
对冲会计法　143
贸易融资　144
利率风险的套期保值　145
相关利率　146
远期利率的预测　147
收益率曲线　147
收益率曲线的剥离　148
小结　154

附录:风险与保险　155

第 5 章　国际金融管理　167
　　资本结构　167
　　在国际证券交易市场交叉上市　170
　　国际流动性与市场一体化　171
　　转移定价　171
　　国际税收　175
　　营运资本管理　178
　　国际并购　180
　　离岸银行业　187
　　国际商务计划:Azteca Café　194
　　最优投资分析　196
　　小结　209

第 6 章　国际金融欺诈与骗局　221
　　金字塔骗局:一个国际视角　221
　　公司治理失效　231
　　2002 年《萨班斯-奥克斯利法案》　237
　　教训　256
　　小结　257

**第 7 章　金融杠杆、道德风险和对手风险:
　　　　　　2007—2009 年的金融危机　261**
　　金融杠杆　262
　　资产证券化　265
　　杠杆化家庭　267
　　政府的角色:房利美和房地美　268
　　房屋所有者权益的上升与下降　269
　　策略违约　274
　　交易对手风险　280
　　杠杆化金融机构　281
　　雷曼兄弟公司的破产　283
　　金融危机的宏观影响　288
　　沃克尔法则　292
　　多德—弗兰克监管法案　295
　　小结　295

附录:货币的时间价值　300
课后习题答案　316
索引　332

Figures

图形列表

2.1 The birth of coinage: Chinese spade monies of the eastern Zhou dynasty 770—256 BC and Ming knife monies, late 5th century BC

2.2 The Lydian Lion Head: 600—575 BC

2.3 The world's first banknote—the Jiaozi of the Song dynasty 1023 AD

2.4 The first European banknote 1661, the riksdalers specie of the Stockholms Banco, Sweden

2.5 The first global money—the Spanish peso or silver dollar

3.1 A floating exchange rate

3.2 Bank profits from the bid-ask spread

3.3 The People's Bank of China buys three million dollars at the lowr intervention rate

3.4 The People's Bank of China sells three million dollars at the upper intervention rate

3.5 The People's Bank of China sells USD

3.6 The People's Bank of China buys USD

3.7 The People's Bank of China sells bonds to neutralize its foreign exchange purchase

3.8 The change in domestic credit, ΔDC, and the change in net foreign assets, ΔFX, of the PBC

3.9 The People's Bank of China buys bonds to neutralize its foreign exchange sale

3.10 Sovereign risk spread over German 10 year sovereigns and the debt to income ratio

3.11 China, the emerging dragon

3.12 Relative purchasing power parity

3.13 Payoff from a short position in gold

3.14 A gain from a short position in gold

3.15 A loss from a short position in gold

3.16 A hedged position in gold

3.17 Covered interest rate parity

3.18 Covered interest arbitrage with a gain

3.19 Uncovered interest arbitrage with a loss

3.20 Triangular foreign exchange arbitrage

3.21 Random investing

3.22 The premium on a foreign exchange call option

3.23 The premium on a foreign exchange put option

3.24 The payoff at maturity from buying a pound call option

3.25 The payoff at maturity from selling a pound call option

3.26 The payoff at maturity from buying a pound put option

3.27 The payoff at maturity from selling a pound put option

4.1 Default risk premium

4.2 A long position in dollars

4.3 A loss on a long position in dollars

4.4 A gain on a long position in dollars

4.5 A forward hedge of a long position in dollars

4.6 A money market hedge of a long position in dollars

4.7 A put option hedge of a long position in dollars

4.8 An unhedged short loss in dollars

4.9 An unhedged short gain in dollars

4.10 A forward purchase of dollars to hedge a short position

4.11 A money market loan of dollars to hedge a short position

4.12 Payoff from buying a call option at the money to hedge a short position

4.13 A collar hedge of accounts receivable in dollars

4.14 A collar hedge of accounts payable in dollars

4.15 An out-of-the-money put option as a partial hedge of a long position

4.16 An out-of-the-money call option as a partial hedge of a short position

4.17 A re-invoicing center

4.18 A natural hedge in dollars

4.19 A foreign exchange swap

4.20 A back-to-back (parallel) loan

4.21 A letter of credit

4.22 The US Treasury yield curve

4.23 An interest rate cap, ignoring the premium paid

4.24 An interest rate cap, including the premium paid

4.25 An interest rate floor, not including the premium

4.26 An interest rate floor, deducting the premium paid

4.27 A collar on an interest payment with equal premium

4.28 A collar on an interest rate receipt with equal premium

4.29 Expected utility with risk aversion

5.1 The weighted average cost of capital and financial leverage

5.2 Transfer pricing

5.3 Abusive transfer pricing

5.4 Working cash balances

5.5 HP acquires 3PAR and suffers the winner's curse

5.6 The winner's curse and synergy

5.7 Offshore banking

5.8 Profit maximization by the firm

5.9 Portfolio diversification and market risk

5.10 The efficient investment frontier

5.11 Capital allocation

5.12 The optimal complete and market portfolios

5.13 A leveraged complete portfolio

5.14   The mutual fund theorem

7.1   The financial crisis of 2008—2009

7.2   The magnification effect of financial leverage on equity gains and losses

7.3   The change in housing prices in the US

7.4   China: Sales price index of residential and commercial buildings in 70 large and medium size cities

7.5   China: Real estate floor space sold

7.6   Optimal strategic default with negative equity

7.7   A credit default swap with no default

7.8   A credit default swap with default

7.9   AIG's default swap insurance to five major Wall Street Banks

7.10   AIG's payments of default swap insurance sold to five major Wall Street banks

7.11   Counterparty risk

7.12   Losses to financial institutions in 2007

7.13   Excess reserves held by US depository institutions

7.14   Total borrowings from the Federal Reserve System

7.15   US GDP growth

7.16   The contributions of consumption and investment expenditure to growth in real GDP

7.17   Annualized quarterly change in GDP for the euro area

7.18   The US economic spending plan of 2009, a consumption smoothing program

A.1   Measuring default risk

Tables

表格列表

2.1 Seigniorage and bond finance by the US Treasury as a percent of GDP

2.2 Negative seigniorage on the US penny and nickel

3.1 Global daily foreign exchange trading in April 2010

3.2 Direct and cross rates in foreign exchange quotations

3.3 The balance sheet of the People's Bank of China

3.4 The Economist's hamburger standard

3.5 Points and outright forward quotations

3.6 European style outright quotations

3.7 Basic arbitrage data

3.8 A five year forecast of the future exchange rate

3.9 Forecasted free cash flows for a UK acquisition in millions of pounds

3.10 Random investment funds

3.11 Direct borrowing rates

3.12 The call and put premium on a foreign exchange option

3.13 Foreign exchange option Greeks

4.1 Valuation of the firm

4.2 Standard and Poor's credit ratings

4.3 Long term sovereign credit ratings by agency

4.4 Treasury spending as a fraction of tax revenues

4.5 US deficits and debt as a fraction of Gross Domestic Product

4.6 Attitudes toward risk

4.7 Fair insurance and risk aversion

5.1 Affiliate located in a high tax jurisdiction

5.2 Affiliate located in a comparable tax jurisdiction

5.3 Affiliate located in a low tax jurisdiction

5.4 Affiliate located in a tax haven

5.5 Foreign Sales Corporations located in a US possessions

5.6 Decentralized cash management

5.7 Centralized cash management

5.8 Standalone values of Firms A and B

5.9 An outright cash acquisition of B by A

5.10 An acquisition of B by A through an incorrect share offer

5.11 An acquisition of B by A through a correct share offer

5.12 An acquisition of B by A through a combination of cash and share offer

5.13 Forecast of the Azteca's free cash flow in new Mexican pesos

5.14 Discounted free cash flow of the Azteca

5. 15   Discounted free cash flow minus existing liabilities of the Azteca

5. 16   A hypothetical complete portfolio

6. 1   A hypothetical Ponzi game with rollover at a quarterly rate of return of 50%

7. 1   Financial leverage of some US tech firms

7. 2   Financial leverage of some industrial manufacturing firms

7. 3   Financial leverage of some financial institutions

7. 4   Rising equity with rising home prices

7. 5   The boom and the bust in Miami's home prices

7. 6   Falling equity with falling home prices

7. 7   China's policies to slow the rise in housing prices

7. 8   Loan to value and financial leverage

7. 9   Bank leverage (Levered Bank, Inc.)

7. 10   Bank leverage and accounting bankruptcy (Levered Bank, Inc.)

7. 11   Residential investment as a share of GDP in the United States: 1999—2009

7. 12   TARP loans to financial and automobile companies

A. 1   Accumulated interest after three years depending on the frequency of interest payments per year

A. 2   The present value of 1,000 dollars paid in year 3 using a discount rate of 5%, depending on the number of conversion periods paying r on P

A. 3   The effective rate of interest depending on the number of conversion payments

A. 4   Accumulated values of an initial payment of $1,000 with continuous versus discrete conversion payments of interest r percent per year paid on P

A. 5   Present values of $1000 paid in each year

A. 6   Present values of free cash flow of $1,000 per year every year for 5 years

A. 7   The internal rate of return

A. 8   The net present value of free cash flow plus terminal value

A. 9   The net present value of a semi-annually paid 5% coupon bond with face value of $1000

A. 10   The net present value of estimated synergies and integration costs

A. 11   The internal rate of return on AT&T's offer to Deutsche Telecom

Abbreviations

重要缩写词

ADR	American depositary receipt
AMEX	American Stock Exchange
AMR	American Airlines Corp.
APA	advanced pricing agreement
BAC	Bank of America, ticker symbol
BFC	British Finance Centre
BIS	Bank for International Settlements
BOA	Bank of America
BSCH	Banco Santander Central Hispano
CAD	covered arbitrage differential
CAOC	China Aviation Oil Corporation
CAOHC	China Aviation Oil Holding Company
CHIPS	Clearing House Interbank Payments System
CDO	Collateralized debt obligation
CSFB	Crédit Suisse First Boston
DJIA	Dow Jones Industrial Average
EDGAR	Electronic Data Gathering and Retrieval
ETF	exchange traded fund
FASB	Financial Accounting Standards Board
FATF	Financial Action Task Force
FCPA	Foreign Corrupt Practices Act
FED	Federal Reserve System
Footsie	Financial Times Stock Exchange
FOREX	foreign exchange
FSC	foreign sales corporation
GAAP	generally accepted accounting principles
GATT	General Agreement on Tariffs and Trade
GKOs	Gosudarstvennye Kratkosrochnye Obligatsii
HLI	highly leveraged institution
IAS	international accounting standard
IBC	international business corporation
IFOC	international financial offshore center

IMF	International Monetary Fund
IPO	initial public offer
IRR	internal rate of return
IRP	interest rate parity
IRS	Internal Revenue Service
L/C	letter of credit
LSE	London Stock Exchange
LTCM	Long Term Capital Management
MBA	mortgage backed asset
MEI	marginal efficiency of investment
MIGA	Multilateral Investment Guarantee Association
NASDAQ	National Association of Securities Dealers Automated Quotations
NCCTs	Non-Cooperative Countries and Territories
NDF	non-deliverable future
NPV	net present value
NYSE	New York Stock Exchange
OECD	Organization for Economic Cooperation and Development
OFC	offshore financial center
OTC	over-the-counter
PPP	purchasing power parity
RER	real effective exchange rate index
RIC	Reuters Instrument Code
S&P	Standard & Poor's
SASAC	State Asset Supervision and Administration Commission
SEC	Securities and Exchange Commission
SIMEX	Singapore International Monetary Exchange
SOES	Small Order Execution System
SOX	Sarbanes-Oxley Act
SSE	Shanghai Stock Exchange
SWIFT	Society for Worldwide Interbank Financial Telecommunications
T-bill	Treasury bill
UAL	United Airlines Corporation
UNCAC	UN Convention Against Corruption
USD	US dollars
WACC	weighted average cost of capital
WTO	World Trade Organization

CHAPTER 1

Features of International Finance 国际金融的特征

In what sense does international finance differ from finance? In fact, there are many.

Currencies

The key distinction between international finance and finance is the exchange rate issue. Issues of valuation, uncertainty about the future exchange rate, its convertibility and transactions costs lead to market segmentation. Consider the important decision to make a foreign acquisition. To value the foreign firm, it is customary to work up an income statement forecasting free cash flow over the next three to five years and estimate a terminal resale value of the acquisition. This is part of due diligence.

When the forecast is in terms of a foreign currency, say the euro, the forward cash flows must then be converted to the home currency, say the dollar, the pound, or the yuan. This task is easy enough using forward rates for the euro up to two years and interest rate parity to forecast the exchange rate through year five. The corresponding conversion of free cash flows is now in home currency for each year, ready to be discounted by the firm's weighted average cost of capital in home currency. If the net present value is positive and higher than alternative investments, the firm may decide to undertake the acquisition.

In doing so, the firm is faced with foreign exchange risk due to unexpected deviations from forecasted exchange rates. This exchange risk takes different forms: transactions risk associated with a specific transaction in foreign exchange, operational risk associated with ongoing operations in the foreign currency, translation risk associated with accounting requirements.

国际金融与金融学的主要差别之一便是不同货币带来的汇率问题。汇率的定价、不确定性、货币的可兑换性问题和外汇的交易成本导致了市场分割。

In addition, reporting requirements are in local currency to the Internal Revenue Service, Inland Revenue, or the Chinese Treasury. In order to hedge exchange risk, there are contractual, operational, and financial hedges, but these add to the costs of risk management of the firm. If done selectively, hedging may lower borrowing costs by reducing the risk of financial distress and bankruptcy.

Accounting rules

影响跨国并购的另一个重要因素是各国会计准则和实务之间的差异。在美国,通用的会计准则是由 FASB 制定实施的美国通用会计准则体系(GAAP),而国际上普遍接受的会计标准是国际会计准则(IAS)。

Another important consideration is the issue of different accounting rules and practices. In the United States, the generally-accepted accounting principles (the GAAP) is used and sanctioned by the Federal Accounting Standards Board. FASB 52 governs currency translation and valuation. Overseas, the standard practice is the international accounting standard (IAS) which depends more on concept and principle than on practice.

In general, reporting and disclosure requirements are higher in the U.S., England, and continental Europe than abroad, particularly when compared to emerging markets. In the U.S., Sarbanes Oxley 2002 (SOX 2002) and Dodd Frank 2010 regulatory bills have significantly increased compliance costs to US firms. SOX 2002 requires the CEO and CFO of publicly listed firms to sign financial and income statements as to their veracity. In principle, this is to reduce accounting fraud in the United States by increasing the liability of officers.

Regulatory Act: The Sarbanes Oxley Act of 2002

Corporate responsibility requires that CEOs and CFOs certify in annual or quarterly reports that:

"the signing officer has reviewed the report; based on the officer's knowledge, the report does not contain any untrue statement of a material fact or omit to state a material fact ... the financial statements, and other financial information included in the report, fairly present in all material respects the financial condition and results of operations of the issuer as of, and for, the periods represented in the report;" It also provides for forfeiture of bonuses and profits as a result of mis-reporting, prohibits insider trades during pension fund blackout periods when the firm suspends the right of more than a majority of participants of pension plans from selling their shares in the company, and provides for "disgorgement" or fair funds for investors whose rights are violated.

While these regulations are a response to the Enron and other corporate scandals, they also raise compliance costs to publicly listed firms. Enron employees were locked into pension plans holding Enron shares, unable to liquidate their pension shares before they became worthless. On the other hand, Enron officers, Kenneth Lay and Jeffrey Skilling sold their shares before the collapse. Europe uses the concept based IAS.

Stakeholders

A related issue is more philosophical; the US firm typically owes its allegiance to its owners, the shareholders. In Europe and elsewhere the firm may have different constituents or stakeholders: the shareholders, management, the government, its unions and its customers. Of course, the government is a majority shareholder in the case of state enterprises. President Dmitry Medvedev of Russia approved a new privatization plan in 2011 reducing the state's participation in 21 enterprises, yet conserving "golden shares" in 6 keeping the government's "right" to veto decisions made by their directors. These six enterprises are the diamond monopoly, Alrosa where the state currently holds 51% of the shares, the largest hydro-electric supplier, Rousguidro, 61% held by the government, Zarouubliejneft foreign drilling and exploration, cereal producer and buyer OZK, and the second largest petroleum company, Rosneft, 75% currently—as of August 5, 2011—controlled by the government. Vladimir Putin, previous president, and candidate in 2012 had implemented several re-nationalizations. Medvedev's argument is that innovation and growth will be higher when the companies are privatized, and will also reduce the fiscal deficit, which was 5% of GDP in 2010. The new plan of privatizations is set for 2017, but is likely to change when Putin is re-elected.

美国企业通常以所有者或股东利益最大化作为经营目标。在欧洲和其他地区,企业可能代表不同委托人的利益,如股东、企业管理人员、政府、工会或顾客。

Legal framework

A number of countries observe Napoleonic rather than Common Law, deriving from the Napoleonic codes which govern business law there. Spain also implanted the Napoleonic codes in most of Latin America. In Islamic countries, interest is prohibited by the Koran, so financial institutions must arrange for profit-sharing with its depositors-owners. As an amendment to the U. S. Securities Act of 1934, the Foreign Corrupt Practices

许多国家遵循拿破仑法律体系,而非英美的普通法体系。

Act of 1997 (FCPA 1977), prohibits making payments to foreign officials for the purpose of securing contracts or licenses, influencing decisions, evading regulations and law, and obtaining business, retaining business, or directing business to any person. If a director, officer, or shareholder of the firm either knows or should know that a payment is being made as a bribe or kickback to favorably influence a decision, it is illegal and subject to civil penalties up to $100,000 and imprisonment for not more than 5 years, or both. There is an exception for routine governmental action "to expedite or to secure the performance of a routine governmental action by a foreign official." This is known as *grease* money, which is not prohibited unless it is so by the local laws.

If a grease payment is not large and is made to expedite governmental action to grant a license to operate a bank that is granted to everyone qualifying for a bank license, there may be no problem. If the payments are made simply to expedite the request, they are not illegal under FCPA 1977. If the official has some discretion, and few applicants are approved, the payment would be illegal. The Organization for Economic Cooperation and Development (OECD) established in February 1999 a Convention Against Bribery of Foreign Public Officials in International Business. The Convention makes it a crime to offer, promise or give a bribe to a foreign public official in order to obtain or retain international business deals. In addition, The UN Convention Against Corruption (UNCAC) is an international treaty that was signed by 113 countries since its launching in December 2003.

Institutional framework

毫无疑问,腐败在每个国家都或多或少地存在。当腐败已经成为实践中制度化的存在时,反腐败的法律已经无能为力。

There is no question that corruption exists everywhere to some degree. Cleptocracies misappropriate profits and wealth, thereby discouraging enterprise and thrift. Instead, bribery and malfeasance are rewarded. It matters little to have laws against corruption, when it is institutionalized in practice. To combat bribery, on November 21, 1997, OECD Member countries and five non-member countries, Argentina, Brazil, Bulgaria, Chile and the Slovak Republic, adopted a Convention on Combating Bribery of Foreign Public Officials in International Business Transactions. The convention was signed in Paris on December 17, 1997. However, Peter Eigen, Chairman of Transparency International puts it this way (January 20, 2001):

"The scale of bribe-paying by international corporations in the developing countries of the world is massive. Actions by the majority of governments of the leading industrial countries to curb international corruption are modest. The results include growing poverty in poor countries, persistent undermining of the institutions of democracy, and mounting distortions in fair international commerce."

Source: www.transparency.org.

Much of the last standby loan to Russia before their sovereign default in 1998 is rumored to have been deposited by Russian officials in an off-shore bank in Jersey, which honors banking secrecy and has no income taxes. "The IMF should learn a lesson from the past five years," the former official, Boris Fyodor, said, referring to the International Monetary Fund. "The IMF was pretending that it was seeing a lot of reforms in Russia. Russia was pretending to conduct reforms. The Western taxpayer was paying for it." (October 1, 1998, I. M. F. Urged by Russian Not to Give More Aid, by Michael R. Gordon, Moscow, © 1998 *The New York Times*). However, "The IMF was surprised by last year's discovery that the central bank was linked to an offshore investment company in the Channel Island of Jersey and that the (Russian Central) bank had misreported its asset levels to the fund. The offshore company, Fimaco, was acquired by a subsidiary of the central bank during Gerashchenko's previous tenure as central bank chief, although the Fimaco operations that have drawn the most attention to date fell during the 1994—1998 period when he did not head the central bank. (Then U. S. Secretary of the Treasury, Larry) Summers continued his public warnings to Russia on Sunday, repeating the line he took at the opening of a congressional inquiry last week into corruption, money-laundering and the still-unsubstantiated charges that IMF funds had been illegally diverted." (Russia Hotly Protests Audits Demanded by I. M. F. for Loans, by David E. Sanger, September 27, 1999, Washington © 1999 *The New York Times*.)

Language

Language barriers can be an important obstacle or alternatively, an advantage in conducting business abroad. Banco Santander Central Hispano of Madrid is now the largest bank in Latin America. It is closely followed by Bilbao Viscaya of Barcelona in size of assets. No doubt the language, cultural similarities, and the use of Napoleonic Law explain, in part, the comparative advantage of Spanish banks in Latin America. Also, their long banking tradition serves them well in emerging markets in Latin America.

Taxation

不同国家的税率不同,这也是造成国际金融与金融学差别的重要原因。

International taxation varies from country to country, ranging from zero corporate income taxes and zero personal income tax in some tax havens to 35% in the United States, the highest corporate income tax reported by Deloitte, *Corporate Taxes: A Worldwide Summary 2011*. When profits of a US company are repatriated, they are converted into dollars and the U. S. corporate tax rate of up to 35% is applied. If the foreign tax rate is lower, say 20%, the company receives a tax credit of 20% paid to the foreign government, and then pays the remaining 15% to the U. S. Treasury. If it pays over 35% in corporate taxes, the firm will get a full offset up to 35%, its marginal tax rate on U. S. earnings, as well as tax credits, possible deferred or for other branches, on the additional excess taxes. In some cases, companies are able to transfer profits out of the U. S. to shell corporations in tax havens to escape taxes by transfer pricing. This is not in principle a legal practice if done solely for the purpose of evading taxes.

FYI: OECD Corporate Tax Rates 2011

OECD member countries Corporate Tax Rates 2011

Country	Rate(percent)	Country	Rate(percent)
Australia	30%	Japan	30
Austria	25	Korea	22
Belgium	33	Luxembourg	26
Canada	26.5/32.5	Mexico	30
Chile	20	Netherlands	21
Czech Republic	19	New Zealand	28
Denmark	25	Norway	28
Estonia	21	Poland	19
Finland	26	Portugal	25
France	33.3	Slovak Republic	19
Germany	30/33	Slovenia	20
Greece	20/24	Spain	30
Hungary	10/19	Sweden	26.3
Iceland	20	Switzerland	8.6/30.5
Ireland	12.5	Turkey	20
Israel	24	United Kingdom	26
Italy	27.5	United States	35

Note: low/high.

Source: Deloitte, 2011.

Corporate tax rates in Asia are generally lower, but not so low as in tax havens at zero percent.

FYI: Asian, and Tax Haven Corporate Tax Rates 2011

Asia		Tax Havens	
Cambodia	25%	Andorra	0
China	25	Anguila	0
Hong Kong(SAR)	16.5	Bahrain	0
Indonesia	25	Bahamas	0
Laos	35	Bermuda	0
Myanmar	30	British Virgin Islands	0
Thailand	30	Cayman Islands	0
Vietnam	25	Jersey	0
Singapore	17	Isle of Man	0
		Maldives	0
Other Asia		Moldova	0
Bangladesh	27.5%	Palau	0
India	30	Vanuatu	0
Pakistan	35	Wallis & Fortuna	0

Source: Deloitte 2011.

Regulatory framework

In the United States, the U.S. Securities and Exchange Commission (SEC) regulates the major exchanges and securities dealers. "The primary mission of the U.S. Securities and Exchange Commission is to protect investors and maintain the integrity of the securities markets. ... The laws and rules that govern the securities industry in the United States derive from a simple and straightforward concept: all investors, whether large institutions or private individuals, should have access to certain basic facts about an investment prior to buying it. To achieve this, the SEC requires public companies to disclose meaningful financial and other information to the public, which provides a common pool of knowledge for all investors to use to judge for themselves if a company's securities are a good investment. The SEC also oversees other key participants in the securities world. ... Typical infractions include insider trading, accounting fraud, and providing false or misleading information about securities and the com-

在美国,美国证券交易委员会(SEC)是监管证券市场参与者的主要机构。虽然新兴市场也强调对交易所、公司、证券交易者的监管,但许多国家的监管并没有被严格执行。

panies that issue them. ... The SEC offers the public ... the EDGAR database of disclosure documents that public companies are required to file with the Commission. " (www. sec. gov, April 30, 2001.) While overseas exchanges, firms, and securities dealers are also subject to scrutiny, in emerging markets many of these are recent and the same disclosure and transparency requirements do not apply. Interestingly, the SEC was created during the great depression (1929—1937), precipitated by the October 1929 stock market crash where half of the $50 billion in new securities offered during the 1920s became worthless. Purchases on margin represented over 10% of the market. The main purposes of the security and exchange law of 1933 can be reduced to two common-sense notions:

 • Companies publicly offering securities for investment dollars must tell the public the truth about their businesses, the securities they are selling, and the risks involved in investing.

 • People who sell and trade securities — brokers, dealers, and exchanges — must treat investors fairly and honestly, putting investors' interests first. (www. sec. gov, April 30, 2001.)

 U. S. publicly listed companies' income statements and balance sheets can be found on the EDGAR database of corporate filings: Here is a lexicon for some of the common filings by publicly traded companies at www. sec. gov.

登录网址 www. sec. gov, 选择"search for company filings"或者"Quick ED-GAR Tutorial"来获取美国上市公司的资产负债表信息。

FYI: The EDGAR database of corporate filings (www. sec. gov)

10K	The official version of a company's annual report, with a comprehensive overview of the business.
10Q	An abridged version of the 10K, filed quarterly for the first three quarters of a company's fiscal year.
8K	If anything significant happens that should be reported before the next 10K or 10Q rolls around, the company files one of these.
12b-25	Request for a deadline extension to file a required report, like a 10K or 10Q. When the late report is ultimately filed, NT is appended to the report's name.
S1	Basic registration form for new securities, most often initial or secondary public offerings. Variants with higher numbers are used for registrations connected with mergers, employee stock plans and real estate investment trusts (REITs).

F6	Foreign companies use similar forms beginning with F; for example, F6 for American Depository Receipts.
Proxy statement	Information and ballot materials for shareholder votes, including election of directors and approval of mergers and acquisitions when required.
Forms 3, 4 and 5	Directors, officers and owners of more than 10 percent of a company's stock report their initial purchases on Form 3 and subsequent purchases or sales on Form 4; they file an annual statement of their holdings on Form 5.

Source: *New York Times*, Sunday June 21, 1998, www. edgar. gov.

The Sarbanes Oxley Act of 2002 in the United States provided for an independent accounting oversight board, independent auditors, corporate responsibility rules, enhanced financial disclosure, regulations on analyst conflict of interest, and increased criminal and civil penalties for executive and accounting fraud. Many of the enhanced penalties are being served in jail and significant fines and disgorgement penalties have been raised.

This did not, however, solve the problem since the Dodd-Frank Financial Regulation bill (The **Dodd-Frank Wall Street Reform and Consumer Protection Act** was signed into law by President Barack Obama on July 21, 2010), following the 2007—2010 financial collapse and economic recession in the United States. In "A New Foundation Outline", the Administration proposed:

The consolidation of regulatory agencies, elimination of the national thrift charter, and new oversight council to evaluate systemic risk;

Regulatory Act: The Dodd-Frank Act of 2009

1. Comprehensive regulation of financial markets, including increased transparency of derivatives (bringing them onto exchanges);
2. Consumer protection reforms including a new consumer protection agency and uniform standards for "plain vanilla" products as well as strengthened investor protection;
3. Tools for financial crises, including a "resolution regime" complementing the existing *Federal Deposit Insurance Corporation* (FDIC) authority to allow for orderly winding down of bankrupt firms, and including a proposal that the Federal Reserve (the "Fed") receive authorization from the Treasury for extensions of credit in "unusual or exigent circumstances";

> 4. Various measures aimed at increasing international standards and co-operation, including in this section were proposals related to improved accounting and tightened regulation of credit rating agencies.
>
> 5. The Volcker rule to separate commercial banking and proprietary trading by investment banks was added in January 2010.
>
> Source: *A New Foundation: rebuilding financial supervision and regulation*, US Congress, Washington, D.C., 2009.

It remains to be seen if the proposed benefits of increased transparency and no more "too big to fail" will outweigh the increased regulatory costs of compliance to the financial industry. There is always the problem of "regulatory capture," where those that are regulated, capture the regulators by more than grease money.

Political risk

政治风险（Political Risk）：由于意料之外的政策变化导致企业的海外分公司遭受经济损失的风险。

Political risk refers to economic exposure to unanticipated changes in governmental policy that affect the earnings and value of your affiliate or subsidiary. Unanticipated nationalization would be an extreme example. The growing global membership in the WTO/GATT has significantly reduced political risk as a signatory nation must adhere to Article III of the GATT, National Treatment on Internal Taxation and Regulation (see Chapter 5). National Treatment requires that a country adhering to the GATT apply the same internal taxes and regulations to foreign firms as it does to national firms. Consequently, a government cannot levy a 25% corporate income tax on national firms and a 35% rate on foreign firms. Of course, in practice informal taxes may be solicited as "fees" from corrupt officials. Even nationalization is possible when a populist government unexpectedly comes to power. The foreign oil companies in Venezuela are facing implicit nationalization by the Hugo Chávez regime through governmental decrees and "purchases" tantamount to nationalization.

The purchases are often done in Venezuelan bolivars at the official rate, thus substantially reducing the compensation for nationalization:

In the News: Political risk in Venezuela

Hugo Chávez, the president of Venezuela, "has ordered the confiscation of 717,000 acres from a British company amid a disagreement over compensation for earlier seizures of ranchland from the firm. Chávez announced the latest takeover after saying that Venezuela refuses to pay compensation in foreign currency to Agropecuaria Flora, a local subsidiary of Britain's Vestey Group. Chávez said the company had demanded the government pay it in dollars for the previous expropriation of tens of thousands of acres. But the government insists in paying in bolivars, Venezuela's currency. It is difficult for foreign companies operating in Venezuela to repatriate profits and other income in bolivars because of foreign currency controls in the South American country."

Source: "Hugo Chávez orders seizure of British company's land for Venezuelan state," AP Caracas, *guardian. co. uk*, Sunday 30 October 2011.

Chavez also imposes price controls, so that a major CEO, Lorenzo Mendoza, the owner of Empresas Polar SA, Venezuela's largest privately held company, complains that Venezuela is "drowning under regulations." (*Bloomberg*, 11/6/2011)

A subsidiary of the World Bank, the Multilateral Investment Guarantee Association (MIGA), provides insurance against investment risk in emerging markets.

Intellectual property rights

Software code, Madonna's latest song, Microsoft's latest Windows operating system, Rolex watches, Lacoste shirts are counterfeited worldwide on a regular basis. In some instances, the copying and manufacture of pharmaceuticals is perfectly legal in the home country, but is prohibited by the GATT/WTO articles of agreement. The Software association publishes a blacklist of countries that pirate the most. Acceding to the WTO requires the signatory country to respect international patents, trademarks and brands. In Latin America, Brazil seems to be the greatest culprit. In Asia, China is taking strong steps to enforce intellectual property rights since it acceded to the GATT/WTO in December 2001. In the smart phone industry, Apple and Samsung are pursuing litigation to prevent copying of intellectual property rights. Kodak, short of liquidity, is selling its patents to earn cash flow. Google bought Motorola Mobility in order to acquire patents to avoid patent litigation. International property rights are extremely valuable in encouraging innovation and spreading it worldwide, especially in our global market connected by the internet.

Trade Related Intellectual Property Rights (TRIPS) were agreed upon in the Final Act of the Uruguay Round of Multilateral Trade Negotiations, April 1994 of the World Trade Organization. A country which has acceded to the WTO must respect patents, trademarks, copyright, and other intellectual property rights. In addition, industrial designs, software programs, and media and inventions of products or processes are protected for 20 years. That means the owners of protected designs can prevent the manufacture, sale or importation of articles bearing or importing a design that is counterfeit—a copy of the protected design.

与贸易有关的知识产权协定(TRIPS):该协定规定了知识产权的保护范围,具体来说,它包括版权及相关权、商标、地域标识、工业品外观设计、专利、集成电路布图设计、未公开的信息等七种知识产权。

Conclusion

International finance involves currency conversion and foreign exchange risk issues. In addition, international taxation, the legal framework, and regulation differ across countries. Most countries have acceded to the GATT/WTO, so are required to extend national treatment to foreign banks and financial institutions, including insurance companies. China acceded to the WTO in December 2001, thus celebrating its tenth anniversary of accession in December 2011. Capital market integration equalizes the risk-adjusted rates of return worldwide, thereby increasing global rates of return and economic growth. Corruption remains a crucial issue in global markets: it is a brake on economic growth and foreign direct investment. Business and finance practices vary widely from country to country. The US dollar is still the world's reserve and settlement currency, but the yuan is taking cautious steps, as if in Deng Xiaoping's words "crossing the river by groping the stones," in establishing offshore markets for the yuan for clearance in settlements and holding as a reserve asset.

Questions and problems

1.1   Suppose there were a single world currency, such as gold, that each country could produce and mint. Would there be any need to study international finance?

1.2 What is the purpose of the SEC requiring publicly listed firms to disclose earnings and the financial condition of the firm in its 10Q and 10K forms?

1.3 What is the purpose the the SOX 2002 act requiring the CEO and the DFO to sign the income and balance sheets as to be correct to the best of their knowledge?

1.4 Why is it that hard currencies, such as gold or silver coins, tend to produce less inflation than fiat or paper monies?

1.5 Why would so many US firms incorporate affiliates in Ireland and not repatriate earnings?

References and suggested reading

Bailay, Rasul (May 16, 2001), "A Ban on Forward Trading Roils Bombay Share Market," *The Wall Street Journal*: A19.

BusinessWeek (February 19, 2001), "Kim's Fall from Grace: Inside Daewoo's Fraud Scandal,": 50—51.

Finance & Development (June 2000), The International Monetary Fund, Washington, D. C.

Fritch, Peter (May 18, 2001), "Sanborns Official Bought CompUSA Stake Before Buyout," *The Wall Street Journal* Friday: A17.

Gordon, Michael R. (October 1, 1998), "I. M. F. Urged by Russian Not to Give More Aid," *The New York Times*.

Leggett, Karby (May 30, 2001), "Lawsuits Flood China's Securities Industry: Shareholders Allege Rife Manipulation," *The Wall Street Journal*: C1.

Luo, Yadong, *Guanxi and Business*, World Scientific, 2nd ed. February 2007.

Sanger, David E. (September 27, 1999), "Russia Hotly Protests Audits Demanded by I. M. F. for Loans," *The New York Times*.

Deloitte, "Worldwide Corporate Tax Rates 2011," www. deloitte. com.

货币和金
融历史

CHAPTER 2

The History of Money, Finance, and Seigniorage

Money serves three important roles in an economy. It is a **unit of account**, a **medium of exchange**, and a **store of value**. As a medium of exchange, money avoids barter of one good for another. Barter, where individuals trade goods, requires a double coincidence of wants. You have a bicycle, but want an iPad, and someone you run into in the market has an iPad and wants a bicycle. When you meet by coincidence, you might exchange the goods. This is called barter, countertrade, or bilateral clearing: trade without a medium of exchange.

In the absence of a stable medium of exchange, countertrade flourishes, bringing oranges from Brazil in exchange for cotton from Uzbekistan or wheat from Kazakhstan. Indeed, Minnesota's Cargill in the US is one of the largest firms engaging in countertrade worldwide. In the newly independent states, the ruble was unstable, losing value over 20% a month, so that half of the trades made in the early and mid-1990s involved bilateral clearing and barter. It is still done, but using a medium of exchange—a hard currency—is far more efficient. A double coincidence of wants is not necessary. If you want an iPad, you take cash to the store and buy it. If you want a bicycle, you can pay cash—or nowadays, use a debit card or a revolving credit card, which involves finance.

Money facilitates exchange. It also provides a unit of account—a yardstick by which we measure the value of goods, assets and foreign currencies. When there is high inflation, money loses its effectiveness both as a yardstick of value and as a medium of exchange. The seller is uncertain about the real amount that will be paid upon delivery since high inflation usually means unstable inflation rates. When a contract calls for payment in thirty days, yet there is 20% inflation in the month, the seller receives

20% less in real value. If the rate of inflation unexpectedly accelerates to 40%, the seller receives 40% less, but if it slows to 10%, the receipt is only 10% less. High inflation sometimes moves economies to indexing for inflation. This reduces the resistance to inflation and makes stopping it more difficult. As a store of value, money is replaced by interest-yielding assets, foreign currency, or durables that rise in value along with inflation.

When the peso rapidly falls in value in Latin America, individuals substitute a more stable currency which they hold as a store of value, medium of exchange, and a stable unit of account. Informal **dollarization** takes place as in Argentina and Peru. When the home currency becomes worthless as a medium of exchange, countries occasionally abolish it and formally adopt another currency as their own. In 2000, Ecuador formally adopted the dollar, abolishing the sucre.

美元化（Dollarization）：是指作为一种政策，一国或经济体的政府让美元取代自己的货币并最终自动放弃货币或金融主权的行动。

Prerequisites of good money

A hard currency, such as gold or silver, costs resources to make. The resource cost ensures that too much money will not be produced, thereby checking inflation. If there is inflation, the intrinsic value of the metal in the coin may surpass its face value as money. At that point, the coins are melted down, thus stopping growth in the money supply. The difference between a coin's value as money and the cost to mint it is called **seigniorage** or mint profits. For example, a penny has one cent as its value as money, yet it costs over a penny to produce it. The cost of materials—zinc and copper—is 0.8 cents, while the manufacturing cost is 0.6 cents. The mint costs are thus 1.4 cents. Consequently, seigniorage is negative, −0.4 cents on a penny. However, consider a $100 bill. To make it difficult to counterfeit, its design requires high quality linen with specks, many colored inks and watermarks, yet the marginal cost of an extra $100 banknote is only about 12 cents. However, its value as money is $100. Seigniorage or mint profits are therefore $99.88. It is no wonder that the $100 bill is the banknote that attracts the most counterfeiters. By law, only the realm can strike coinage. That is, a sovereign country enjoys the monopoly issue of the national currency. It consequently enjoys also the seigniorage profits associated with the issue of currency. The US Treasury benefits from the world reserve status of the dollar and its use as a substitute money around the world. It collects seigniorage from the use of the dollar as a store of value and medium of exchange in other countries. Approximately half of the printed US 100 dollar bills are held abroad. Ecuado-

铸币税（Seigniorage）：硬币作为货币的价值与铸造它所耗费成本的差额，被称为铸币税或铸币利润。

rians, for example, ship coffee and shrimp to the US to earn the $100 bill.

To avoid inflation, the Charter of central banks usually establishes the independence of the Central Bank from the Treasury. That way, the Treasury cannot simply order the Central Bank to purchase its bonds in exchange for the issue of new money, i. e. the printing press, to finance its deficits. However, central bank independence is not always observed.

As a medium of exchange, a good money must be divisible, even down to a penny. This allows a near continuum of prices to be settled upon rather than discrete price increments or the exchange of money plus some candy or gum, as has been the case in Italy in bygone days. It is a nickels or dimes problem. A ten dollar bill is divisible into two fives, a five into five ones, a one into twenty nickels, ten dimes, four quarters, or 100 pennies. This divisibility criterion is important to facilitate transactions. Cigarettes have been used in exchange in prisoner of war camps, as well as script that signify money. The U. K. shilling being worth 12 pence and 20 shillings equal to one pound made for an awkward division and became obsolete with decimalization on February 15, 1971.

不兑现纸币（Fiat money）：由政府发行的不能兑换成黄金或白银的纸币。它的目的在于节省采掘金银带来的成本。

Fiat money, paper money not exchangeable for a commodity, such as silver—came about to save on the mint costs of mining gold and silver. It also is easier to change denominations and carry around paper money rather than heavy coin. The first paper money was issued in China during the 11th century, around 1023. Seigniorage is greater with paper money than coin. In some countries, such as Argentina in the early 2001, protestors wore signs in protest of "No mas papel pintado" or "No more painted paper" to voice their opposition to the over-issue of money, the freezing and confiscation of bank accounts, and the ensuing inflation. It is always tempting for government to finance a deficit. The broader the currency zone of a money, and the fewer the transactions costs of conversion, the more useful it is. The use of the U. S. dollar in the fifty US states and the euro in 12 European countries makes the liquidity of these currencies greater. Stable monetary policy is the key to having a currency substituted for those that depreciate rapidly in value. Price stability in a currency increases the zones that the particular money is used in. Fiscal convergence within the same monetary zone is also proving to be a necessary condition to avoid financial crises such as those occurring in Europe.

Money and exchange rates

Great central banks, such as the Bank of England and the Banque de

France, had gold windows where they bought and sold gold at a fixed currency price in the 19th century. In doing so, their currency rates were fixed. For example, if the Bank of England sets ten pounds per ounce of gold as the buy/sell rate and the Banque of France 100 francs, the equilibrium exchange rate is set at 100 francs per 10 pounds or 10 francs a pound.

Arbitrage in gold kept the exchange rates within a narrow band of **gold points**. Let's say the exchange rate falls to 9.5 francs a pound. A gold arbitrageur purchases 10 pounds for 95 francs, presents the 10 pounds to the Bank of England gold window in exchange for an ounce of gold. The arbitrageur then insures and ships the gold to the Banque de France, selling it for 100 francs, pocketing 5 francs less insurance and shipping as profits. This gold arbitrage kept the exchange rates within narrow margins known as gold points, the points at which profitable gold arbitrage took place. Consequently, countries that were on the gold standard had fixed exchange rates between themselves.

黄金输送点（Gold Points）：对于黄金的套利使得汇率在黄金输送点确定的狭窄范围内波动。

Similarly, countries in Asia were on the silver standard so that their currencies were pegged to one another and had corresponding silver points. However, since there was usually no fixed relationship between the price of gold and silver, China, a silver standard country, floated its exchange rate with respect to the gold standard currencies. The silver depreciation kept Chinese exports up during the great depression in the West until 1934, when the US passed the Silver Purchase Act to monetize silver at a significantly higher price. The implicit Chinese revaluation of 25% destroyed their export and import competing industries, sending them into a major recession that caused famine in the countryside (see Milton Friedman, 1992).

History of monies

The first money originated in China during the Shang dynasty from the 13th to the 12th century BC. It was in shell form, cowls connected by string, bone, and copper objects shaped in the form of grain or shells. From 770 to 256 BC, mostly in the later Zhou dynasty, bronze and copper coins in the shapes of small spades, chisels, hoes and knives were used in place of the articles themselves as hard-bodied money in some of the warring states. Figure 2.1 illustrates the Chinese spade monies of the eastern Zhou dynasty and the Ming knife monies.

历史上第一枚货币出现在公元前 13 世纪到公元前 12 世纪的中国商朝。

Figure 2.1   The birth of coinage: Chinese spade monies of the eastern Zhou dynasty 770—256 BC and Ming knife monies, late 5th century BC

It is legitimate to regard Chinese tool coins as the first coinage since they were used as a medium of exchange, unit of account, and store of value. Glyn Davies (1994) believes that Chinese spade, hoe, and knife money preceded Lydian coinage of 600—575 BC but refers to them as "quasi-coins." Many Zhou period coins have characters indicating denomination in liangs, the Chinese ounce or *tael*, but they weigh only about 77% of their official value, indicating a seigniorage system where coins are made to a weight below their circulating value. The seigniorage profits offset the cost of minting, showing a small profit to the minting authority.

The earliest known European coins appeared in Lydia, now Asia Minor, part of Turkey, circa 600—575 BC. These early coins were made of electrum, a precious alloy of gold and silver that: " ... consists of about 54 percent gold, 44 percent silver, 2 percent copper, and trace amounts of iron and lead. " Figure 2.2 illustrates the Lydian Lion Head, an early electrum coin.

最早所知的欧洲硬币出现在大约公元前 600 年到公元前 575 年的利迪亚古国(现在小亚细亚和土耳其的一部分)。它是由琥珀制成的。

Figure 2.2   The Lydian Lion Head: 600—575 BC

Source: "A Case for the World's First Coin: The Lydian Lion", http://rg. ancients. info/lion.

The electrum coins were used to finance transactions between City States based on their weight. Greek coinage followed. The first bronze coins did not appear in Europe until the fifth century BC. Alexander the Great introduced uniform coinage to all the territories he conquered. He confiscated the gold and silver treasuries in these countries and minted coins from them. At this time, the Romans were developing their own metal monies. The Romans reduced the metal content of their coins, making them lighter, but maintaining the same value as money. The government saved precious metals in this way to meet its debts by making greater seigniorage profits: the difference between value as money and mint costs.

The silver penny was first introduced around AD 760 in Britain. Following the Norman invasion in 1066, William the Conqueror continued to mint the Saxon pennies. He introduced the "sterling silver" standard. Silver was the coin of England from the Norman invasion until 1920. The gold sovereign appeared circa 1500. It was called a sovereign because the coin bore the picture of Henry VII on the royal throne. It was minted until the outbreak of World War I.

Jiaozi, the first uniform paper money in the world, was printed in 1023 AD by the Song dynasty. Later dynasties issued paper money, but most were over reliant on seigniorage—the printing press—to finance their expenditures. Hyperinflation resulted. Eventually, even the government would not accept paper money in payment of taxes. Round copper and bronze coins replaced paper, but lost their worth due to ease of production and widespread counterfeiting. One ounce silver ingots, called *taels* meaning one ounce, supplanted paper and copper money since silver was a better asset not subject to ease of coining. It was also a good international medium of exchange, used in trade payments. Figure 2.3 illustrates the world's first banknote, the Song dynasty's Jiaozi.

中国的宋朝发明了世界上第一张纸币——"交子"。

In 1661, the first European bank note appeared in Sweden. The Swedish riksdaler banknote is illustrated in Figure 2.4. Before the end of the 17th century, bank notes were being printed and issued in England. London goldsmiths originated the bank note when they began to act as bankers. People deposited gold with them for safe keeping, and the goldsmiths would give them a receipt. The words "or bearer" were added after the name of the depositor in 1670. This meant that the goldsmith would deliver metallic money to the person who presented the note for redemption; thus the notes were used as money.

Figure 2.3 The world's first banknote—the Jiaozi of the Song dynasty 1023 AD

Figure 2.4 The first European banknote 1661, the riksdalers specie of the Stockholms Banço, Sweden

January 30, 1666 note

Johan Palmstruch, founder and director of the Stockholms Banco obtained a Royal Decree to print banknotes in 1661, agreeing to share the profits of the bank with the Crown. However, overissue of the new banknotes was a problem. When presented in 1664 for redemption in terms of copper coins, redemption was refused and the bank was taken over by the government.

The first global money: the Spanish peso 1497 to the 1900s

1497 年到 19 世纪的西班牙比索是世界上第一种世界货币。

The Spanish peso or dollar, contained 0.821791 troy ounce (25.560 grams) pure silver and was also used as domestic money in China, having been minted in the new world in Mexico, Peru, and Spain, then used in commerce. The so called "pieces of eight," referred to their value of 8 *reales*. The Spanish dollars were manufactured in Mexico and Peru, as well as in Sevilla, and transported in bulk back to Spain to pay for wars and commerce. The Manila Galleon shipped Mexican silver to Manila, where it would be exchanged for Chinese goods, since silver was the only foreign commodity money Chinese merchants would accept. Spanish dollars were often stamped with Chinese characters known as "chop marks", indicating that the coin had been assayed by a respected merchant and determined to be genuine. Figure 2.5 shows a 1739 Spanish silver dollar.

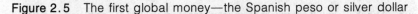

Figure 2.5 The first global money—the Spanish peso or silver dollar

The use of *taels* reduced significantly the risk of inflation in terms of the silver price of goods because it was widely hoarded as a store of wealth. The weight of a piece of silver determined its value as money, so it had the desired divisibility property. Furthermore, silver was also held in

the form of jewelry, thereby reducing its supply as a medium of exchange. Under the silver standard, China experienced 300 years of price stability (Ray Huang, 1974). Paper money was used again from 1875 to 1908 during the Qing dynasty, the last feudal dynasty in China. It was colorful and ornate and difficult to counterfeit, resembling modern banknotes.

When the first pilgrims arrived in America they found the Indians using strings of shell beads, cowls or "wampum" as money. The colonists traded goods with the Indians, but also adopted wampum as money. The Spanish dollar coming from Mexico was held as a store of value and used as a medium of exchange for large transactions. The colonists met their everyday needs by paying with sugar and tobacco—commodity monies. Bricks of salt were used elsewhere as commodity money.

The American colonists requested a supply of coins from Britain, but the British Treasury declined: So they set up the first mint in Boston, producing shillings, sixpences, and three-penny pieces in 1652. Each state issued its own money, both paper and coin, until the Civil War of 1861—1865, when both the greenback and the confederate dollar were newly printed to finance the war efforts of the North and the South respectively. At the end of the war, the confederate currency was worthless and the greenback dollar evolved into the modern currency used in the United States. It still has a green back, but is smaller in size than the original issue. The Federal Reserve System was created in 1913, splitting seigniorage profits between the 12 districts.

The latest prominent currency is the euro, created by the Maastricht Treaty whereby Western European countries increased integration of their economies by adopting a common currency. On January 1, 1999, the exchange rates of the existing currencies were irrevocably set and the euro was introduced as a legal currency. Euro area member states began implementing a common monetary policy, but diverged in fiscal policy, debt and borrowing. The eleven existing currencies of the participating member states were converted to euros and withdrawn from circulation January 1, 2002. Greece joined on January 1, 2001, though it required accounting smoke and mirrors. Now 12 member states share the new euro banknotes and coins, but the European sovereign debt crisis of 2011 and 2012 is putting the euro in jeopardy. It is proving difficult to reform spending greater than tax revenues, thus putting no upper bound on debt in countries like Greece. A structured default of Greek sovereigns is taking place, but even then the fiscal deficit must be eliminated.

Foreign exchange history

Foreign trade was initially conducted by barter or with the currency of the importing country acting as the medium of exchange. Foreign merchants accepted payment in local currency and spent the proceeds on the purchase of local goods. Foreign exchange emerged when uniform metallic coins bearing the marks and seal of a banker or merchant came into being. Having gold, silver and copper as the units of account facilitated valuation and conversion, but did lead to some counterfeiting, as modern monies do.

Bills of exchange made their appearance in Babylonia and Assyria centuries before the invention of marked coinage in Lydia. The bill of exchange was used primarily in international trade, and is a written order by one person to pay another a specific sum on a specific date in the future. Since carrying large amounts of coins was risky, bills of exchange were used in order to facilitate currency and trade transactions. The text of some bills of exchange indicates that payment was made in locations other than those of issue. The bill of exchange allowed trade to take place without the use of coinage, a precursor of the modern letter of credit (L/C). Furthermore, the bills were traded as financial instruments in trade fairs. They were discounted and converted into foreign units of account. The trade fairs were of the precursors of modern stock and foreign exchanges.

The first semblance of foreign exchange trading consisted of meeting places in commercial centers. The discrepancies in the relative values of metals were exploited by foreign merchants when choosing their means of payment, a version of Gresham's Law where merchants use the lower valued money in exchange, and hoard the higher valued one. It also confirms the "law of one price" through arbitrage. The role played by money-changers greatly increased in importance during the centuries of Roman debasement of the coinage.

During the Middle Ages and the Renaissance, the bill of exchange could be used to disguise payments of interest in foreign exchange. Since they were discounted, their yield to maturity represented interest payments. These disguised loans were referred to as "fictitious exchange", whereas conventional bill exchanges were referred to as "real exchange". The convention was to quote foreign exchange rates in terms of bills payable at settlement. The pound was quoted in terms of foreign currencies.

汇票 (**Bill of exchange**) : 汇票主要用在国际贸易中,是由一人开出的要求某人在将来某一特定时间支付特定金额给他人的书面命令。它是现代信用证(L/C)的前身。

Thanks to interest-bearing loans disguised as a foreign exchange transaction, merchants and financiers were able to make loans evading usury laws using a sequence of two bill transactions—a precursor of today's foreign exchange swap.

An important 16th century development was the appearance of a system of "betting" on future exchange rates: a **non-deliverable forward market**. The betters made forecasts on future exchange rates. The difference between the realized rate and the forecasted rate determined who won the bet and how much the loser would pay the winner. This form of forward exchange still exists today in the form of non-deliverable futures (NDFs) in the Chinese yuan, formally the Renminbi, the "People's Currency," in Singapore and Hong Kong SAR.

不可交割的远期外汇市场（Non-deliverable forward market）：下注者对将来一个特定时期的外汇汇率作出预测。预期汇率与真实汇率之间的差别决定了在这场预期的博弈中谁是赢家，输家要支付多少给赢家。这种远期外汇交易今天仍然以无本金交割远期（NDFs）的形式在新加坡和中国香港市场上存在，并仍以人民币计价。

As Rudiger Dornbush noted, Spanish writers of the 16th century discovered the basics of the purchasing power parity theory. They noticed the relationship between the prices of goods exported from Spain to the new World. By the time they reached their destination, the price of these goods was higher, owing to the cost and risk in transport. The purchasing power parities represented the difference between the prices of these goods in Spain and in Mexico and Peru, adjusting for costs of transport. In the 19th century, Paris and London became the leading markets, dealers being in contact throughout business hours. Forward currencies were widely traded. During the U.S. colonial period, no business in dollars was transacted in London, so that trade with Britain was financed exclusively in sterling. Many of the transactions in sterling bills were done in New Orleans where bills earned by cotton traders were sold.

1944 年布雷顿森林体系（The 1944 Bretton Woods system）：是指二战后以美元为中心的国际货币体系。其主要内容包括美元与黄金挂钩，成员国货币和美元挂钩，实行可调整的固定汇率制度。

The 1944 Bretton Woods, New Hampshire system of pegged but adjustable exchange rates triggered automatic foreign exchange intervention in spot markets, but occasional discretionary intervention in forward markets. Forward intervention often inflicts great losses to the Central Banks buying their currency forward "high" when it eventually goes "low". Thailand did this at great loss, initiating the South East Asia crisis of the 1990s. The era of fixed exchange rates came to an end in 1971—1973, in particular when US President Richard Nixon closed the gold window in 1971 and Britain floated the pound in 1973. With the euro's launch in 1999, fixed rates have returned for many countries in the form of a common currency.

The London FOREX market

By the early 1920s, London was considered to be the world's leading foreign exchange center (Atkin, 2005). Floating exchange rates began in the early 1970s, the resulting desire of multinational businesses to hedge their currency exposures caused the rapid growth of foreign exchange trading. London is still by far the largest FOREX market today in terms of daily foreign exchange turnover. Banks located in the United Kingdom accounted for 37% of global foreign exchange market turnover in April 2010, followed by the United States (18%), Japan (6%), Singapore (5%), Switzerland (5%), Hong Kong SAR (5%) and Australia (4%). (Source: *Triennial Central Bank Survey*, "Foreign exchange and derivatives market activity in April 2010", Bank for International Settlements.)

Banks and banking

In 3,000 B. C, the temples in Babylon are reported to have accepted deposits of money and made loans. In the Greek states of the 5th and 4th centuries B. C. the temples, the city authorities and private individuals engaged in banking (Jones, 1973). In the 12th century banking started again in some Italian cities after the fall of the Roman Empire. Risky lending by banks led to a demand for a bank that would transfer funds for its customers, but not make loans. The first *giro* or transfer banks came into being. These started in the great Italian trading cities: Florence, Siena, and Venice. German cities followed, but Amsterdam and London eventually became the most important financial centers. The first modern bank was the Bank of Amsterdam, founded in 1609. The Amsterdam bank was quickly followed by other major cities. The Bank of Hamburg was formed in 1619 and the Bank of Sweden in 1656. As noted, Sweden issued the first European paper bank notes in 1661.

Until 1640 the Tower of London provided merchants with a reliable deposit service. Other banking services, money transmission and accounting, were provided by scriveners, essentially accountants. The development of "goldsmith bankers" came about when the goldsmiths persuaded the scriveners to deposit money with them in return for a small interest payment. The main purpose was apparently to have an opportunity to pick over the coins. (Atkin, 2005)

Charles I seized the assets deposited in the Tower in 1640 when refused a goldsmith loan of 300,000 pounds. The Tower was no longer a safe depository. The goldsmiths become commercial bankers, providing loans of revolving cash balances. The Bank of England was founded in 1694 as a commercial bank by William Paterson with the right to issue notes up to the amount of its capital, initially £ 1. 2 million. It was nationalized by Parliament in 1946. The shareholders received compensation and the Bank of England thereafter ceased its private business, becoming the banker of government and, since 1977, taking responsibility for monetary policy. Prudential oversight of the British commercial banking system was simultaneously transferred to the Securities and Investments Board.

The Federal Reserve System

联邦储备体系(The Federal Reserve System) :即美国的中央银行体系,它由设在华盛顿特区的联邦储备理事会和位于全国一些主要城市的 12 个地区联邦储备银行构成。地区银行的总裁由每个银行的理事会选择,理事会成员一般来自当地银行和企业界。

The First Bank of the United States was established in 1791, but collapsed in 1811. The Second Bank of the United States was established in 1816 and survived only until 1836. Thereafter, until 1862, only state-chartered banks existed. They issued notes against gold and silver and were regulated by the states in which they were chartered. The National Banking Act of 1863 in the middle of the U. S. Civil War created a system of national banks with higher banking standards than state banks. It also created a national currency, the greenback dollar. National banks were required to accept each others' notes at par. The government imposed a tax on state banks, forcing most to become national banks. Also, the use of checking accounts grew: by the turn of the century, 90% of narrow money, currency outside banks plus demand deposits, was in the form of checking accounts.

In 1907, a banking panic in the U. S. accompanied by runs on deposits bankrupting banks, led to arguments for the establishment of a U. S. central bank with an elastic currency to provide liquidity to commercial banks in the event of crises. The Federal Reserve Act established the Federal Reserve System (the FED) in 1913 with 12 districts. The Federal Reserve Banks provide liquidity, control the money supply, clear transactions and supervise member banks. The FED was established primarily as a reserve institution, a lender of last resort to prevent bank runs and liquidity crises. The FED has developed into a supervisory institution for member banks and savings and loan associations that pay a premium to the Federal Deposit Insurance Corporation, established in 1933, and the Federal Savings and Loan Insurance Corporation, established in 1934. The FSLIC's functions were transferred to the FDIC in 1989.

The FED is also responsible for U. S. monetary policy: open market operations, primarily Federal Funds targets, rediscount rate setting, and reserve requirements of commercial banks. The FED system also serves as a clearinghouse for the transfer of monies by check and draft between banks within the United States and abroad. By law, the FED also has the objective of promoting maximum employment, but cannot achieve this "real" objective with monetary policy, even if it sacrifices its dual goal of price stability.

The international monetary institutions

The International Monetary Fund(IMF) was established in 1944 at the Bretton Woods Conference in New Hampshire. Its purposes were:
   • to establish orderly exchange rate arrangements based on a par value system,
   • to eliminate exchange controls, especially for current account transactions, and
   • to provide temporary short term balance of payments assistance via loans to member countries that are short of foreign exchange reserves.

The IMF provided for a pegged exchange rate system with central bank intervention required in the foreign exchange market when the rate approached narrow margins around the official, par value. Rather than imposing exchange controls, it was deemed better to make balance of payments adjustment loans that impose macro-economic policy conditions on the sovereign country that agrees to the conditions. If it agrees to the IMF's loan conditions, the finance minister and the governor of the central bank typically sign a memorandum of understanding with the IMF. The loan is disbursed in several "tranches" or slices and satisfaction of the loan conditions is monitored between disbursements. Extended stand-by-loans have a maturity of 36 months and are essentially lines-of-credit that the country can draw from should it wish to or need to do so. There have been several criticisms leveled recently at the role of the IMF in the international financial system. Just before the Russian default, a multi-billion dollar disbursement was made. The IMF country economist called it a FIEF (foreign investor relief facility) since the dollars were sold for 6 rubles shortly before the Russian default and floating of the exchange rate to 18 rubles a dollar. A substantial portion of the IMF loan was also rumored to have been diverted by government officials into their private accounts in the Jersey Islands. (See Blustein, 2001) The argument is that the IMF creates "moral hazard", encouraging investors to invest in risky, high return

国际货币基金组织(The International Monetary Fund) :国际货币基金组织与世界银行并列为世界两大金融机构之一,其职责是监察货币汇率和各国贸易情况、提供技术和资金协助,确保全球金融制度运作正常;其总部设在华盛顿。

jurisdictions knowing that the IMF will bail them out. In a crisis, the IMF often will lend foreign reserves to the central bank, which then dumps them in the foreign exchange market at discount prices before the ultimate depreciation takes place. Similarly, in the case of Argentina's currency board crisis of 2001, due to excessive foreign debt, provincial deficits, and spending before a Presidential campaign, the IMF lent to the Argentine government anyway. In response to criticism, the IMF established an "Independent Internal Evaluation" unit. It is now trying to rescue Europe by lending more to insolvent European nations that are not reforming—a harsh example of moral hazard. The Germans are reluctant to finance the deficit of other spendthrift Europeans.

世界银行（The World Bank）：世界银行作为 IMF 的姐妹机构创建于 1944 年的布雷顿森林会议，其一开始的使命是帮助在第二次世界大战中被破坏的国家的重建。今天它的任务是资助国家克服穷困，联合向发展中国家提供低息贷款、无息信贷和赠款，各机构在减轻贫困和提高生活水平的使命中发挥独特的作用。

The World Bank, a sister institution of the IMF, created in 1944 at the Bretton Woods Conference, initially made long term development loans for projects such as dams, airports, rubber and concrete production, water systems, and the like. It got involved in Structural Adjustment Loans (SALs) in the 1990s in tandem with the IMF requiring structural adjustments to economic policy. This could mean privatization of state enterprises, lifting price and exchange controls, and improving monetary and fiscal policies, for instance. Some of its large scale loans for dams in particular were criticized by environmentalists and human rights activists because of damage to the environment by immediate flooding of the dam area, and the wholesale removal of villagers in the way of the projects. In modern times, World Bank lenders are more sensitive to the environment, as is the IMF to corruption, so they go in for micro-lending at the wholesale level. Many economists think IMF and World Bank loans do more harm than good to the residents of the countries that receive them. Ultimately, the loans are the taxpayer's liability. Portfolio investors often count on the multilateral lenders to bail out a country from bankruptcy, a so-called "moral hazard" investor play where the country is guaranteed not to fail by the lenders. The multi-lateral institutions have also not successfully prevented the wholesale theft of loans by officials in corrupt environments: the former Zaire's Mobutu built palaces in the Congo, France, and Switzerland. Of course, maybe the money did not come from IMF and World Bank loans.

The Bank of International Settlements (BIS) is often referred to as the bank of central banks. It was established May 17, 1930 at the Hague convention. As such, it is the oldest international monetary organization. It does not do business with private individuals or corporations; only with central banks and international institutions. The head office is in Basel, Switzerland. In their role of fostering international monetary cooperation, the General Manager of the BIS has seen the need to address issues of the growth of Offshore Financial Centres (OFCs), Highly Leveraged Institutions (HLIs), Large and Complex Financial Institutions (LCFIs), deposit insurance and the spread of money laundering and accounting scandals.

In his statement to the Financial Stability Forum (FSF), Mr. Crockett, then General Manager, specifically mentions Long Term Capital Management (LTCM), a Connecticut hedge fund, as an example of the near-collapse of a highly leveraged institution. He also singles out Enron as an accounting scandal with financial risks. These are the issues that need to be addressed by the international monetary institutions in his view. Additionally, offshore financial centers need to "facilitate efforts to strengthen supervisory, information sharing and cooperation practices in OFCs, which have taken on increased urgency following 11 September and the global efforts to combat terrorism financing." (Crockett, 2001).

国际清算银行（The Bank of International Settlements）：国际清算银行常被视为中央银行的银行。它于 1930 年 5 月 17 日成立于海牙会议中，因而它是最古老的国际货币组织。

History of the stock exchanges

Adam Smith warned in 1776 about mismanagement of companies that issue shares to finance their operations, the primary role of the stock exchanges. He raises the principal-agent problem, where the shareholders are the principals or owners and the managers are the agents:

Applying the Concept: **The Principal-Agent problem**

"The directors of such (joint stock) companies, however, being the managers rather of other people's money than of their own, it cannot well be expected that they should watch over it with the same anxious vigilance with which the partners in a private copartnery frequently watch over their own. Like the stewards of a rich man, they are apt to consider attention to small matters as not for their master's honour, and very easily give themselves a dispensation from having it. Negligence and profusion, therefore, must always prevail, more or less, in the management of the affairs of such a company. It is upon this account that joint stock companies for foreign trade have seldom been able to maintain the competition against private adventurers. They have, accordingly, very seldom succeeded without an exclusive privilege, and frequently have not succeeded with one. Without an exclusive privilege they have commonly mismanaged the trade. With an exclusive privilege they have both mismanaged and confined it. "

Source: Adam Smith, *An Inquiry into the Wealth of Nations*, Ch.1, "Of the Expences of the Sovereign or Commonwealth" : 107.

Yet, large corporations with many owners are able to limit the liability of the owners to the value of the shares they hold. The shareholder can enter a venture by buying shares, and exit it by selling them. The manager acts as the shareholders' agent. Under agency law, a corporation is a single entity, a "person" that may sue or be sued without its members being held liable. It is chartered by the state in which it is located. A corporation is a business in which large numbers of people are organized so that their labor and capital are combined in a single venture. Corporations can list and sell their shares on a number of exchanges. This is known as equity finance versus debt finance. Some of these exchanges use the "open-outcry" form of trading where the trader has to continuously shout his or her order until they are out of breath. If a trader stops shouting, the order is assumed no longer in effect. Since many are shouting at the same time, a system of hand signals has come about that effectively convey the order to the pit manager. While some argue that the presence of specialists and market makers on the floor aid in the conveyance of information, others welcome the transparency of the electronic exchanges that are taking business away from the open-outcry exchanges. Indeed, the NYSE has acquired Archipelago, a state of the art electronic trading system, no longer using open outcry trading.

The main global stock exchanges

The New York Stock Exchange was established May 17, 1792 on Wall Street. Traders met at the old wooden wall, no longer in existence, but giving its name to the street. The Dow Jones Industrial Average (DJIA) started out with 12 stocks in October 1928. Only General Electric remains of the original twelve. The S&P 500 Index covers the 500 most widely held companies. The exchange is now NYSE-Euronext following its merger on September 22, 2000 with the Amsterdam, Brussels, and Paris exchanges. It has moved to all electronic trading using Archipelago with five trading posts, and various brokers arranged along the side of the exchange. Specialists still monitor trading activity and the brokers send their orders wirelessly.

The **NASDAQ** is an acronym for National Association of Securities Dealers Automated Quotations. An online stock exchange, it began operations in 1971.

纳斯达克证券交易所（NASDAQ）：NASDAQ 是全国证券商协会自动报价系统的缩写。作为在线证券交易所，它于 1971 年开始交易。

The American Stock Exchange (AMEX) is a subsidiary of the National Association of Securities Dealers. The AMEX index is a composite index of the 739 stocks listed.

The London Stock Exchange was established in 1773, formerly Jonathan's Coffee House where trades met. Trading has since moved off the floor with the introduction of the Stock Exchange Automated Quotations (SEAQ) system. The Footsie 100 Index is the Financial Times Stock Exchange Index of the 100 largest companies listed on the London Stock Exchange.

The Tokyo Stock Exchange was established on May 15, 1878. Japan's Nikkei 225 Index is an average of stock market prices similar to the Dow Jones Industrial Average.

The Paris Bourse was established in Paris by the order of the Royal council in 1724. In 1986, the futures exchange—Le MATIF—was established. The CAC 40 Index is the acronym for "Compagnie des Agents de Change 40 Index," 40 French companies listed on the Paris Stock Exchange.

The Shanghai Stock Exchange (SSE) was founded in 1904, mainly dealing in rubber shares. The Japanese occupation brought an end to its operations. The modern Shanghai Stock Exchange was founded in 1990. The Shanghai Composite Index is a composite of foreign currency denominated B shares sold to qualified foreign institutions and yuan-denominated A shares sold to Chinese citizens and institutions. This market segmentation combined with capital controls makes the Shanghai exchange less linked to international exchanges.

The Shenzhen Stock Exchange (SZSE) was founded in 1990. Owned by the Shenzhen Securities Clearing Corporation (SSCC), it is under the regulatory supervision of the China Securities Regulatory Commission. The SZSE has grown significantly to become the second-largest exchange in

China after the Shanghai Stock Exchange. It is now owned by the China Securities Depository and Clearing Co. , the parent company of the Shanghai Stock Exchange. By May 2008 the SZSE listed 897 securities in 697 companies. In 2009, it agreed with S&P to produce benchmark investible indices on the Chinese market. Chinese institutional investors will also be able to invest in a listed fund based on the S&P 500 Index.

点 心 债 券 (Dim sum bonds): 点心债券是在中国香港地区发行的以人民币计价的债券,因其相对于整个人民币债券市场规模很小,所以被称为点心债券。

The Hong Kong Stock Exchange was established in 1891. The Industrial and Commercial Bank of China (ICBC) and the Bank of China (BOC) along with other commercial banks from China were listed on the Hong Kong Security Exchange by issuing H shares denominated in HK dollars. An H share is a share of a company incorporated in the Chinese mainland but listed on the Hong Kong Stock Exchange or another foreign exchange. H-shares are regulated by Chinese law, but when listed on the HKSE are denominated in Hong Kong dollars and trade the same as other equities on the Hong Kong exchange. ICBC was simultaneously listed on both the HKSE and Shanghai Stock Exchange on October 27, 2006. It was the world's largest initial public offer (IPO) at that time, valued at US $ 21.9 billion. However, in 2010, the Agriculture Bank of China broke its record and became the world's largest IPO by raising $22.1 billion. ICBC raised at least US $14 billion in H shares and another US $5.1 billion in A shares. The BOC was listed on the HKSE on June 1, 2006, raising US $9.7 billion in H shares. The total value of their IPO was US $11.2 billion.

The great virtue of offering shares on the Hong Kong Exchange in HK $ is the currency board of the Hong Kong Monetary Authority. The HK currency board has a rigidly fixed exchange rate pegged to the USD since 1983 with a parity rate of HK $7.8 per USD, though it may float between 7.75 and 7.85. Consequently, the shares are effectively USD shares. Under the Special Administrative Law (SAL), Hong Kong retains financial independence for 50 years following its reunification with China in 1999.

Futures exchanges in China

There are four official exchanges in mainland China.

The Shanghai Futures Exchange (SFE) trades futures contracts in copper, aluminum, zinc, plumbum, fuel oil and natural rubber. It was established in 1998 in a merger of four previously separate commodity exchanges.

The Dalian Commodity Exchange, established February 28, 1993, trades futures contracts in corn, No. 1 Soybeans, No. 2 Soybeans, Soybean meal, Soybean Oil, LLEPE, RBD Palm Olein, PVC, and Coke.

The Zhengzhou Commodity Exchange was established in 1990, and is one of the four official exchanges decided by the restructuring of 1998. Its futures contracts are in Hard White wheat, Strong Gluten Wheat, Cotton, Sugar, PTA, Rapeseed Oil, Early Long-grain Nonglutinous Rice.

The China Financial Futures Exchange, established in Shanghai in 2006, trades in CSI 300 Index Futures.

In the News: SHANGHAI yuan options

In the latest liberalizing step for its foreign-exchange market, China is loosening the rules on yuan options—offering banks and businesses more ways to hedge currency risks, which have grown in recent months with the increasing volatility in the yuan's value. The move could be a shot in the arm for the nascent yuan-options market, virtually dormant since its launch in April. The new risk-reversal option structure, introduced by a State Administration of Foreign Exchange statement dated November 8, 2011 will allow investors to buy and sell options simultaneously, starting December 1, 2011. Under the current rules, investors can buy options only from banks; they can sell options only to exit the position established by their earlier option purchase. To limit risk exposure under the new rules, the cost of the option—called the premium—that the investor sells can't exceed the cost of the option the investor buys. Selling options is riskier than buying them—the buyer's risk is limited to the premium paid. Restricting investors' options sales—or selling a put or a call—is a typical measure adopted in emerging economies, Chinese regulators said.

Source: Esther Fung and Shen Hong, "China Eases Yuan-Option Rules", *Wall Street Journal*, November 11, 2011.

The Frankfurt Stock Exchange dates from the 9th century when trade fairs were authorized. In 1585 it was organized as a bourse to fix exchange rates and by 1894 had become a formal stock exchange. Its main index, the DAX, consists of the 30 largest issues traded on the exchange.

The performances of the international stock markets indices are related. In fact, this is one aspect of the increased globalization of international trade and finance. The major stock indices are positively correlated, suggesting the globalization of the international financial markets. Since we are dealing with the monthly real rates of return adjusted for inflation, the positive and significant correlations suggest that arbitrage is keeping the real rates of return in line. Also, many real shocks are worldwide.

Why is money important?

When the money supply is unstable, prices are unstable. This often happens when the printing press becomes the finance of last resort of the Treasury's deficit. A financing identity illustrates the fact that the printing press can be used for residual finance of the deficit that is not financed by a sale of bonds to the public:

$$H_t - H_{t-1} \equiv [G_t + rB_{t-1} + V_t - T_t] - [B_t - B_{t-1}] \qquad (2.1)$$

where $H_t - H_{t-1}$ is new base money issued by the central bank.

$[G_t + rB_{t-1} + V_t - T_t]$ is the total fiscal deficit, including interest on the national debt, rB_{t-1}, V_t transfer payments (entitlements), G_t government purchases of goods and services, and T_t total tax revenues.

$[B_t - B_{t-1}]$ is the amount of the fiscal deficit financed by new borrowing, i. e. the sale of new debt by the Treasury to the public.

The residual of the deficit that is not financed by new bond issue is the printing press, $H_t - H_{t-1}$, the sale of new debt to the FED.

This is a tautology, an identity that must hold. When there are shocks to the deficit or spending greater than tax revenues that cannot be financed by new borrowing, the printing press is engaged and inflation typically follows. As a fraction of GDP, the financing equation can be written as:

$$\frac{H_t - H_{t-1}}{Y_t} \equiv \frac{G_t + r_t B_{t-1} + V_t - T_t}{Y_t} - \frac{[B_t - B_{t-1}]}{Y_t} \qquad (2.2)$$

or in terms of small letters:

$$h_t - \frac{h_{t-1}}{(1+\gamma)} = g_t + v_t + \frac{r}{(1+\gamma)} b_{t-1} - \tau_t - \left(b_t - \frac{b_{t-1}}{(1+\gamma)} \right) \qquad (2.3)$$

where γ is the growth rate in GDP, since $Y_t = (1+\gamma)Y_{t-1}$. If we define the total deficit as a fraction of GDP by d_t as the fiscal deficit as a fraction of GDP, we have:

$$d_t = g_t + \frac{r}{(1+\gamma)} b_{t-1} + v_t - \tau_t \qquad (2.4)$$

or:

$$h_t - \frac{h_{t-1}}{(1+\gamma)} = d_t - \left(b_t - \frac{b_{t-1}}{(1+\gamma)} \right) \qquad (2.5)$$

The world reserve and settlement status of the U.S. dollar is put in jeopardy by large deficits financed by the printing of seigniorage, as reported in Table 2.1.

Table 2.1 Seigniorage and bond finance by the US Treasury as a percent of GDP

表 2.1 给出了 2010 年和 2011 年美国新发货币和新发国债占美国 GDP 的比重。

	2010	2011
g_t	9.3	9.0
v_t	13.2	13.5
$\left(r/(1+\gamma)\right)b_{t-1}$	1.4	1.5
$g_t + \left(r/(1+\gamma)\right)b_{t-1} + v_t$	23.8	24.1
τ_t	14.9	15.4
$d_t = g_t + \left(r/(1+\gamma)\right)b_{t-1} + v_t - \tau_t$	8.9	8.7
$b_t - b_{t-1}/(1+\gamma)$	10.1	7.4
$h_t - h_{t-1}/(1+\gamma)$	-1.2	1.3

Source: Calculated from US Congressional Budget Office, Budget Tables, 2011.

Printing money equal to 1.3% of GDP is a bad omen. Hopefully, the US dollar will not suffer the fate of the Zimbabwean dollar!

In the News: The end of the Zimbabwean dollar

Zimbabwe slashed 12 zeros from its currency as hyperinflation continued to erode its value, the country's central bank announced. The move means that 1 trillion in Zimbabwe dollars now will be equivalent to one Zimbabwe dollar. The old notes—with the highest being 100 trillion dollars—not enough to buy a loaf of bread—will remain valid until June 30, 2009 after which they will cease to be legal tender. One U.S. dollar is trading above 300 trillion Zimbabwe dollars. Since many traders no longer accept the ZWD, the acting finance minister authorized payments in foreign currency.

Source: cnn.com/world.

While seigniorage is typically positive, it can indeed be negative, such as on the US penny. In 2011, the unit cost of a penny was 2.4¢ and the unit cost of a nickel was 11.2¢! (Source: *Coin Update*)

Applying the Concept: Negative seigniorage—US Mint Cost to Produce the Penny and Nickel

For the past four years, it has cost the **United States Mint** more than face value to produce the penny and the nickel. The cost of the coins was recently 1.62 cents to produce each penny and 5.79 cents to produce each nickel ... Seigniorage arises from the difference between the face value and the cost to manufacture and distribute the coins. Amounts earned through seigniorage—are transferred to the United States Treasury General Fund. However, since 2006, it has cost more than face value to produce the cent and nickel due to the increased costs of base metals—the cent is 2.5% copper and 97.5% zinc, and the nickel is 75% copper and 25% nickel.

Table 2.2 calculates the negative seigniorage realized by the US Treasury on the one cent and nickel coins since 2005.

Table 2.2 Negative seigniorage on the US penny and nickel

Cost of producing the US penny			Cost of producing the US nickel		
Fiscal Year	US Mint Cost (US ¢)	Seigniorage (USD millions)	Fiscal Year	US Mint Cost (US ¢)	Seigniorage (USD millions)
2009	1.62	($19.80)	2009	5.79	($2.20)
2008	1.42	($22.20)	2008	8.77	($24.80)
2007	1.67	($40.10)	2007	9.49	($58.50)
2006	1.21	($18.30)	2006	5.97	($14.60)
2005	0.97	$2.00	2005	4.84	$2.40

Source: February 3, 2010, *Coin Update.*

While the US Mint lost a combined $22 million on production of the cent and nickel, the gains from other denominations more than made up for this amount. Last year, the United States Mint shipped a total of $777.6 million in circulating coins, earning $427.8 million in seigniorage. Profitable seignorage is earned from the international circulation of banknotes. While the cost of printing a $100 banknote is 12 cents, foreigners must supply goods and services—coffee, shrimp, and tourism, for instance—at the face value of the note. The $100 banknote is held abroad because the entity values it as a *store of value* because of mistrust of the local currency and as *a unit of account* and *medium of exchange* for settling both legal and illegal transactions. The Federal Reserve Board of Governors Flow of Funds reports that at the end of March 2009, $313 billion (36.7 percent) of U. S. currency was held abroad. Feige estimates that "over the past two decades seigniorage revenues from foreigners have averaged $6—$7 billion dollars per year". Foreigners are thus paying a high seigniorage tax to the US Treasury.

截至 2009 年 3 月, 3130 亿美元(约 36.7%)的美国货币被外国持有。

The negative seigniorage on the penny and the nickel are a wise investment by the US Treasury in maintaining the dollar as a good unit of account and medium of exchange. Rather than exchanging chewing gum to round up or down transactions, the reliable penny is there as the unit of account and means of payment.

Conclusion

Money serves as a medium of exchange, a unit of account, and a store of value. Different monies must be converted into the same unit of account by the exchange rate in order to compare prices and rates of return. This currency conversion gives rise to foreign exchange risk in investing and operating internationally. The foreign exchange markets have arisen to deal with spot and forward transactions in different monies, as well as currency options to either hedge or speculate. The largest FOREX market remains London, accounting for 36% of daily turnover in the foreign exchanges. The exchange costs on the FOREX market are mainly the difference between the *ask* and the *bid* price of foreign currency—*the bid-ask spread*—as well as any commission associated with the conversion. These costs are not insignificant, amounting to approximately a billion USD daily.

The world financial market is becoming increasingly integrated. The adoption of the euro by twelve countries as the same currency has removed conversion costs from the financial landscape of Europe, but has not prevented greater credit risk in the *PIIGS* sovereign bonds—Portugal, Ireland, Italy, Greece, and Spain. Greater openness in trade has brought with it greater openness in finance since current account deficits must be financed, and surpluses provide foreign lending. The decade of the 1990s brought all of Latin American into the WTO-GATT, and in December 2001, China became a signatory as well. Russian is acceding in 2012. There have been great foreign direct investment flows that follow trade, as well as portfolio investments. On the other hand, China still has not liberalized the capital account to permit foreign portfolio diversification, though large direct foreign investments and acquisitions have been approved since Deng Xiaoping's pivotal 1978 policy of moving toward the socialist market economy and opening the Chinese economy. There is increasing financial integration in the world financial markets, making for a more efficient distribution of worldwide capital. Shocks to the financial system are now global in nature.

Questions and problems

2.1 The functions of money

a. What are the three main functions of money? (that is, define and explain the different roles of money in an economic system.)

1.

2.

3.

b. How does high inflation damage each of the main roles that money plays?

1.

2.

3.

2.2 Gold arbitrage

Assume country A's central bank has a gold window where it freely sells and/or buys an ounce of gold for 2 dollars of currency, while Country B buys and/or sells an ounce of gold for one pound of currency. There is no bid-ask spread in purchases or sales of gold at the Central Bank.

a. Using the cross rate, what is the par price of the pound in terms of the dollar?

b. If the price of the pound rises to $2. 01 on the foreign exchange market, will gold arbitrage take place assuming no costs of arbitrage?

c. If so, explain the steps in a "round trip" beginning and ending in the same currency. That is, explain each transaction in gold arbitrage and indicate your profits:

1. Sell one pound for $2. 01 on the foreign exchange market

2.

3.

4.

5.

    d. Since gold moves from one country to another, what is the automatic effect on the money supply of the country that receives gold, and on the money supply of the country that loses gold?

    e. Could these monetary effects of gold flows be neutralized? How?

References and suggested reading

Aliber, Robert Z. (2002), *The International Money Game*, Chicago: The University of Chicago Press.

Atkin, John (2005), *The Foreign Exchange Market of London: Development Since 1900*, London & New York: Routledge.

Bahng, Seungwook (2003), "The Response of the Indian Stock Market to the Movement of Asia's Emerging Markets: From Isolation Toward Integration," *Global Economic Review*, 32(2): 43—58.

Bank of International Settlements (2011), *Trienniel Central Bank Survey: Foreign Exchange and Derivatives Activity in 2010*, Basel, Table E4:56.

Blustein, Paul (2001), *The Chastening: Inside the Crisis that Rocked the Global Financial System and Humbled the IMF*, New York: Public Affairs.

Chown, John F. (1994), *A History of Money: From AD 800*, London & New York: Routledge.

Damme, Ingrid Van (April 1998), "The Cradle of the European Banknote Stood in Sweden," Museum of the National Bank of Belgium.

Davies, Glyn (1994), *A History of Money: From Ancient Times to the Present Day*, Cardiff: University of Wales Press.

Donaldson, R. Glen (1993), "Financing Banking Crises: Lessons from the Panic of 1907," *Journal of Monetary Economics*, 31(1): 69—95.

Einzig, Paul (1970), *The History of Foreign Exchange*, New York: Macmillan.

Jones, J. P. (1973), *The Money Story*, New York, Drake Publishers.

Friedman, Milton (1992), "FDR, Silver and China," in *Money Mischief: Episodes in Monetary History*, Orlando, Florida and San Diego, California: Harcourt Brace and Company.

Huang, Ray (1974), *Fiscal Administration During the Ming Dynasty*, London: Cambridge University Press.

Poitras, Geoffrey (2000), *The Early History of Financial Economics, 1478—1776: From Commercial Arithmetic to Life Annuities and Joint Stocks*, Cheltenham & Northhampton: Edward Elgar.

Racine, M. D. and Lucy F. Ackert (2000), "Time Varying Volatility in Canadian and U.S. Stock Index and Index Futures: A Multivariate Analysis,"

Journal of Financial Research, 23(2): 129—143.

Smith, Adam (1776), *An Inquiry into the Wealth of Nations*, London: Methuen and Co., Ltd., ed. Edwin Cannan, 1904 (5th ed.).

Spahn, Heinz-Peter (2001), *From Gold to Euro: On Monetary theory and the History of Currency Systems*, Berlin & New York: Springer.

Westermann, Frank (2002), "Stochastic Trends and Cycles in National Stock Market Indices: Evidence from the U.S., U.K. and Switzerland," *Swiss Journal of Economics and Statistics*, 138(3): 317—328.

CHAPTER 3 The Foreign Exchange Market

外汇交易
市场

According to the Bank of International Settlements (BIS), average net daily turnover in the over-the-counter (OTC) foreign exchange market in 2010 was nearly 4 trillion US dollars—spot transactions of $1.49 trillion, forwards of $475 billion, foreign exchange swaps of $1.8 trillion, and options of $207 billion. That makes foreign exchange trading one of the largest financial markets in existence. Table 3.1 reports the daily foreign exchange turnover in April 2010.

Table 3.1 Global daily foreign exchange trading in April 2010

OTC foreign exchange turnover in April 2010
(Daily averages, in millions of USD)

Spot	1,490,205	37%
Outright forwards	475,007	12%
Foreign exchange and currency swaps	1,808,076	45%
Options	207,264	5%
Total foreign exchange contracts	$3,980,552	100%

Source: Bank of International Settlements, Triennial Central Bank Survey of Foreign Exchange and Derivatives Market Activity in 2010, December 2010.

This chapter outlines floating and fixing the exchange rate in the spot market, forward and futures markets, as well as the options market in foreign exchange. As always, it is supply and demand that determines the equilibrium in each market, but arbitrage plays an important role in setting an equilibrium price in both the spot and futures markets. Broadly understood, **arbitrage** is buying low in one market and selling high in another, thereby bringing prices into equilibrium. No further profitable arbitrage is

套利(Arbitrage):一般来说,套利是指在低价市场上买进再到高价市场上卖出,从而调节市场价格达到均衡,在此价格上任何套利行为都将不再盈利。

possible.

A floating exchange rate system

浮动汇率制度（Floating exchange rate system）：在浮动汇率制度下，外汇市场的供给和需求决定了均衡汇率。央行不进行外汇买卖活动从而不对汇率进行干预的汇率制度称为自由汇率制度。

买入价（The bid）：买入价是银行买入一单位外汇的价格。

卖出价（The ask）：卖出价是银行卖出一单位外汇的价格。

欧式标价法（European quotation）：一单位美元买卖人民币的数量，这种标价法被称为欧式标价法。

美式标价法（American quotation）：一单位人民币买卖美元的数量，这种标价法被称为美式标价法。

With a floating exchange rate, supply and demand in the foreign exchange market determine the equilibrium exchange rate. When the central bank neither purchases nor sells foreign exchange, it is said to be a freely floating exchange rate system.

The bid is what a bank pays for a unit of foreign exchange, **the ask** is the price at which it sells the same unit of foreign exchange. Individual firms and persons will pay the ask rate which is slightly higher, and they will receive the slightly lower bid rate. The bank earns the bid-ask spread.

In Figure 3.1, at a spot price of S, the supply and demand for foreign exchange are reconciled, so S is the equilibrium exchange rate in terms of yuan/dollar. This is known as a **European quotation**—foreign currency unit per USD. When a currency is quoted as USD per unit of foreign currency, it is known as an **American quotation**. The equilibrium quantity bought (and) sold is Q.

Figure 3.1   A floating exchange rate

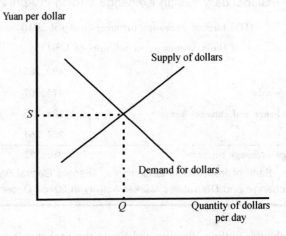

有管理的浮动汇率制度（Managed float）：中央银行有时会通过增加或减少外汇市场上外汇供给数量的办法来干预外汇市场，这样的浮动汇率制度被称为有管理的浮动汇率制度。

Central banks occasionally intervene in the foreign exchange market by increasing or decreasing the supply of foreign exchange. With intervention, the float is said to be a **managed float**. Foreign exchange dealers quote customers a *bid* and an *ask* (or offer) rate for foreign exchange. A dealer purchases at the bid rate and sells at the offer rate. The *bid-ask* *spread* (the difference between the ask and the bid rates) represents profits to the foreign exchange dealer.

Day trading in foreign exchange is not likely to be profitable. For one thing, the speculator pays fees per trade and, for another, buys at the ask and sells at the bid when trading. Consider a simultaneous purchase and sale of foreign exchange by a day trader: the trader buys high at the ask and simultaneously sells low at the bid, paying the exchange spread plus any commission on the trade. Table 3. 2 indicates the bid and ask rates from a foreign exchange trading platform.

Table 3.2   Direct and cross rates in foreign exchange quotations

	CNY	USD	EUR	JPY
CNY		Bid: 0.15660284 Ask: 0.15699355	Bid: 0.11358405 Ask: 0.11385380	Bid: 12.03100014 Ask: 12.05799961
USD	Bid: 6.36968851 Ask: 6.38558027		Bid: 0.72516000 Ask: 0.72531998	Bid: 76.80491303 Ask: 76.80491303
EUR	Bid: 8.78319424 Ask: 8.86405314	Bid: 1.37870185 Ask: 1.37900601		Bid: 105.91000366 Ask: 105.91999817
JPY	Bid: 0.08293250 Ask: 0.08311861	Bid: 0.01302000 Ask: 0.01302000	Bid: 0.00944000 Ask: 0.00944000	

Source: XigniteCurrencies, September 17, 2011.

CNY indicates the yuan or renminbi, while USD, EUR, JPY indicate respectively the United States dollar, the euro, and the Japanese yen respectively. The CNY bid for the USD is 6. 36968851, while the ask is 6.38558027, so the bid ask spread is (6. 38558027 – 6. 36968851) = 0.0158918 or 159 **basis points or** *pips*—measured as the fourth decimal.

The bank is a market maker, ready to either buy or sell dollars. Assume that it trades 10 billion USD per day: That is, it buys 10 billion at 6.36968851 and sells them at 6.3855807, closing out its net position in dollars at the end of the day. Its profits from the spread are thus:

$$1,000,000,000 \times \frac{0.01589176}{} = 15,891,760$$

Profits in terms of CNY are indicated in Figure 3.2:

基 点 (**Basis points or** *pips*): 基点, 亦即外汇术语中的"pips", 指的是 0.0001。

Figure 3.2 Bank profits from the bid-ask spread

American and European quotations

A forex quotation may be in American terms—USD per unit of foreign currency or in European terms—units of foreign currency per dollar. The European quotation of the dollar is:

	CNY
USD	Bid: 6.36968851
	Ask: 6.38558027

while the American quotation of the CNY is:

	USD
CNY	Bid: 0.15660284
	Ask: 0.15699355

美式标价法与欧式标价法之间的转换(Conversion between American and European quotations):一种标价法下的买入价的倒数即为另一种标价法下的卖出价;同样,一种标价法下的卖出价的倒数即为另一种标价法下的买入价。

The **conversion between American and European quotations** is simple since 1/bid in one quotation equals the ask in the other. Similarly, 1/ask equals the bid when changing the style of quotation. To be sure, the ask must always exceed the bid after conversion.

A fixed exchange rate system

A fixed exchange rate system usually has a ceiling and a floor (intervention points). The central bank purchases foreign exchange at the floor and sells it at the ceiling to maintain the exchange rate within a narrow band. When the supply of dollars is greater than the demand for dollars at the floor price, the central bank purchases dollars at the floor price and adds them to its foreign exchange reserves. To facilitate international adjustment, the central bank that purchases dollars with say yuan lets the domestic yuan money supply rise, thus enabling inflation. Occasionally, central banks "sterilize" or "neutralize" the monetary effects of forex purchases by simultaneously selling domestic currency bonds or raising required reserve ratios to take back the increase in the supply of yuan (Hanke, 2002). This neutralizes adjustment and the surplus or deficit continues until policy or a shock changes the circumstances.

固定汇率制度(A fixed exchange rate system)：在固定汇率制度下,汇率的变动通常有一个上限和下限,即干预点。央行在汇率变动的下限买入外汇,并在上限卖出外汇,以使汇率稳定在一个狭窄的区间内。

A central bank purchase of dollars

When the supply of dollars is greater than the demand for dollars at the floor price, the central bank purchases dollars at the floor price and adds them to its foreign exchange reserves. For example, in Figure 3.3 the supply of dollars exceeds the demand for dollars at a floor price of 6.3697 yuan per dollar. This triggers central bank intervention (that is, purchases of 3 million dollars by the central bank) at 6.3697 yuan per dollar. The equilibrium exchange rate is thus 6.3697 yuan per dollar, including the central bank's demand for 3 million dollars at the floor rate. Normally, the 3 million dollars are added to central bank reserves in the form of US Treasuries. However, the central bank could sterilize the immediate impact on the domestic money supply by selling 6.3697 × $3,000,000 yuan of domestic bonds on the open market.

央行买进美元(A central bank purchase of dollars)：在下限上,美元的供给大于需求时,央行以下限价格买进美元用以增加外汇储备。

Figure 3.3   The People's Bank of China buys three million dollars at the lower intervention rate

Notice that a central bank's ability to purchase foreign reserves is unlimited since it can always print or supply more domestic money. This is not the case when it comes to selling foreign reserves to support the home currency. It cannot print foreign currency.

A central bank sale of dollars

央行卖出美元（A central bank sale of dollars）：美元的供给小于需求，于是央行动用外汇储备，以上限价格卖出美元。

When the demand for dollars is greater than the supply of dollars at the ceiling price, the central bank draws from its reserves of dollars and sells them at the ceiling price. In Figure 3.4, the demand for dollars exceeds the supply of dollars at a price of 6.3856 yuan per dollar, triggering a sale of dollars by the central bank at the ceiling rate. The sale of reserves just equilibrates supply and demand at a price of 6.3856 yuan per dollar. Neutralization would entail a purchase of domestic bonds equal to 6.3856 × 3,000,000 yuan. With a fixed exchange rate that has a ceiling and a floor the central bank purchases foreign exchange at the floor and sells it at the ceiling to maintain the exchange rate within a narrow band. By appreciating the rates slowly, the central bank can appreciate the currency, yet provide some certainty to exporters.

Figure 3.4 The People's Bank of China sells three million dollars at the upper intervention rate

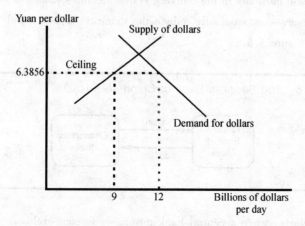

A central bank's holdings of foreign reserves are limited. Consequently, it may sell reserves until it has sold all its reserves and exhausted its ability to borrow reserves to support its currency, if it chooses to do so. At that point, it must float (or worse yet, impose exchange controls, in which case the parallel market rate floats) its exchange rate.

At that point, speculators who had "Bet against the Bank" make their profits. Most empirical studies show that by taking a position opposite to central bank intervention, small systematic profits can be made (Taylor, 1982). The reason for this is that central banks often " lean against the wind", that is, resist changes in the fundamental equilibrium rate. In the case of the People's Bank of China, the purchase of foreign exchange on the exchange market has led to over three billion dollars of reserves in September 2011. A managed floating exchange rate system allows the exchange rate to float according to the laws of supply and demand, but there are discretionary sales and/or purchases of foreign exchange to maintain the equilibrium exchange rate within small margins.

The effect of a sale in foreign reserves on the domestic money supply

When the demand for money declines, say due to a crisis in confidence in the home currency, the Central Bank must sell foreign exchange reserves, thereby reducing the supply of home currency. **The effect on**

央行所持有的外汇储备是有限的。因此，它可以选择卖出外汇储备，直至外汇储备全部耗尽而且无法借入外汇储备来支持本币。在这个时候，央行只能够允许其汇率浮动。

对本国货币供给的影响
（The effect on the do-
mestic money supply）：
央行在卖出外汇储备的
同时，购进了本国货币。
因此，银行体系中的本币
减少了，卖出外汇储备便
自动减少了本币的供给。
当央行购进外汇以增加
外汇储备时，同时向银行
体系中注入了本币，因此
本币供给自动增加。

the domestic money supply is direct: when the Central Bank sells foreign exchange reserves, it simultaneously buys domestic currency. Consequently, domestic currency in the banking system declines. Sales of foreign exchange reserves automatically reduce the domestic money supply as illustrated in Figure 3.5.

Figure 3.5   The People's Bank of China sells USD

Similarly, when a central bank purchases foreign exchange and adds to reserves, it simultaneously sells domestic currency to the banking system. Consequently, the domestic money supply rises automatically. The effect on the domestic money supply in China can be illustrated in Figure 3.6.

Figure 3.6   The People's Bank of China buys USD

Naturally, the ability of a Central Bank to maintain a fixed exchange rate depends on its holdings of foreign reserves. From the point of view of the balance sheet of the Central Bank in Table 3.3, we have a simplified T-account:

Table 3.3   The balance sheet of the People's Bank of China

Assets (RMB)	Liabilities (RMB)
Foreign reserves	Currency held by the public
Domestic credit	Commercial bank reserves
Base money	Base money

On the asset side, foreign reserves are net foreign assets held by the central bank; domestic credit represents loans made by the Central Bank, usually to the Treasury. On the liability side, the bank issues domestic currency to the public and it takes in deposits of commercial banks as required reserves. Commercial banks are also allowed to count cash on hand ("vault cash") as part of their reserves.

A decline in the demand for money is reflected by a decline in the demand for base money. By selling its foreign reserves at the spot rate, the Central Bank accommodates the decline in the demand for money by buying the excess domestic supply. Otherwise, the Central Bank could contract domestic credit to reduce base money supply.

Notice that if the demand for money were constant, base money is constant. Any attempt by the Central Bank to expand domestic credit (say to finance a fiscal deficit) under a fixed exchange rate regime would come at the expense of a loss in foreign reserves. The central bank would have to repurchase the excess supply of money on the foreign exchange market. This is the so called "monetary anchor" role of a fixed exchange rate. In principal, a fixed exchange rate prevents the Central Bank from financing the fiscal and quasi-fiscal deficit. An independent expansion of the money supply by the Central Bank triggers excess demand in the foreign exchange market, requiring a sale of foreign exchange reserves to maintain the fixed exchange rate. The Central Bank thus expands credit and hence the money base, but contracts the base by the same amount when it sells foreign exchange reserves. Consequently, a fixed exchange rate serves as a "monetary anchor" on expansionary monetary policy.

Neutralization policy

When the People's Bank of China purchases US dollars to stabilize the exchange rate, it increases the yuan base money supply in the commercial banking system. Normally, this leads to an increase in the yuan money supply and ultimately a higher rate of inflation in China. To offset the effect of the purchase of dollars on the yuan money supply, the PBOC can neutralize by selling Chinese bonds to the commercial banks, or by increasing the domestic required reserve ratio that commercial banks must maintain. Neutralization is thus illustrated in Figure 3.7.

冲销政策(**Neutralization policy**):当中国人民银行购入美元来稳定汇率时,商业银行系统中的人民币数量增加。通常,这会导致人民币供给增加和更高的通货膨胀率。为了抵消这一效果,中国人民银行可以通过出售中国国债或提高存款准备金率来降低人民币供给数量。

Figure 3.7   The People's Bank of China sells bonds to neutralize its foreign exchange purchase

In theory, we know from Mundell (1968) that a central bank can *either* fix the exchange rate and let the money supply float, *or* fix the money supply and let the exchange rate float, but not *both*.

From the simplified balance sheet of the PBC, a change in monetary base, H, the liabilities of the central bank, equals the change in its assets, either caused by a change in net foreign assets, FX, or a change in net domestic assets, DC.

$$\Delta H \equiv \Delta DC + \Delta FX \qquad (3.1)$$

This identity suggests that an increase in foreign assets, due to the PBC's purchase of foreign exchange, other things constant, tends to increase the monetary base, and hence the overall money supply. However, to limit the impact of an increase of net foreign assets on monetary base, the central bank can neutralize the monetary effects by reducing domestic credit. A direct way to measure the effectiveness of PBC's neutralization is to test how domestic assets respond to a change in net foreign assets.

Neutralization can be characterized by a sterilization coefficient, θ, representing the fraction of the change in net foreign assets that is neutralized:

$$\Delta DC = -\theta \Delta FX \quad \text{where} \quad 0 \leqslant \theta \leqslant 1 \qquad (3.2)$$

The coefficient of $\theta = 1$ implies full monetary neutralization, or $\Delta DC = -\Delta FX$ so $\Delta H = 0$, while $\theta = 0$ implies no monetary neutralization. Here we define the sterilization coefficient narrowly from the central bank balance sheet perspective. It is the fraction of a change in net foreign assets that is neutralized by a reduction in the PBC's domestic credit.

We can also test the impact of an increase in net foreign assets on broader monetary supply such as M2. Recall that the money supply M equals monetary base times the money multiplier m:

$$M = mH \qquad (3.3)$$

which implies, for a constant multiplier:

$$\Delta M = m\Delta H = m(\Delta FX + \Delta DC) \qquad (3.4)$$

Substituting equation (3.2) into equation (3.4), we have:

$$\Delta M = m(1 - \theta)\Delta FX \qquad (3.5)$$

where ΔM denotes the change in commercial banks' domestic credit due to a change in net foreign assets, ΔFX, and $m(1 - \theta)$ is the *effective* money multiplier, which de-multiplies the effect of the purchase of net foreign assets on the money supply. Note that in the case of perfect neutralization $\theta = 1$, so the effective money multiplier for purchase of foreign exchange $m(1 - \theta) = 0$. In general, $m(1 - \theta) > 0$.

On the complete sample from period, 1999:7 to 2011:6, OLS regressions yield an estimated sterilization coefficient of 0.66, significant at the 5% level, suggesting that the PBC only neutralizes 66% of the change in net foreign assets effectively. This is illustrated by the negative slope of the estimated neutralization equation and the regression line in Figure 3.8.

$$\Delta DC = -0.66\,\Delta FX + 0.03 \qquad (3.6)$$
$$\quad (0.02) \qquad\qquad (0.02)$$

Note: Standard errors are reported in parentheses.

Figure 3.8   The change in domestic credit, ΔDC, and the change in net foreign assets, ΔFX, of the PBC

The estimated money multiplier is 4.04. This implies an *effective* money multiplier of 1.4, that is, a one yuan increase in net foreign assets would lead to a 1.4 yuan increase in the money supply due to sterilization. From July 1999 to June 2011, China's foreign reserves rose by 66.9 trillion yuan, at the nominal exchange rate. Given an effective money multiplier of 1.4, this led to an increase of 27.3 trillion yuan increase in the money supply, which is 41% of the total increase of 66. 9 trillion yuan during the same period. In other words, 41% of money growth is accounted for by the growth of foreign reserves alone. This high percentage suggests that the PBC cannot effectively neutralize the change in its net foreign assets, contrary to previous results.

Indeed, if we divide the whole sample into two subsamples using the 2005 currency reform as the break point, the results suggest that the size of the sterilization coefficient decreases considerably in the second period, and the degree of statistical significance is lower, indicating it has become more difficult for the PBC to pursue a policy of neutralization since August 2005. The estimates are significant at 5% level except for the sterilization coefficient in the second subsample, whose p-value is less than 0. 12. Estimated sterilization coefficients for these two subsamples are 0. 82 and 0. 57 respectively. In the face of rapid growth of foreign reserves, neutralization in China is becoming increasingly difficult, consistent with Mundell's hypothesis.

When a Central Bank has an expansionary monetary policy (say to finance the fiscal deficit via the printing press), it continuously loses reserves until they are exhausted, usually by a sudden speculative attack or a run against remaining Central Bank reserves. At that point, the exchange rate must float since no further support of the exchange rate is possible—foreign exchange reserves are no longer available. Often, the central bank sees no alternative but to expand domestic credit to as the financier of last resort of the Treasury's deficit. Monetary policy becomes dependent on the deficit of the Treasury. Thus foreign exchange reserves are spent until they run out.

Under neutralization or sterilization policy: a central bank sells a million dollars of foreign currency and simultaneously buys with the proceeds a million dollars worth of Treasury Debt. In doing so, it neutralizes the natural fall in the money supply triggered by the sale of foreign exchange. Neutralization of the monetary effects of a sale of foreign exchange reserves is illustrated in Figure 3. 9.

Figure 3.9　The People's Bank of China buys bonds to neutralize its foreign exchange sale

The Euro—"irrevocably fixed" exchange rates

Robert A. Mundell, Professor at Columbia University and 1999 Nobel Prize Laureate in economics noted in his "A Theory of Optimum Currency Areas" that the "... economists of the nineteenth century were internationalists and generally favored a world currency. Thus John Stuart Mill wrote: 'So much of barbarism, however, still remains in the transactions of most civilized nations, that almost all independent countries choose to assert their nationality by having, to their own inconvenience and that of their neighbors, a peculiar currency of their own.'" John Stuart Mill clearly had in mind transactions costs involved in having separate monies. Not only the bid-ask spread and commissions in foreign exchange, but also problems of exchange controls and currency risk that impede trade, investment, and factor mobility. Rigidly fixed exchange rates under a gold standard provided a nearly universal money for most of the 19th century, although Asia was mainly on a silver standard.

As Mundell put it succinctly: "Money, in its role of medium of exchange is less useful if there are many currencies; although the costs of conversion are always present, they loom exceptionally large under inconvertibility or flexible exchange rates." (AER, 1961). In 1973, he proposed a European currency in "A Plan for a European Currency" and has become known as the "father of the euro." His plan extolled the benefits of a common currency: reserve pooling, less costly more transparent financial intermediation, and policy coordination. The larger the zone of a common currency, the greater are its advantages.

罗伯特·蒙代尔（Robert A. Mundell）：美国哥伦比亚大学教授，1999 年诺贝尔经济学奖获得者，因提出"最优货币区理论"和推动欧洲货币一体化而被誉为"欧元之父"。

The launching of the euro

On January 1, 1999 the euro was launched. The 11 member states launching the euro were Belgium, Germany, Spain, France, Ireland, Italy, Luxembourg, the Netherlands, Austria, Portugal and Finland. On January 1, 2000 Greece became the 12th member state to adopt the euro. At inception, the euro was worth $1.18, sank to $0.85, and then rose to a peak of $1.45, before stabilizing somewhat at $1.35. From a purchasing power point of view, it is still overvalued. Costs of conversion are disappearing. The bid-ask spread has gone to zero for banknotes and coins, and wire transfers are less expensive. In addition, exchange rate uncertainty under separate European currencies had led to an active market in London in foreign exchange options, futures, forwards and swaps in cross currency trading in Europe. With the adoption of a single currency, forex risk management is no longer necessary in the euro zone. Exchange rate volatility is zero, so options are worthless. European interest rates initially converged since currency risk in the euro zone was eliminated. However, they have diverged significantly in 2011 due to large fiscal deficits in Portugal, Ireland, Greece, and Spain. As a direct consequence of the deficits, sovereign debt in these countries pays a high default risk premium over German sovereigns of the same maturity. Matters have significantly worsened since 2010, but even then the risk spread was high. On December 27, 2011, Italian 10-year sovereign debt has a yield to maturity of 7%, making debt service more expensive.

截至 2011 年 11 月,希腊 10 年期主权债券的利率 已上升至约 30%。

In Figure 3.10, as debt rises to income in Europe, the interest rate on sovereigns rises to reflect the increased risk of default. Greece has the highest interest rates. The current plan is to restructure Greek debt by increasing its maturity to 15 years, and to ask banks holding Greek debt to mark it down 52.5%. This represents a sovereign default. In any case, European banks, especially French and Greek ones that hold billions of euros worth of Greek sovereigns have suffered write downs in these assets of 52.5%. The share price of these banks has plummeted.

Figure 3.10   Sovereign risk spread over German 10 year sovereigns and the debt to income ratio

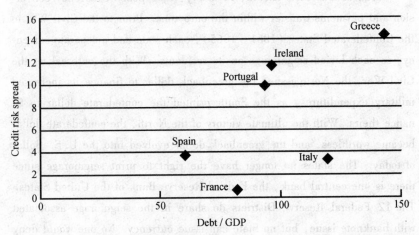

Source: *Eurostat*, debt to GDP 2011, *Les Echos*, interest spread on July 21, 2011.

The interest rate is being targeted at 3.5% for new debt that is bought by the European Financial Stability Facility, and commercial banks in Europe have written down their debt 52.5%, representing a default.

In the News: The euro and the Greek debt crisis

The Greek crisis hasn't proved that the euro was a mistake. But the political reaction to it has placed the experiment in serious danger by abandoning the no-bailout principle and replacing it with a doctrine that sovereign default in a currency zone is unthinkable. This policy makes no more sense than saying that bankruptcy should be impossible, because no one will lend to a company if it might go bust. What's worse is that Europe's leadership has adopted this view for the sake of defending the Greek government from the consequences of its irresponsibility on spending and mendacity about its true level of deficit and debt. The solution is not a return to monetary "sovereignty." Countries don't need unfettered monetary freedom. Only governments do, to bail themselves out of their own bad policies. If the euro should fail, it will be because those governments did too little to hold themselves to the discipline that a hard currency, albeit a paper one, demanded.

Source: *Wall Street Journal*, October 7, 2011.

Benefits of currency unification

货 币 一 体 化 的 收 益
（ Benefits of currency
unification）：理论上，欧
元区内由货币转换和支
付转换所产生的交易成
本应该消失。

Transactions costs should, in theory, disappear in currency conversion and payments transfer within the euro zone. Prior to the Civil War in the Confederated States (1861—1865), each state had a separate currency, so each levied seigniorage on its residents. With the outbreak of the Civil War, the North issued the greenback dollar to finance its increased military expenditures, as the South printed the confederate dollar to finance theirs. With the ultimate victory of the North, the confederate dollar became worthless, and the greenback dollar evolved into the U. S. dollar of today. The states no longer have the right to print seigniorage since there is one central bank, the Federal Reserve Bank of the United States. The 12 Federal Reserve Districts do share in the seigniorage associated with banknote issue, but no State can issue currency. No one would deny the benefits from currency and trade integration of the 50 United States. Capital market integration and liquidity effects have led to a low cost of capital, investment and growth in the United States. The U. S. Constitution prohibits taxes on trade among the states, and a banknote issued in New York is legal tender in California. Similarly, a note issued in San Francisco is accepted in New York.

This is now the case in Europe with the euro. Seigniorage is spread among the member countries by the issue of slightly different banknotes and coins. All are acceptable as the medium of exchange in the member countries. However, the countries within the Euro zone have not met the convergence conditions in terms of budget deficits less than 3% of GDP, and a national debt less than 60% of GDP established by the Maastricht Treaty. National macro-economic policy is supposed to be subjected to the monetary anchor of a common currency. European sovereign debt is denominated in euros, but it is not the common obligation of the European states, but rather the sovereign obligation of each country that issues the debt. There is little chance, however, that an individual country, such as Italy or Greece, would forego the benefits of the common currency zone to be able to run a higher deficit, financed by seigniorage through the printing press. A sovereign country can run a higher deficit, but it then faces default risk since it has difficulty financing its bonds on the open market. When Greece faced a default on its debt obligations in May 2010, the European's established a European Stabilization Fund hand in hand with the IMF to lend to Greece with conditionality. A second loan has been established for Greece, which may not meet the conditions required for further disbursement. The euro has depreciated, but further loans to Greece will, in all likelihood, postpone further default but make matters worse since Greek debt will be·larger. Greece does not credibly seem able to reduce its deficit below 8% of GDP. Further borrowing seems necessary. Since the debt to GDP ratio of Greece cannot go to infinity, a second restructuring will be necessary, sooner or later. Technically, Greece would not need to leave the euro zone by re-issuing the drachma, though this is not ruled out.

The Chinese yuan

The following essay makes the case for China maintaining a fixed exchange rate for stability and growth in the Chinese economy, despite much clamor for yuan revaluation of up to 35%. We take the position that a large devaluation would cause a major recession in China, much as the ever-appreciating yen caused recession, a housing and stock market slump, and a liquidity trap as in Japan where interest rates approached zero.

In the News: China Syndrome

In the 1980s and early '90s, Japan bashing was the favorite pastime in Washington. Japan's sin: its large "contribution" to a growing U. S. trade deficit. To solve this "problem," the U. S. demanded that Japan either strengthen the yen or face trade sanctions. Japan reluctantly complied. In Tokyo, "voluntary" export quotas and an ever-appreciating yen policy became orders of the day. But that one-two policy punch missed its target. Both the U. S. trade deficit and Japan's surplus continued to grow. The "strong" yen wasn't benign, however. It created a monster of a problem in Japan—a deflationary slump.

Figure 3.11 China, the emerging dragon

David Klein

Today, the U. S. trade deficit is almost double what it was five years ago. This time around China is the fingered culprit; it accounts for almost 25% of the deficit. To deal with China, Washington has dusted off the same defective game plan used to bash Japan.

Senators Charles Schumer (D. , N. Y.) and Lindsey Graham (R. , S. C.) have led the mercantilist charge on Capitol Hill. They claim that China manipulates its currency, the yuan. As a result, the yuan is undervalued and Chinese exports are subsidized. To correct for China's alleged unfair trade advantage, Senators Schumer and Graham have sponsored currency revaluation legislation and the Senate has agreed to give it an up or down vote by July. If it becomes law, the Chinese would be given six months to negotiate a yuan revaluation with the U. S. Absent a satisfactory revaluation, all China's exports to the U. S. would be slapped with a 27.5% tariff—a rate equal to the alleged yuan undervaluation.

Not to be outdone, members of the House have also laid the U. S. trade deficit at the yuan's doorstep. Congressmen Duncan Hunter (R. , Calif.) and Tim Ryan (D. , Ohio) have introduced the China Currency Act. It defines "exchange rate manipulation" as a "prohibited export subsidy" which, if deemed harmful, could—under Article VI of the General Agreement on Tariffs and Trade—trigger an antidumping or countervailing duty to offset the "subsidy." Furthermore, if currency manipulation injured the U. S. defense industry, the importation of Chinese defense products would be prohibited.

The clamor for a yuan revaluation is loud. At one time or another, everyone from President Bush to the G-7 has had a hand in the noisemaking. But the yuan quick fix might just be neat, plausible and wrong. Let's investigate:

• Does China manipulate its currency? It is not possible to give a categorical response to this question because "currency manipulation" is simply not an operational concept that can be used for economic analysis. The U.S. Treasury admitted as much in a March 2005 report that attempted to clarify the statutory meaning of currency manipulation for the Committees on Appropriations.

• Is the yuan undervalued vis-à-vis the dollar? No. The nominal yuan/dollar rate has been set in stone at 8.28 since June 1995. Adjusting for inflation in China and the U.S., the real value of the yuan has depreciated by only 2.4% during the last decade. And today the yuan is in equilibrium in the sense that China's inflation rate has converged to the U.S. rate. Not surprisingly, the IMF's most recent Country Report on China concluded that "it is difficult to find persuasive evidence that the renminbi [yuan] is substantially undervalued."

• Would a yuan revaluation reduce the U.S. trade deficit? Not much, if at all. After a yuan revaluation, the U.S. demand for foreign goods would simply be shifted from China to other countries.

• Would the House and Senate bills comport with international agreements and U.S. obligations? No. The yuan revaluation required by the Schumer-Graham bill would violate China's rights and sovereignty. Under the IMF Articles of Agreement (Article IV, sec. 2(b)), a member country is free to choose its own currency regime, including a fixed exchange rate. The bill's revaluation mandate would also throw a wrench into what has been an incredibly successful economic performance. Over the last decade, China avoided the great Asian financial maelstrom of 1997—1998 and has realized stable prices and an annual growth rate of over 9%. The yuan's fixed exchange rate against the dollar has provided the linchpin for that outstanding record.

According to Nobelist Robert Mundell, who is honorary president (along with Xu Jialu, vice chairman of the Standing Committee of the People's Congress) of Beijing's Mundell International University of Entrepreneurship, a substantial yuan revaluation would cut foreign direct investment, cut China's growth rate, delay convertibility, increase bad loans, increase unemployment, cause deflation distress in rural areas, destabilize Southeast Asia, reward speculators, set in motion more revaluation pressures, weaken the external role of the yuan and undermine China's compliance with World

Trade Organization rules. In consequence, a forced revaluation would violate Article IV, sec. 1(i) of the IMF Articles of Agreement, which states that a member shall "endeavor to direct its economic and financial policies toward the objective of fostering orderly economic growth with reasonable price stability."

● If China failed to revalue the yuan, the across the board 27.5% tariff triggered by Schumer-Graham would violate China's Most Favored Nation status under Article I of the GATT. Both the tariff and import prohibition features of the Hunter-Ryan China Currency Act would also violate the MFN treatment of China and would be ruled illegal by the WTO.

● Would it be in China's interest to revalue and get the U.S. politicos off its back? No. The effect of a yuan revaluation—deflation and recession—would even be more damaging to China than trade sanctions. We estimate that a 25% yuan revaluation against the dollar would result in a deflation of at least 15%. China would be forced to relive the terrible economic conditions induced by the 1930s yuan revaluation. In 1934, the U.S. Silver Purchase Act monetized silver. This effectively revalued the yuan by 24% because China was on the silver standard. The price of the yuan against the dollar went from 33 cents at the end of 1933 to 41 cents in 1935. As Milton Friedman concluded in his classic study Money Mischief: "Because silver was China's money, the rise in the price of silver had produced a major deflation, which in turn had led to severely troubled economic conditions."

It is time for the U.S. to stop rushing to judgment based on false premises. Antagonizing the world's most populous country—and doing so by illegal means to boot—is both irrational and dangerous.

Source: Steve H. Hanke and Michael Connolly, *The Wall Street Journal*, May 9, 2005. (reprinted by permission of the *WSJ* © 2005.)

The SWIFT international clearing system

SWIFT 清算系统（SWIFT clearing system）: 各国的银行间清算系统被 SWIFT 清算系统联系起来,这个系统为一千多个成员提供安全的电子汇款和信息传输。中国银行(Bank of China)是其成员之一。

In 1977, national inter-bank clearing systems were linked internationally through the **SWIFT clearing system**: an acronym for The Society for Worldwide Interbank Financial Telecommunications. The system has over a thousand members for whom it provides secure electronic transfer of monies and communication of messages internationally. Each member bank has an electronic identification and some handshaking goes on through the international computer centers for identification. When the bank ID is confirmed, transactions and communications can take place swiftly and securely since the computer system is a dedicated one. The CHIPS (Clearing House Interbank Payments System) clearing system in the United States handles tens of thousands of transactions and transfers many billions of dollars internationally per day. Member banks make electronic payments in CHIP dollars during the day and at the end of the day the master system nets out the sums to be paid, then transfers only the net amount of real money. This system is connected to the SWIFT system and is run by dedicated computers and member banks having strict code identification. Verification, confirmation, and authentification of transactions is also carried out by the CHIPS system.

Theories of the long-run movement of exchange rates

During World War I, a Swedish economist, Gustav Cassel corresponded with John Maynard Keynes, then editor of the *Economic Journal*. Cassel's position was that movements in exchange rates reflected movements in their relative purchasing power. He plotted monthly changes in prices in different countries and compared those to the movements in exchange rates at the same time period. Countries with higher inflation suffered currency depreciations. He dubbed his theory the "Purchasing Power Parity" (PPP) doctrine of the exchange rate in 1918. The PPP theory fit well the wartime facts of high inflation and currency depreciation in the belligerent nations.

Purchasing power parity

If a commodity can be purchased in one place and sold in another without any transport costs, tariffs, nor transactions costs, its price should be the same in both markets. This is the law of one price. It is an arbitrage relationship: arbitrageurs buying low and selling high will equalize commodity prices. That is:

$$P_{us} = SP_j \tag{3.7}$$

where the price of the product in yen is multiplied by the spot dollar price of the yen to yield the same price in the United States.

购买力平价理论 (**Purchasing power parity**):购买力平价理论要求汇率等于两种货币购买力之比。

Absolute purchasing power parity

绝对购买力平价理论
（Absolute purchasing
power parity）：如果所有
商品均可以被用于无成
本的套利活动，那么根据
任何一种同质商品用不
同货币所表示出的价格
便能够推导出两种货币
之间的即期汇率。这个
购买力平价理论的一般
形式就被称为绝对购买
力平价。

By the same token, if all goods are costlessly arbitraged, the spot exchange rate can be deduced from the ratio of any identical commodity price in each currency, or:

$$S = \frac{P_{us}}{P_j} \qquad (3.8)$$

This strong version of purchasing power parity (PPP) is known as absolute PPP, where the prices correspond to consumer price indices of similar commodities in each country.

The spot exchange rate can be inferred from commodity prices in different markets.

This is the reasoning embodied in the *Economist's* Big Mac hamburger standard.

In the News: The Big Mac standard

"ITALIANS like their coffee strong and their currencies weak. That, at least, is the conclusion one can draw from their latest round of grumbles about Europe's single currency. But are the Italians right to moan? Is the euro overvalued? Our annual Big Mac index suggests they have a case: the euro is overvalued by 17% against the dollar. How come? The euro is worth about $1.22 on the foreign-exchange markets. A Big Mac costs € 2.92, on average, in the euro zone and $3.06 in the United States. The rate needed to equalize the burger's price in the two regions is just $1.05. To patrons of McDonald's, at least, the single currency is overpriced. The Big Mac index, which we have compiled since 1986, is based on the notion that a currency's price should reflect its purchasing power. According to the late, great economist Rudiger Dornbusch, this idea can be traced back to the Salamanca school in 16th-century Spain. Since then, he wrote, the doctrine of purchasing-power parity (PPP) has been variously seen as a "truism, an empirical regularity or a grossly misleading simplification." Economists lost some faith in PPP as a guide to exchange rates in the 1970s, after the world's currencies abandoned their anchors to the dollar. By the end of the decade, exchange rates seemed to be drifting without chart or compass. Later studies showed that a currency's purchasing power does assert itself over the long run. But it might take three to five years for a misaligned exchange rate to move even halfway back into line. Our index shows that burger prices can certainly fall

> out of line with each other. If he could keep the burgers fresh, an ingenious arbitrageur could buy Big Macs for the equivalent of $1.27 in China, whose yuan is the most undervalued currency in our table, and sell them for $5.05 in Switzerland, whose franc is the most overvalued currency. The impracticality of such a trade highlights some of the flaws in the PPP idea. Trade barriers, transport costs and differences in taxes drive a wedge between prices in different countries. More important, the $5.05 charged for a Swiss Big Mac helps to pay for the retail space in which it is served, and for the labour that serves it. Neither of these two crucial ingredients can be easily traded across borders. David Parsley, of Vanderbilt University, and Shang-Jin Wei, of the International Monetary Fund, estimate that non-traded inputs, such as labour, rent and electricity, account for between 55% and 64% of the price of a Big Mac. The two economists disassemble the Big Mac into its separate ingredients. They find that the parts of the burger that are traded internationally converge towards purchasing-power parity quite quickly. Any disparity in onion prices will be halved in less than nine months, for example. But the non-traded bits converge much more slowly: a wage gap between countries has a "half-life" of almost 29 months. Seen in this light, our index provides little comfort to Italian critics of the single currency. If the euro buys less burger than it should, perhaps inflexible wages, not a strong currency, are to blame."
>
> Source: "Fast food and strong currencies"? *The Economist* Newspaper Limited, London (June 11, 2005).

Table 3.4 measures over and undervaluation of different currencies based on the Big Mac standard. It is a whimsical index, not to be taken seriously.

Table 3.4   The Economist's hamburger standard

	Big Mac price in dollars*	Implied PPP[†] of the dollar	Under(−)/ over(+) valuation against the dollar, %		Big Mac price in dollars*	Implied PPP[†] of the dollar	Under(−)/ over(+) valuation against the dollar, %
United States[‡]	3.06	—	—	Aruba	2.77	1.62	−10
Argentina	1.64	1.55	−46	Bulgaria	1.88	0.98	−39
Australia	2.50	1.06	−18	Colombia	2.79	2.124	−9
Brazil	2.39	1.93	−22	Costa Rica	2.38	369	−22
Britain	3.44	1.65[§]	+12	Croatia	2.50	4.87	−18
Canada	2.63	1.07	−14	Dominican Rep	2.12	19.6	−31
Chile	2.53	490	−17	Estonia	2.31	9.64	−24

（续表）

	Big Mac price in dollars*	Implied PPP† of the dollar	Under(−)/ over(+) valuation against the dollar, %		Big Mac price in dollars*	Implied PPP† of the dollar	Under(−)/ over(+) valuation against the dollar, %
China mainland	1.27	3.43	− 59	Fiji	2.50	1.39	− 18
Czech	2.30	18.4	− 25	Georgia	2.00	1.19	− 34
Republic				Guatemala	2.20	5.47	− 28
Denmark	4.58	9.07	+ 50	Honduras	1.91	11.7	− 38
Egypt	1.55	2.94	− 49	Iceland	6.67	143	+ 118
Euro area	3.58**	1.25‡	+ 17	Jamaica	2.70	53.9	− 12
Hong Kong SAR	1.54	3.92	− 50	Jordan	3.66	0.85	+ 19
Hungary	2.60	173	− 15	Latvia	1.92	0.36	− 37
Indonesia	1.53	4.771	− 50	Lebanon	2.85	1.405	− 7
Japan	2.34	81.7	− 23	Lithuania	2.31	2.12	− 24
Malaysia	1.38	1.72	− 55	Macau SAR	1.40	3.66	− 54
Mexico	2.58	9.15	− 16	Macedonia	1.90	31	− 38
New Zealand	3.17	1.45	+ 4	Moldova	1.84	7.52	− 40
Peru	2.76	2.94	− 10	Morocco	2.73	8.02	− 11
Philippines	1.47	26.1	− 52	Nicaragua	2.11	11.3	− 31
Poland	1.96	2.12	− 36	Norway	6.06	12.7	+ 98
Russia	1.48	13.7	− 52	Pakistan	2.18	42.5	− 29
Singapore	2.17	1.18	− 29	Paraguay	1.44	2.941	− 53
South Africa	2.10	4.56	− 31	Qatar	0.68	0.81	− 78
South Korea	2.49	817	− 19	Saudi Arabia	2.40	2.94	− 22
Sweden	4.17	10.1	+ 36	Serbia &	2.08	45.8	− 32
Switzerland	5.05	2.06	+ 65	Montenegro			
China Taiwan	2.41	24.5	− 21	Slovakia	2.09	21.6	− 32
Thailand	1.48	19.6	− 52	Slovenia	2.56	163	− 16
Turkey	2.92	1.31	− 5	Sri Lanka	1.75	57.2	− 43
Venezuela	2.13	1,830	− 30	Ukraine	1.43	2.37	− 53
				UAE	2.45	2.94	− 20
				Uruguay	1.82	14.4	− 40

Source：McDonald's, *The Economist*.

Notes：

* At current exchange rates. † Purchasing-power parity. ‡Average of New York, Chicago, San Francisco, and Atlanta. § Dollars per pound. ** Weighted average of member countries. # Dollars per euro.

Source："Fast food and strong currencies" ? *The Economist* Newspaper Limited, London（June 11, 2005）.

Arbitraging Big Macs

Let's follow the *Economist's* suggestion and buy Big Macs low in yuan and sell them high in USD! As the article suggests, the costs of arbitrage are high. Firstly, we have to buy yuan to purchase a Big Mac in Shang-hai. We pay the ask price of the yuan to the bank. Secondly, with our yuan, we buy the Big Mac in China. Thirdly, we pay insurance and freight charges to ship the Big Mac to New York. Fourthly, we pay any U. S. customs duties on prepared foods. Finally, we sell the Big Mac in Manhattan, paying the sales tax there. Let's write a formula for our arbitrage profits:

$$\pi = P_{us}(1 - t_{us}) - S_{ask}P_c(1 + \tau_{us} + t_{c-us}) \qquad (3.9)$$

When our transactions costs are reckoned in, arbitrage profits are likely to be nil. We incur these additional arbitrage costs:

1. We pay the ask rate, S_{ask}, a premium, for the yuan—these are currency exchange costs.

2. We pay the cost of shipping and insuring the Big Mac, t_{c-us}.

3. We pay US customs rate on the Big Mac, τ_{us}.

4. Finally we pay the NY excise tax, t_{us}.

Net of these costs, we will not make a dime since arbitrage assures that the law of one price holds, assuring that arbitrage profits are zero, $\pi = 0$: or

$$P_{us}(1 - t_{us}) = S_{ask}P_c(1 + \tau_{us} + t_{c-us}) \qquad (3.10)$$

The bid-ask spread is part of the transactions costs that the arbitrageur must cover in order to make the arbitrage profitable. The other transactions costs—import duties and transport costs—are more obvious, but they must also be covered to make arbitrage profitable.

The strict law of one price

For the law of one price to exactly hold, taxes, transports costs, import duties, and the bid-ask spread all must be zero, in which case arbitrage (in either direction) imposes the strict law of one price, or:

$$P_{us} = SP_c \qquad (3.11)$$

With non-traded goods (in which no arbitrage takes place due to high transport costs or prohibitive duties), this condition cannot be satisfied. In general, the spot exchange rate, whether bid or ask, will not exactly satisfy the law of one price due to the presence of duties and transport costs on traded goods as well as the prohibitive costs of arbitraging non-traded goods. A weaker form of purchasing power parity-relative PPP—however, may save the day.

Relative purchasing power parity

Relative PPP does not require that the level of the exchange rate equal the ratio of purchasing powers, but that the change in the spot rate

严格的一价定律（The strict law of one price）：如果要使一价定律严格成立，那么税收、运输费用、进口关税和外汇的买卖价差必须为零。在这种情况下，任何方向的套利活动都会使严格的一价定律成立。一般说来，即期汇率可能会因为可贸易商品的关税、运输费用以及不可贸易商品的存在而不严格地满足一价定律。

相对购买力平价理论（Relative purchasing power parity）：相对购买力平价理论不要求汇率等于两种货币购买力之比，而是要求即期汇率的变化反映通货膨胀率的差异。

reflect the inflation rate differential. In other words, there is no change in the real exchange rate. Relative PPP states:

$$E\left(\frac{S_{t+1} - S_t}{S_t}\right) = E\left(\frac{P_{t+1}^{us} - P_t^{us}}{P_t^{us}}\right) - E\left(\frac{P_{t+1}^{j} - P_t^{j}}{P_t^{j}}\right) \qquad (3.12)$$

where the left-hand side of equation (3.12) is the expected appreciation of the foreign currency in terms of home currency and the right-hand side is the expected inflation rate differential: that is, the expected rate of inflation at home less the expected rate of inflation abroad (Japan). The relative purchasing power parity theory of the exchange rate is depicted in Figure 3.12.

Figure 3.12   Relative purchasing power parity

When inflation at home is expected to be 1% greater than abroad, the expected price of foreign currency rises 1%. In fact, whenever the shocks are mainly monetary in nature, the purchasing power parity theory provides a good forecast of future exchange rates. It is not an arbitrage equation; rather it says that movements in currencies reflect movements in their relative purchasing power.

The monetary approach to the exchange rate

If different movements in price levels cause movements in the exchange rate, it is natural to ask what causes different inflation rates internationally. The old view that "inflation is too much money chasing too few goods" is not far from the truth. When money grows faster than income, prices tend to rise. Consequently, countries that inflate their money supply relative to the supply of goods experience higher inflation and greater depreciation of their currencies. This is known as the monetary approach to the exchange rate.

It follows from **the quantity theory of money**:

$$MV = Py \qquad (3.13)$$

Where M is the money supply (currency plus checking deposits), V is the income velocity of circulation of money, P is the price level, in this case the implicit GDP deflator, and y is real GDP. The price level is thus determined by:

$$P = \frac{MV}{y} \qquad (3.14)$$

An equivalent but insightful way of defining income velocity as the inverse of the demand for money as a fraction of income, that is $k = 1/V$ we may express the price level as the ratio of money supply to money demand:

$$P = \frac{M}{ky} \qquad (3.15)$$

where M is the money supply and ky is the demand for money. The higher the money supply relative to money demand, the higher the price level.

In terms of percentage changes, the rate of inflation is determined by growth in the money supply relative to growth in money demand:

$$\frac{\Delta P}{P} = \frac{\Delta M}{M} - \frac{\Delta y}{y} - \frac{\Delta k}{k} \qquad (3.16)$$

Inflation is caused by "too much money chasing too few goods", $\frac{\Delta M}{M} - \frac{\Delta y}{y}$, compounded by any percentage fall in the demand for money relative to income, $\frac{\Delta k}{k} < 0$, or, equivalently, an acceleration in the income velocity of money, $\frac{\Delta V}{V} > 0$.

In a sense, money is the root of all inflationary evil. It helps to understand why inflation bursts out here and there periodically. In principle, any third grader as Governor of the Central Bank could follow a simple Friedman rule to maintain a low, constant rate of growth in the money supply to avoid inflation. The problem is that the issue of money, seigniorage,

货币数量理论（The quantity theory of money）：认为货币数量变化与物价变化之间存在因果关系。其核心思想是，当其他因素不变时，货币数量增加会导致物价增加。用公式表示为$MV = Py$，其中 M 为货币供应量，V 为货币流通速率，P 为价格水平，y 为 GDP 水平。

式(3.16)表明通货膨胀率由货币供给相对于货币需求的增长率所决定。

68   International Financial Management

is often the finance of ultimate resort of the fiscal deficit. For example, if the fiscal deficit is 10% of GDP, and 3% can be financed by borrowing at home through the sale of bonds domestically, and 2% can be financed by borrowing abroad by the sale of bonds to foreigners, the residual finance must come from the "printing press" or seigniorage finance, 5%. New money must be issued. That is:

除了征税和发行国债,政府还可以通过启动印钞机器来弥补财政赤字。新发行货币的数量如式(3.17)所示。

$$\frac{dM}{dt} = (G + rD + V - T) - \left(\frac{dB}{dt} + \frac{dB^*}{dt}\right) \qquad (3.17)$$

or new seignorage, dM/dt, must finance the unfinanced residual of the fiscal deficit, $(G + rD + V - T) - (dB/dt + dB^*/dt)$. where G is government spending on goods and services, rD is interest payments on the public debt, V transfer payments, and T taxes. The change in the debt equals the sum of sales of new bonds to the domestic and foreign public: $\frac{dD}{dt} = \frac{dB}{dt} + \frac{dB^*}{dt}$. Another way of expressing inflationary finance is as the inflationary tax, multiplying and dividing the left hand side of (3.17) by M:

$$M\left(\frac{1}{M}\frac{dM}{dt}\right) = (G + rD + V - T) - \left(\frac{dB}{dt} + \frac{dB^*}{dt}\right) \qquad (3.18)$$

where $(1/M)(dM/dt)$ is the percentage inflationary tax rate and M is the base of the inflationary tax. There is a limit to the amount of inflationary tax since high inflation renders money a poor store of value, so money demand collapses i. e. velocity accelerates. This exacerbates inflation. Inflationary episodes such as in Peru in the late 1980s were the result of collapsing real GDP, a fiscal deficit residual equal to 20% of GDP, financed almost solely my new money issue, and accelerating velocity. Inflation made the *inti* worthless, so the currency had to be changed. In the context of the exchange rate, countries that rely more heavily on inflationary finance have greater depreciations than those that do not. This suggests that the purchasing power parity relationship has as its foundation the growth of money supply relative to the growth of money demand.

Applying the Concept: Inflation in China in 2005

The percentage increase in China's Consumer Price Index in 2005 was only 1.8%, despite high money growth 17.6%. This is due to some prices being controlled, particularly fuel and gasoline. The implicit price deflator, a broader measure, rose however 3.4% more accurately reflecting inflation in China. A strong factor keeping inflation down, in addition to 9.9% real growth in GDP, is the rise in demand for money relative to income in China, 4.3%, a sign of financial deepening in Ronald McKinnon's terminology. There is greater financial intermediation due to an income elasticity of demand for money equal nearly to 2. Here is the summary for 2005.

- Increase in Implicit GDP Deflator 3.4%, $\frac{\Delta P}{P}$.

- Increase in Money supply (Money + Quasi - Money) 17.6%, $\frac{\Delta M}{M}$.

- Increase in Real GDP 9.9%, $\frac{\Delta y}{y}$.

- Increase in demand for money as a fraction of Nominal GDP 4.3%, $\frac{\Delta k}{k}$.

Had money demand not increased relative to income by 4.3%, the inflation rate would have been 7.7%. In terms of the actual outcome:

$$\frac{\Delta P}{P} = \frac{\Delta M}{M} - \frac{\Delta y}{y} - \frac{\Delta k}{k} \quad \text{or} \quad 3.4 = 17.6 - 9.9 - 4.3$$

Source: Author's calculations.

The great advantage of the quantity theory of money is that it provides a basis for estimating the difference in expected inflation rates, thus providing a foundation for the theory of purchasing power parity. The level of the exchange rate in terms of the monetary approach is given by the ratio of internal prices. Consequently:

$$S = \frac{\dfrac{M}{ky}}{\dfrac{M^*}{k^* y^*}} \tag{3.19}$$

That is, the level of the exchange rate is determined by the relative money supplies and money demands.

In general, relative purchasing power parity as a monetary phenomenon can be expressed as:

$$\frac{\Delta S}{S} = \left[\frac{\Delta M}{M} - \frac{\Delta y}{y} - \frac{\Delta k}{k} \right] - \left[\frac{\Delta M^*}{M} - \frac{\Delta y^*}{y} - \frac{\Delta k^*}{k} \right] \quad (3.20)$$

—more rapid monetary growth at home causes the home currency to depreciate, as does slower real economic growth. By the same token, a fall in domestic money demand compared to foreign money demand also depreciates the home currency. This is known as the monetary approach to the exchange rate.

实际汇率（Real exchange rate）:实际汇率是指将现实汇率经过相对物价指数调整后得到的汇率。

Deviations in exchange rates from purchasing power parity can, however, result from real shocks and changes in the terms of trade. For that reason, it is useful to have a measure of the *real exchange rate* to capture changes in the exchange rate relative to the *PPP* rate. The concept of the real exchange rate is a simple one, measuring the costs of one country's goods in terms of another's. A bilateral real exchange rate is defined as:

$$RER = \frac{P}{SP^*} \quad (3.21)$$

Where P is the price level at home and SP^* is the foreign price level expressed in terms of home currency. When domestic prices rise relative to foreign prices, a real appreciation is said to take place. This means home goods can buy more foreign goods because a positive deviation from purchasing power parity has taken place. A dramatic example of the real depreciation of the dollar in terms of the euro has been the increase in the dollar price of the euro from \$0.90 to \$1.37 from 2005 to 2008, while there has been little difference in the inflation rates. The euro has thus experienced a real appreciation, while the dollar has suffered a real depreciation.

Naturally, there are many currencies, so the best *RER* measurement is one that takes into account the weight of each currency in terms of trade. The IMF provides such a calculation.

The IMF's real effective exchange rate

IMF 的真实有效汇率（The IMF's real effective exchange rate）:IMF（国际货币基金组织）的真实有效汇率指数是一个指数加权指数。这个指数用外国商品来衡量本国商品的价格。

The International Monetary Fund's (IMF) real effective exchange rate index, *RER*, (line rec, International Financial Statistics) is an exponentially-weighted index which measures the price of a home country's goods in terms of foreign goods. This type of index has excellent properties and is known as a *harmonic index*, having exponential weights that sum to one:

$$RER = 100 \prod_{i=1}^{n} \left(\frac{P}{S_i P_i} \right)^{w_i}$$

$$= 100 \left(\frac{P}{S_1 P_1}\right)^{W_1} \left(\frac{P}{S_2 P_2}\right)^{W_2} \left(\frac{P}{S_3 P_3}\right)^{W_3} \cdots \left(\frac{P}{S_n P_n}\right)^{W_n} \quad (3.22)$$

As the RER rises, the home currency is said to experience a real appreciation while if RER falls, a real depreciation is said to occur. The Π symbol stands for the product of the i terms, in the same way that the Σ stands for the sum of various terms in a summation expression. P indicates the consumer price index of the home country, S_i indicates the home currency price of currency i, and the P_i indicates the consumer price index in country i. The exponential weights for each currency i are the w_i terms and must sum to unity (i. e. the equation is homogeneous of degree one so that a doubling of domestic prices relative to all exchange rate adjusted foreign prices leads to a doubling of the index). The w_i can represent simply trade weights with different countries, or in the case of the IMF's RER, the weights are known as effective trade weights.

Essentially, if the USA trades heavily with China and Mexico, the weights for the yuan and the peso would be relatively high in the US's RER. The International Financial Statistics are published in CD-ROM format monthly by the IMF, but lags in the data are a problem. Bloomberg contains more current financial data on the real exchange rate.

Foreign currency futures versus forward contracts

Futures are standard contracts per currency traded on the floor of an organized exchange. Maturities are usually less than one year and have fixed maturity dates. Prices are determined by the Chicago method of "open outcry". In Francesca Taylor's words: "This is very colorful to watch, and conveys 'price transparency' by allowing every trader equal access to the same trade at the same price. Technically the meaning of open outcry is that your bid or your offer is good 'whilst the breath is warm.' What this actually means is that each trader on the exchange will shout out what trade he is trying to execute. He is not able to just shout it once and assume everyone has heard him, he must keep shouting. If he stops shouting, it is assumed that he no longer wishes to execute his trade at that price level. Everyone around him is also shouting, resulting in a lot of noise without too much clarity. The consequence of this is that not only do traders have to shout continuously what trades they are trying to fill, but they must also 'hand-signal' their trades, in case a trader a long way away

期货合约（Futures）：期货合约是在有组织的某种交易所内进行交易的某种标准化合约。合约的期限一般低于一年，并且有固定的到期日。

cannot hear clearly. The hands and the mouth must say the same thing. Traders cannot just trade with hand signals and they must take examinations to comply with the requirements of the respective exchanges. " (p. 26)

In the futures market, initial margin is required and the position is " marked to market" daily. Delivery rarely takes place—the purchase of an offsetting position unwinds the contract. A single commission is paid for the round trip purchase and sale. There is no counterparty risk as the exchange guarantees the contracts. Trading hours are regular exchange hours, but recently electronic trading takes place on a 24 hour basis. While liquid, the futures market is small in size.

远期合约(Forwards): 远期合约没有固定的合约规模,合约期限也可以超过一年。

Forwards, on the other hand, are any size desired, with maturities occasionally longer than a year. Trading occurs between firms and banks in the interbank market, with prices determined by bid ask quotes—the spread providing profits for the banks. Standing bank " relations" are necessary, but not margin collateral. In the forwards market, banks are connected 24 hours a day via the SWIFT system and negotiate forward prices directly. In volume, the forwards market dwarfs the futures markets. As a practical matter, international businesses hedge their risks through the forward market, through money market hedges, and foreign exchange swaps. Forwards give them the flexibility in terms of size of contract, maturity terms, and does not require the firm to tie up working balances in margin deposits. Money market hedges allow for a matching of streams of payments and receipts in a foreign currency, thus reducing exchange rate exposure. Foreign exchange swaps do the same thing, but allow each firm to take advantage of its comparative advantage in borrowing in its local currency, swapping the obligations of the loans through a swap dealer. Both borrowers are able to hedge their ongoing exposure through swaps at a lower cost. Nevertheless, the bid-ask spreads in foreign exchange and interest rates allows the swap dealer to make profits.

In forward markets, money markets, and swap markets, there is counterparty risk, broadly defined as non-fulfillment or downgrading, either partial or complete, of the terms of financial contract.

Points quotations

A point is the last digit of a quotation. Thus, a point in foreign exchange quotations is typically equal to 0.0001 or 1/10,000 because currencies are usually quoted to four decimal points. A point is sometimes called a *pip* by foreign exchange traders. Consequently, when a forward quotation is given in terms of forward points (also known as swap points), it is necessary to adjust the spot quotation accordingly to obtain an outright forward quotation. For example, consider the following outright spot quotations on the pound sterling and the one, two, three, six and twelve month forward point quotations in Table 3.5, as well as the corresponding outright forward rates.

Table 3.5   Points and outright forward quotations

Spot rate GBP/USD = 1.76048/1.76242.

	Forward points			Outright forward quotation(£ / $)	
Period	Bid	Ask	Period	Bid	Ask
1 Month	−0.00195	−0.00185	1 Month	1.75853	1.76057
2 Months	−0.00354	−0.00313	2 Months	1.75694	1.75929
3 Months	−0.00440	−0.00410	3 Months	1.75608	1.75832
6 Months	−0.00599	−0.00541	6 Months	1.75448	1.75702
12 Months	−0.00619	−0.00541	12 Months	1.75428	1.75702
2 Years	−0.00639	−0.00541	2 Years	1.75408	1.75702

Source: OzForex Foreign Exchange Services, July 14, 2005.

As a general rule:

• When the bid in points is larger than the offer in points, the reference currency is at a discount, so the points are subtracted from the spot quotations to obtain the outright forward quotation.

• When the bid in points is smaller than the offer in points, the reference currency is at a premium, so the points are added to the spot quotations to obtain the outright forward quotation. Notice again that the reciprocal of the American bid equals the European ask quotation. Likewise, the reciprocal of the American ask equals the European bid. This is obviously the case since when bidding pounds for dollars, a bank or trader is simultaneously offering dollars for pounds. The corresponding European quotation is reported in Table 3.6.

Table 3.6 European style outright quotations

Outright forward quotation(£/$)

Period	Bid	Ask
1 Month	0.56800	0.56866
2 Months	0.56841	0.56917
3 Months	0.56872	0.56945
6 Months	0.56915	0.56997
12 Months	0.56915	0.57003
2 Years	0.56915	0.57010

Source: OzForex Foreign Exchange Services, July 14, 2005.

Forwards and futures in commodities

Like futures, forward contracts are agreements to exchange an underlying asset, such as gold, at an agreed price at some future date. Consequently, futures and forward contracts may be used either to manage risk or for speculative purposes. However, there are important differences between forwards and futures that bear recalling:

1. A forward contract is negotiated directly between counterparties and is therefore tailor-made, whereas futures contracts are standardized agreements that are traded on an exchange.

2. Although forward contracts offer greater flexibility, there is a degree of counterparty risk, whereas futures contracts are guaranteed by the exchange on which they are traded.

3. Because futures contracts can be sold to third parties at any point prior to maturity, they are more liquid than forward contracts.

4. Futures prices are determined by the carrying costs at any time. These costs include the interest cost of borrowing gold plus insurance and storage charges.

5. The cost of a futures contract is also determined by the "initial margin", the cash deposit that is paid to the broker.

Speculative positions in forward contracts

A speculative position in a forward contract is the forward purchase or sale of an asset or commodity for delivery at some specified date in the future at a price, F, determined today. If a speculator who sold

远期合约的投机头寸（A speculative position in a forward contract）：投机头寸是指以今天决定的价格 F 在未来某一特定交割日交割某一特定资产或商品。

gold short, purchases gold spot upon the delivery date at a price, S, to cover the short position, the profits/losses per unit of gold are $F - S$. Gold is usually traded forward in large units—metric tons. On the other hand, if the spot price of gold is greater than F the trader loses $S - F$ in covering the forward contract. The payoff for a forward sale of gold at the price F is illustrated in Figure 3.13.

Figure 3.13 Payoff from a short position in gold

A long position in gold is a purchase of gold for forward delivery. Consequently, if the spot price upon maturity of the forward purchase is higher than the forward price, a speculator gains $S - F$. If the spot price is less, the trader loses. A gold mining company that sells its gold forward may not be perfectly hedged. If the spot price of gold rises before maturity, the company may be forced to sell its forward contract at a loss if it is illiquid. Similarly, if it has production problems, it may not be able to deliver the gold, so may end up buying and selling spot at the same time.

The cost of carry and the forward arbitrage price

The forward price of an asset may be computed by the cost of carry and a no-profit arbitrage condition. Consider the following steps:

持仓成本和远期套利价格 (**The cost of carry and the forward arbitrage price**): 资产的远期价格可以通过无套利原则和持仓成本来计算。

- Borrow S today at interest rate r.
- Purchase today one unit of the security at price S.
- Sell forward today one unit of the security at price F for delivery at time T.
- At maturity T, cash in the dividend, k, on the security, and

- Deliver the security at maturity T at agreed upon price F.
- Pay off loan at T.

The profit from this arbitrage can be computed as the forward sale price, plus the dividend received, less the principal and interest on the borrowed funds. That is:

$$\pi = F + [(1+k)^T - 1]S - (1+r)^T S \qquad (3.23)$$

Zero arbitrage profits imply: $F = [(1+r)^T - (1+k)^T + 1]S$

Or, subtracting S from both sides of the equation yields *the cost of carry*:

$$F - S = [(1+r)^T - (1+k)^T]S \qquad (3.24)$$

When $T = 1$, the cost of carry is simply:

$$F - S = [r - k]S \qquad (3.25)$$

The **carry trade** requires that the forward price be at a premium when the borrowing rate is greater than the dividend rate or $r > k$. When the security has zero coupon $k = 0$, or is a commodity with storage costs, $k < 0$, arbitrage pricing requires a premium over spot on the forward sale.

Let's take a few examples. First, suppose you sell 500 ounces of gold short for delivery in the futures market at \$1,680 in three months. In a short sale, an investor borrows shares or gold from a brokerage firm and sells them, hoping to profit by buying them back at lower prices. If they rise, the investor faces a loss. Uncovered short sales are those shares or gold that have been borrowed and sold, but not yet covered by repurchase. If the spot price falls to \$1660, three months later when you cover your short position, gaining \$20 per ounce or \$10,000, as illustrated in Figure 3.14.

Figure 3.14 A gain from a short position in gold

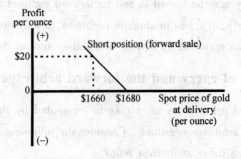

However, if the price of gold rises in the spot market to \$1,700, you will lose \$2 an ounce, or \$10,000, as shown in Figure 3.15.

Figure 3.15   A loss from a short position in gold

Since the forward rate is centered at the expected future value of gold, it is as likely you will gain at least $11,000 as you will lose at least $11,000. **A hedged position** combines a short with a long position, guaranteeing neither gains nor losses. However, you will pay the ask for the long forward and receive the bid for the short forward—that is, you will pay the spread. In addition, there is a commission. Since the hedged position is the combination of a long and a short position for the same amount and maturity of a security or asset, what is gained on the long position is lost on the short position, and vice versa. Graphically, the hedged position, ignoring transactions costs, is the sum of the long and short positions, yielding the horizontal axis in Figure 3.16—a zero payoff.

对冲头寸(**A hedged position**)：一个对冲头寸将一个多头头寸与一个空头头寸结合起来，从而保证既无收益也无损失。

Figure 3.16   A hedged position in gold

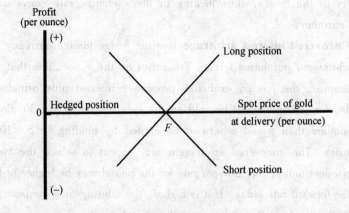

By the same token, a long position—i. e. a forward purchase, gains when the spot price rises and loses upon covering when the spot price falls.

Gold is a hedge against inflation, as evidenced by these observations: "Crude's coming back up, and gold is getting more buying," said Frank McGhee, head trader at brokerage Alliance Financial LLC in Chicago. 'Oil's stability is allowing gold to regain some of the price that it shed,' he said. Gold futures for August delivery rose 50 cents to $420.70 an ounce at noon on the Comex division of the New York Mercantile Exchange." (Source: Jennifer Itzenson, *Bloomberg*, July 15, 2005.) Of course, this writer was right, gold is currently in December 2011 $1,560 a troy ounce.

Arbitrage determination of the spot and future rates

Arbitrage-buying low, selling high and profiting from differences in price when the same security, currency, or commodity is traded on two or more markets. An arbitrageur simultaneously buys one contract of say gold in New York and sells one contract of gold in Chicago, locking in a small profit because at that moment the price on the two markets is different. Arbitrageurs perform the economic function of making markets trade more efficiently by eliminating different prices for the same item. **Covered interest arbitrage** hedges the foreign currency risk, thus covering the arbitrage from exchange rate losses in the future spot market. The hedge takes the form of a forward sale for foreign currency today at an agreed upon rate for delivery in the future, thus locking in the exchange rate conversion to home currency.

Uncovered interest arbitrage does not hedge foreign currency risk. The arbitrageur purchases foreign Treasuries on the expectation that when they mature, the foreign exchange proceeds—interest plus principal in pounds, for example—will be sold on the spot market in say 30 days for more dollars than would otherwise be earned by holding U. S. 30 day Treasuries. The uncovered arbitrageur may expect to sell at the forward rate in effect today, but the spot rate for the pound may be higher or lower than the forward rate today. If it is higher, the arbitrageur-speculator gains by selling pounds at the higher rate, but if it is lower, there are unantici-

抛补套利 (Covered interest arbitrage): 抛补套利能够对冲外汇风险，通过这种办法可以抵补在未来即期外汇市场上的潜在汇率损失。

非抛补套利 (Uncovered interest arbitrage): 非抛补套利不对冲外汇风险。

pated losses on the exchange conversion. Since the arbitrager does not cover foreign exchange exposure by selling pounds in the forward market, this type of interest arbitrage is called uncovered.

Covered interest arbitrage

Let's jot down some preliminary notation. To focus on strict interest rate parity, we will initially ignore the foreign exchange and Treasury bid-ask spreads. As we shall later see, these spreads are not insignificant and add substantially to the cost of arbitraging for an individual investor. Banks and financial intermediaries trading on their own accounts are spared the spreads and can arbitrage large amounts to take advantage of small deviations from interest rate parity.

Spot rate for the pound: $S = (\$/\pounds)$ spot = number of dollars paid today for one British pound sterling today. One month forward rate for the pound: $F = (\$/\pounds)$ forward = number of dollars received in three months for the sale of one pound sterling. This rate is agreed upon today.

The U. S. Treasury bill three month rate: r_{us} = the interest rate on the three month US Treasury bill (the quarterly rate). U. S. Treasury bills are issued with maturities of three months in denominations beginning at $1,000. Treasury bills do not bear interest nor pay coupons. Instead, investors purchase bills at a discounted price from their face value. At maturity, the Treasury redeems the bills at full face or par value. The difference between the discounted price paid and the face value of the bill is paid when redeemed. T-bills are also quoted by price. An investor pays the ask when buying T-bills and receives the bid when selling them. For the moment, we set the bid-ask spread at zero. The U. K. Treasury bill interest rate: r_{uk} = interest rate on a three month U. K. Treasury bill. To simplify the notation, this is the three-month interest rate, i. e. the quarterly rate, not the interest rate per annum. To convert the annual interest rate to a 90 day interest rate, the convention is to multiply the annual rate by 90/360 or 1/4 to convert to a quarterly rate: that is, just divide by four.

To take advantage of small profit opportunities by arbitraging short term liquid capital, take the following two steps:

- **Step I. Compare dollars to dollars**

1. Route one: With one million dollars, buy 90 day US Treasury bills. At maturity, they will yield principal plus interest of $(1 + r_{us})$ million dollars. Each dollar invested yields $1 + r_{us}$ dollars in 90 days.

2. Route two:

a. Buy $[1/(S)]$ million pounds sterling in the spot market at S.

b. Invest $[1/(S)]$ pounds sterling in 90 day U. K. T-bills, yielding $[(1/S)(1+r_{uk})]$ million pounds in three months.

c. Sell $[(1/S)(1+r_{uk})]$ pounds sterling in the forward market at F, yielding $F[(1/S)(1+r_{uk})]$ million or $\left(\dfrac{F}{S}\right)(1+r_{uk})$ dollars at settlement in three months.

- **Step II. Select higher dollar return**

If $(1+r_{us}) > \left(\dfrac{F}{S}\right)(1+r_{uk})$, place short term capital in US Treasuries due to the higher yield. That is, sell pound Treasuries from your portfolio, buy dollars spot, buy 90 day U. S. Treasuries, sell the proceeds 90 days forward. You have completed a round trip in pounds and gained the covered arbitrage differential.

If $(1+r_{us}) < \left(\dfrac{F}{S}\right)(1+r_{uk})$, place short term capital in UK Treasuries due to the higher yield. That is, sell 90 day U. S. Treasuries from your portfolio, buy pounds spot, buy U. K. 90 day Treasuries, sell the pound proceeds forward for delivery in 90 days. You have completed a round trip and gained the covered arbitrage differential.

However, if

$$(1+r_{us}) = \left(\dfrac{F}{S}\right)(1+r_{uk}) \tag{3.26}$$

covered interest rate parity holds: there are no unexploited arbitrage profit opportunities, so do nothing!

Covered interest parity can be expressed in terms of the percentage interest rate differential versus the percentage premium or discount on the forward pound. Subtract $(1+r_{uk})$ from both sides of the interest rate parity equation and simplify:

$$(r_{us} - r_{uk}) = \left(\dfrac{F-S}{S}\right)(1+r_{uk}) \tag{3.27}$$

which says that the interest rate differential in favor of U. S Treasuries is just (approximately) offset by the premium on the pound sterling. If interest rates on US Treasuries are two percent higher than on UK Treasuries, the forward pound will be at a 2% premium. Covered interest rate parity can be illustrated in Figure 3.17.

Figure 3.17   Covered interest rate parity

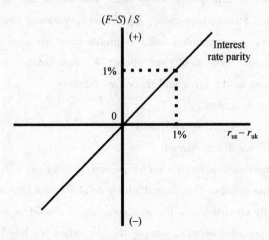

抛补的利率平价（Covered interest rate parity）：如图 3.17 所示，在利率平价曲线上，把短期资金投资于美国国库券和英国国库券没有差别；在利率平价曲线的右边，投资于美国国库券会获得抛补套利收益；在利率平价曲线的左边，投资于英国国库券会获得抛补套利收益。

Along the interest rate parity line, it does not matter whether you invest your short term funds in U. S. Treasuries or UK Treasuries. To the right of the interest parity line, the covered arbitrage differential is in favor of U. S. Treasuries. To the left, the CAD is in favor of U. K. Treasuries.

The covered arbitrage differential

The covered arbitrage differential (CAD) in favor of 90 day U. S. Treasuries is measured by:

$$CAD = (1 + r_{us}) - \left(\frac{F}{S}\right)(1 + r_{uk}) \qquad (3.28)$$

抛补套利差异（The covered arbitrage differential）：投资美国国库券的抛补套利差异可以为正也可以为负。如果为正，则应该卖出英国国库券，买入美国国库券；如果为负，则应该卖出美国国库券，买入英国国库券。

which may be positive or negative. If positive, sell U. K. T-bills, buy dollars spot with the pound proceeds, buy U. S. T-bills, sell the dollars forward (buy pounds forward), thus gaining the CAD in the round trip arbitrage. If negative, sell U. S. T-bills, buy pounds spot, buy U. K. T-bills and sell pounds forward (buy dollars forward), to gain the CAD in favor of U. K. Treasuries.

Transaction costs

Of course, there are transactions costs since the investor must pay the ask when buying and receives the bid when selling, effectively paying the bid-ask spreads on forex to the financial institution. Similarly, when buying US or UK Treasuries, the investor pays the ask price, while when selling, the investor receives the bid. For this reason, slight deviations from interest rate parity do not trigger covered arbitrage movements, except pos-

套利成本（Arbitrage costs）：在本节的例子中，存在外汇与国库券的三次买卖价差以及一次佣金。它们分别是：外汇买卖价差、美国国库券的买卖价差、英国国库券的买卖价差以及外汇和国库券买卖佣金。

sibly by financial institutions. Ignoring transactions costs, capital will arbitrage until interest rate parity holds since the assets are risk-free. The CAD, including transactions costs, equals zero, yielding covered interest parity. Otherwise, unexploited risk less profits from arbitrage would exist.

Just what are these **arbitrage costs**? We can identify three spreads and commissions in the forex and treasuries markets:

1. The forex spread.

2. The U.S. T-bill spread, and

3. The U.K. T-bill spread.

4. Commissions on foreign exchange and Treasuries.

Taking into account the rates at which an individual transacts, the interest rate parity condition is a bit more complex. It should be borne in mind that when you purchase pounds, you pay the ask, when you buy UK treasuries you again pay the ask, but when you sell pounds forward you receive the bid. That is, there are transactions costs in short term money arbitrage.

An example of covered interest arbitrage

When the interest differential does not exactly offset the forward discount, it is possible to make small gains by arbitraging money. Consider an example of either investing $10,000 in three-month US Treasury Bills, or converting into euros, purchasing European Treasury Bills, and selling the euro proceeds in the three month futures market. The basic data are given in Table 3.7.

Table 3.7 Basic arbitrage data

US T-bill rate(3 months)	0.9625
Euro T-bill rate(3 months)	0.9000
Sport price of the euro	1.2500
Forward price of the euro(3 months)	1.2700

In this case, the interest rate differential against euro Treasuries is less than the percentage future premium on the euro. Consequently, small gains ($33.41) can be made by arbitraging toward euro T-bills, and selling the euro proceeds three months forward. Once again, we are covered in the futures market. Thus this risk less arbitrage (buying low-selling high) will eliminate arbitrage gains. The steps in covered interest arbitrage are illustrated in Figure 3.18.

Figure 3.18   Covered interest arbitrage with a gain

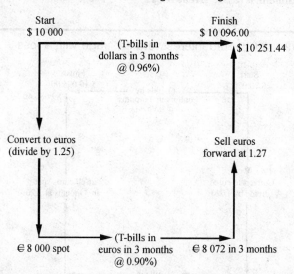

For arbitrage activity to be truly profitable to the investor, the correct rate quotation must be used for each transaction. When US T-bills are sold, the bid rate is received, when pounds are bought spot, the dollar bid—pound ask rate is used, the ask rate for UK T-bills is paid and the forward bid price of the pound is received (or equivalently, the forward ask price of the dollar is paid.) Every transaction has a transactions cost. The round-trip must cover all the transactions costs to be worthwhile.

It is also possible to buy and hold euro T-bills for three months, then at maturity sell the euro proceeds in the spot exchange market. This type of arbitrage is called uncovered interest arbitrage because it is subject to unexpected gains or losses.

Uncovered interest arbitrage equilibrium occurs when the expected returns are equal. When there are riskless assets, it is generally true that $E(S_{90}) = F_{90}$. Consequently, when covered interest arbitrage equilibrium holds, the uncovered interest arbitrage equilibrium condition does too. Figure 3.19 illustrates an example of realized uncovered interest arbitrage where the euro proceeds are multiplied by the actual spot exchange rate realized after three months.

If the realized spot rate of the euro is higher than the expected rate in one year, there are unanticipated gains, while if it is less, there are unanticipated losses. Hence, the term uncovered interest arbitrage. In Figure 3.19, the spot price of the euro has unexpectedly fallen to $1.20, so the arbitrage return is only $9,686.40. A loss of $409.85 is realized relative to the investment is U.S. Treasuries.

Figure 3.19 Uncovered interest rate arbitrage with a loss

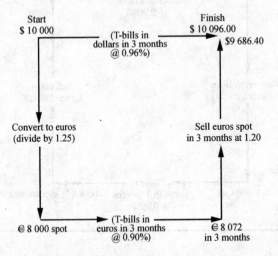

Of course, the arbitrageur could liquidate the position at any time before maturity, thereby locking in any gains or losses. In general, we may define the unanticipated gain (+)/loss (−) by the difference between the spot price of the euro in 90 days (the bid) S_{90} and the future bid price of today. The unanticipated gain, if positive, or loss, if negative, in uncovered interested arbitrage activity is measured as $S_{90} - F_{90}$ per unit of foreign exchange. We must still bear in mind that the rates refer to the dollar bid price of the euro in the spot and futures markets respectively, i. e. American quotation, and that the bid-ask spread is also paid on Treasuries.

Cross rates and triangular arbitrage

三角套利（Triangular arbitrage）：三角套利能够消除两种货币之间的直接汇率与交叉汇率的不一致，从而确保一价定律的成立。它能够使即期与远期外汇市场上的汇率保持一致。

Another type of arbitrage that is done by multinational financial institutions is known as **triangular arbitrage**. Triangular arbitrage eliminates inconsistencies between direct and cross rates between two currencies, thereby enforcing the law of one price. It can take place in the spot or the futures markets to keep rates consistent.

• The direct rate for the purchase of pounds by dollars is simply the American style quotation $/£ . For an investor, this is the ask in dollars for one pound.

The cross rate, American quotation, between dollars and pounds via the yen is indicated by ($/ ¥)(¥ /£) since this is the number of pounds obtained by buying yen for dollars, then buying pounds with the yen.

Naturally, an investor pays the ask rate in dollars for yen, then the ask price in yen for pounds.

Triangular arbitrage equilibrium

There are no profit opportunities via triangular arbitrage when: ($/ ¥)(¥ /£) = ($/£).

Whenever this condition is not satisfied, profit opportunities exist. Consider the following inconsistent quotations:

Direct rate:

Dollars per pound sterling ($/£)　　　　　　1. 7669

Cross rate:

Dollars per Japanese Yen ($/ ¥)　　　　　　0. 009434

Japanese yen per pound sterling (¥ /£)　　　186. 3543

Therefore, the cross rate is (0. 009434)(186. 3543) = 1. 7581

An arbitrage opportunity exists! Buy yen with dollars, then pounds with yen. This will cost you $ 1. 7581 per pound. Sell the pounds at $1. 7669, earning one half of a US penny per pound. If you trade $1,000, your net profits are $5. 02.

In Figure 3. 20, start with $1,000 in the upper right hand starting position. Buy yen with dollars, then pounds with yen. At the end of the triangular arbitrage, you will have made about one cent per pound.

Figure 3. 20　Triangular foreign exchange arbitrage

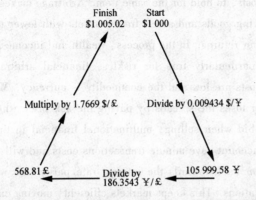

Profitable arbitrage will eliminate this price inconsistency, establishing the law of one price. Arbitrageurs take advantage of these opportunities until profit disappears and arbitrage equilibrium is satisfied, increasing the dollar price of the yen and the yen price of the pound, until no further arbitrage profits exist.

Consider another arbitrage example: You have two prices for a pound:

$$(\$/¥)(¥/£) = \$1.7669$$
$$(\$/£) = \$1.7642$$

In this case, buy a pound directly with dollars, and then sell it indirectly through yen for dollars, earning profits of (\$1.7669 − \$1.7642) = 0.0027 dollars per pound. Recall that you will pay the forex spread three times in converting currency in this example.

The law of one price

一价定律 (The law of one price):当同种商品在不同的市场有不同的价格时,那么就存在套利机会。低价买进而高价卖出的套利活动使得商品价格在不同的市场上趋于一致。这就是一价定律。

Interest rate arbitrage is another way of looking at the law of one price. A dollar is a dollar is a dollar. You should only pay one dollar for it! In general, the same item must have the same price, adjusting for transactions and shipping costs. An ounce of gold is worth the London fixing price all over the world. Even gold panners in Brazil know the day's market price of gold.

When prices for the same item are out of line, that is, are different in two markets, an arbitrage opportunity exists. Buy low in the low market and sell high in the high market, making sure your transactions and/or transportation costs are covered in doing so. Buying in the low market makes the price rise there and selling in the high market makes the price fall there. The equilibrium requires the law of one price, accounting for transactions costs, to hold for the same item. Arbitrage makes markets more efficient, moving goods and assets from markets with lower returns to markets with higher returns. In the process, wealth and income are increased.

This is particularly true for riskless financial arbitrage where the transactions costs are low and the commodity is currency. While the individual investor loses the spreads by paying the ask price when buying and receiving the bid when selling, multinational financial institutions trading on their own account have minute transactions costs and will therefore push the equilibrium back towards the interest rate parity line whenever there are slight deviations. This keeps markets efficient, moving capital from low return environments to high return environments. Bear in mind, naturally, that we are speaking of riskless assets that are otherwise identical.

When riskless assets do not exist, the interest differential is no longer a good predictor of the percentage rate of depreciation because a risk premium is imbedded into the risky asset. For emerging markets, therefore, expected inflation rate differentials (e. g. relative purchasing power parity) is a more reliable indicator of expected depreciation.

Exchange rate forecasting

If a forward rate, F, exists, it is centered at the expected exchange rate. Consequently, just buy the *Wall Street Journal* or the *Financial Times* and look up the forward rate. In the euro and the pound, there are futures up to two years. Consequently, today's forward quotations provide every bit of known information about the future, so they are unbiased predictors of the future spot exchange rate.

However, forward and futures markets do not always exist for future delivery of foreign currency and their maturity is only up to two years. A forward bid and ask quotation could be gotten from a foreign exchange dealer, but the spread would be greater, the further the quote is in the future. The foreign exchange dealer limits risk by widening the spread.

Forecasting the future exchange rate is conveniently done by the interest rate parity equation. First, let's create a hypothetical one year Treasury Bill that is composed of a six month bill rolled over for an additional six months. That is: $(1 + r_{us_{180}})(1 + r_{us_{180}}) = (1 + r_{us_{360}})$ yields an estimate of the comparable risk free one year rate, r_{us}. Alternatively, we could strip the interest rate futures to predict the 180 to 360 day six month T-bill forward rate, or we could use the rate on a 2 year T-bill with one year to maturity remaining. The main point of the exercise is to construct a one year riskless Treasury rate, r_{us}.

According to interest rate parity one year forward:

$$\left(\frac{F}{S}\right) = \frac{(1 + r_{us})}{(1 + r_{uk})} \tag{3.29}$$

Or equivalently

$$F = S \frac{(1 + r_{us})}{(1 + r_{uk})} \tag{3.30}$$

We can therefore use the interest rate parity equation to forecast the forward spot rate in one year—it is a no profit arbitrage condition that must hold. Similarly, by rolling over the Treasury asset an additional year or in general, n, years, we can forecast the future spot rate in n years by repeated application of interest rate parity.

汇率预期（Exchange rate forecasting）：我们可以利用利率平价公式来预测远期汇率——即能够使套利利润为零的远期汇率。

式(3.31)给出了预测 n 年后即期汇率的公式。

$$F = S \left[\frac{(1 + r_{us})}{(1 + r_{uk})} \right]^n \qquad (3.31)$$

All information needed to make a five year forecast of the future spot rate of the pound is available today: the spot rate, a one year riskless interest rates in the U. S. and the U. K.

For example, if one year risk less rate were 3.5% in the United States and 4% in the U. K, interest rate parity implies that the dollar would be expected to appreciate approximately one half of a percent in a year relative to the pound. By rolling over the riskless pound investment each year, the successive dollar pound future spot rates can be predicted using interest parity. That is, given the spot bid of $1.7609 per pound, we may predict the future spot bid rates by applying the n period forward interest parity formula, yielding a five year forward forecast of the price of the pound in Table 3.8.

Table 3.8　A five year forecast of the future exchange rate

$$F_1 = 1.75243$$
$$F_2 = 1.74401$$
$$F_3 = 1.73562$$
$$F_4 = 1.72728$$
$$F_5 = 1.71898$$

The use of interest rate parity conditions—that is, the no expected profit arbitrage condition—as a forecasting tool is powerful and based in the best available finance theory. Despite the absence of a futures market five years ahead, a market based forecast is still possible. It can be used to convert expected future cash flows in foreign currency, for instance.

An application to international capital budgeting

Free cash flow is defined as earnings after tax, plus depreciation, a non-cash expense, minus changes in net working capital, minus capital expenditures. Table 3.9 indicates the forecasted free cash flows for a possible expansion in the United Kingdom by a U. S. firm in millions of pounds.

自由现金流（Free cash flow）:定义为税后收入加上折旧（非现金费用）再加上净营运资本的变化。

Table 3.9   Forecasted free cash flows for a UK acquisition in millions of pounds

	Year						Terminal
	0	1	2	3	4	5	value
Earnings before financing charges and taxes	—	£10.0	£12.5	£15.0	£16.5	£18.0	
Taxes*	—	—	3.5	4.4	5.3	5.8	
Earnings before financing charges, after taxes	—	10.0	9.0	10.6	11.2	12.2	
Depreciation expense†	—	5.0	5.0	5.0	5.0	5.0	
Capital expenditures	£(50.0)	(4.0)	(4.4)	(5.0)	(5.3)	(5.7)	
Investment in net working capital	(6.0)	(0.6)	(0.7)	(0.9)	(1.0)	(1.1)	
Total free cash flow	£(56.0)	£10.4	£8.9	£9.7	£9.9	£10.4	£78.0‡

* Taxes are incurred locally at the full marginal corporate tax rate of 35 percent, and paid 9 months following the end of the tax year. US Inc. receives a tax credit on income remitted from UK plc up to the full marginal U.S. corporate tax rate of 35 percent.

† Initial capital expenditures of £50 million are depreciated on a straight-line basis over 10 years, beginning in the first year.

‡ Estimated as a level, no-growth perpetuity of £11.7 million that begins in the sixth year of the project.

Source: "Note on Cross Border Valuation," *Case Problems in International Finance*, W. Kester & T. Luehrman, McGraw-Hill 1993.

Their approach is to estimate foreign-currency cash flows, then discount to the present at the weighted average cost of capital in pounds, assumed to be 15%. Table 3.9 estimates the cost of acquisition of a subsidiary in the U.K. at 50 million pounds. In the first year of operations, it will generate a free cash flow of £10.4 million, then to £10.4 in its fifth year of operations. During its fifth year, the firm is sold. Its terminal value is estimated to be £78.0 (a £11.7 million perpetuity discounted at 15%, the pound discount rate). Alternatively, the terminal value could be the scrap value of the operation. Then discount at the firm's cost of borrowing in pounds, given as 15%. This yields a positive net present value of £15.76 million, representing a 20% internal rate of return (the rate of discount of free cash flows in pounds that sets the net present value of the investment equal to zero). Clearly, this expansion is worthwhile.

Random investing

Are darts better than financial advisors? Consider the following three tosses of a true (fair) coin that has a fifty percent (0.5) probability of landing heads and a fifty percent probability of landing tails. There are 8 possible outcomes after three tosses as illustrated by the binomial tree illustrated in Figure 3.21.

Figure 3.21 Random investing

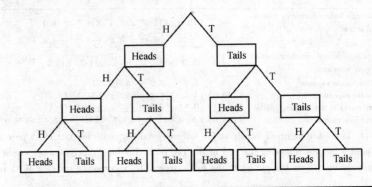

There are eight investment funds associated with each branch of the binomial tree in Table 3.10. *Ex ante*, before the coin tosses, each has a 12.5% chance of winning the forecast, assuming three tosses of a fair coin. *Ex post*, after the coin tosses, there will only be one winner.

Table 3.10 Random investment funds

	Branches	Probability	Investment Fund
1.	HHH	12.5%	Fudelity
2.	HHT	12.5%	Local
3.	HTH	12.5%	Simpleton
4.	HTT	12.5%	Dubious
5.	THH	12.5%	Ponce de Leon
6.	THT	12.5%	GuarVan
7.	TTH	12.5%	T. Rut Price
8.	TTT	12.5%	Christopher Columbus

Only one of the investment funds will be the successful investor, the others will be wrong. Nevertheless, the outcome was randomly determined. This random-walk view of investment suggests that indexed funds managed passively with low fees will do better on the average than actively managed funds with high fees (Reinker and Tower, 2004). This is the efficient market hypothesis. For instance, if the winner gets $100, a fair investment would be $12.50. Notice that this example is a "fair" investment—neither bid-ask spread, nor fees associated with it—each investor pays the expected value of investing. However, the house usually charges an entry fee and an ask price, so the investment is biased against the investor. This is especially true when a portfolio is actively managed and charges management fees. Yes, darts are better than financial advisors, unless the advisor uses expert witnesses to trade on inside information.

Stock options

A call option contract carries the right, but not the obligation, to buy a specified amount of shares of stock at an agreed upon price at settlement on or before a specified future date. **A put option** contract carries the right, but not the obligation, to sell a specified amount of shares of stock at a settlement price on or before a set future date.

The specified price is called the option's exercise or strike price. The specified future date is called the option's expiration date or maturity. Options are therefore derivatives whose value derives from the value of an underlying asset.

An *American* style option can be exercised anytime between the moment the option is purchased and its expiration. A *European* style option can be exercised only on its expiration date. The terms *American* and *European* refer to the existence of the early exercise feature or not of the options, not to where they are traded.

The cost of an option is known as the **premium**, which has both an intrinsic value and a time value. The **intrinsic value** is the profit from an immediate exercise of an option if it is in the money, i. e. profitable if exercised. Otherwise, the intrinsic value of the option is zero. Mathematically, intrinsic values can be easily summarized by the follow expressions:

$$\text{Intrinsic value of a call} = \max(S - X, 0)$$
$$\text{Intrinsic value of a put} = \max(X - S, 0)$$

where S is the stock price and X is the exercise price of the option.

The time value of an option is also called the speculative value of an option. It is the difference between the option premium and the option's intrinsic value. Because the option holder does not have to exercise the option immediately, the time value reflects the holder's right to exercise the option on a later date when the stock price moves higher.

An option is **in the money** if its intrinsic value is positive. An option is at the money when the underlying stock price is equal to the option's exercise price and an option is **out of the money** when it is not profitable to exercise.

The buyer of an option pays a premium to purchase the option, but

看涨期权（Call option）：是指在合约到期日或者之前，按照一定的执行价格，购买特定数量的标的资产的权利。

看跌期权（Put option）：是指在合约到期日或者之前，按照一定的执行价格，卖出特定数量的标的资产的权利。

美式期权（American style option）：美式期权可以在到期日之前的任意时点执行。

欧式期权（European style option）：欧式期权不能在到期日之前执行。

期权费（Premium）：购买期权的成本。

期权的内在价值（Intrinsic value）：是指执行期权时所获得的正的收益。如果执行期权不能获得正的收益，那么期权的内在价值为零。

期权的时间价值（The time value of an option）：也称作期权的投机价值。它是期权费与期权内在价值之间的差额。期权的时间价值体现了投资者继续持有期权以在将来获得更大收益的权利。

实值（In the money）：如果在某一时刻执行期权能够获得正的收益，那么期权此时为实值。

虚值（Out of the money）：如果在某一时刻执行期权不能获得正的收益，那么期权此时为虚值。

does not risk any further monies. If the option finishes at the money or out of the money, the buyer loses 100% of the initial investment. The maximum payoff of a put option is the option's exercise price when the underlying stock becomes worthless. The maximum payoff of a call option is unlimited because the underlying stock price can, in principle, be infinite.

The seller of an option receives a premium for selling, or writing the option. In exchange for the option premium, the seller agrees to stand ready to satisfy an option exercise if the buyer chooses to do so. As the option moves further into the money, the seller's liability increases. As the option moves further out of the money, his liability decreases. If the option finishes in the money, the buyer will exercise and the seller must fulfill the exercise and lose the intrinsic value of the option.

The maximum loss to a put option seller, or writer, is the exercise price should the underlying stock becomes worthless. The seller of a call option faces potentially unlimited losses as the price of the asset could conceivably rise towards infinity.

Options are risky investments for two reasons. First, option positions are highly leveraged and consequently, small changes in the underlying stock may cause large percentage changes in the option price. Second, since the life of the option is usually no longer than nine months, option traders are forced to close out their positions at expiration. They don't have the ability to continue to hold their positions until the market "recovers or comes back."

交易所（Exchange）：投资者可以在交易所购买期权,交易所内进行的期权交易是标准化的,交易所内进行的期权交易不存在违约风险,因为清算所保证了这种交易的顺利进行。

If an investor buys an option on an **exchange**, the buyer does not run counterparty risk since a clearinghouse for the exchange guarantees the option. Options cannot be bought on margin since there is no supporting stock. Instead, the full premium must be paid. The seller (writer) of the option has to post a margin account, which is marked-to-market by the clearinghouse on a daily basis. Stock options are traded on a number of U. S. exchanges, including the Chicago Board Options Exchange (http://www. cboe. com/), the Pacific Exchange (http://www. pacificex. com/) in San Francisco, the Philadelphia Stock Exchange (http://www. phlx. com/), and the American Stock Exchange (http://www. amex. com/). Exchange-traded options are standardized options in terms of underlying asset, contract size, expiration dates, exercise prices, delivery, and exercise settlement, among others. The cost of an option is always known as the premium. The contract size is a pre-specified amount of the underlying asset. The quoted exercise price is per unit of the underlying asset, for example per share. Standardization of options dramatically increases the liquidity of options. Because the Options Clearing Corporation (OCC) (http://www.optionsclearing.com/) guarantees the performance of every option, exchange-traded options essentially do not carry any counterparty default risk.

Over-the-counter (OTC) options are sold by financial institutions to institutional buyers and are tailored to their needs in terms of amount (notional principal), delivery conditions, and expiration date. These are mainly hedging transactions between enterprises and banks. There is counterparty risk of non-performance if an option is purchased over-the-counter from a dealer, broker, or bank, since these can go bankrupt or default.

场外期权交易（Over-the-counter（OTC）options）：场外期权是金融机构向机构投资者销售的,它根据投资者的需要来确定金额和到期日。场外期权交易存在交易对手风险。

The Black-Scholes formula for a call option premium, C, is given by:

$$C = SN(d_1) - Xe^{-rT}N(d_2) \text{ where} \qquad (3.32)$$

$$d_1 = \frac{\ln(S/X) + (r + \sigma^2/2)T}{\sigma\sqrt{T}}$$

$$d_2 = d_1 - \sigma\sqrt{T}$$

This result is derived from the basic relationship that the value of the option today is the discounted value of the expected payoff at expiration:

$$C = e^{-rT}E[\max(0, S_T - X)] \qquad (3.33)$$

The Black-Scholes formula for a put option premium, P, is given by:

$$P = Xe^{-rT}N(-d_2) - SN(-d_1) \qquad (3.34)$$

This is similarly derived from the discounted value of the expected payoff of the put at expiration:

$$P = e^{-rT}E[\max(0, X - S_T)] \qquad (3.35)$$

The notation for the call and put options on a share is:

C = the value of the European call option

P = the value of the European put option

T = the time to maturity (when the option matures, in years)

e = exponent, base of the natural logarithm (the number 2.718281828 where $\frac{de^x}{dx} = e^x$)

S = the spot market price of the underlying asset

X = the exercise or strike price of the underlying asset

r = the continuously compounded risk-free interest rate

σ = volatility (the standard deviation of the returns on the underlying asset)

$N(d)$ = the cumulative normal distribution function (see Equation

3. 36 below)

ln = the natural logarithm ($\ln e^x = x$).

For any number z, where z can be negative, $N(z)$ is indicated by the area under the normal distribution to the left of the value z. Due to the symmetry of the normal distribution, the following relation holds for the cumulative normal distribution function: $N(z) = 1 - N(-z)$.

That is:

$$p(z < d) = N(d) = \frac{1}{\sqrt{2\pi}} \int_{-\infty}^{d} e^{-z^2/2} dz \qquad (3.36)$$

which is indicated by the mass of the area under the normal distribution to the left of the value d.

The probability of a critical value less than d can be looked up in the cumulative normal distribution tables, or consulted in Microsoft Excel under the function wizard, f_x, as NORMSDIST(d), where you are prompted to enter the d value. Simply enter the d value you are seeking to input into the Black-Scholes formula. For example, if you input the value -1 into the NORMSDIST function, your result is 15. 8655%. That is:

= NORMSDIST(-1) in Excel displays 0. 15865526

meaning that the probability of an observation being below one standard deviation from the mean is about 16%. NORMSDIST (1) yields 0. 84134474, so that $1 - N(1) = 1 - 0. 84134474 = 0. 15865526 = N(-1)$. Similarly, $N(-2) = 0. 022750062$, so that the probability of an observation falling outside two standard deviations is about 2. 3%, or nearly 5% for a two-tailed test.

The more general NORMDIST(x, mean, standard deviation, cumulative) in Excel gives the probability of a value being less than, given the mean and standard deviation specified and whether it is cumulative (true) or not (false). This is essentially the JPMorgan's Riskmetrics approach. That is, indicate True when prompted for cumulative or False if it is the probability density distribution, rather than the cumulative distribution. For example:

= NORMDIST(80,100,10,TRUE) = 0. 022750062

indicates that if the mean or expected value is 100 and the standard deviation (volatility), there is a probability of a value of less than 80 of 2. 3%. The logical statement TRUE is to indicate that we are dealing with the cumulative normal distribution.

If FALSE were indicated, it would be the standard normal distribution and would indicate the probability of an observation equaling 80. With

FALSE, the probability of 80 equals 0. 005399097 or approximately 0. 54%.

Table 3. 11 provides a numerical example of options pricing of a stock.

Table 3.11   The call and put premium on a stock option

Equity options		
Strike Price	X	100
Time to expiry	T	0. 25
Spot price	S	100
Interest rate	r	0. 05
Volatility	σ	0. 3
	d_1	0. 1583
	d_2	0. 0083
Call	C	6. 5831
Put	P	5. 3409

This non-dividend paying option for settlement in 90 days at a strike price of 100 yields a call option premium of 6. 58 and a put option premium of 5. 34.

Foreign currency options

A foreign currency call option is the right, but not the obligation, to buy a specified amount of foreign currency, known as the contract size, at an exercise price on or before the expiration date. A forex put option is the right to sell a specific quantity of foreign currency at a strike price on or before maturity. Therefore, foreign currency options are derivatives whose value derives from the value of the underlying foreign currency. Like options on stocks, a European style option cannot be exercised before the expiration date, while an American style option can be exercised anytime between the moment it is written and its expiration.

- A call is an option to buy a foreign currency
- A put is an option to sell a foreign currency

The buyer of a foreign currency option pays a premium to purchase the option, but does not risk any further monies beyond the premium paid. Holding option positions can be risky and expensive. If the option expires "out-of-the-money," not profitable if exercised, the buyer loses all of the investment in the option premium. If the option expires "in-the-money," profitable if exercised, the buyer realizes a positive profit if the payoff of the option exceeds its cost, the premium.

外汇期权（Foreign currency options）：是指在合约到期日或者之前,按照一定的执行价格,购买（或卖出）一定数量的外汇的权利。

The seller or writer of a foreign exchange option must honor the option contract if it is presented for exercise. Consequently, the seller of a put option risks the amount equal to the exercise price times the option contract size, should the currency become worthless. The seller of a call option faces potentially unlimited losses as the spot price of the underlying foreign currency could conceivably rise to infinity.

Exchange options in foreign currency are traded on the Philadelphia Stock Exchange (http://www. phlx. com/) , and the International Money Market of the Chicago Mercantile Exchange (http://www. cme. com/). Exchange-traded options are standardized. The price of the option on an exchange is known as the premium. The contract is for a specified amount and the quoted exercise price is per unit of the underlying foreign currency, for example per pound sterling. Exchange-traded foreign exchange options do not carry default risk as the clearing house guarantees their performance.

Over-the-counter (OTC) options are sold by financial institutions to institutional buyers and are tailored to their needs in terms of amount (notional principal) and expiration date. These are mainly hedging transactions between multinational enterprises and banks. Once again, with over-the-counter options, there is counterparty risk—the risk of deterioration in the terms of repayment, including default.

The valuation of European style foreign exchange options

An option is worth its expected present value. The Fischer-Black and Myron-Scholes formula is used for the valuation of a European style option, and there are binomial tree pricing models for the valuation of American style options.

If the foreign interest rate is indicated by φ and the domestic interest rate by r, interest rate parity is expressed:

$$F = Se^{(r-\varphi)T} \tag{3.37}$$

The Black-Scholes formula can then be written as:

$$C = Se^{-\varphi T}N(d_1) - Xe^{-rT}N(d_2) \text{ where} \tag{3.38}$$

$$d_1 = \frac{\ln(S/X) + (r - \varphi + \sigma^2/2)T}{\sigma\sqrt{T}}, \quad d_2 = d_1 - \sigma\sqrt{T}$$

C = the value of the European style FX call option

T = the time to option's maturity, in years

S = the spot price of the underlying foreign currency

X = the option's exercise price

r = the continuously compounded US risk-free interest rate

φ = the continuously compounded foreign risk-free interest rate

σ = volatility (the standard deviation of the returns on the exchange rate)

Graphically, the premium on a foreign exchange call option is illustrated in Figure 3.22.

Figure 3.22   The premium on a foreign exchange call option

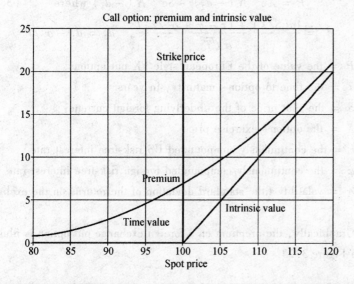

In general, the expected value of the underlying asset is given by its forward price. Its volatility or standard deviation indicates how likely it is that the subsequent spot rate deviates from its expected value. The greater the volatility of the underlying asset, the greater is the likelihood of large movements in its value. With large movements, options are more likely to be "in the money". Therefore, they are worth more, the greater the volatility of the underlying asset.

The further away from expiration, the greater the volatility of the underlying asset. Consequently, for the same reason, options further away from expiration are worth more. Indeed, as the option expiration date approaches, the volatility approaches zero so that at the time of expiration, the option is worth only its intrinsic value—the value if immediately exercised. The time value of the option is extinguished at expiration.

The value of an option equals the sum of its intrinsic value and its time value. The intrinsic value is its value if exercised immediately. It is zero if the option is out of the money, then rises cent for cent as the option moves into the money. The time value is the difference between the premium and the intrinsic value. It reflects the possibility that the option could move into the money or even further into the money.

A put option on foreign exchange

The put option formula also uses continuous interest rate parity in the Black-Scholes equation:

$$P = Xe^{-rT}N(-d_2) - Se^{-\varphi T}N(-d_1) \text{ where} \qquad (3.39)$$

$$d_1 = \frac{\ln(S/X) + (r - \varphi + \sigma^2/2)T}{\sigma\sqrt{T}}, \quad d_2 = d_1 - \sigma\sqrt{T}$$

P = the value of the European style FX put option

T = the time to option's maturity, in years

S = the spot price of the underlying foreign currency

X = the option's exercise price

r = the continuously compounded US risk-free interest rate

φ = the continuously compounded foreign risk-free interest rate

σ = volatility (the standard deviation of the returns on the exchange rate)

Graphically, the premium on a foreign exchange put option is illustrated in Figure 3.23.

Figure 3.23   The premium on a foreign exchange put option

We use a call option on pounds sterling to demonstrate the terminal profit to a long (buy) and a short (sell) call option position. Suppose that the call option premium is 1¢ per pound when the option positions were established. The exercise price of the call option is $1.77 per pound. Figure 3.24 demonstrates the profit/loss to an investor who bought the call option and held it to the option's expiration date. As we can see, the payoff is a negative 1¢ per pound when the option expires at $1.77 per pound or lower. The more the call option is in the money, the higher is its payoff. The breakeven point is at $1.78 per pound, which is the sum of the exercise price and call option premium. The payoff is potentially unlimited because the exchange rate could go to infinity.

Figure 3.24   The payoff at maturity from buying a pound call option

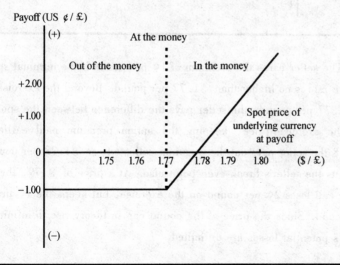

At expiration at a spot price of $1.79 per pound, the call holder exercises the call option, buying pounds at $1.77 and selling them spot at $1.79, making 2¢ per pound. Net profits are one cent since the holder paid a premium of 1¢ per pound. The break-even point is $1.78 per pound. At a spot price of $1.75 per pound, the option would finish out of the money. The call expires unexercised, leaving the holder with a net cost of 1¢ per pound of notional value. Because options are zero-sum games to their buyers and sellers, the seller of the call option has a profit diagram mirroring that of the buyer, but opposite in value, as in Figure 3.25.

Figure 3.25 The payoff at maturity from selling a pound call option

The seller earns the premium of 1¢ per pound if the terminal spot exchange rate is no higher than $1.77 per pound. Beyond the exercise price of $1.77 per pound, the seller pays the difference between the spot price and the exercise price, keeping the option premium paid earlier. At $1.78 the seller pays out the premium collected, so $1.78 per pound represents the seller's break-even point also. At a price of $179, the seller of the call loses 2¢ per pound on the exercise, but keeps the 1¢ premium per pound. Since the price of the pound can in theory rise to infinity, the seller's potential losses are unlimited.

Profits from a foreign exchange put option

We use a put option on pounds sterling to demonstrate the terminal profit to a long and a short put option position. Suppose that the put premium was 1¢ per pound when the put option position was bought. The exercise price of the put option is $1.77 per pound. The put holder paid 1¢ per pound for the put. On expiration, the holder benefits if the spot exchange rate drops below $1.76 per pound, the breakeven point. The lower the terminal spot rate, the higher are profits. The maximum profit is $1.77 per pound when the pound exchange rate drops to zero. The holder's maximum loss is the put option premium, 1¢ per pound if the put expires out of the money—above $1.77 spot at maturity, as shown in Figure 3.26.

Figure 3.26　The payoff at maturity from buying a pound put option

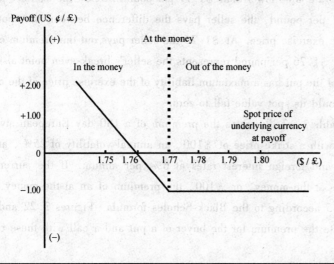

The put seller collected 1¢ per pound of premium, which is the maximum profit the seller can expect to realize. If the put option finishes out of the money (when the spot exchange rate is more than $1.77 per pound), the seller keeps the premium without any further obligation. However, as the spot exchange rate decreases, so does the seller's liability up to $1.77 per pound. Because of the symmetry in payoffs, the seller's profit break-even point is also $1.76 per pound. Figure 3.27 illustrates the payoff for the seller of a put option.

Figure 3.27　The payoff at maturity from selling a pound put option

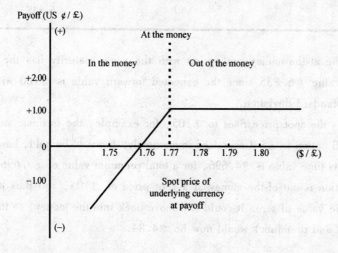

The seller earns the premium of 1¢ per pound if the terminal spot exchange rate is no lower than $1.77 per pound. Below the exercise price of $1.77 per pound, the seller pays the difference between the spot price and the exercise price. At $1.76 the seller pays out the premium collected, so $1.76 per pound represents the seller's break-even point also. The seller of the put has a maximum liability of the exercise price of the currency, should its spot value fall to zero.

Table 3.12 illustrates the premium of a 180 day European style call option with a strike price of $100, an annual volatility of 25%, and domestic and foreign interest rates at 6% per annum. If the current spot price is at-the-money, or $100, the premium of an at-the-money call is $6.835 according to the Black-Scholes formula. Figures 3.22 and 3.23 illustrate the premium for the buyer of a put and a call with these characteristics.

Table 3.12 The call and put premium on a foreign exchange option

Foreign exchange option		
Strike price	X	100
Time to expiry	T	0.5
Spot price	S	100
Domestic interest rate	r	0.06
Foreign interest rate	φ	0.06
Volatility	σ	0.25
	d_1	0.0884
	d_2	-0.0884
CALL	C	6.835
PUT	P	6.835

The at-the-money put option with the same maturity has the exact same value $6.835 since the expected forward value is $100 with the same standard deviation.

As the spot price rises to $105, for example, the intrinsic value of the call option is $5 if exercised immediately. It would be held, however, since its time value is $4.696, for a total premium value of $9.696. The put option is out-of-the-money at a spot price of $105, and thus has an intrinsic value of zero. It could still move back into the money, so its time value (and premium) would now be $4.84.

Foreign exchange option *Greeks*

In general, the value of a call option is summarized in Greek terms. Option Greeks measure the sensitivity of option price changes with respect to small changes in underlying parameters. For example, by raising the spot price of the foreign currency a very small amount, the call option premium rises. The rate at which the call option premium rises with respect to small increases in the underlying spot price of the currency is known as the option's delta. Table 3.13 summarizes the effect of changes in various parameters and the change in an option premium.

Table 3.13 Foreign exchange option Greeks

Greek	Meaning	Interpretation
Delta	The change in the option premium due to a small change in the spot rate	The higher the delta the more (less) likely a call (put) option will move into the money
Theta	The change in the option premium due to a small change in the time to expiry	Premia deteriorate in value as the time to expiration approaches
Vega	The change in the option premium due to a small change in volatility of the asset	An increase in volatility increases the value of call and put premia
Rho	The change in the option premium due to a small change in the domestic interest rate	An increase in the domestic interest rate causes rising call and falling put premia
Phi	The change in the option premium due to a small change in the foreign interest rate	An increase in the foreign interest rate causes falling call and rising put premia

Note: Vega is not a Greek language term, but is used for convenience.

Options may be used to hedge foreign exchange exposure, as we will see in Chapter 4 on hedging techniques.

Conclusion

The foreign exchange market is huge: average net daily turnover in the over the counter foreign exchange market in 2010 was nearly 4 trillion US dollars. These transactions facilitate trade and finance, and allow hedging of both transactional and operational exposure. We have tried to emphasize the idea that there is a bid-ask rate for nearly every forex transaction, as well as a commission. Unanticipated changes in exchange rates can cause large financial losses to unhedged international businesses. Yet hedges are not free. It is too costly to hedge all risk, but prudent risk management is in order when the firm has substantial foreign exchange revenues from transactions and operations. Often natural or matching hedges will do the trick, at less cost.

The Bank for International Settlements, the central bank's bank, has called for global currencies as we had under the silver and gold standards. So has Nobel Laureate Robert Mundell of Columbia University. This would remove exchange rate risk and reduce transactions costs considerably. However, nations would have to forego seigniorage, an important source of tax revenue for many. Their monetary and fiscal policies would also have to converge, a seemingly Sisyphean task in Europe, thus giving up discretionary economic policy. In the meantime, as an asset, good monies will drive out bad monies and various currency unions are to be expected.

Questions and problems

3.1 The time value of money

Consider the following cash flows from today (year zero) to year 3 in pounds sterling.

Cash flow in pounds sterling	Year
− 100	0
50	1
50	2
50	3

Your interest rate (or discount rate) in pounds is 10%.

a. Compute the net present value (NPV) at a 10% discount rate and the internal rate of return of this investment in pounds.

b. If you were to sell this investment today (its NPV in pounds), how much would it be worth in USD at 1.76 dollars per pound?

3.2 The equilibrium exchange rate

Consider the following quantity of dollars demanded and supplied in millions as a function of the dollar's peso price, S.

$$\text{Quantity demanded} \quad Q_D = 90 - 2S$$

$$\text{Quantity supplied} \quad Q_S = -10 + 3S$$

a. Solve for the equilibrium exchange rate under a freely floating exchange rate regime, S (pesos per dollar). What is the quantity sold at the equilibrium price?

b. If the Central Bank maintained a fixed exchange rate of 15 pesos per dollar, how many millions of dollars of foreign reserves would it have to sell to maintain the fixed exchange rate regime? (Hint: Solve for $Q_D - Q_S$ at $S = 15$ pesos per dollar.)

c. If the Central Bank only had $15 million left in foreign reserves, what would its policy alternatives be?

d. If it instead wished to add $10 million to its holdings of foreign reserves, to what exchange rate would the Central Bank have to devalue the peso?

3.3 Intervention in the foreign exchange market

Argentina pegged its currency, the peso, to the US dollar at a rate of 1 to 1 from April 1991 to November 2001. Under the rules of the currency board, the central bank must intervene to buy and sell dollars at this rate. For this reason, the Banco de la Republica Argentina backed its domestic currency issue with foreign exchange by the *Convertibility Law*, principally dollars. The supply and demand for dollars is indicated below. Answer the following questions.

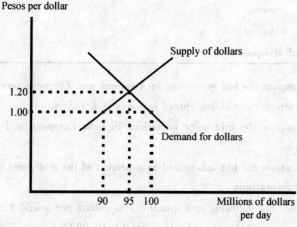

a. What amount of dollar reserves must the central bank of Argentina sell to the foreign exchange market daily in order to maintain its rigidly fixed exchange rate to the US dollar?

b. What is the impact of the sale of dollars on the Argentine money supply? Does this cause any adjustment process?

c. When the Argentine government abandons the currency board, what is the equilibrium exchange rate and the volume of dollars traded daily?

3.4 The bid-ask spread

In the table below, consider the following bid and ask spot quotations in dollars per pound ($/£), *i. e* in American terms.

	European terms(£ / $)		American terms($/£)	
	Bid	Ask	Bid	Ask
Spot			1.7669	1.7675
Spread				
Mid-point				

a. Compute the bid and quotations in European terms, i. e. in pounds per dollar (£ / $).
b. Compute the bid-ask spread in terms of £ and $.
c. Compute the mid-point quotations in both European and American terms (Hint: mid-point = (bid + ask)/2).
d. Compute the bid-ask spread as a percent of the mid-point quotation.

3.5 The bid-ask spread

Consider the following spot quotations in pounds per dollar (£ / $) and dollars per pound ($/£) in the table below.

	Bid	Ask	Bid	Ask
Spot		0.5660		1.7675
Spread				
Mid-point				
Spread/Mid-point(%)				

a. Compute the bid quotations in American and European terms.
b. Compute the bid-ask spread in terms of £ and $.
c. Compute the mid-point quotations in both European and American terms.
d. Compute the bid-ask spread as a percent of the mid-point quotation.

3.6 Point quotations

Consider the following spot quotations in dollars per pound ($/£) and the forward quotations in basis points (1/10,000).

	American terms($/£)	
	Bid	Ask
Spot	1.7669	1.7675
Points	Bid	Ask
1 month	214	220
2 months	283	298
3 months	388	416

On the basis of the points quotations above, derive the outright quotations.

3.7   Interest rate parity

Consider the figure below indicating (approximately) the difference between interest rates in the United States (U. S.) and the United Kingdom (U. K.), $r_{us} - r_{uk}$, on a one year Treasury Bill (i. e. a two year Bill with one year left to maturity) on the horizontal axis, and the forward premium on the pound for delivery in one year, $(F - S)/S$ on the vertical axis. If you wish, assume you already hold a portfolio of both Treasuries. Note:

F is the US dollar price of the British pound for delivery in 1 year (the bid)

S is the US dollar price of the British pound for spot delivery (the ask)

r_{us} is the interest rate on a hypothetical US one year Treasury Note (the ask)

r_{uk} is the interest rate on a hypothetical UK one year Treasury Note (the bid)

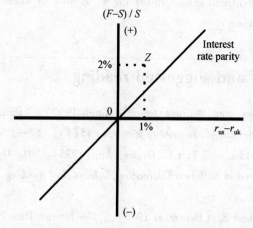

a. At point Z, in what direction will short term arbitrage capital flow and what will be the arbitrage profits?

b. What steps will arbitrageurs take from point Z in order to make their profits and what will be the consequences on the forward discount on the pound and the interest rate differential?

3.8 Purchasing power parity

You are given the following data on prices in local currency in the United States, Mexico, and England:

	Shoes	Hats	Haircuts
U. S.	$20	$10	$5
England	£10	£10	£3
Mexico	N $200	N $100	N $20

Suppose that a representative consumer bundle of these goods is:

Shoes	Hats	Haircuts
2	1	2

a. What are the rates of currency exchange suggested by the absolute version of the purchasing power parity doctrine?

b. Would you be surprised to learn that the equilibrium exchange rates were 0.566 pounds per dollar and 11 pesos per dollar?

c. Why might the PPP prediction for the peso be further off than for the pound?

d. Now suppose that all prices doubled in the U. S. and tripled in England and Mexico in the next 10 years. What would you predict to be the equilibrium exchange rates in 10 years?

e. How might real shocks to say the world price of wheat or oil modify your answer?

References and suggested reading

Abuaf, Niso, and Philippe Jorion (March 1990), "Purchasing Power Parity in the Long Run," *Journal of Finance*, 45(1): 157—174.

Ahtiala, Pekka, and Yair E. Orgler (April 1995), "The Optimal Pricing of Exports Invoiced in Different Currencies," *Journal of Banking and Finance*, 19(1): 61—77.

Aliber, Robert Z. (December 1973), "The Interest Rate Parity Theory: A Reinterpretation," *Journal of Political Economy*, 81(6): 1451—1459.

Antl, Boris ed. (1983), *Swap Financing Techniques*, London: Euromoney Publications.

Beidelman, Carl R. (1991), *Cross-Currency Swaps*, Homewood, IL: Irwin.

Bilson, John F. O. (1983), "The Evaluation and Use of Foreign Exchange Rate Forecasting Services," in *Management of Foreign Exchange Risk*, R. J. Herring, ed. Cambridge, UK: Cambridge University Press, 149—179.

Black, Fisher and Myron Scholes (May-June 1973), "The Pricing of Options and Corporate Liabilities," *Journal of Political Economy*, 45(1): 637—659.

Cassell Gustav (1918), "Abnormal Deviations in International Exchanges," *Economic Journal*, 81(3): 413—415.

Cincibuch, Martin (2004), "Distributions implied by American currency futures options: a ghost's smile." *Journal of Futures Markets*, 24(2): 147—178.

Connolly, Michael, Alvaro Rodriguez and William Tyler (1994), "The Use of the Exchange Rate for Stabilization: A Real Interest Arbitrage Model Applied to Argentina", *Journal of International Money and Finance*, 13(2): 223—231.

Connolly, Michael and Dean Taylor (1984), "The Exact Timing of the Collapse of an Exchange Rate System," *Journal of Money, Credit and Banking*, 16(2): 194—207.

Connolly, Michael (1983), "Optimum Currency Pegs for Latin America," *Journal of Money, Credit and Banking*, 15(1): 56—72.

Connolly, Michael, (1982), "The Choice of An Optimum Currency Peg for a Small, Open Country," *Journal of International Money and Finance*, 1(2): 153—164.

Cox, J. C., Stephen A. Ross, and M. Rubinstein (1979), "Option Pricing: A Simplified Approach," *Journal of Financial Economics*, 7(3): 229—263.

DeRosa, David F. (1992), *Options on Foreign Exchange*, Chicago: Probus Publishing.

Giddy, Ian H. and Guner Dufey (Fall 1995), "Uses and Abuses of Currency Options," *Journal of Applied Corporate Finance*, 8(3): 49—57.

Fama, Eugene F. (October 1976), "Forward Rates as Predictors of Future Spot Rates," *Journal of Financial Economics*, 3(4): 361—377.

Fernald, Julia D. (Winter 1993—1994), "The Pricing and Hedging of Index Amortizing Rate Swaps," *Quarterly Review of the New York Federal Reserve Bank*, 18(4):71—74.

Frenkel, Jacob A., and Richard M. Levich (April 1975), "Covered Interest Arbitrage: Unexploited Profits?" *Journal of Political Economy*, 83(2):

325—338.

Friedman, Milton and Anna Jacobson Schwartz (1993), *Monetary History of the United States: 1867—1960*, Princeton: Princeton University Press, 1—14.

Geman, Helyette (2005), *Commodities and Commodity Derivatives*, John Wiley & Sons.

Giddy, Ian H. (Winter 1979), "Measuring the World Foreign Exchange Market," *Columbia Journal of World Business*, 14(4): 36—48.

Globecom Group, LTD. (1995), *Derivatives Engineering: A Guide to Structuring, Pricing and Marketing Derivatives*, Homewood, IL: Irwin.

Goodhart, Charles A., and Thomas Hesse (1993), "Central Bank Forex Intervention Assessed in Continuous Time," *Journal of International Money and Finance*, 12(4): 368—389.

Hanke, Steve. H. (2002), "On Dollarization and Currency Boards: Error and Deception," *Journal of Policy Reform*, 5(4): 203—222.

Hull, John, C., *Options, Futures, and Other Derivatives*, 3rd ed., (1997) Prentice Hall, Upper Saddle River, N. J.

Kester, W. & T. Luehrman (1993), "Note on Cross Border Valuation," *Case Problems in International Finance*, McGraw-Hill.

Lessard, Donald R. (1979), "Evaluating Foreign Projects: An Adjusted Present Value Approach," in D. R. Lessard, ed. *International Financial Management*, Boston: Warren, Gorham & Lamont.

Levich, Richard M. (1998), "Interest Rate Parity and the Fisher Parities," *International Financial Markets: Prices and Policies*, Boston: Irwin-McGraw-Hill.

Mahlotra, D., Rand Martin and Vivek Bhargava (2004), "An Empirical Analysis of yen-dollar currency swap market efficiency," *International Journal of Business*, 9(2): 143—158.

Marshall, John F., and Kenneth R. Kapner (1993), *The Swaps Market*, Miami, FL: Kolb Publishing.

Melvin, Michael (2004), *International Money and Finance*, Addison-Wesley.

Melvin, Michael, and David Bernstein (December 1984), "Trade Concentration, Openness, and Deviations from Purchasing Power Parity," *Journal of International Money and Finance*, 3(3): 369—376.

Mill, John Stuart (1848), *Principles of Political Economy*, London: John W. Parker, West Strand, Book Ⅲ, Chapter XX: 10.

Mundell, Robert A. (September 1961), "A Theory of Optimum Currency Areas," *American Economic Review*, 51(4): 657—665.

Mundell, R. A. (1968), "Barter theory and the monetary mechanism of adjustment," *International Economics*, New York: Macmillan, 130—133.

Mundell, Robert A. (1973), "Plan for a European Currency" in *The Economics of Common Currencies*, eds. Harry G. Johnson and Alexander K. Swoboda, Cambridge, Massachussets: Harvard University Press.

Officer, Lawrence H. (March 1976), "The Purchasing Power Parity Theory of Exchange Rates: A Review Article," *IMF Staff Papers*, 23 (1): 1—60.

Ong, Li Lian (2003), *The Big Mac Index: Applications of Purchasing Power Parity*, Palgrave MacMillan.

Pan, Ming-Shiun, Angela Y. Liu, and Hamid Bastin (August 1996), "An Examination of the Short-Term and Long-Term behavior of Foreign Exchange Rates," *Financial Review*, 31(3): 603—622.

Popper, Helen (August 1993), "Long-Term Covered Interest Parity: Evidence from Currency Swaps," *Journal of International Money and Finance*, 12(4): 439—448.

Reinker, Kenneth and Edward Tower (Summer 2004), "Index Fundamentalism Revisited," *The Journal of Portfolio Management*, 30(4): 37—50.

Riehl, Heinz and Rita Rodriguez (1989), *Foreign Exchange and Money Markets*, Englewood Cliffs, N. J.: Prentice-Hall.

Rolnick, Arthur J., Bruce D. Smith, and Warren E. Weber (2001), "Establishing a Monetary Union in the United States," *Federal Reserve Bank of Minneapolis*.

Rosenberg, Michael (2003), *Exchange Rate Determination: Models and Strategies for Exchange Rate Forecasting*, McGraw-Hill.

Sercu, Piet, Raman Uppal, and Cynthia Van Hulle (1995), "The Exchange Rate in the Presence of Transaction Costs: Implications for Tests of Purchasing Power Parity," *Journal of Finance*, 50(4): 1309—1319.

Shapiro, A. C. (Spring 1978), "Capital Budgeting for the Multinational Corporation," *Financial Management*, 7(1): 7—16.

Solnik, Bruno (Spring 1990), "Swap Pricing and Default Risk: A Note," *Journal of International Financial Management and Accounting*, 2(1): 79—91.

Stapleton, Richard C., and Marti Subrahmanyam (May 1997) "Market Imperfections, Capital Asset Equilibrium, and Corporation Finance," *Journal of Finance*, 32(2): 307—319.

Sweeney, Richard J., and Edward J. Q. Lee (1990) "Trading Strategies in Forward Exchange Markets," *Advances in Financial Planning and Forecasting*, 4: 55—80.

Tan, Zhuo and Shenggang Yang (2012), "Neutralization in China: Evidence from the Balance Sheet of the People's Bank of China," *Journal of Economic Policy Reform*, 15(1): 25—31.

Taylor, Dean (April 1982), "Official Intervention in the Foreign Exchange Market, or Bet Against the Bank," *Journal of Political Economy*, 90(2): 356—368.

Taylor, Francesca (1996), *Mastering Derivatives Markets*, London: Financial Times-Pitman Publishing.

Wong, Kit (2003), "Currency hedging with options and futures." *European Economic Review*, 47(5): 833—839.

4 Hedging Foreign Exchange Risk

CHAPTER 4

外汇风险的套期保值

Hedging defined

A firm or an individual hedges by taking a position, such as acquiring a cash flow, an asset, or a contract, including a forward one, that will rise (or fall) in value to offset a drop (or rise) in value of an existing position. A *perfect* hedge is one eliminating the possibility of future gain or loss due to unexpected changes in the value of the existing position.

Why hedge? Shareholders can, in principle, perform any foreign exchange hedging that the corporation can. Consequently, the corporation need not devote resources to the elimination of diversifiable or hedgeable risk. Indeed, hedging might be counterproductive by harming the interests of shareholders. Similarly, a firm which takes over other firms in different industries might displease shareholders who can diversify their portfolio directly by purchasing shares themselves in those industries.

When there are neither transactions costs, nor bankruptcy costs, shareholders with perfect information on the firm's foreign exchange exposure can undertake any hedging they feel necessary. In short, a cogent argument can be made that the firm should not hedge foreign exchange risk—that is, exposure to unexpected changes in the exchange rate.

However, the majority of international firms hedge foreign exchange risk selectively, if not completely. Furthermore, shareholders do not have the same information that the firm has regarding its foreign exchange risk. Or it would involve considerable search costs to ascertain the foreign exchange risk exposure of the firm. This is a question of asymmetric information. It is unlikely that pension fund managers, for example, have any i-

套期保值(Hedging):公司或个人建立一个新的头寸,并通过它的价值的上升(或下跌)来抵消一个现有头寸价值的下跌(或上升),我们则称公司或个人在进行套期保值。

完全的套期保值(Perfect hedge):如果套期保值能够完全消除由于现有头寸价值的意外变动而在将来获利或受损的可能性,那么他被称为完全套期保值。

dea about the currency flows involved in global operations of firms such as IBM, General Motors or Ford.

A counterargument in favor of foreign exchange hedging is made by Ian Giddy:

> "Exchange-rate volatility may make earnings volatile and thus increase the probability of financial distress. If hedging reduces the nominal volatility of the firm's earnings, it will in turn reduce the expected value of the costs of financial distress (including bankruptcy) ... Some of these costs are borne by creditors, in which case a reduction in expected distress costs will reduce lenders' required rate of return. In addition, for a given level of debt, lower earnings volatility will entail a lower probability of bankruptcy."
>
> (Source: Ian H. Giddy, *Global Financial Markets*, © DC Heath and Company 1994: 481.)

In bankruptcy, there is a discrete drop in the return to creditors. Their return declines more as the value of its assets is further downgraded. For instance, under Chapter 7 or liquidation proceedings, the return on the dollar to creditors deteriorates the lower the value of remaining assets to be liquidated by the court.

Increased volatility in earnings and the risk of financial distress, in general, lead creditors to charge a higher risk premium on loans to the firm. Greater leverage becomes more expensive and thus there are lower gains from tax shields. As Giddy argues:

货币配对 (Currency matching):货币配对降低了财务困境的可能性,它允许公司使用更高的财务杠杆进而获得更多的税盾收益和更低的借款成本。

> "The double taxation of corporate income and the worldwide practice of tax deductibility of interest payments provide an incentive for debt finance. This incentive is weakened, however, by the direct and indirect costs of financial distress and bankruptcy; the greater the volatility of earnings, the greater the costs. More leverage means more volatile earnings, so the tax shield gains from leverage are, at some point, offset by the deadweight costs of financial distress. The greater the probability of distress, the lower the leverage level that is optimal for the firm and the lower the tax shield. Because **currency matching** reduces the probability of financial distress, it allows the firm to have greater leverage and therefore a greater tax shield and lower borrowing costs. Thus, the greater the degree of bankruptcy-cost-hedging, the greater the value of the firm and the lower the cost

of capital. "

(Source: Giddy, *op. cit.*: 482)

In this simple framework, the value of the firm to shareholders can be
divided into the parts in Table 4.1:

Table 4.1   Valuation of the firm

	The value of a firm to shareholders
equals	the value of existing assets
less	the value of existing debt and obligations
less	the present value of the expected costs of financial distress
less	the present value of the cost of hedging
plus	the present value of tax shields
plus	the present value of lowered borrowing costs
plus	the present value of growth and operating options

Consequently, in comparison to the unhedged firm, Giddy argues that
a firm which hedges selectively may increase its net worth rather than reducing it. This would be the case when the reduced costs of financial distress and the lowered borrowing costs offset the costs of the hedges. Indeed, if this were true, the total cost of hedging would be negative, Giddy
argues. While possible, this is unlikely since managing risk usually entails
a cost.

Another way of putting the argument is that foreign exchange hedging
reduces the β, or market risk, of a company by reducing the volatility of
its earnings, thus reducing the risk premium at which expected earnings
are discounted. With hedges, a company's β is lower so its risk premium
is lower.

To summarize the arguments: On the one hand, expected earnings
are discounted at a lower interest rate; On the other hand, earnings may
also be lower due to the costs of the hedges. The firm's net worth could
therefore conceivably be higher or lower. The theory of comparative advantage should shed some light on this unsettled issue. A firm that does not
hedge its foreign exchange exposure is not only producing goods and services, but is also a currency speculator by taking unhedged positions in foreign currencies. It may have a comparative advantage in producing its
goods, but surely does not as a currency speculator. To focus on its core
business, production, it should selectively hedge through foreign exchange
forwards, swaps, and offsetting currency flows that do not leave it exposed

to large unexpected losses in foreign exchange that could put it in financial distress.

Consider now a specific example of long exposure to dollars by a Chinese battery firm, Corum batteries. Corum has an ongoing automobile battery contract for delivery of one thousand units each month in exchange for monthly payment of one million dollars upon delivery. Corum's reporting and functional currency is the Chinese yuan, so it is exposed to the risk that the dollar might continuously depreciate, Corum may not want to run the risk of large losses, and consequently could hedge by a number of means, such as a sequence of forward sales of the one million dollars on the forward over-the-counter market with a bank. However, a better way to hedge ongoing flow of receipts in dollars is by a foreign exchange swap of yuan for dollars, thus giving it a debt obligation to service in terms of dollars: In other words, an offsetting currency flow. Each million dollars of accounts receivable monthly could be used to pay one million dollars of interest and principal on the dollar denominated loan. Any losses on dollar depreciation from accounts receivable would be recouped by gains on the loan payments in dollars.

Credit ratings

信用评级（Credit rating）:信用评级是对公司债务（股份权益或公司债券）、机构债券或政府（包括中央、省级或地方政府）债务信誉的评估。

In addition to foreign exchange risk, there is also credit or default risk. Credit ratings are an assessment of the creditworthiness of a corporation's debt, whether equities or corporate bonds, agency debt or that of sovereign, state and local governments. The definitions of creditworthiness are based on how likely the firm, agency, or government is to default and the protection that creditors receive in the event of a default. The creditworthiness is rated by Standard & Poor's, Fitch, and Moody's.

The highest rating a firm or government can have is AAA or Aaa, and such debt is judged to be the best quality and to have the lowest degree of risk. This rating is not awarded very often; AA or Aa ratings indicate very good quality debt and are much more common. Low quality, speculative and "junk" (below BBB –) bonds have higher probabilities of default than investment grade (BBB – or above) bonds. S&P reduced General Motors two notches to BB and Ford to BB + , both junk bond statuses. This following their low earnings, high pension liabilities and outstanding debts, caused their bonds to plunge in value. (*New York Times*, May 6, 2005.)

Applying the Concept: The bankruptcy of General Motors

On June 1, 2009, General Motors filed for Chapter 11 Bankruptcy. The filing reported US $82.29 billion in assets and US $172.81 billion in debt, with US $2 billion cash in hand. The company received debtor-in-possession financing of US $15 billion from the US Treasury to complete the bankruptcy. The "new GM" is mostly owned by the United States Government, whose further Treasury loans of $50 billion gave the government a 60.8% stake. The Canadian Government owns 11.7% and the United Auto Workers, a further 17.5% through its health-care trust. The remaining 10% is held by unsecured creditors. Under the reorganization process, a *363 sale* (for Section 363, Title 11, Chapter 3, United States Bankruptcy Code) the purchaser of the assets of a company in bankruptcy proceedings is able to obtain approval for the purchase from the court prior to the submission of a re-organization plan, free of liens and other claims. On November 17, 2010 the new General Motors Co. realized the biggest initial public offering in U.S. history, raising $20.1 billion. The new GM sold 478 million common shares at $33 each, raising $15.77 billion, as well as $4.35 billion in preferred shares. On December 28, 2011, its common shares were worth $20.07 on the NYSE, nearly 40% below the IPO price.

Source: *Reuters*, November 17, 2010; *Yahoo Finance*, December 28, 2011.

In the 1980s, a growing part of corporate borrowing has taken the form of low-grade, or "junk" bonds. The lowest corporate rating is D for debt that is in default. For sovereign debt that is in default, the rating is SD. Both Moody's and S&P use adjustments to these ratings. S&P uses plus and minus signs: an A + is higher than an A rating and an A − is lower. Moody's uses a 1, 2, or 3 designation, with 1 being the highest. A favorable creditworthiness rating reduces the interest that a borrower has to pay for new loans because the risk premium is lower, while an unfavorable rating increases the interest that investors require. Table 4.2 illustrates the twenty-one notches of the Standard and Poor's ratings.

Table 4.2 Standard and Poor's credit ratings

	S&P	Standard and Poor's Credit Rating Notches
Upper Investment Grade	AAA	Capacity to pay interest and principal is extremely strong.
	AA +	Very strong capacity to pay interest and repay principal.
	AA	
	AA −	
	A +	Strong capacity to pay, but susceptible to adverse economic conditions.
	A	
	A −	
Lower Investment Grade	BBB +	Adequate capacity to pay, but likely to have weakened ability to pay.
	BBB	
	BBB −	
Non Investment Grade	BB +	Speculative or "junk" with respect to payment.
	BB	
	BB −	
Lower Non-investment Grade	B +	Large uncertainties regarding ability to pay. Some issues in default.
	B	
	CCC +	
	CCC	
	CCC −	
	CC	
	C	Income bonds on which no interest is being paid.
Default	D	Default, payment of interest and or principal is in arrears.

Source: Standard and Poor's.

Table 4.3 shows several long term bond sovereign ratings by agency in July 2011.

如表 4.3 所示，标准普尔在近期下调了美国国债评级，将其从 AAA 级降至了 AA + 级。

Table 4.3 Long term sovereign credit ratings by agency

	Moody's	Standard & Poor's	Dagong
China	Aa3	AA −	AA +
United States	Aaa	AA +	A +
Canada	Aaa	AAA	AA +
Russia	Baa1	BBB +	A
United Kingdom	Aaa	AAA	A +
France	Aaa	AAA	A +
Belgium	Aa1	AA +	A +
Italy	Aa2	A +	A −
Spain	Aa2	AA	A
Greece	Ca	CC	BB
Portugal	Ba2	BBB −	A −

Source: *Natixis*, *Bloomberg*, *Les Echos*, July 29/30, 2011.

The Natixis study supports the Chinese rating agency's lower credit rating of the United States in light of the fiscal deficit of 10% of GDP in recent years, as well as the projected low growth of 1.6%. Independent sources expect growth in spending surpassing growth in revenues. Cuts in US discretionary spending will not suffice since tax revenues do not even cover mandatory spending on entitlements plus interest on the national debt. Both Moody's and S&P had a negative outlook, however, on the AAA rating of U.S. Treasuries. In the event, S&P reduced the credit rating of US Treasuries by one notch to AA +, while maintaining the negative outlook, suggesting that further downgrades are likely. The S&P forecast of future deficits was immediately challenged by the US Treasury, but the Chinese Agency, Xinxua, pointed out that when a state "issues new debt to finance repayment of old debt" ... it is taxing Peter to pay Paul. In their words: Xinhua said in a commentary that Mr. Biden—who visited China—had repeatedly told Chinese leaders and students that its U.S. dollars assets were safe.

"Yet that is far from enough to soothe the concerns of China and the world as concrete actions are badly needed from the United States to honor its promises," the commentary said. It urged Washington to "end its excessive reliance on overseas borrowing, make substantial reforms and cuts to its bloated entitlement programs, reduce budget deficits and restructure its economy." (Source: *Wall Street Journal*, August 22, 2011). The Chinese government, whose People's Bank of China holds of over a trillion dollars worth of U.S. Treasuries, wants "concrete measures."

Applying the Concept: A US Treasury Ponzi Game

The largest Ponzi game in world history, far surpassing that of Bernie Madoff, is being run by the US Treasury. Worse yet, the People's Bank of China may be left holding the bag. When cash flow from operations is not sufficient to cover interest and redemptions, and old debt is being repaid by funds from new borrowing, we have "Ponzi finance" as defined by MIT's Charles Kindleberger. In terms of sovereign debt, Ponzi finance is the issue of new debt to finance mandatory spending on entitlements plus net interest on existing debt. This occurs when current tax revenues to not cover mandatory spending-social security, medicare, medicaid, income security, civilian and military retirement, veterans income security, and net subsidy costs of the TARP, Fannie Mae and Freddie Mac, and other programs, as well as

庞 氏 骗 局 （ Ponzi Game）：庞氏骗局实质上是将后一轮投资者的投资作为投资收益支付给前一轮的投资者，以此类推，使卷入的人和资金越来越多。当投资者和资金难以为继时，庞氏骗局便会骤然崩溃。

interest payments on Treasuries. Failure to make an interest payment would represent a sovereign Treasury default.

The "non-partisan" U. S. Congressional Budget Office (CBO) suggests that the U. S. Treasury is currently running a pyramid scheme. Treasury debt held by the public (52% US residents, 48% foreign) is projected to nearly double in the next 10 years as a percent of U. S. GDP, rising from 53% in 2009 to 90% in 2020. Surprisingly, these projections are optimistic ones, not including the costs of new health spending and the regulatory costs of policing the financial system. Furthermore, real GDP growth in the U. S. is assumed by the CBO to be 4.3% per annum in the next ten years. This will not happen! As tax rates and new borrowing increase the effective tax burden in the U. S. , and debt rises quickly relative to GDP, economic growth will be slow. Uncertainty kills business investment and new hiring.

When growth slows, tax revenues slow in proportion and government spending rises through automatic stabilizers—unemployment compensation, payments to the needy and dependent. Assume instead that U. S. real growth will average 2% , that tax revenues will be two percent lower, and government spending 1% higher. An adjusted forecast shown in Table 4.4 is alarming:

Table 4.4 Treasury spending as a fraction of tax revenues

	2009	2010	2011
Mandatory spending & interest payments	108.3	109.1	100.5
Total spending	167.1	175.3	158.6

Note: As a percentage of total tax revenues.

Table 4.5 reports the deficits as a fraction of Gross Domestic Product.

Table 4.5 US deficits and debt as a fraction of Gross Domestic Product

	2009	2010	2011
Deficit (−) or Surplus	−9.9	−11.2	−9.9
Debt Held by the Public	53.0	65.2	74.3

Note: As a percentage of Gross Domestic Product.

Source: Revised CBO projections, March 5, 2010 by the authors.

Bear in mind that new health and regulatory costs are not included, nor are "unexpected" future Fannie Mae, Freddie Mae, AIG, General Motors, and GMAC subsidies. The likely consequence of this Ponzi Game is US Treasury default, either explicitly by failing to make a payment when due or implicitly by a burst of unexpected inflation. When U. S. bondholders, domestic and foreign, reach a maximum US debt they are willing to hold, new borrowing by the Treasury must be financed by the "lender of last resort," the Federal Reserve Bank by printing of new seignorage. Printing press finance of the Treasury deficit will catch bondholders by surprise, erasing the real value of their bonds by the percentage that realized inflation exceeds expected inflation. This is the warning of Sargent and Wallace (1982). There are hardly enough Treasury Inflation Protected Securities (TIPS) to save bondholders. Inflationary finance could come as early as 2016.

Source: By Michael Connolly, Finance, Hunan University and Wei Lai, Economics, Shenzhen Polytechnic.

Default risk premium

Consider a corporate coupon bond with a face value of $100 and a coupon of $5 payable at maturity in one year. The risk free rate is 5% for T-bills with one year before expiration. If there is no default risk, its present value is $100:

$$PV = \$100 = \frac{\$105}{1.05} \qquad (4.1)$$

违约风险溢价(Default risk premium):为了吸引投资者,债券的收益率通常会高于同期的市场无风险利率,两者之差即为该债券的违约风险溢价。

Now consider the same coupon bond, but having a probability of complete default of p, in which case nothing is paid, and a probability of $(1 - p)$ of no default in which case $105 is paid at maturity. The expected payment is a weighted average of zero with weight p and $105 with weight $(1 - p)$. That is:

$$E(V) = p \times (0) + (1 - p) \times 105 = (1 - p) \times 105 \qquad (4.2)$$

For instance, suppose that the probability of default is 0.3 or 30%. Then the expected value of the payment at maturity is given by:

$$E(V) = 0.7 \times (105) = \$73.5 \qquad (4.3)$$

Therefore the present value of the expected payment at maturity is:

$$PV = \frac{\$73.5}{1.05} = \$70 \qquad (4.4)$$

This should equal the market value of the bond, given that there is a 30% chance of full default. Accordingly, the yield to maturity, r, is given by the internal rate of return which sets the present value of face plus coupon equal to the market price of the bond, or:

$$\$70 = \frac{\$105}{1 + r} \quad \text{or} \quad r = \frac{105}{70} - 1 = 0.5 = 50\% \qquad (4.5)$$

Therefore the default risk premium, ρ, for this bond is approximately 45% since: 50% – 5% approximately yields the risk premium. The exact risk premium, found by solving $(1 + R)(1 + \rho) = (1 + r)$, is 42.9%, very close to the approximate value, 45%, given by the rule of thumb.

An equivalent technique for measuring the default risk premium on a corporate bond is to simply use the market price discount of the bond to compute the risk premium. That is:

(1) compute the present value of the riskless bond and compare it to the market price of the risky bond.

(2) Compute the risk premium, ρ, from the ratio of the market price of the asset to its present value discounted at the risk free rate, and subtract one.

Default risk graphically

違 约 风 险 (Default Risk): 违约风险可由一种资产的市场价值比上它的报酬以无风险利率（例如美国国库券利率）贴现获得的现值所得到的折扣百分比来度量。

Default risk is measured by the percentage discount of the market value of an asset relative to the present value of its payments at a risk-free interest rate (say U. S. Treasury rate). In Figure 4.1, the present value of the bond is indicated along the horizontal axis, discounted by the risk-free rate. If there is no default risk, the market value of the bonds plotted on the vertical axis would be the same, as plotted along the 45 degree line from the origin. When there is default risk, the market value falls below the risk free value indicated along the 45 degree line.

Figure 4.1   Default risk premium

As indebtedness increases, holding other things such as income constant, it becomes more difficult to service the foreign debt, so a discount emerges. It is entirely conceivable that additional debt might reduce the expected present value of repayment—more debt would have in fact less market value. In that case, the market value curve slopes downward. In the previous example of a risky coupon bond with a present value of $100 at the risk free rate, the present value of expected repayment is only $70 in one year since there is a 30% chance of full default.

In general, bonds that are rated poorly have a high yield to maturity, incorporating a risk premium.

Hedging foreign exchange transactions exposure

A firm may have foreign currency exposure, either long or short, due to a future receipt or payment of a specified amount in a foreign currency. For example, when a Chinese firm has accounts receivable in dollars at some point in the future, say 90 days, it is exposed to transactions exposure—losses or gains due to unexpected changes in the exchange rate—in the yuan price of the dollar. The Chinese firm is said to be long dollars. If the firm has accounts receivable in dollars, it will have to sell them for yuan—renminbi (CNY)—at the bid rate for the dollar in yuan. Let's indicate the expected exchange rate (yuan price of the dollar) in 90 days by F_{90}, the futures or forward bid rate. If a forward rate does not exist, just forecast the rate using interest rate parity. In 90 days, there will be a realized spot rate, S_{90}, the bid spot rate for the dollar.

Consequently, the unanticipated change in the exchange rate or forecast error is indicated by: $F_{90} - S_{90}$. This represents the gain or the loss per dollar in which the firm has foreign exchange exposure. If the firm is long 1,000,000 dollars, accounts receivable, for example, it will gain if the spot price of the dollar is above the forward price upon receipt and sale of the dollars. If the spot price is less than the forward, the firm will lose: $(F_{90} - S_{90})1,000,000$ in terms of yuan. If unhedged, the long position in dollars due to accounts receivable has the following payoff diagram in Figure 4.2.

Figure 4.2   A long position in dollars

For example, let's say the 90 day yuan bid price of the dollar is 6.380. This would be the expected rate of settlement of the $1,000,000 accounts receivable. If the firm goes unhedged, it risks possible losses or gains from unanticipated changes in the exchange rate. For instance, the dollar may fall in the spot market to 6.300 so we would lose ¥0.08 per dollar, or eight fen, when we sell in the spot market. On $1,000,000, this amounts to ¥ -80,000. This is illustrated in Figure 4.3.

图 4.3 显示了美元多头的损失,如果公司不进行套期保值,90 天后即期市场中的美元汇率跌至 6.30,则公司将在每美元上损失 0.08 元人民币。

Figure 4.3   A loss on a long position in dollars

On the other hand, by going unhedged, the firm also may gain from a rise in the spot price of the dollar, to say 6.46 CNY per USD. In this case, the firm would gain ¥ +80,000 from the sale of our dollar receipts, eight fen per dollar. This is illustrated in Figure 4. 4.

Figure 4.4 A gain on a long position in dollars

图 4.4 显示了美元多头的获利,如果公司不进行套期保值,90 天后即期市场中的美元汇率升至 6.46,则公司将在每美元上获利 0.08 元人民币。

With $1,000,000 accounts receivable in 90 days, a one-time transaction, the hedging choices would be to acquire one of the following contractual hedges:

- A forward market sale of $1,000,000,
- a money market hedge by borrowing the present equivalent of $1,000,000, or
- purchase a put option on $1,000,000.

These three contracts would be short positions offsetting the initial long position in USD.

持有 90 天期的 100 万美元应收账款,对于一次性交易,可以选择如下的合约套期保值策略:在远期市场上出售 100 万美元;采取货币市场套期保值,借入 100 万美元的现值;为 100 万美元购买一份看跌期权。

A forward market sale

To hedge the long position in dollars using a forward market hedge, sell $1,000,000 in the forward market for delivery in 90 days. The forward sale is a short position in dollars that exactly offsets the existing long position from accounts receivable. What is gained on the short position is lost on the long position. Or what is gained on the long position is lost on the short position. The combined position is perfectly hedged—no chance of either gain or loss from unanticipated movements in the dollar. The forward market sale is illustrated in Figure 4. 5.

远期市场出售（A forward market sale）:利用远期市场对美元多头进行套期保值,在远期市场上出售 90 天后交割的 100 万美元。远期卖出形成一个美元多头,正好抵消应收账款产生的已存在的多头。

Figure 4.5 A forward hedge of a long position in dollars

What is lost on the long position—accounts receivable—is just offset by gains on the short position—the forward sale—if the spot price of the dollar falls to 6.30 CNY in 90 days, for example. The horizontal axis is the hedged position, the sum of the long and the short positions, showing neither gains nor losses, independent of the subsequent spot rate in 90 days.

A money market hedge

货币市场套期保值（Money market hedge）：利用货币市场对美元多头进行套期保值,今天借入 90 天期美元,并在即期市场马上出售。90 天后用 100 万美元应收账款归还贷款。

To hedge the long position in dollars using a money market hedge, borrow dollars today for 90 days, and then sell them immediately in the spot market. In 90 days, repay your loan with the $1,000,000 accounts receivable. How many dollars would you need to borrow today? That would depend on the cost of borrowing. Say you can borrow dollars for 90 days at 2% quarterly interest. Borrow exactly $1,000,000/1.02 = 980,392.16$ dollars today, repay the loan with $1,000,000 in 90 days. This is a perfect hedge using the money market. Be sure to sell the dollars you borrow in the spot market—otherwise you acquire another long position in dollars. Your intent is to acquire a short position, the payment of the dollar loan, to offset your existing long position, accounts receivable in dollars in 90 days.

The money market hedge is depicted graphically in Figure 4.6, exactly as the forward sale is illustrated, assuming the firm can borrow or lend at the risk free rate.

Figure 4.6 A money market hedge of a long position in dollars

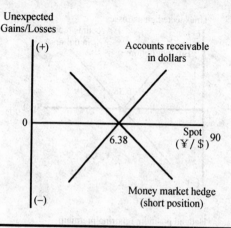

Buying a put option

Buying a put option at a strike price of 6.38 CNY per USD would be a hedge against unforeseen losses, while retaining the possibility of unexpected gains. The cost of the hedge is the option premium. Figure 4.7 illustrates a put option hedge of a long position in dollars.

When the positive put option and the losing position below 0.638 per dollar are added, and a hypothetical cost per dollar of 1 *jiao* or 10 *fen* of the hedge is subtracted, the net position of the put option hedge is illustrated in Figure 4.7. The breakeven point is at a spot price of the dollar of 6.48, the ten fen gain in the long position in accounts receivable just offsetting the cost of the option.

An existing short position in dollars

Consider now a short position in dollars. If your firm has a $1,000,000 accounts payable in 90 days, the choices are as follows:

• Do nothing, remaining unhedged, or acquire one of the following contractual hedges:

• buy dollars for delivery in 90 days, a forward market hedge,

• buy 3 month US Treasuries, a money market hedge, or

• purchase call options for $1,000,000.

买入一个执行价格为 6.38 元人民币/美元的看跌期权 (put option), 这是一个针对意外损失的套期保值, 但仍然保留了意外获利的可能性。

如果你的公司 90 天后有 100 万美元的应付账款, 你可以选择不进行套期保值, 或者你可以选择下列合约套期保值中的一种: 购买 90 天后交割的远期美元, 这是远期市场保值; 购买 3 个月美元国库券, 这是货币市场套期保值; 为 100 万美元购买一份看涨期权。

Figure 4.7 A put option hedge of a long position in dollars

Remain unhedged

The payoff diagram if unhedged is a straightforward short position in dollars, as illustrated in Figure 4.8. The expected spot rate in 90 days is the forward ask rate for the dollar in terms of yuan, which, for simplicity, we assume is 6.39 yuan per dollar. This is because we are short dollars and will have to pay the ask price in yuan when we purchase dollars spot in three months. The difference between the bid and the ask rates is typically around less, but this facilitates the analysis. As drawn in Figure 4.8, we lose 0.08 yuan per dollar when we cover our short position in dollars at a spot price of 6.47, once again amounting to a loss of 80,000 yuan.

Figure 4.8 An unhedged short loss in dollars

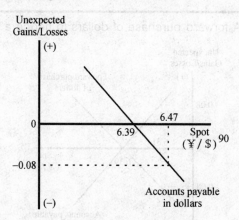

如图 4.8 所示,如果公司不进行套期保值,90 天后即期市场上的美元汇率成为 6.47 元人民币/美元,我们在每美元上损失 0.08 元人民币。

On the other hand, if we do not hedge, we may cover our short position at a lower spot price, say 6.31 yuan per dollar, should the dollar fall 0.08 yuan on the spot market as illustrated in Figure 4.9.

Figure 4.9 An unhedged short gain in dollars

如图 4.9 所示,如果公司不进行套期保值,90 天后即期市场上的美元汇率成为 6.31 元人民币/美元,我们在每美元上获利 0.08 元人民币。

In this case, we gain ¥ +80,000 by not hedging our short position.

A forward hedge

远期套期保值（Forward hedge）：我们只要以 6.39 元人民币/美元的价格买入远期美元 100 万，就可以弥补我们的空头。

We can simply cover our short position by a forward purchase of $1,000,000 at 6.39 yuan per dollar. That is, by acquiring an offsetting long position in dollars, we have a perfect hedge. Any loss made in one position is recovered in the other position, as illustrated in Figure 4.10.

Figure 4.10   A forward purchase of dollars to hedge a short position

As illustrated in Figure 4.10, the gains from the short position—accounts payable in dollars—are just offset by the forward purchase of dollars, the long position.

A money market hedge

货币市场套期保值（Money market hedge）：公司可以通过发放一笔货币市场贷款来弥补美元空头。

The short position in dollars could be covered by a money market loan made by the firm. It would simply lend enough principal in dollars so that principal plus interest repaid in 90 days would represent $1,000,000. If the rate of return were 1% quarterly, the firm would have to lend $1,000,000/1.01 or $990,099.01.

The money market hedge is illustrated in Figure 4.11.

Figure 4.11   A money market loan of dollars to hedge a short position

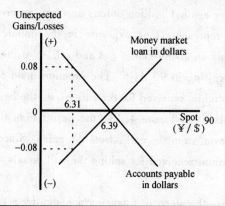

The payoff from the money market hedge exactly cancels any gains or losses from the short position in accounts payable.

Buying a call option

Finally, we sketch the purchase of a call option with a strike price of 6.39 costing 10 fen per dollar. To simplify, we only sketch the net position in Figure 4.12 with a breakeven point of 6.29 yuan per dollar.

Figure 4.12   Payoff from buying a call option at the money to hedge a short position

Collars as hedges

A **collar** is an options hedge that simultaneously limits a loss in one direction by giving up a gain in the other direction. A **zero premium**

买入一个执行价格为 6.39 元人民币/美元、期权费为 10 分人民币/美元的看涨期权（call option）。这是一个针对意外损失的套期保值，但是仍然保留了意外获利的可能性。

领子期权（Collar）：领子期权是一种期权套期保值，它在放弃一个方向上的获利的同时，限制另一个方向上的损失。

零期权费领子期权（Zero premium collar）：零期权费领子期权是一种套期保值，它出售一个期权所获的期权费，正好用于支付购买一个相反期权所需的期权费。

collar is a hedge in which the premium received from selling one option exactly offsets the premium paid for purchasing an opposing option. For example, consider again 1 million dollars accounts receivable in 90 days. This transaction represents long exposure in the dollar. The firm could simultaneously buy an at-the-money put and sell an at-the-money call for 1 million dollars expiring in 90 days. The premium paid for the put would just equal the premium received for the call—i. e. the hedge is known as a zero premium collar. In Figure 4.13, the payoff from the put eliminates losses and the payoff from the call offsets the gains. Since both are at-the-money, the premium received for selling the call equals the premium paid for the put.

To summarize the steps in financing a hedge by a collar: The initial position is long dollars—accounts receivable of $1,000,000 in 90 days. Buy an at-the-money put to sell $1,000,000 in 90 days at-the-money-rate. Simultaneously sell an at-the-money call for $1,000,000 in 90 days. The collar is equivalent to a sale of dollars at the forward price, with the exception that the sale of the call finances the purchase of the put. IBM uses this financing strategy for its hedges.

Figure 4.13   A collar hedge of accounts receivable in dollars

领子期权可以被用来对外汇空头进行套期保值。考虑一个美元空头,例如90天后的应收账款100万美元。为一个外汇空头风险进行套期保值,公司同时出售一个看跌期权、购入一个看涨期权,期限都为90天。如果售出的看跌期权和购入的看涨期权都是平值的,那么期权费相同。因此,出售看跌期权为购买看涨期权提供了资金,这是一种零期权费领子期权。

Hedging a short position in dollars by using a collar

A collar can be used to hedge a short position in foreign exchange. Consider one-million dollars accounts payable in 90 days, a short dollar position. To hedge short foreign exchange exposure, the firm simultaneously sells a put and buys a call, both with 90 days maturity. If the sale of the put and the purchase of the call are both at-the-money, the premi-um is the same. Thus, the sale of the put finances the purchase of the call—another zero premium collar. This collar is illustrated in Figure 4.14.

Figure 4.14   A collar hedge of accounts payable in dollars

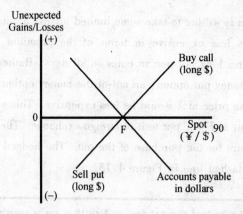

Related techniques for hedging foreign exchange risk

Risk-shifting by currency invoicing

By invoicing in pounds, the British firm can shift the foreign currency exposure to the European importer. The pound may be specified as the currency of payment in the letter of credit. However, the shifting of the FX exposure the European importer may risk the loss of the contract since it raises its cost the European firm. The latter may shift its source of supply to another European firm.

Risk-sharing by currency contingency clauses

In the terms and conditions of the letter of credit, a risk-sharing cur-rency clause may pass part of the currency risk onto the European firm. For instance, if the euro declines by more than 10% between today and settlement, the European firm may agree in advance to pay 5% more euros at settlement. Thus, at settlement, the European firm pays 5% more in euros and the European firms receives 5% less in pounds if the euro declines more than 10%.

A single large transaction involving foreign currency can be best and efficiently hedged by a contractual hedge. However, when the accounts receivable or payable are on an ongoing, operational basis, a natural, matching flow of offsetting amounts of the foreign currency is more appropriate.

Out of the money options hedges

If your firm is willing to take some limited losses, an out of the money options hedge is less expensive in terms of the premium paid. For instance, consider a long position in euros in 90 days. Rather than purchasing an at-the-money put option, an out-of-the-money option to sell the euros at an exercise price of X would be less expensive. This would limit losses to the amount of $F - X$ per unit of foreign exchange. The idea is to pay a smaller premium for the purchase of the put. The hedged position is indicated by the dashed line in Figure 4.15.

Figure 4.15   An out-of-the-money put option as a partial hedge of a long position

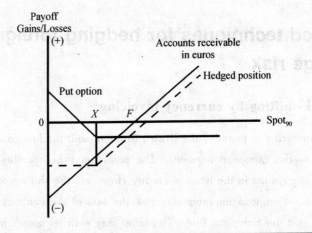

Similarly, if you had a short position in euros, say accounts payable in 90 days, you could purchase an out-of-the-money call at a strike price of X, thus saving on the premium paid to buy the call, and limiting potential losses to $X - F$. The hedged position is indicated by the dashed line in Figure 4.16.

Figure 4.16 An out-of-the-money call option as a partial hedge of a short position

Hedging operating exposure

Operating exposure measures the changes in the net present value of a firm due to unexpected changes in exchange rates. It is a forward looking concept which re-estimates the discounted cash flow in home currency from overseas operations in a local currency following an unexpected change in the exchange rate. Nissan Motor experienced unexpected losses from its overseas automobile sales in US dollars:

经营风险（**Operating exposure**）：经营风险测量汇率意外变动导致的公司净现值的变动。

In the News: The dollar eats into Nissan's profits

Nissan Motor Co.'s chief operating officer said Tuesday that the auto maker is working "with a sense of crisis" to lessen the impact of the strong yen on its business, as the currency's surge threatens to eat into profits in one of Japan's key export industries. "We can't adequately express our concern about the sharp yen rise on our earnings by simply saying … We are worried about it. The company is now working with a sense of crisis," Toshiyuki Shiga said at a news conference for the hybrid version of Nissan's Fuga luxury sedan. The comments are the latest in a series of warnings from Japanese companies ahead of the country's fiscal second-fiscal-quarter earnings season, which starts this week. The dollar fell to 80.41 yen against the yen Monday, its lowest since April 1995 and near its record low of 79.75 yen, before rebounding Tuesday. Each one-yen fall in the dollar slashes Nissan's operating profit by 15 billion yen, the company has said. Mr. Shiga declined to comment on whether the company would change its assumption for the dollar for this fiscal year from the current 90 yen, saying only that Nissan will explain further when it reports its July-September earnings on Thursday next week.

Nissan said in July that it earned nearly half its expected operating profit for the full fiscal year in the first quarter, but it didn't lift its full-year forecast at the time partly because of the difficult outlook for the yen. The auto maker is reducing exports from Japan while increasing imports as a short-term measure to cope with the strong yen, Mr. Shiga said. The company needs to speed up shifting production overseas in the long term, he added. The car maker plans to produce 1.1 million vehicles in Japan during the current fiscal year through March.

Source: Yoshio Takahashi, "Nissan Tries to Blunt Yen 'Crisis'," *Wall Street Journal* (October 27, 2010).

日产汽车的美元多头头寸,给其带来了经营风险。具体表现在当日元相对美元升值时,日产汽车以日元计价的利润减少。

Nissan motor's problem is that it is long dollars in its operational exposure. Its profits in dollars have been reduced in yen by the yen appreciation (dollar depreciation) relative to expectations. In its fiscal year business plan, Nissan used 90 yen to the dollar but has unexpectedly received 80 yen per dollar, suffering an unexpected 11% loss from its U.S earnings. While much of Nissan's earnings are in dollars, the lion's share of its costs are in yen since it produces automobiles in Yokohama. This operational exposure to the US dollar can be dealt with in several ways, including economical, financial and operational hedges.

Economic hedges

Nissan can make economic decisions in its operations to offset the effect of the change in the exchange rate on its earnings when translated into dollars. Firstly, Nissan can raise the dollar price of its automobiles sold in the US market. If it were able to raise the price 11%, yet sell the same volume, it would recoup its foreign exchange losses. This would be more feasible if other auto prices were rising in dollars in the United States.

日产汽车可以进行以下商业计划的调整:通过提高价格,增加以美元计价的利润;通过增加产量,提高美元收入;提高价格与增加产量相结合。

Alternatively, Nissan could hold the line on prices, yet sell 11% more automobiles in the US. If its costs in yen remain the same, it could recoup its exchange rate losses this way. However, it may require Nissan acquiring a larger share of the US market. Thirdly, it could pursue a strategy of both raising dollar prices somewhat and increasing sales.

The change in Nissan's business plan can involve:

- A rise in the profit margin in dollars by raising prices
- A rise in revenues in dollars by expanding the volume of output,

or

- A combination of higher prices and increased output

Free cash flow in dollars could conceivably increase to offset the unanticipated dollar depreciation.

Each of the three cases is plausible since the devaluation of the dollar will be inflationary, so all goods and services prices will rise. However, other operational hedges are available.

Diversifying operations

The firm can diversify its production, sourcing and sales internationally. As suggested in Mr. Shiga's remarks, Nissan can import more parts from abroad, export fewer automobiles from Japan, and speed up its plans to locate and produce abroad, as other Japanese automobile companies, notably Honda and Toyota have done. Nissan could shift the production and assembly of its automobiles to the United States, purchasing parts, renting plants, and hiring labor there. Nissan could then use the dollars from its sales to pay for parts, assembly, distribution and after-sales service on a matching basis. This is a natural operational hedge. Nissan's net income would be less adversely affected by the yen appreciation relative to the dollar. The decline in yen revenue due to dollar devaluation is offset in large part by the decline in costs when reckoned in yen. Net income, however, is still adversely affected, particularly since the Japanese auto makers have difficulty increasing their price due to competition from US auto makers.

生产、原料供应与销售的国际化分散(International diversification of production, sourcing and sales):以日产汽车公司为例,日产汽车公司可以从国外进口更多部件,减少汽车出口,还可以加速海外建厂与生产的步伐。

Another example of operational hedging is the low cost US carrier, Southwest Airlines. In the first quarter of 2005, "Southwest said it saved $155 by capping 86% of its fuel expenses at the equivalent of just $26 a barrel of crude oil, close to half the actual cost of oil during the quarter." (*Wall Street Journal*, April 15, 2005 p. A2). Its fuel hedges run through 2009, but cover a smaller portion of its fuel needs. In 2006, an estimated 60% of fuel use is capped at the equivalent of $30 a barrel, falling to 20% at $35 in 2009. In hindsight, these hedges have led to Southwest being one of the few profitable airlines in 2004 and 2005.

Risk-shifting by currency invoicing

By invoicing in yen, Nissan could in principle shift the foreign cur-

通过选择计价货币转移风险(Risk-shifting by currency invoicing):通过以日元计价,日产汽车公司原则上可以将外汇风险转嫁给美国分公司的批发采购商。

rency exposure to the wholesale purchasers and distributors in the United States. The yen would be specified as the currency of payment. However, the shifting of foreign exchange exposure to the wholesale purchasers imposes currency risk on the importer, requiring the importer to take hedging actions and costs.

Risk-sharing by currency contingency clauses

通过货币或有条款分散风险（Risk sharing by currency contingency clauses）：在信用证的诸多条款中，一项风险分担货币条款可以将部分货币风险转移给国外进口商。

In the terms and conditions of a letter of credit, a risk-sharing currency clause may pass part of the currency risk onto the foreign importer. For instance, if the dollar declines by more than 10% between today and settlement for exports of the automobile, the importer may agree to pay 5% more dollars for the automobiles at settlement. Thus, at settlement, the importer pays 5% more in dollars and Nissan receives 5% less in yen if the dollar declines more than 10%.

Leads and lags in currency payments

提前或延期支付（Leads and lags in currency payments）：在"软币"的预期贬值尚未发生之前，一个公司可以用"软币"提前偿还它的以"硬币"计算的外币债务。

A firm can pay its "hard" foreign currency commitments early with "soft" currency before the latter's anticipated devaluation. The idea is to spend the "soft" currency before it loses value.

Similarly, it can delay paying its "soft" currency liabilities by lagging the payment so as to purchase the soft currency after it loses value. That is, it delays its payment, waiting to purchase the currency at a lower rate. Leading and lagging payments on liabilities benefits the firm actively managing the timing of the transfer of funds, but worsens the position of the corresponding firm. If the latter is a subsidiary that is affected, the profits are transferred from the subsidiary to headquarters. If it is between the firm and a totally separate firm, the latter could easily be bankrupted from currency losses and delays in payments. This procedure may also be used to transfer profits to a subsidiary for example. Early repatriation of profits by Nissan could save the company some unanticipated exchange rate losses.

Re-invoicing centers

再开票中心（Re-invoicing centers）：再开票中心是一家公司的分支机构，它并没有存货，而只是负责开具发票和集中管理经营风险。

A re-invoicing center is a corporate subsidiary that has no inventory but centralizes invoices and manages operating exposure in one center. Manufacturing affiliates ship goods directly to distribution affiliates, but invoice the re-invoicing center that then receives title to the goods and invoices the distribution affiliate in a separate currency.

Transactions exposure thus resides in the re-invoicing center. Naturally, some of its accounts receivable and accounts payable will be in the same currency, providing a natural hedge. The invoicing center thus centralizes the net exposure to each currency.

A re-invoicing center could also transfer profits from a high tax affiliate to a low tax affiliate, i. e. practice aggressive transfer pricing. This is not the purpose of the re-invoicing center and it violates "arm's length" pricing rules established by the US Internal Revenue. A re-invoicing center's purpose is to centralize and manage foreign exchange risk in one place. Diagrammatically, Figure 4. 17 depicts the flow of invoices and payments.

Figure 4.17　A re-invoicing center

Diversifying financing

Natural hedges

A firm that has an ongoing inflow of foreign currency as accounts receivable, can borrow the same currency so as to have a matching accounts payable as a natural hedge. This is illustrated in Figure 4. 18, where a Chinese firm sells goods for dollars in the U. S. , but offsets its operating exposure by obtaining a loan in U. S. dollars. This would be a natural hedge of its earnings in dollars—the cash inflow from its sales in dollars would be a cash outflow of offsetting payment of interest and principal in dollars. The loan, when disbursed in dollars, should be immediately sold for yuan to avoid a long cash position in USD.

自然套期保值 (Natural hedge) :如果一家公司有一笔提供持续外币收入的应收账款,那么它可以借入该种外币,产生一个相匹配的应付账款,从而形成一个自然的套期保值。

Figure 4.18   A natural hedge in dollars

Foreign currency swaps

外汇互换（Foreign currency swaps）：外汇互换是一份协议,协议的双方互换数额一定的两种货币的本金,并且约定在将来相互偿还两种货币的本息和。

A foreign currency swap is an agreement between two parties to exchange a given amount of one currency for another and to repay these currencies with interest in the future. One counterparty borrows under specific terms and conditions in one currency while the other counterparty borrows under different terms and conditions in a second currency. The two counterparties then exchange the net receipts from their respective issues and agree to service each other's debt. Diagrammatically, the currency flows of a foreign exchange swap are illustrated in Figure 4.19.

Figure 4.19   A foreign exchange swap

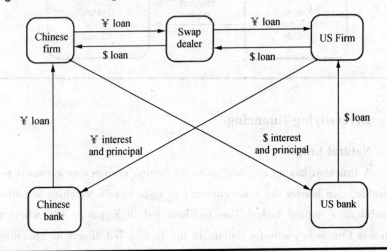

In Figure 4.19, an American firm borrows dollars, a Chinese firm borrows yuan. The two firms exchange the debt obligations through the swap dealer, agreeing to service each other's debt. This swap arrangement benefits each due to their comparative advantage in borrowing in their respective national markets. The swap enables both firms to have lower borrowing costs in foreign currency. The Chinese firm may have dollar receipts from its exports and the American firm may have yuan receipts from its exports, so the swap dealer arranges for matching payments in foreign currency at a lower interest rate. Thus, a currency swap is a way of managing foreign exchange risk. The swap dealer captures some of the lowered borrowing costs by earning the bid-ask spread on foreign currency, the interest rate spread, and other fees from serving as an intermediary. Alternatively, the two firms had they known of each other's matching needs and maturities, could have done the swap directly with each other, but then would have counterparty risk. A swap dealer can provide insurance against non-performance of the counterparty as well as general intermediation.

Back-to-back (parallel) loans

Indirect financing can be done by a Chinese firm lending yuan to the US affiliate in China and simultaneously a US firm lends dollars to the Chinese affiliate in the United States. At an agreed upon time, each return the other's currency. A parallel loan is also known as a credit swap loan since the firms are borrowing each other's currency for a specified period of time. It is illustrated in Figure 4.20.

背对背（平行）贷款
（ Back-to-back (parallel) loans)：我们可以通过中国企业向美国企业的中国分公司提供人民币贷款，同时美国企业向中国企业的美国分公司提供美元贷款的形式，在两家企业之间开展间接融资。背对背贷款或平行贷款又被称为信用互换贷款，因为公司彼此借入对方的货币，使用一定期限。

Figure 4.20 A back-to-back (parallel) loan

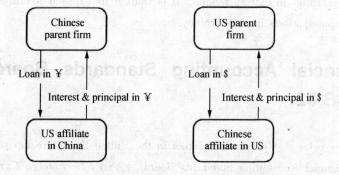

The firms do not go through the foreign exchange market, so do not pay the foreign exchange spread, nor fees. Neither firms wish to hold the cash in foreign currency disbursed by the loan, they are mainly interested in acquiring the interest and principal as an offsetting liability. Consequently, they sell the proceeds from the loan on the spot market.

The firms also benefit from lowered interest rates. In short, they save intermediation costs and benefit from comparative advantage in lending. At the same time, they may use a parallel loan to hedge their foreign exchange risk. Naturally, there is counterparty risk, but the right of offset exists. A swap dealer is better able to match the size, timing, and condition of foreign exchange swaps by avoiding the "double coincidence of wants" implicitly involved in direct counterparty swaps.

Accounting exposure

会计风险（Accounting exposure）:汇率变动导致母公司净值发生变化,从而产生了会计风险。会计风险又称为转换风险,因为它与外币资产和负债的转换相联系。

Accounting exposure arises from changes in the parent's net worth due to changes in exchange rates. Accounting exposure is also known as translation exposure since it is associated with the translation of foreign currency assets and liabilities. Foreign currency financial statements must be translated into the parent company's reporting currency to consolidate worldwide financial and income statements. If exchange rates have changed since the previous reporting period, the restatement of financial and income statements that are denominated in foreign currencies will result in foreign exchange gains or losses. Re-measurement of different line items using different exchange rates results in changes in current income or equity reserves.

A firm is long in a currency if its net exposed assets in the currency are positive (i. e. its exposed assets in a currency are greater than its exposed liabilities in that currency.) It is short if its exposed liabilities exceed exposed assets in the currency.

Financial Accounting Standards Board—FASB 52

The rules that govern translation in the United States are devised by the Financial Accounting Standards Board. FASB 52—*Foreign Currency Translation* established US translation standards, requiring a functional currency and a reporting currency. A functional currency must be selected for each subsidiary. That is the currency of its primary working environment. Any foreign currency income is translated into the functional currency at current exchange rates if measured at current cost and at historical rates if measured at historical cost. Then, all amounts are translated at the current exchange rate from the functional currency into the reporting currency. The reporting currency is the currency in which the parent firm prepares its own financial statements: that is, U.S. dollars for a U.S. firm. In the case of a hyperinflationary country—defined as one that has cumulative inflation of approximately 100% or more over a three-year period—the functional currency of a U.S. affiliate must be the dollar. Translation gains and losses bypass the income statement and are accumulated in a separate equity account on the parent's balance sheet called a *cumulative translation adjustment*.

Translation methods vary from country to country, but most use a cumulative translation adjustment equity line to account for translation gains or losses.

A simple technique is to multiply the difference between exposed assets and exposed liabilities by the change in the exchange rate in each currency. The resulting number is the gain/loss due to translation exposure in that currency. That is:

$$(A_i - L_i)(S_i^2 - S_i^1) \qquad (4.6)$$

Where $(A_i - L_i)$ represents the net position in currency i. If $A_i > L_i$, the firm is long in currency i, if $A_i < L_i$, the firm is short in currency i, while if $A_i = L_i$, the firm is hedged in currency i from an accounting point of view. $(S_i^2 - S_i^1)$ represents the change in the spot price of currency i terms of USD or the home currency between re-measurement periods.

The total gain or loss between reporting periods due to translation at new exchange rates is the sum of the gains or losses in each individual currency, or:

$$\sum_{i=1}^{n} (A_i - L_i)(S_i^2 - S_i^1) \qquad (4.7)$$

This amount is added to or subtracted from the cumulative translation adjustment item.

Hedge accounting

Hedge accounting refers to the inclusion of gains and losses in earnings from financial hedge instruments at the same time losses and gains from changes in the value of the asset are recorded. FASB 52, paragraph 21 indicates that the financial hedge must be designated as and be effective as a hedge of a firm, foreign currency commitment. That is, the value of the hedge must move opposite to the value of a definite foreign currency commitment.

对冲会计法（Hedge accounting）：是指在记录由资产价值变化导致的损益的同时，包含由套期保值金融工具产生的损益。

Trade finance

Trade finance can play a useful role in hedging. A letter of credit specifies, for example, the currency of payment as well as the conditions of payment. When it is confirmed, the bank substitutes its credit for that of the importer should the importer default on payment. Naturally, there are fees associate with a letter of credit, but it assures the payment for international trade, a very important role in the world trade and financial system.

In general, trade can be financed by:

预付现金 (Cash-in-advance):发货前卖方从买方处收取现金。这将信用风险转移给了买方。

• **cash-in-advance**: the seller receives cash from buyer prior to shipment.

This shifts the credit risk to the buyer.

赊销 (An open account):货物先被发送给买方,然后再付款。这将信用风险转移给了卖方。

• **an open account**: goods are shipped to the buyer then payment made to account. This shifts the credit risk to the seller.

托收 (Collections):货物发送给买方,卖方的汇票以及运输单据则由其银行递交给买方的付款行索偿货款。在这种情况下,信用风险由双方共同承担。

• **collections**: goods are shipped to the buyer, the seller's draft and documents covering the shipment are presented through his/her bank to the buyer's bank for payment. In this case, both share in the credit risk.

信用证(A letter of credit):卖方收到一张信用证并满足其所列款项后,将发送货物。在确认信用证的条款得到满足后,信用证开证行通过对信用证进行保兑向卖方提供付款保证。经过保兑的信用证是可以转让的。

• **a letter of credit**: After the seller receives a L/C with acceptable terms, the seller ships the goods. The bank which issued the L/C assures the seller of payment when the terms of the L/C are met by confirming the letter of credit. A confirmed letter of credit is a negotiable instrument.

Steps in obtaining a letter of credit

1. The importer obtains a letter of credit promising to pay on the importer's behalf.

2. The bank promises the exporter to pay on behalf of the importer by advising and/or confirming the letter of credit.

3. The exporter "ships to the bank" trusting the bank's promise.

4. The bank pays the exporter.

5. The bank "turns over" the merchandise to the importer.

Diagrammatically, a letter of finance can be depicted in Figure 4.21.

Figure 4.21   A letter of credit

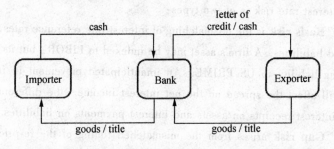

Documents in trade finance

• Letters of credit are documentary or standby, irrevocable or revocable, confirmed or unconfirmed, and revolving or non-revolving. A letter of credit may be transferable to a second party, i. e. discounted on a secondary market. It is typically irrevocable and confirmed to be marketable on the secondary market.

• The exporter ships the merchandise to the importer's country. Title to the merchandise is given to the bank on an order bill of lading.

• The exporter asks the bank to pay for the goods and the bank (or its correspondent or affiliate) does so. The document to request payment is a sight draft (also known as a bill of exchange). The bank passes title to the importer. At that time, or later, depending upon the terms of the agreement, the importer reimburses the bank.

• Both sight drafts and time drafts are negotiable instruments, if properly drawn. When a time draft is drawn upon and accepted by a bank, it becomes a banker's acceptance. When a time draft is drawn on and accepted by a business firm, it becomes a trade acceptance.

• Countertrade takes place when " . . . the sale of goods and services by a producer is linked to an import purchase of other goods and services. " Countertrade is thus a form of barter or bilateral clearing resulting from shortages of hard currency, central planning, political risk, and barriers to international trade and investment. It also is a vehicle for avoiding taxation.

Hedging interest rate exposure

Foreign and interest rate risk management focuses upon hedging existing or anticipated cash flow exposures of the firm. Treasurers have the job of managing interest rate expenses and exposures.

Interest rate risk is of two types:

- **Basis risk** is the mismatching of interest rate reference rates on assets and liabilities. A firm's asset may be indexed to LIBOR, but its corresponding liability to US PRIME. An unanticipated movement in interest rates will affect the spread on the net interest income—the difference between interest receipts on assets and interest payments on liabilities.

- **Gap risk** arises from the mismatched timing of the re-pricing of interest rate referenced liabilities and assets. A bank may possess long term interest sensitive assets but be funded by a large amount of short term interest sensitive debt. Thus, the bank has financial exposure to an unanticipated rise in short term interest rates when it has to frequently rollover or re-set its short term debt. For example, the Fed's "operation twist" of the U.S. yield curve involves a purchase of long term debt and a corresponding sale of short term Treasury debt. The purpose of the operation is to lower long term rates. The banks, however, suffer when short term rates rise and long term rates fall due to gap risk.

Interest rate practices

Interest rate practices vary but the *international practice* (and US practice) is to use the exact number of days for the day count and 360 days in a year. Consequently, 180 days represents half a year.

On the other hand, the United Kingdom, while using the exact number of days for the day count, has 365 days in a year. The Swiss have 30 days in a month and 360 days in a year.

Reference rates

Reference rates such as US dollar LIBOR are used in quotations and loan agreements. **LIBOR** is the London Interbank Offered Rate determined by the British Banker's Association as the mean of 16 multinational banks' interbank offered rate at approximately 11:00 am London time.

Yen LIBOR and DM LIBOR are calculated at the same time in London using an average of interbank yen and DM offer rates. Other financial centers have interbank offer reference rates, such as PIBOR (Paris Interbank Offer Rate), MIBOR (Madrid Interbank Offer Rate), and FIBOR (Frankfurt Interbank Offer Rate), which refer to reference rates on do-

基本风险（Basis risk）：是利率风险的一种，是指由于资产和负债的利率基准不匹配而引起的风险。

缺口风险（Gap risk）：如果一家银行的贷款期限长于存款期限，即借短贷长，那么该银行市场价值的变动方向将与市场利率的变动方向相反。如果该银行的贷款期限短于存款期限，即借长贷短，那么该银行市场价值的变动方向将与市场利率的变动方向一致。

伦敦同业拆借利率（LIBOR）：它是伦敦的一流银行之间短期资金借贷的利率，是国际金融市场中大多数浮动利率的基础利率。

mestic currency agreements in those countries.

Forecasting forward interest rates

The first step in managing interest rate risk is to formulate a forecast of forward interest rates. For this, a strip of the yield curve is the standard technique. Second, a firm's net cash flow exposure to unanticipated changes in the interest rate is measured, then hedged.

The yield curve

The yield to maturity curve depicts the term structure of interest rates. It plots the yields of bonds of the same class (corporates, treasuries, etc.) with maturities that range from the shortest to the longest term. The curve indicates whether short-term interest rates are higher or lower than long-term interest rates.

In general, the yield curve has a positive slope because investors usually receive a higher yield for the extra risk of tying up their money long term. Figure 4.22 depicts the current yield curve for US Treasuries. In the year 2011, the yield curve exhibits a positive slope with higher long term interest rates on the *long bond* (30 year Treasury) than on the 10 year Treasury.

收益曲线 (The yield to maturity curve): 收益曲线表现了利率的期限结构。它刻画了同种类型但有不同到期期限的债券的收益率。

Figure 4.22   The US Treasury yield curve

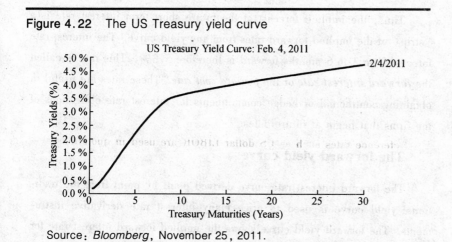

Source: *Bloomberg*, November 25, 2011.

A strip of the yield curve

Consider a 5.125% per annum yield on a 6 month US Treasury bill versus a 4.850% p. a. yield on a 3 month US Treasury bill. It would be possible to hold the 3 month T-bill, then roll it over for a second three months. Ignoring transactions costs, arbitrage pricing should yield the same rate of return. That is:

$$\left(1 + r_{90} \left[\frac{90}{360} \right] \right) \left(1 + r_{90,180} \left[\frac{90}{360} \right] \right) = \left(1 + r_{180} \left[\frac{180}{360} \right] \right) \quad (4.8)$$

or

$$r_{90,180} \left[\frac{90}{360} \right] = \frac{\left(1 + r_{180} \left[\frac{180}{360} \right] \right)}{\left(1 + r_{90} \left[\frac{90}{360} \right] \right)} - 1$$

$$= \frac{1.025625}{1.012125} - 1 = 0.013338 \quad (4.9)$$

or 1.3338 percent.

Multiplying by 4, we have

$$r_{90,180} = 5.333531\% \text{ p. a.}$$

In continuous time, the answer differs slightly.

$$(1 + r_{90})^{1/4} (1 + r_{90,180})^{1/4} = (1 + r_{180})^{1/2} \quad (4.10)$$

yielding

$$r_{90,180} = 5.401\% \text{ p. a.}$$

Thus, the implicit forecast of the future short term interest rate is a "strip" of the implied forward rates from any yield curve. The interest rate forecast from 3 to 6 months forward is therefore 5.3%. This rate is called the *forward interest rate* or the *forward spot rate*. These rates are useful in obtaining contractual or hedge commitments for interest rate obligations of the firms that begin at future dates.

远期利率（Forward interest rate）：远期利率是指隐含在给定的即期利率之中，从未来的某一时点到另一时点的利率。

The forward yield curve

The forward interest rate curve derived point by point from the traditional yield curve is used to price many interest rate derivative instruments. The forward yield curve shows the implied forward interest rate for each period covered by the yield curve.

Outright techniques

- Mismatched maturities—a firm interested in locking in a future rate on investments that are more attractive than current rates can borrow short and lend long. With a positive sloping yield curve, a firm could reduce its borrowing costs by borrowing short and lending long, rolling over its short term debt continually. A firm wishing to borrow at a fixed rate from 6 to 12 months in the future can borrow now for one year, then lend for six months, thereby locking in the future interest rate.

• **Forward rate agreement**—a contract settled in cash to buy or sell interest rate payments on a notional principal. The buyer of an FRA locks in an interest rate for a desired term that begins at a future specified date. The seller of the FRA pays the buyer the increased interest cost on a nominal amount of money if the interest rate rises above a specified rate, but the buyer pays the seller the interest differential if the interest rate falls below the agreed rate. The contract is priced on the basis of the strip rates of the yield curve.

远期利率协定（Forward rate agreement）：是指交易双方约定在未来的某一日期,交换由协议期间的一定名义本金分别以合同利率和参考利率计算的利息的金融合约。

• A foreign currency swap—Two offsetting forwards with different maturities can lock in a future interest rate in a foreign currency. Consider two simultaneous forward contracts：

  • Buy 100 euros 180 days forward at $1. 15 per euro.
  • Sell 100 euros 360 days forward at $1. 17 per euro.

The firm receives 100 euros in 180 days then returns them in 360 days, effectively borrowing the euros forward for 6 months (and lending dollars forward for 6 months). Because the exchange rate is specified on both ends of the contract, the cost of the forward euro funds has been locked in. The actual net cost of the euro funds to the firm is calculated by the internal interest rate that equates the dollar amount put up at the beginning of the 6 month period with the funds returned at the end of the 12 month period. The net interest rate for this foreign currency swap is thus (the difference between the US interest rate and the euro interest rate, from interest rate parity)：It is also known as the "cost of carry."

$$\frac{1.17}{1.15} - 1 = 0.171913 \approx 3.49\%$$

or

$$\frac{F_{360} - F_{180}}{F_{180}} = r_{180,360}^{usd} - r_{180,360}^{euro} \tag{4.11}$$

Interest rate uncertainty is thus removed by the foreign currency swap.

互换（Swap）：互换是指双方按照商定条件,在约定的时间内,交换一系列现金流的合约。

利率互换（Interest rate swap）：利率互换是指交易双方以一定的同种货币作为名义本金,将该本金产生的以固定利率计算的利息收入（支出）流与对方的以浮动利率计算的利息收入（支出）流相交换。

• Interest rate swaps—A **swap** is a contract to exchange debt service obligations. An **interest rate swap** is an agreement to exchange fixed for

货 币 互 换 (Currency swap) : 利率互换是相同货币债务间的调换,而货币互换则是不同货币债务间的调换。

floating interest rate payments in the same currency. A **currency swap** is an agreement to swap interest obligations in different currencies. In both types of swaps, each borrower obtains a payment structure that is preferred, while still retaining the obligation for the principal payment.

Options based interest rate hedging techniques

● Caps, floors and collars are traded over the counter and on the exchanges. Interest rate options have a specified maturity, in practice up to ten years for the over-the-counter market and from one to five years in the options market, and *reset dates* or *fixings*, for instance every three months during the lifetime of the interest rate option.

利率上限 (Interest rate cap) : 通过购买利率上限,购买者可以锁定短期利息支付的最大值。

An **interest rate cap** is an option to fix a ceiling or maximum on a short-term interest rate payment. The buyer pays a premium to the seller of the cap. If the market interest rate rises above the strike rate, the buyer receives a cash payment equal to the difference between the actual market interest rate and the cap strike rate on the notional principal. If the market rate falls below the strike rate, the option expires out of the money and is not exercised. A cap on an interest rate payment is depicted in Figure 4.23.

Figure 4.23 An interest rate cap, ignoring the premium paid

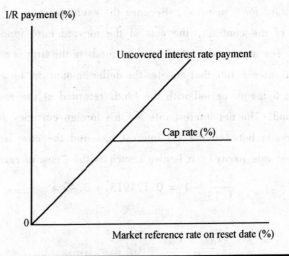

I/R payment (%)

Uncovered interest rate payment

Cap rate (%)

0

Market reference rate on reset date (%)

Ignoring the premium paid at the initial purchase of a cap option, the effect of the cap is to reset the interest payment at the fixing when the market rate of interest is above the strike rate. The interest rate payment is thus capped at the strike rate. The borrower pays the market interest rate but receives from the seller of the cap a payment equal to the difference between the market rate and the strike rate. Effectively, therefore, the interest rate payment is capped.

When the market rate of interest is below the strike rate, the borrower pays the market rate of interest since the cap is out-of-the-money. There are thus no compensating interest payments from the seller of the cap to the buyer. The buyer thus loses the option paid for the purchase of the cap. Figure 4.24 illustrates the effect on interest payments at a fixing date of an interest rate cap.

Figure 4.24 An interest rate cap, including the premium paid

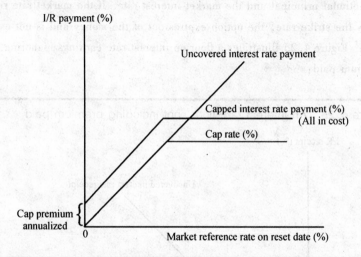

An interest rate guarantee (*IRG*) is similar to a cap but differs in that it provides interest rate protection for a single period. There is thus at most one interest rate resetting. An interest rate cap provides for multiple reset dates. The premium is paid in full upon the purchase of the interest rate cap, but may be annualized to arrive at an all-in-cost (all included) interest rate payment. The standard amortization formula is used to derive a quarterly or annual amortized premium equivalent.

$$\text{Period payment} = \frac{\text{premium}}{\left[\frac{1}{r} - \frac{1}{r(1+r)^t}\right]} \qquad (4.12)$$

which is the amortized loan payment formula for a fixed interest rate r where the premium is the equivalent of the current loan amount, and t is the number of periods or resets. The amortization allows the calculation of the premium on a quarterly or annual basis, for instance, to measure an all-in-cost—the resulting amortized payment that services both principal and interest in a single cash payment per period. Figure 4.24 depicts the all-in-interest payments with the interest rate cap.

The value of an interest rate cap is determined by three factors: (1) the uncovered interest payment, (2) the amount of the cap payment if the reference rate rises above the cap rate, and (3) the annualized cost of the cap.

利率下限（Interest rate floor）：通过购买利率下限，购买者可以锁定短期利息收入的最小值。

An **interest rate floor** is an option to fix a floor or minimum on a short-term interest rate receipt. The buyer pays a premium to the seller of the floor. If the market interest rate falls below the strike rate, the buyer receives a cash payment equal to the difference between the strike rate on the notional principal and the market interest rate. If the market rate rises below the strike rate, the option expires out of the money and is not exercised. Figure 4.25 illustrates a floor on interest rate earnings, ignoring the premium paid:

Figure 4.25   An interest rate floor, not including premium paid

In Figure 4.26, we deduct the interest paid for the premium for a floor on an interest rate receipt.

When an interest rate collar is constructed by the purchase of a cap to protect interest payments and the simultaneous sale of a floor with an equal premium, the combined position is depicted in Figure 4.27.

Figure 4.26   An interest rate floor, deducting the premium paid

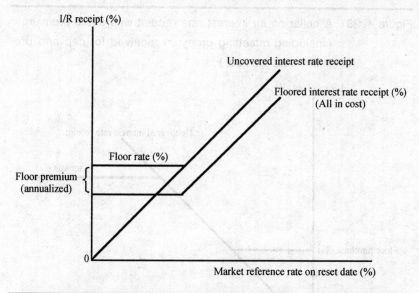

Figure 4.27   A collar on an interest rate payment with equal premium
(including offsetting premium paid for cap and received
for floor)

A foreign exchange collar is the simultaneous purchase of a call option
and sale of a put option, or the purchase of a put option and the sale of a
call option. A zero-cost foreign exchange collar would have equal premi-

ums so there is zero initial payment.

Figure 4.28   A collar on an interest rate receipt with equal premium
(including offsetting premium received for cap and premium paid for floor)

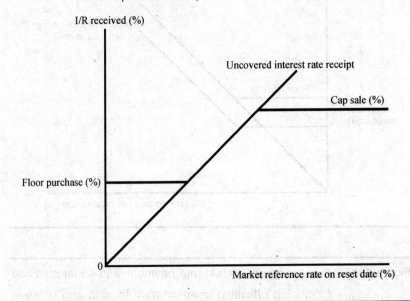

• Swap options. A swap option gives the firm the right to enter into a swap on a predetermined notional principal at some defined future date at a specified strike rate. A firm might purchase a *payer's* swap option giving it the right to enter into a swap in which it pays the fixed rate and receives the floating rate. (Eitemann *et al.* : 810). A firm might sell a *swapoption*, a *receiver's swap option*, giving the purchasing bank or swap dealer the right to receive the fixed rate from the firm. When the swap is exercised for cash, it is said to be *swap settled*. Cash settlement for the intrinsic value of the swap eliminates ongoing counterparty risk. The firm purchasing a swap option can lose at most its initial premium, ignoring counterparty risk.

• Options on interest rate futures are essentially *caps, collars and floors* but traded via an exchange using futures.

Conclusion

A firm's free cash flow from overseas operations is subject to exchange rate risk. By changing economic variables or seeking offsetting matching currency flows, the firm can hedge against exchange rate losses. To hedge, there are contractual hedges, operational hedges, and trade documents that cover against unexpected changes in exchange rates. The contractual hedges are mainly useful for one-time large future receipts or expenses in foreign exchange, while operational hedges provided matching natural offsetting flows in foreign currency on an ongoing basis. Accounting hedges insulate the balance sheet and income statement from translation losses, and trade finance can set up risk sharing contingency clauses or invoicing in the reporting currency of the exporter. While the case for hedging may be debated, large multinational businesses hedge their foreign exchange exposure on a routine basis. Their core business and comparative advantage is in the production of goods and services, not in speculating on movements in the exchange rate by implicitly taking long or short positions in different currencies.

Appendix: Risk and Insurance

Consider a risky investment project that has a good return indicated by $(1 + r_a)$ and a bad return indicated by $(1 + r_b)$. The good outcome has probability p while the bad outcome has probability $(1 - p)$. The expected return from the project is thus indicated by:

$$E(W) = p(1 + r_a) + (1 - p)(1 + r_b) \qquad (4.13)$$

Figure 4.29 indicates the levels of utility associated with the two returns, d and h, as well as the utility associated with the expected return, $E(W)$.

Figure 4.29   Expected utility with risk aversion

Risk aversion

风险厌恶（Risk aversion）：假设给定具有同样收益水平和不同风险水平的证券，风险厌恶的投资者会选择风险最小的证券；或者说，对于更高的风险水平，理性的投资者会要求更高的回报。

Risk aversion refers to the assumption that, given the same return and different risk alternatives, a risk averse investor will seek the security offering the least risk—or, put another way, the higher the degree of risk, the greater the return that a rational investor will demand.

When there is diminishing marginal utility of wealth, $U''(W) < 0$, the individual, a proprietor of a firm, for example, is risk averse. This is the case depicted in Figure 4.29 where the utility curve is concave downward. The expected utility is indicated by point f, while the utility of the expected outcome is indicated by the point g. Risk aversion is seen graphically since the utility of the expected outcome is greater than the expected utility, or $U[E(U)] > E(U)$. That is:

$$U[p(1 + r_a) + (1 - p)(1 + r_b)] > pU(1 + r_a) + (1 - p)U(1 + r_b)$$
$$(4.14)$$

The coefficient of relative risk aversion, Θ, is indicated by:

$$\Theta = - \frac{U''(W)}{U'(W)} W \qquad (4.15)$$

where $U'(W)$ is the first derivative of the utility function, which is always positive, while $U''(W)$ is the second derivative, which is negative with risk aversion. Consequently, the coefficient of risk aversion is positive when the individual is risk averse.

Attitudes towards risk

风险中性（Risk neutral）：风险中立者通常既不回避风险，也不主动追求风险。他们选择资产的唯一标准是预期收益的大小，而不管风险状况如何。

风险偏好者（Risk lover）：风险偏好者通常主动追求风险，他们选择资产的原则是当预期收益相同时，选择风险大的，因为这会给他们带来更大的效用。

When the second derivative of the utility function is zero, the individual is said to be **risk neutral**. The utility function is a straight line, linear in wealth. When there is rising marginal utility of wealth, $U''(W) > 0$, and $\Theta < 0$, the individual is said to be a **risk lover**. When the second derivative is negative, $\Theta > 0$, the utility function displays diminishing marginal utility of wealth. In this case, the individual is said to be risk averse. Naturally, the individual could have an S-shaped utility function, being a risk lover over some range of wealth and being a risk hater over another.

The certainty equivalent ratio

The certainty equivalent level of wealth is indicated by $(1 + r)$ where r is the risk free rate of return. The certainty equivalent approach yields a certain dollar equivalent ratio between zero and one that is equal to:

$$\alpha = \frac{(1 + r)}{E(W)} \qquad (4.16)$$

or

$$\alpha = \frac{(1 + r)}{p(1 + r_a) + (1 - p)(1 + r_b)} \qquad (4.17)$$

The profits, Π, from a risky project may be multiplied by α, then discounted by the risk free rate, that is, divided by $(1 + r)$:

$$\text{NPV} = \sum_{i=1}^{n} \frac{\alpha \Pi_i}{(1 + r)^i} \qquad (4.18)$$

The higher the risk of the project, the lower the certainty equivalent, α. This can be seen by increasing the variance of the project, so that the good outcome involves higher wealth, while the bad outcome involves lower wealth, yet preserving the expected wealth level—the mean. As a result of the risk-increasing spreading of outcomes, the certainty equivalent level of income falls, therefore α declines.

A risk adjusted interest rate

A risk-adjusted interest rate can be used instead by adding a risk premium, ρ, to the risk-free rate of interest, and then discounting by the risk-adjusted interest rate. That is, let:

$$\alpha = \frac{1}{1 + \rho}$$

where ρ is the risk premium. Multiplying by Π yields:

$$\alpha \Pi = \frac{\Pi}{1 + \rho}$$

Consequently, a stream of uncertain receipts may be equivalently discounted at the rate $(1 + r)(1 + \rho)$ to calculate the net present value of the risky project using:

$$\text{NPV} = \sum_{i=1}^{n} \frac{\Pi_i}{[(1 + r)(1 + \rho)]^i} \qquad (4.19)$$

Once again, profits from projects with higher risk—greater standard deviations—are discounted at a higher risk premium.

Now consider the square-root utility function:

$$U = \sqrt{\Pi} = \Pi^{1/2}$$

高风险的项目（也即收益具有更高标准差的项目）需要用更高的风险溢价率来折现。

The coefficient of relative risk aversion can be computed to be $1/2$ from equation (4.14).

Constant risk aversion

In general, if the utility function has the following form:

$$U = \Pi^\theta \quad \text{where} \quad \theta > 0$$

The coefficient of relative risk aversion is indicated by:

$$\Theta = 1 - \theta$$

which yields the constant coefficients of relative risk aversion given by table 4.6.

Table 4.6 Attitudes toward risk

θ	Θ	Attitude toward risk
1/2	1/2	risk averse
3/4	1/4	risk averse
1	0	risk neutral
3/2	-1/2	risk lover
2	-1	risk lover

Risk aversion and fair insurance

An individual or firm owns an asset, say a house or an office building, that is worth \$100 thousand, but, if uninsured, risks a fire with a 10% probability of reducing the building's value to \$9 thousand (i. e. a loss of \$91 thousand). Consequently the expected loss is $0.1 \times \$91 = \$9.1$ thousand. The expected value of the asset is $\$100 - 9.1 = \$90.9$ if uninsured. This is a single proprietorship with a square root utility function:

$$U = \sqrt{\Pi} = \Pi^{1/2}$$

That is, utility rises as the square root of the value of the building. Consequently, if uninsured the entrepreneur in the good state (no fire) enjoys utility of $\sqrt{100} = 10$ and in the bad state (fire) enjoys $\sqrt{9} = 3$ utils. Expected utility is therefore $(0.9 \times 10) + (0.1 \times 3) = 9.3$ utils.

This entrepreneur displays risk aversion due to the diminishing marginal utility of his/her utility function, and would therefore seek insurance against fire to protect against the low state of utility (3 utils). An insurance company might offers a premium rate per dollar of losses equal to γ, so that full insurance against the loss would cost $\gamma 91$ thousand dollars. Consider the expected profit, Π_c, of the insurance company. It is equal to the premium less the expected payout, $p91$, if a fire occurs.

$$\Pi_c = \gamma 91 - p91$$

Fair insurance

A "fair" insurance policy would imply zero profits for the insurance company and thus the premium per dollar of insurance would be 10% in a competitive insurance industry. That is, $\gamma = p = 0.10$ or 10%. To insure the building against fire, the entrepreneur would therefore pay a premium of $9.1 to enjoy a certain value of the home of $90.9, after payment of the premium. Instead of an expected value of utility of 9.3 utils, he/she now enjoys a certain utility level of 9.53, which is preferred.

It is optimal for the risk averse manager/entrepreneur to fully insure when insurance rates are "fair". However, this entrepreneur would be willing to pay up to $13.51 or a rate of 13.51% per dollar of insurance since this would yield a certainty-equivalent after-premium value of the building equal to $86.49. This would be the value that corresponds to an expected value of $90.9.

To summarize the states of nature and the choices of this risk averse manager (Mr./Ms. Square Root!), Table 4.7 summarizes expected wealth and utility outcomes when the entrepreneur is uninsured, and then computes the outcomes with fair insurance.

公平保险 (Fair insurance):如果保险公司设定的保险费率能够保证保险公司的期望利润为零,则称这种费率为公平保险费率,这种保险就是公平保险。

Table 4.7 Fair insurance and risk aversion

State of nature	Probability	Wealth (no insurance)	Utility
Good(No fire)	90%	100	10
Bad(Fire)	10%	9	3
		90.9	**9.3**
		Expected wealth uninsured	Expected utility uninsured

State of nature	Probability	Wealth (fair insurance)	Utility
Good(No fire)	90%	90.9	9.53
Bad(Fire)	10%	90.9	9.53
		90.9	**9.53**
		Expected wealth fair insurance	Expected utility fair insurance

With fair insurance, the manager fully insures.

Key concepts in insurance

● **Adverse selection** occurs when higher risks seek insurance clai-

逆向选择 (Adverse selection):保险投保者的投保意愿与其面临的风险正相关,通常低风险承担者不愿意投保,而高风险承担者愿意投保,保险公司难以甄别每类人群所面临的风险。

ming to be low risks. Low risks may not see the need to insure. Often, insurance companies deny insurance to those they identify as high risks (an example is the denial of new homeowner insurance and the huge increase in homeowner's premium after Hurricane Andrew in 1992 in South Florida.)

道德风险(**Moral hazard**):当某人获得保险后,其行为方式可能发生改变。例如,房屋拥有者可能不安装烟雾探测器,因为他已经购买了火灾险。

• **Moral hazard** occurs when the owner of the building does not install fire detectors, hoses, etc. since he/she has insured against fire. An extreme case of moral hazard would be the owner of the building burning it down for its insurance value when its market value falls from $100 thousand to below $91 thousand.

• **Risk diversification** can be accomplished by purchasing assets or pursuing projects that tend to vary oppositely in value. Let $Z = X + Y$ be the sum of two random variables, stock Y and stock X for example. The variance of Z is indicated by:

$$V(Z) = V(X) + V(Y) + 2\text{Cov}(X, Y) \qquad (4.20)$$

Consequently, reducing US portfolio holdings from 100% to 80% by acquiring 20% foreign assets that vary negatively with US assets, the expected rate of return can be increased at the same time the overall portfolio volatility (the square root of the variance) reduced (see example below).

In general, a simplifying formula for the variance of a random variable, Z, is given by

$$V(Z) = E(Z^2) - [E(Z)]^2 \qquad (4.21)$$

• **Risk-spreading or pooling** in the example above, individuals faced with a risk of fire could self-insure in a cooperative insurance arrangement. If say 1,000 individuals faced the same risks as above, they could all agree in advance to pay $91 thousand to any of its members that suffer from a fire. Similarly, a stock market allows owners to spread the risk of the firm among many shareholders.

Other decision making rules under uncertainty

• The **maximin criterion** has the manager determine the worst possible outcome under each strategy, then choose the strategy that provides the best of the worst possible outcomes. This is a very conservative, pessimistic decision rule.

• The **minimax regret criterion** postulates that the decision maker should select the strategy that minimizes the maximum regret or opportunity cost of the wrong decision, whatever the state of nature that actually occurs. Regret is measured as the difference between the payoff between a given strategy and the best strategy under the same state of nature. This is a more optimistic decision rule than the maximin criterion.

Questions and problems

4.1   Hedging

There are several schools of thought regarding hedging and its impact on the value of the firm. One school argues that if the owners of the firm wish to hedge, they can do so in their own portfolios. If the firm hedges, the costs outweigh any benefits. Another school argues that the comparative advantage of the firm is production of goods and services, and that if it does not hedge, it is essentially speculating. However, not all risk can be hedged by contracts and the cost of reducing some risks is prohibitively expensive. Write two short essays defending the following opposing positions:

a. "I never hedge, since it reduces my bottom line!"

b. "I always hedge, since I cannot take the risk of exchange rate losses bankrupting my firm."

4.2   Default risk

Consider the following basic data on a one-year Ecuadorian Brady Bond (dollar denominated sovereign obligation). It has a face value of USD 100 payable at maturity, but no coupon. Today it is trading at $80. Your risk free rate is 5%. Answer the following questions:

a. What is the Brady Bond's "yield to maturity" (that is, its internal rate of return)?

b. What is its "risk premium"?

4.3   Stock options as executive compensation

You were hired by Sparkle. com, a telecommunications company, last year (exactly a year ago today). The company agreed to pay you £12,000 annual salary plus an option to buy in one year (i. e. today) 1,000 shares in Sparkle. com at £80. Today's share price on the market is £50. Answer the following:

a. What was your total annual compensation?

b. What percent of your compensation was in the form of stock options? Now answer questions a. and b. above on the assumption that today's share price is £100 instead.

4.4   Foreign exchange options

a. Claudia Speculator, IB Investments LTD bought a 100 euro call options at $0.01 per option (i. e. one cent per option) with a strike price of $1.25. She exercised them and sold the proceeds at a spot price of $1.27. How much profit did Claudia make?

b. Thomas Banker, NPI Bankers, sold 100 Euro put options with a strike price of $1.25, receiving a premium of $.005 (i.e. one-half of one cent per option). The put expired when the spot price was $1.20. Answer the following:

1. Was the put in or out of the money from the point of view of the buyer?

2. How much money did Tomas make or lose as the seller (what is his P/L on the put he sold)?

3. Did he have to honor the put?

4.5 Hedging

Martha Exporter, *Miami Baking*, LTD. exports her delicious Martha's Brownies to the United Kingdom and has accounts receivables in pounds sterling of £100 thousand in 90 days. What are the various contractual hedges that Martha might purchase to hedge her pound exchange exposure?

You are given the following basic data:

U.S. interest rate at which Martha can borrow dollars 10% p.a.

U.K. interest rate at which Martha can borrow pounds 8% p.a.

Spot price of pound $1.7603, bid

Spot price of pound $1.769, ask

Forward bid price of pound $1.78 for 90 day delivery

Premium on £ put option at $1.78 (at-the-money) strike price $0.0028 per £

Now suppose that Martha decides to invoice British Baking Imports in US dollars to shift the exchange rate exposure to the importer. She thus invoices $178 thousand dollars deliverable in 90 days. British Baking is assumed to face the same market conditions as Martha's Brownies, namely:

U.S. interest rate at which British Baking can lend dollars 10% p.a.

U.K. interest rate at which BB can borrow pounds 8% p.a.

The spot ask price of the dollar is £0.56527 per dollar

The forward ask price of the dollar is £0.5618 per dollar for 90 day delivery

A £0.5618 at-the-money call option to buy dollars costs £0.0028 per dollar

What are the various contractual hedges that British Baking might purchase to hedge their dollar exchange exposure?

4.6 Balance sheet hedging

Gateaux Antoinette, Société Anonyme, a subsidiary of Antoinette Cakes,

Inc., New York, had cash of 100,000 euros and accounts receivable of 100,000 euros each on its books (or 200,000 euros in total) when the euro suddenly appreciated from $1 per euro to $1.20.

a. Indicate what effect of the revaluation would have on the translation of these assets into US dollars on the consolidated balance sheet of the US parent firm.

b. How could Antoinette Cakes have acquired a "balance sheet" hedge for its cash and accounts receivable in euros prior to the revaluation (even though it benefited from the exposure in this instance)?

4.7   Operating exposure

You are a French company exporting widgets to the U.S. from your plant in France where the widgets are produced. You sell them for dollars in the United States. Last year you sold 100,000 widgets in the US for 10 dollars a widget, converting your dollar revenues to euros at 0.90 euro per US dollar. Next year you expect the dollar to be worth less, 0.8 euros but to export 110,000 widgets to the U.S. You are considering selling them at $10 a widget, but may reconsider the U.S. price.

a. Are you subject to operating exposure in dollars for the next year? If so, by how much?

b. What are some techniques you can use to hedge against this operating exposure in the United States?

4.8   Operating exposure

Tiny Tots Toys of Miami, Florida projects second quarter 2006 sales in Argentina to be 10,000 pesos, and expects the exchange rate to be $0.5 per peso (dollar earnings are therefore expected to be $5,000).

a. If the exchange rate unexpectedly changes to $0.25 per peso and Tiny Tots has not hedged, what are losses due to "operating exposure"?

b. How could Tiny Tots eliminate its operating exposure?

c. Suppose that Tiny Tots relocates production to Argentina and expects second quarter costs of production and distribution to be 5,000 pesos, leaving a net profit of 5,000 pesos if sales remain constant. Would you recommend that Tiny Tots hedge the entire 10,000 pesos?

d. In either event, what will Tiny Tots hedging activity do to the expected profitability in US dollars and in Argentine pesos of Tiny Tots? Explain.

4.9   Accounting exposure

Your European subsidiary has cash and accounts receivable of 100 and 300 euros respectively, and accounts payable and short term debt of 100 and 200 euros respectively. U.S. headquarters re-measures these line items in dollars on November 1, when the dollar price of the euro rose from $1.20 per euro to $1.30 per euro.

a. Did headquarters experience translation losses or gains in terms of US dollars?

b. How are any such translation gains or losses entered into the balance sheet?

c. How could the European subsidiary have acquired balance sheet hedge against losses or gains from translation exposure?

References and suggested reading

Akemann, Michael and Fabio Kanczuk (2005), "Sovereign Default and the Sustainability Risk Premium Effect," *Journal of Development Economics*, 76(1): 53—69.

Aliber, Robert Z. and C. P. Stickney (January 1975), "Accounting Measures of Foreign Exchange Exposure: The Long and Short of It," *Accounting Review*, 50(1): 44—57.

Ball, Ray (Fall 1995), "Making Accounting International: Why, How, and How Far Will it Go?" *Journal of Applied Corporate Finance*, 8(3): 19—29.

Banks, Gary (June 1983), "The Economics and Politics of Counter-trade," *World Economy*, 6(2): 159—182.

Bilson, John F. O. (1994) "Managing Economic Exposure to Foreign Exchange Risk: A Case Study of American Airlines" in *Exchange Rates and Corporate Performance*, Y. Amihud and R. Levich, eds., Burr Ridge, IL: Irwin Publishing.

Bishop, Paul, and Don Dixon (1996), *Foreign Exchange Handbook: Managing Risk and Opportunity in Global Currency Markets*, New York: John Wiley & Sons, Inc.

Clark, Ephriam (2004) *Arbitrage, hedging, and speculation: the foreign exchange market*, Praeger, New York.

Donnenfeld, Shabtai and Alfred Haug (2003), "Currency invoicing in international trade: An empirical investigation," *Review of International Economic*, 11(2): 332—345.

Eiteman, David K., Arthur I. Stonehill, and Michael H. Moffett (2000), "Translation Exposure," in *Multinational Business Finance*, 10th edition, Massachusetts: Addison-Wesley Publishing Company, Reading.

Euromoney Publications (1988), *The Guide to Export Finance London*.

Financial Accounting Standards Board (1981), *Foreign Currency Trans-*

lation, *Statement of Financial Standards No. 52*, Stamford, Connecticut.

Francis, Dick (1987), *The Countertrade Handbook*, Westport, Conn: Quorum Books.

Friedman, Milton, and Leonard Savage (August 1948), "The Utility Analysis of Choices Involving Risk," *Journal of Political Economy*, 56(4): 279—304.

Giddy, Ian H. (1994), *Global Financial Markets*, D. C. Heath and Co., Lexington, Massachusetts.

Handbook of Currency and Interest Rate Risk Management (1990), New York Institute of Finance, 3—14.

Heckerman, Donald (January 1972), "The Exchange Rate Risks of Foreign Operations," *Journal of Business*, 45(1): 42—48.

Henderson, Callum (2002), *Currency Strategy: The Practitioner's Guide to Currency Investing, Hedging, and Forecasting*, New York: John Wiley & Sons.

Jesswein, Kurt R., Chuck C. Y. Kwok, and William R. Folks, Jr. (Fall 1995), "Corporate Use of Innovative Foreign Exchange Risk Management Products," *Columbia Journal of World Business*, 30(3): 70—82.

Jokung, Octave (2004), "Risky assets and hedging in emerging markets," *Economic and Financial Modelin*, 11(2): 66—98.

Kerkvliet, Joe and Michael H. Moffet (December 1991), "The Hedging of an Uncertain Future Foreign Currency Cash Flow," *Journal of Financial and Quantitative Analysis*, 26(4): 565—578.

Lecraw, Donald J. (Spring 1989), "The Management of Countertrade: Factors Influencing Success," *Journal of International Business Studies*, 20(1): 41—59.

Lintner, J. (February 1965), "The Valuation of Risk Assets and the Selection of Risky Investments in Stock Portfolios and Capital Budgets," *Review of Economics and Statistics*, 47(1): 13—37.

Pilbeam, Keith (2004), "The stabilization properties of fixed and floating exchange rate regimes." *International Journal of Finance and Economics*, 9(2): 113—23.

Ross, Stephen A., Randolph W. Westerfield, and Jordan (2003), *Corporate Finance*, 5th ed., McGraw Hill-Irwin.

Sharpe, W. F. (September 1964), "Capital Asset Prices: A Theory of Market Equilibrium Under Risk," *Journal of Finance*, 19(3): 425—442.

Smith, Clifford W., Jr., and Rene M. Stulz (December 1995), "The Determinants of Firms' Hedging Policies," *Journal of Financial and Quantitative Analysis*, 20(4): 391—405.

Soenen, Luc A. (1991) "When Foreign Exchange Hedging Doesn't Help," *Journal of Cash Management*, 11(6): 58—62.

Solnick, Bruno (Spring 1990), "Swap Pricing and Default Risk: A Note," *Journal of International Financial Management and Accounting* 2(1): 79—91.

Stultz, Rene M. (June 1984), "Optimal Hedging Policies," *Journal of Financial and Quantitative Analysis*, 19(2): 127—140.

Stultz, Rene M. (Fall 1996), "Rethinking Risk Management," *Journal of Applied Corporate Finance*, 9(3): 8—24.

5
CHAPTER

International Financial Management

国际金融
管理

International financial management deals with valuation of cross border acquisitions, cash pooling, offshore accounts, transfer pricing, international taxation, and other matters that impact the global firm's balance sheet, income statement, and its business plan. Special tax regimes are considered, as well as the issue of repatriation of profits earned abroad. A concluding section extends the Markowitz (1952) optimal investment portfolio analysis to international portfolio investments taking into account foreign currency risk.

Capital structure

Apart from internal savings, there are two ways to finance your firm: by contracting debt (business loans) or issuing equity (shares). Creditors have senior debt that must be paid in full, except in the case of bankruptcy. They only share in bankruptcy risk. Shareholders participate in ownership of the firm, so they share in both business risk and risk of bankruptcy, in which case they usually get nothing. Due to the greater risk, shareholders typically require a higher rate of return to their equity. Interest payments to creditors are treated as an expense, so they are a "tax shield" for the firm. **The cost of capital** is thus a weighted average of the after-tax cost of borrowing (D) and the cost of issuing equity (E):

$$\text{WACC} = r_D(1 - t_C)\left(\frac{D}{D + E}\right) + r_E\left(\frac{E}{D + E}\right) \qquad (5.1)$$

- where WACC indicates the weighted average cost of capital, the cost of debt, r_E, the cost of equity, $D/(D + E)$ **the degree of financial leverage**, the ratio of debt to the value of the firm, E the value of equity

税盾（Tax shield）：支付给债权人的利息在财务上是按照费用来处理的，所以它们是公司的税盾。

资本的成本（The cost of capital）：资本的成本是税后举债成本（D）以及发行股票成本（E）的加权平均。

金融杠杆度（The degree of financial leverage）：$D/(D + E)$ 为负债与资产的比率，是三种金融杠杆度之一。

shares in the firm, and t_c the marginal corporate tax rate. For example, assume your corporation has 30% debt and 70% equity. It can borrow at 10% by selling its corporate bonds. Its shareholder require a return on investment based on the market risk premium. The cost of equity can be estimated using the Capital Asset Pricing Model (CAPM):

$$r_E = r_f + \beta_E [E(r_m) - r_f] \tag{5.2}$$

Where r_f is the risk-free Treasury Rate, β_E is the covariance between the equity return, r_E, and the market rate of return, r_M divided by the variance of the market, and $[E(r_m) - r_f]$ is the market risk premium. The equity's β_E or *beta* is thus a measure of the degree of market risk of the equity. It is measured as $\text{Cov}(r_E, r_M)/\text{Var}(r_M)$. With a 5% risk free rate, an equity *beta* equal to one, and a market risk premium of 10%, yielding an r_E equal to 14%, the weighted average cost of capital is:

$$11.05\% = 10\%(1 - 0.35)(0.3) + 14\%(0.7)$$

Due to the tax shield of borrowing and to the low degree of risk to the initial loans, the WACC initially declines with greater financial leverage, $[D/(D+E)]$. With a high degree of financial leverage, $[D/(D+E)]$ approaching one, the risk of financial distress and bankruptcy increase. This causes both the borrowing rate and the equity rate to rise sharply. Consequently, there is an **optimum capital structure** which minimizes the weighted average cost of capital, indicated in Figure 5.1.

最优的资本结构(Optimal capital structure): 能够最小化资本加权成本的资本结构。

Figure 5.1　The weighted average cost of capital and financial leverage

The optimal degree of leverage appears to be around 40% in Figure

5.1. The degree of curvature is exaggerated for illustration purposes. In practice, the WACC is likely to have fairly flat ranges. Start-ups are often too leveraged and fail to reach their break-even point due to fixed interest and principal payments on debt. Equity-based finance is less risky to the firm because shareholders participate in operational and economic risk. Dividends need not be paid out should profits be small or negative. However, venture capitalists often seek management fees and some management control, in addition to 40% of ownership control. Marketing is often the greatest challenge to the start-up firm. The four *Ps* of marketing: product design, pricing, promotion and placement (distribution), are critical in generating positive cash flow as soon as possible.

Tight financial controls are indispensable. A monthly, if not weekly, profit/loss statement (*P/L*) should be accurately done, including the opportunity cost of the owners, if they are involved in the management. Positive cash flow is the aim of the firm and its owners. Records must be kept and discussed at regular meetings of the board of directors and managers.

This is what gives value to the firm and ultimately dividends to its owners. The managers can enjoy their jobs. But as **agents**, they must be loyal to the principals, taking decisions that increase the value of the firm. Revenue growth is good, but costs should grow at a lower rate. The tax shield advantage of additional debt must be weighed against the rising cost of financial distress. Theoretically, a firm has an optimal level of debt which balances increased value of the tax shield against the increased cost of borrowing with financial distress.

代理人(Agent):代理人受委托人委托,必须忠于后者,采取措施增加公司价值,而不是利用权利为自己谋利。

International capital structure

Some basic rules apply to the optimal capital structure from an international point of view. First, the basic rule for conversion of the WACC in dollars to say pounds for purposes of discounting pound cash flows, the interest rate parity rule is

$$\left(\frac{1 + \text{WACC}_£}{1 + \text{WACC}_\$}\right) = \left(\frac{1 + r_{uk}}{1 + r_{us}}\right) \quad (5.3)$$

or equivalently:

$$\text{WACC}_£ = (1 + \text{WACC})\left(\frac{1 + r_{uk}}{1 + r_{us}}\right) - 1 \quad (5.4)$$

在这里,我们遵循利率平价原则将以美元计价的资本的加权平均成本转化成以英镑计价。

If your weighted average cost of capital is 10.7% in USD, $r_{us} = 4.5\%$ in GBP, and $r_{uk} = 3\%$, the WACC in GBP is 10.9%, reflecting the lower expected inflation in the UK. That is:

$$10.9\% = (1.1105)\left(\frac{1.03}{1.045}\right) - 1$$

The key idea is to seek the lowest $WACC$ in whatever currency it is the least, and then use the conversion rule to measure the $WACC$ in the other currency. It is important to use the interest rate on risk-free Treasury Bills for conversion purposes. Even though U. S. Treasuries are rated by S&P at AA +, they are still default risk free. Their real value may be depreciated by inflation, but the Treasury will not miss a payment. The FED will purchase excess debt that cannot be sold to the public, so there is a risk of implicit default by seignorage, leading to high unexpected inflation. That allows the costs of capital to be adjusted for different inflationary expectations, as in the Fisher equation. It is appropriate to consolidate all debt and equity at current exchange rates in order to correctly measure the debt-to-equity ratio for global operations.

Cross-listing on foreign stock exchanges

在国外证券交易所交叉上市（Cross-listing on foreign stock exchanges）：指既在境外证券市场上市，又在境内证券市场上市。

By cross-listing its shares on foreign stock exchanges—despite additional disclosure, listing and reporting costs—a firm can improve the liquidity of its existing shares by making it easier for foreign shareholders to acquire shares at home in their own currencies. Cross-listing may also increase the share price by overcoming mispricing in a segmented, illiquid, home capital market.

There are other advantages to cross-listing: (1) It may also provide a liquid secondary market to support a new equity issue in the foreign market and, (2) establish a secondary market for shares used to acquire local firms or to compensate local management and employees in foreign affiliates.

American Depositary Receipts (ADRs)

美国存托凭证（American Depositary Receipts, ADRs）：美国存托凭证是美国本土银行所发行的代表基础股份的可转让凭证，以信托的形式由托管银行保存。

Cross listing is often accomplished by depositary receipts. In the United States, many foreign shares are traded through American Depositary Receipts, or ADRs. These are negotiable certificates issued by a U. S. bank in the United States to represent the underlying shares of stock, which are held in trust. "Sponsored" ADRs are created at the request of a foreign firm wanting access to equity finance in the United States. The firm applies to the Securities and Exchange Commission and a U. S. bank for registration and issuance. The firm bears the costs of creating sponsored

ADRs. However, a U. S. bank may issue "unsponsored" ADRs if the foreign firm does not wish to sponsor them.

International liquidity and market integration

By seeking access to international capital markets, a firm can benefit from two distinct, important effects: first, increased liquidity of its own securities, and second, overcoming market segmentation. Both effects tend to lower the cost of capital to the firm compared to borrowing from solely domestic sources. The firm has a list of investment projects ranked according to the marginal rate of return on investment, sometimes called the marginal efficiency of investment (MEI). High return projects are taken on before low return projects. As the firm spends more of its capital budget, the marginal efficiency of investment declines. Its level of capital expenditure therefore is constrained by the marginal cost of borrowing. Increased liquidity increases the supply of capital at existing interest rates, so that an increase in borrowing causes a smaller rise in the cost of borrowing. In addition, market integration overcomes market segmentation, thus additionally lowering the cost of borrowing.

Transfer pricing

Transfer pricing refers to pricing of the transfer of goods, services, and technology between related units of the firm. Transfer pricing takes place both domestically and internationally. In the case of the international firm, several considerations come into play. In principle, there is an optimal transfer price to provide the right incentives to the affiliate to supply the appropriate quantity of the intermediate input.

转移定价(Transfer pricing):指的是对于国内外相关公司间转移商品、劳务和技术进行定价,它同时存在于国内和国外的交易中。

Optimal transfer prices

Assume there are a marketing division and a production division. Each unit of output requires one unit of marketing production, that is, marketing and production are joint products. The marketing division purchases the intermediate input from the production division, then markets the final product. The intermediate input is neither sold to other firms, nor bought from other firms, by assumption. In Figure 5.2, the marginal cost of the marketing and the production divisions are summed vertically to yield the marginal cost of the final product. Setting marginal cost of the final product equal to its marginal product yields the profit-maximizing level of production, 100, and a price of $8.

在图 5.2 中,最优转移价格所对应的产出水平是使利润最大化的产量。

Figure 5.2 Transfer pricing

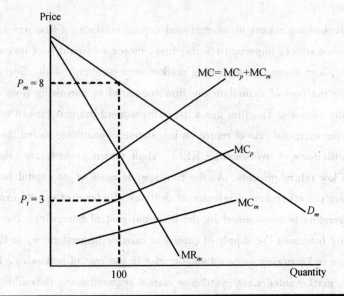

To provide the correct incentives to the production division, a transfer price of $3 is optimal. In its production decisions, the production division sets marginal cost equal to $3 to maximize profits. It produces exactly the required amount of intermediate inputs and sells them to the marketing division. Any other transfer price would distort the incentives of the overseas affiliate.

Transfer pricing with external sales or purchases

When there is a possibility to buy or sell the intermediate input externally to other firms at a fixed price, the firm should regard this price as the opportunity cost of the intermediate input. In this case, the marketing department will maximize profits by having a transfer price equal to the market price of the intermediate input. Any excess supply of the intermediate input at the market price would be sold externally, while any excess demand for the intermediate input would be outsourced: that is, purchased externally.

Imperfectly competitive market for the intermediate good

When the market for the intermediate good is not competitive, the marketing division should set a higher transfer price to its internal division, and restrict its purchases slightly from the external market. Indeed, profit-maximization requires:

$$\frac{P_t}{P_x} = 1 + \frac{1}{\varepsilon} \qquad (5.5)$$

where P_t represents the transfer price, P_x represents the price at which the firm purchases the input on the external market, and ε the elasticity of supply of the intermediate input to the marketing division. Equation (5.5) reflects the fact that by curtailing purchases on the external market somewhat, the marketing division pays a lower price for outsourced intermediate goods. For example, if $\varepsilon = 2$, the transfer price would be 50% higher than the external price, If the external market were perfectly competitive, ε approaches infinity, and the optimal transfer price equals the market price of the intermediate good.

If the production division produces more of the intermediate input than sold to the marketing division and has monopoly power in the market for the intermediate input, its optimal transfer price is below the price at which it sells the intermediate input to the external market.

$$\frac{P_t}{P_x} = 1 - \frac{1}{\eta} \qquad (5.6)$$

where η is the absolute value of the elasticity of market demand for the intermediate good. For example, if $\eta = 2$, the optimum transfer price is 50% below the price at which the intermediate input is sold on the external market. Again, if the external market were perfectly competitive, η approaches infinity, and the optimal transfer price would equal the market price of the intermediate good.

Transfer pricing may also a technique by which funds may be relocated. A lowering of transfer prices may finance the foreign affiliate. On the other hand, a parent firm wishing to transfer funds out of a particular country can charge higher prices on goods sold to its affiliate there, thus evading exchange controls by setting transfer prices to shift taxable income from a country with a high income tax rate to a jurisdiction with a low income tax rate, the firm may also lower its taxable income. It may do so legally since profits earned in the lower tax jurisdiction may not be taxed until repatriated under some circumstances. However, according to the IRS guidelines, the "correct transfer price," is one that reflects an arm's-length price for a sale of the same goods or service to an unrelated customer. An advanced pricing agreement (APA) may be negotiated with the tax authorities of both home country and host country. An APA may save trouble and litigation resulting from an IRS challenge to transfer prices. The incidence of import duties may also offset the favorable income taxes in transfer pricing, an additional consideration.

The aggressive use of transfer pricing can transfer profits from high tax jurisdictions to **tax havens**, thereby reducing global tax liabilities. Profits can be accumulated in an offshore tax haven, no income taxes being paid in the home country of headquarters. Say you are a hardware equipment manufacturer, *XYZ* Hardware Corp., USA where you are not only subject to federal taxes, but also state and local taxes. You export hardware equipment to Europe through a Foreign Sales Corporation in Nassau, the Bahamas. Take a hammer, for example, that costs a constant $2.00 per unit to produce. *XYZ* Hardware sells it to the FSC in Nassau for $1.00, thereby incurring losses of $1.00 per hammer exported. Thus far, headquarters has saved $0.35 in corporate income taxes. Next, the FSC sells it in euros to its affiliate in Europe for $5.00 which in turn distributes it for $3.75, or €2.64, losing $1.25 per hammer.

Consequently, the affiliate's taxes are down approximately $0.44. The FSC bought the hammer at $1.00 and sold it to the affiliate at $5.00, making $4.00 in profits on each hammer. These profits are deposited in an offshore bank and are not subject to income taxes until repatriated, if ever. If this sounds like eating your cake and having it too, it is! Taxes are down $0.79, and the affiliate accumulates $4.00 of untaxed profits in Nassau. These can be used to make payments or deposits of one sort or another. Clearly, this would be an example of abuse of the national and international laws of taxation. Yet, it takes place. Figure 5.3 depicts this example of abusive transfer pricing.

Figure 5.3   Abusive Transfer pricing

XYZ Hardware Corp. could be fined.

International taxation

The General Agreement on Tariffs and Trade（GATT）of the World Trade Organization（WTO）governs the tax treatment of branches and subsidiaries located abroad. If a branch or subsidiary is located in a signatory country, it is entitled to "national treatment": that is, tax and regulatory treatment no less favorable than that accorded to national enterprises. Article III *National Treatment on Internal Taxation and Regulation* explicitly forbids discrimination against foreign subsidiaries. Consequently, a firm with a foreign subsidiary may appeal any discriminatory treatment to the GATT/WTO in Geneva, Switzerland. Its corporate income tax cannot be higher than that of local companies, it cannot be charged higher duties to import intermediate goods, nor be required to purchase inputs locally to protect domestic production.

关贸总协定（The General Agreement on Tariffs and Trade）：世界贸易组织（WTO）的关贸总协定规定了国外分支机构和子公司应享受的税收待遇。

U. S. taxation of foreign income

Income derived from a minority-controlled foreign affiliate is taxed when remitted to the U. S. parent. This treatment sometimes leads to tax avoidance by the creation of tax-shelter affiliates such as Foreign Sales Corporations（FSCs）and International Financial Offshore Centers（IFOCs）located in offshore banking havens.

Foreign sales corporations

A foreign sales corporation（FSC）allows firms having export operations to enjoy exemption of most export income from U. S. taxes, even when the good is produced in the US. Exempt foreign trade income derives from "export property" sold, leased, or rented outside the United States by the FSC. The portion of income exempted is either 34% when arm's length pricing is used, or 17/23（approximately 74%）if the transfer price is set by administrative pricing rules applicable to FSCs. The WTO has ruled that the FSC amounts to an export subsidy and as such violates Article VI *Anti-Dumping and Countervailing Duty* rules of the GATT/WTO.

Examples of taxation of international operations

A foreign majority-controlled branch is treated as part of the parent firm and thus must repatriate profits and pay home taxes contemporaneously. A subsidiary incorporated locally need not repatriate profits, nor pay home country taxes unless it remits the profits. Foreign income tax credits apply in both cases. The value-added tax and sales taxes are deducted from income, and thus treated as expenses. The following examples attempt to capture these various aspects of international taxation. Country A, where the affiliate is located is a high-tax country, so that the home country, assumed to be the US, issues an excess tax credit to the parent firm in Table 5.1.

Table 5.1 Affiliate located in a high-tax jurisdiction

	Country A (exemption)*	Country A (credit)*
Foreign income	100	100
Foreign taxes paid	40	40
Home taxes paid	0	0
Net Income	60	60

* Excess tax credit of 5.

Country B in Table 5.2 is a comparable tax country.

Table 5.2 Affiliate located in a comparable tax jurisdiction

	Country B (exemption)	Country B (credit)
Foreign income	100	100
Foreign taxes paid	35	35
Home taxes paid	0	0
Net Income	65	65

No U.S. taxes would be paid, the firm receiving a full tax credit for the 35% corporate income tax. The tax burden would thus be the same as in the U.S.

Table 5.3 depicts a low tax country.

Table 5.3 Affiliate located in a low-tax jurisdiction

	Country C (exemption)	Country C (credit)
Foreign income	100	100
Foreign taxes paid	15	15
Home taxes paid	0	20
Net Income	85	65

A U. S. subsidiary that re-invested dividends in the host country would be exempt from U.S. taxes; a branch would receive a tax credit of 15, and pay an additional 20 to the US Treasury on its repatriated profits. The tax treatment of affiliates located in tax havens is shown in Table 5.4.

Table 5.4　Affiliate located in a tax haven

	Country D (tax haven, no deferral)	Country D (tax haven with deferral) *	Country D (tax haven, no repatriation)
Foreign income	100	100	100
Foreign taxes paid	0	0	0
Home taxes paid	35	0	0
Net Income	65	100	100

* Taxes paid upon repatriation.

In some instances, special regimes are applied to a tax-haven, thereby further lightening the tax burden. Table 5.5 illustrates the special cases of Foreign Sales Corporations locate in tax havens which benefit either from 34% exemption, or 17/23 exemption of foreign source income depending on whether arm's length pricing or administrative rules pricing is applied. The total exemption of foreign source income or possessions derived investment income is also shown in Table 5.5.

Table 5.5　Foreign Sales Corporations located in a US possession

	Foreign Sales Corp. (arm's length pricing)	Foreign Sales Corp. (administrative rules)	US possession income from foreign sources or possessions source investment income
Foreign income	100	100	100
Foreign taxes paid	0	0	0
Home taxes paid	23.1	9.13	0
Net Income	76.9	90.87	100

A U.S. parent firm can take advantage of these special regimes, but may be tempted to abuse them. In these cases, the IRS takes a "guilty until proven innocent" approach. The firm may end up tricking itself, especially if it uses aggressive transfer pricing to shift profits into the tax haven, then does not repatriate the profits, thus evading corporate income taxes in the US altogether. A U. S. amnesty was applied in the 2005 tax year to permit a repatriation of accumulated overseas funds at a 5% rate, ostensibly to encourage investment in the United States. Large sums were repatriated on these favorable terms by companies such as Hewlett Packard.

The value-added tax (VAT) is treated as an expense, so that the firm cannot receive a full deduction for value added taxes paid. The VAT is imposed on the value of the final product less the cost of the intermediate inputs: that is, on the value that is added by the firm. Suppose a firm adds 10 euros of value to a product, and pays a value-added tax of 20%, or 2 euros. If it is in the 35% marginal corporate tax bracket, it would receive a tax reduction of $0.35 \times 2 = 0.70$ euros, about one dollar at current exchange rates.

Working capital management

营 运 资 本 净 额（Net working capital）:营运资本净额包括现金、应收账款、存货减去应付账款以及流动负债。

Net working capital consists of cash, accounts receivables plus inventories less accounts payable and other current liabilities. A firm must have operating balances to manage its receivables, inventories and payables. Its net working capital finances the cash conversion cycle from raw inputs to final product and sale. As indicated in Figure 5.4, short term borrowing and repayment plays an important role in the cash management process.

Figure 5.4 Working cash balances

In addition, the international firm may hold cash reserves for its anticipated cash needs (*transactions motive*) and its unanticipated cash needs (*speculative motive*). A multinational firm with many affiliates may, for example, reduce its cash reserves by pooling them in a centralized facility (Eitemann *et al.*).

Cash pooling maintains the same level of protection, while reducing the amount of cash necessary to hold. Take the example in Table 5.6 of three subsidiaries whose operations have different expected cash requirements.

Table 5.6　Decentralized cash management

	Expected cash requirement	Three standard deviations	Cash management pool
Subsidiary A	100	12	112
Subsidiary B	50	6	56
Subsidiary C	200	18	218
		Total	386

When the three subsidiaries hold one common cash pool, they are able to hold $13.56 less while maintaining the same level of protection, as illustrated in Table 5.7.

Table 5.7　Centralized cash management

	Expected cash requirement	Three standard deviations	Cash management pool
Subsidiary A	100	12	
Subsidiary B	50	6	
Subsidiary C	200	18	
		Total	372.45

集中的现金管理(Centralized cash management):通过集中的现金管理,减少了所需的现金持有额,同时保证了相同的安全等级。

The analysis assumes that the cash requirements of each subsidiary are independent, normal distributions so that the standard deviation of the sum of the expected cash requirement, σ, equals:

$$\sigma = \sqrt{4^2 + 2^2 + 6^2} = \$7.48 \qquad (5.7)$$

Consequently, a centralized cash reserve facility need only hold the sum of the expected cash needs, plus three standard deviations of the sum, or:

$$\$350 + 3(\$7.48) = \$372.45$$

While the cash requirements may be positively correlated, provided they are not perfectly so, gains to pooling can be realized.

Cash netting

现金净额交易（Cash netting）：现金净额交易可以减少现金交易的次数，从而降低拥有多个分支机构的跨国公司的结算成本。

Cash netting may also reduce the settlement costs of a multinational firm with several affiliates having separate foreign exchange transactions between themselves and the parent firm. For instance, if subsidiary A must pay 150 euros to subsidiary C for widgets, and C must may A 100 euros for intermediate inputs for assembling widgets, rather than having two separate transactions, subsidiary A (or a centralized facility) can simply pay subsidiary C 50 euros. The single transaction netting the payment saves the multinational firm transactions and spread fees in its cash operations. In short, the cash management process attempts to not tie up cash unnecessarily, without risking liquidity crises. A centralized invoice center can facilitate cash netting considerably.

International mergers and acquisitions

International mergers and acquisitions are not for the faint of heart. Political risk, hostile trade unions, and governmental regulations protecting employment and working conditions are fraught with pitfalls. Every foreign investor is guaranteed "national treatment" by the WTO/GATT, meaning the same treatment as domestic firms, but in most cases this is not particularly business friendly. The firm's cultures may differ significantly in terms of goals and means of communication, introducing an additional layer of difficulty in managerial decision-making. The tax burden is invariably higher in developed countries, especially high payroll taxes to finance social programs—health, unemployment, retirement, and disability. As a result, the growth of temporary employment agencies in Europe, for example, is phenomenal. Temporary workers do not "benefit" from the same high payroll tax treatment. In emerging markets, securing large contracts—for example, the exploitation of mineral rights, or the acquisition of a state enterprise that is being privatized—is often a matter of putting a bundle of cash on the President or Minister's desk, or depositing some percent of the contract in an offshore bank account in his or her name (or that of his wife or sons or daughters), or some numbered account. Under the Foreign Corrupt Practices Act of 1997, these practices are illegal for U. S. corporations as well as under the **OECD** Anti-Corruption Agreement. Consequently, an acquisition of a former state-enterprise in a rigged bid involving bribery of government officials would not be admissible. Political risk is great as it may damage the firm's global reputation, for example in the case of the sale of computers by IBM, Argentina to the Banco de la Nación, Argentina.

On the other hand, there are potential gains to mergers and acquisitions:

- **Economies of scale** (global output may be maintained by reducing inputs or output may be expanded at reduced average costs.)

- **Marketing economies** (advertising costs are spread over the merged firm.)

- **Economies of scope** (wider and complementary product range.)

- Economies of global standardization of product and manufacturing processes.

- Exploitation of comparative advantage within the merged firm by greater vertical integration.

- Leapfrogging of import barriers by producing, distributing and marketing locally.

- Anti-competitive acquisitions (reduce market competition and increase market share, but risk of violating anti-trust laws.)

- Acquisition of technologies.

- Economies of R&D (sharing fixed costs).

- Diversifying the risk of R&D (exploring competing technologies within the merged firm).

- Restructuring (takeover, eliminating inefficient management, and cost reducing).

- **Natural hedging** (acquiring accounts payable in a currency in which there are accounts receivable.)

- Tax gains from the acquisition of tax shields from net operating losses, unused debt capacity, and surplus funds.

- Vertical integration and avoidance of double marginalization—a downstream retailer charging a higher than profit maximizing price to earn a positive margin (See problem 5.14).

经济合作和发展组织（**OECD**）：是由34个市场经济国家组成的政府间国际经济组织，旨在共同应对全球化带来的经济、社会和政府治理等方面的挑战，并把握全球化带来的机遇。

规模经济（**Economies of scale**）：在总产出不变的情况下降低了投入，或者在平均成本降低的情况下增加了产出。

营销经济（**Marketing economies**）：并购公司得以分摊广告费用。

范畴经济（**Economies of scope**）：更加广泛、互补的产品范围。

自然对冲（**Natural Hedging**）：在拥有一种货币的应收账款时，获得该货币的应付账款。

Mergers and acquisitions

并购 (Mergers and Acquisitions) : 指兼并和收购。兼并 (Merger) 是指两家或者更多的独立企业合并组成一家企业。收购 (Acquisition) 是指一家企业用现金或者有价证券购买另一家企业的股票或者资产,以获得对该企业的全部资产或者某项资产的所有权,或对该企业的控制权。

协同效应 (Synergy) : 是指并购后竞争力增强,导致净现金流量超过两家公司预期现金流量之和,又或合并后的公司业绩比两个公司独立存在时的预期业绩高。

A merger is the absorption of one firm by another. Firm A might acquire firm B by offering two shares in A for each share of B. B would then cease to exist. Typically, two thirds of the voting shares of each firm must approve the merger. In general, a merger is only worthwhile if there is some **synergy** in combining the firms:

$$V_{AB} > V_A + V_B \qquad (5.8)$$

that is to say, the value of the merged firm should be greater than the individual firms taken alone. When firm A and firm B consolidate into a new firm C, in general it should be true that:

$$V_C > V_A + V_B \qquad (5.9)$$

In practical terms, a consolidation is equivalent to a merger. Synergy itself is measured by:

$$V_{AB} - V_A - V_B \qquad (5.10)$$

That is, the value of the merged firm less the sum of the standalone values.

Acquisition by cash

Consider a simple example in Table 5.8.

Table 5.8 Standalone values of Firms A and B

	Firm A	Firm B
Value	$100	$50
Shares outstanding	20	10
Share value	$5	$5

Let's say that after the acquisition, the combined firms are worth $170. Synergy is thus $20. Firm A could acquire Firm B by paying $60 in cash, a premium of $10 over its market value in order to secure the 2/3 vote necessary of B's shareholders. Each share would be tendered at $6 while it was previously worth $5. For Firm A to benefit from this, the combined value of the firms must increase to more than $160 (the sum of their values, $150, plus the premium offered, $10.) After the acquisition, the combined firms are worth $170. The value of Firm A after the acquisition will therefore be $170 minus the $60 paid to B's stockholders. Firm A is thus worth $110 after the acquisition, or in Table 5.9.

Table 5.9   An outright cash acquisition of B by A

	Firm A
Value	$110
Shares outstanding	20
Share value	$5.5

The acquisition has a positive net present value, increasing shareholder's value. The price of the share rises to $5.50. Shareholders of both firms benefit and should go along with the merger. The firms share equally in the synergy. Notice that if the NPV of firm B were $50, but it had present value of debt of $10, firm A could equivalently offer cash of $50 and assumption of debt of $10.

Acquisition by stock

It would seem that the same purchase price of $60 could be paid by the issue of 12 shares of A in exchange for the 10 shares of B. At the current market value of $5 for A's shares, this would be equivalent to $60. However, this is not correct, because due to the rise in the value of A after the merger, 12 shares would be worth more than $60. To see this, consider the exchange ratio 12:10. Firm A would then look like this in Table 5.10.

Table 5.10   An acquisition of B by A through an incorrect share offer

	Firm A
Value	$170
Shares outstanding	32
Share value	$5.31

Former stockholders in B, would now own $5.31 × 12 = $63.75 worth of A's stock, receiving more than the purchase price of $60 in cash. How many shares should A therefore offer to B's shareholders? The correct amount would equal the ratio: α 170 = 60, giving them shares worth $60. That is, α =60/170 =0.352941176 of the combined company. Setting this ownership share equal to the fraction of new shares in the merged company, we can solve for n_w the number of new shares issued in addition to the existing number of shares, $n = 20$.

$$\alpha = \frac{n_w}{n + n_w} \qquad (5.11)$$

or solving for n_w:

$$n_w = \frac{\alpha n}{(1 - \alpha)} = 10.90909 \qquad (5.12)$$

Firm A's situation is now shown in Table 5.11.

Table 5.11   An acquisition of B by A through a correct share offer

	Firm A
Value	$170
Shares outstanding	30.91
Share value	$5.50

The 10.91 shares offered to shareholders of B are worth exactly $60 at the new market price of $5.50!

Acquisition by stock and cash

Suppose firm A acquires firm B by an offer of both cash and stock, for instance, $30 in cash and the rest in stock. How many shares of stock will firm A have to offer? Firm A will therefore be worth $140 after the cash payment of $30. In this case $\alpha = 30/140 = 0.21428571429$, or inputting the basic data directly into equation 5.12.

$$n_w = \frac{\left(\frac{30}{140}\right)20}{\left(1 - \frac{30}{140}\right)} = 5.45455 \qquad (5.13)$$

By offering exactly 5.45455 shares and $30 in cash, Firm A would be offering the same premium as with pure cash or pure stock. Notice that the 5.45455 new shares are worth exactly $30 at the new share price of A, $5.5. Firm A's new situation would be as follows in Table 5.12.

Table 5.12   An acquisition of B by A through a combination of cash and share offer

	Firm A
Value	$140
Shares outstanding	25.45
Share value	$5.5

赢者诅咒 (The winner's curse)：在拍卖中，由于拍卖品的价值是不确定的，赢得拍卖品的中标者出价高于其他竞标者，但他很可能对拍卖品估价过高，支付了超过其价值的价格，从而赢得的拍卖品的收益会低于正常收益甚至为负。

The winner's curse and synergy

When a firm has an "intrinsic, common" value that is not known to bidders in an auction, the winner values the firm at more than other bidders and more than its intrinsic value. This is known as the "winner's curse." Consider the recent September 2010 bidding by HP and Dell for the relatively small cloud computing firm 3PAR. The share price of 3PAR was around $10 before the bidding war began, culminating in a winning bid of $33 a share by HP. We can therefore put a lower bound on the intrinsic value of 3PAR of $10 and an upper bound of $33. If the intrinsic value is uniformly distributed between $10 and $33, as suggested in Dixit et al., the probability distribution may be drawn in Figure 5.5 as:

Figure 5.5 HP acquires 3PAR and suffers the winner's curse

The area of the rectangular probability distribution is one, its height is 1/23, and its expected value is $21.5, that is ($33 + $10)/2. In fact, 3PAR had indicated a willingness to accept an $18 per share offer from Dell and paid a $3 per share contingency fee for terminating the sale to Dell. An intrinsic value of $21.5 seems reasonable. Consequently, the winner's curse is estimated to be $33 − $21.5 = $11.50.

If the winner's curse is offset by sufficient synergy as a percent of the intrinsic value, ϕ, HP will anticipate increased profits from its acquisition:

$$(1 + \phi)\left(\frac{a + b}{2}\right) > b \quad \text{or} \quad (1 + \phi)\frac{(33 + 10)}{2} > 33$$

That is, synergies as a percent of the estimated intrinsic value must be greater than the amount of the winner's curse:

$$\phi > \frac{33}{21.5} - 1 = 53.4\%$$

The winner's curse is $b - \frac{a + b}{2}$.

Figure 5.6 illustrates the relationship between the winner's curse and the synergy required to overcome the curse.

Figure 5.6 The winner's curse and synergy

In general, if b is the winning bid, and a is the initial share value, the winner's curse is measured by:

$$b - \frac{a + b}{2}$$

为了抵消"赢者诅咒"的负效应,协同效应所带来的价值增加必须大于"赢者诅咒"的损失。

To offset the winner's curse, synergy, ϕ, as a percent must satisfy:

$$(1 + \phi)\left(\frac{a + b}{2}\right) > b$$

or

$$\phi > \frac{b - a}{a + b} \qquad (5.14)$$

If the market is convinced that synergy is greater than the winner's curse, the share price of the acquiring firm should rise. In the case of HP's acquisition of 3PAR, it fell several dollars.

In the News: **HP activist shareholder to become member of board of directors**

Hewlett-Packard Co. said it will give an activist shareholder a seat on its board, as new Chief Executive Meg Whitman tries to right the big technology company after a more than a year of instability. Relational Investors LLC co-founder Ralph Whitworth, who will take the seat, wants to focus on improving H-P's discipline on spending, particularly in the area of acquisitions, people familiar with the matter said. Many of H-P's shareholders, including Relational, have been concerned about how much the company has been spending on deals, saying it often overpays for companies. In August, H-P announced an $11.7 billion acquisition of Autonomy Corp., representing about an 80% premium to Autonomy's share price the day before the deal was announced. At the same time H-P announced that it was exploring a spinoff of its PC business. Relational wasn't in favor of the spinoff idea, according to

a person familiar with the matter. In October (2011), Ms. Whitman said H-P
was going to keep its PC business.

Source: "H-P Grants Activist Shareholder Board Seat" by Ben Worthen
and Gina Chon, *Wall Street Journal*, 11/18/2011.

The coinsurance principle

The increased value of the firm from an acquisition benefits both
shareholders and bondholders. The reduced variability in the sum of the
value of the firms (due to less than perfect correlation) reduces the cost of
borrowing and thus mainly benefits bondholders at the expense of shareholders. The reduced likelihood of financial distress mainly benefits creditors. Some consider the co-insurance effect as a cost to shareholders
(Ross, Westerfield and Jordan: 844—845).

共同保险原则(The co-
insurance principle):并
购后公司价值的增加将
使得股东和债券持有者
同时获益。

Alternatives to acquisition

• Joint ventures involve local partners who share in the managerial
and financial decision-making in the local venture. This has both advantages in their knowledge of the local market, but may not properly align the
motivation of firm and local managers. In the case of China, until 2006 foreign companies typically had to be minority partners in joint ventures.

• Direct licensing agreements and management contracts allow headquarters to share in some of the profits from a locally owned operation. On
the other hand, direct foreign investment should be considered as an alternative.

• A strategic alliance takes place when two firms exchange stock and
form a separate joint venture to develop and manufacture a product or
service.

Offshore banking

Offshore banking refers to deposits and loans that are made in a country other than the depositor's or borrower's country of origin. The Euro-
dollar market was one of the earliest examples of an offshore banking market.

Diagrammatically, an offshore deposit or loan is simply characterized
in Figure 5. 7.

离岸银行业务(Offshore
banking):指的是在存款
人和借款人的本国之外
进行的存储业务。

Figure 5.7   Offshore banking

The key differences between offshore banking and domestic banking are the currency of denomination, the tax jurisdiction and the regulatory framework. For accounts payable and hedging purposes, it is often convenient to hold cash balances in a foreign currency. In some cases, however, offshore banking is used for money-laundering. A recent example is a shell Argentine bank in the Cayman Islands which had no personnel in the Cayman Islands, but was used to launder money. It was ordered closed recently by the Cayman banking regulators. The Bank of New York has experienced regulatory trouble resulting from the alleged laundering of Russian monies, as have some Swiss Banks.

埃奇法案银行(**Edge Act Bank**):是外国银行的分支机构,该银行可以吸收离岸存款,但是不能吸收国内存款。

In the United States, an **Edge Act Bank** is a branch of a foreign bank that is allowed to take in offshore deposits, but not domestic deposits. Edge banks are subject to the regulation and the supervision of the US monetary authorities (the Federal Reserve Bank and the Comptroller of the Currency), who are keen to discover money laundering and close the offending banks.

An Edge bank may make US and foreign loans and investments for its offshore clients. Examples are Banco Santander Central Hispano which has Edge Act facilities for private banking in New York and Miami. Its depositors are mainly from Europe, primarily Spain, and Latin America. It complies with international and U.S. banking regulation and best banking practice which it has observed since the 15th century. Today, Banco Santander Central Hispano has the greatest volume of assets of any bank in Latin America. Its policy is to acquire 100% of existing or new banks, and to install BSCH management to avoid taking the risk of a partner doing illegal or irresponsible banking. Additionally, they take no deposits from politicians nor former-politicians from Latin America.

International Financial Offshore Centers

The primary purpose of an International Financial Offshore Center (IOFC) is to centralize, net, and track international cash flow and defer taxes on profits before repatriation or investment. It may also serve as an invoicing center. The Internal Revenue Act of 1962 and the Tax Reform Act of 1984, which created Foreign Sales Corporations (FSCs), permit this in an attempt to reduce the tax burden on exports from the United States.

However, by the use of aggressive transfer pricing, shell banks and corporations, IOFCs have been vehicles for tax avoidance rather than deferment, and, even worse, money laundering. The Edge Act for the US created IOFCs inside the US for the rest of the world, so this is not a statement only about a few small Caribbean islands. The larger jurisdictions, the United States and Europe, are pressuring smaller offshore banking centers to remove coveted banking secrecy laws that have shielded money laundering. However, it is clear that a great deal of money is laundered through New York and Miami, despite mandatory notification to the Treasury of deposits over $10,000, an amount so small that it triggers too many notifications.

离岸国际金融中心（International financial offshore center）：它的主要目的是集中、结算并追踪国际现金流，以及延迟汇回或投资前利润的税收。

Other special regimes

A US Possessions Corporation is not subject to US income tax on income received in the US possession, provided it is not received in the United States. This is an incentive for US firms to set up separate corporations in the US possessions. These special incentives are being phased out gradually.

Blacklisted countries (Non-Cooperative Countries and Territories)

The Financial Action Task Force(FATF) to combat money laundering and terrorist financing, an international body created by the G-7 to deter money laundering—the movement of profits from illicit activities through the banking system or legitimate business—has established a blacklist of countries that do not take enough action to curb money-laundering. It also requires greater identification of customers involved in wire-transfers to combat terrorism. The FATF removed the Cook Islands, Indonesia, and Philippines from the Non-Cooperative Countries and Territories (NCCTs)

金融特别行动组（The Financial Action Task Force）：由七国集团成立的一个旨在反洗钱及反恐怖主义融资的国际组织。

list in February 2005. The currently blacklisted countries are few. Iran and North Korea are listed as not taking enough measures against money laundering and the transfer of terrorist monies. Ten others are listed as having deficiencies in this regard: Cuba, Bolivia, Ethiopia, Kenya, Myanmar, Nigeria, São Tomé and Príncipe, Sri Lanka, Syria and Turkey. While the FATF cites considerable progress in this respect, there is no hard evidence that money laundering or terrorist finance has abated. More worrisome, in their 2005 NCCT Report, they welcome the substantial progress made by Myanmar, Nauru, and Nigeria in enacting legislation that addresses money laundering deficiencies. (June 2005 NCCTs Report: 5, FATF/OECD, Paris.)

An international business plan

The principal ways of organizing a business are:

- a **sole proprietorship** involves an individual acting on his or her own behalf in a business context. It is the least specially regulated and least complex form of business, but has greater asset exposure.

- a **partnership** formed by the independent action of the partners whose rights and duties are spelled out in business charters.

- a **limited partnership** involves one or more investing partners and at least one operating partner. There are restrictions on the formation of limited partnerships that are designed to ensure that creditors are aware that an investing partner will be liable only to the extent of that partner's investment.

- a **corporation** is a single entity, a "person" that may sue or be sued without its members being held liable. It is chartered by the jurisdiction in which it is located. A corporation is a business in which large numbers of people are organized so that their labor and capital are combined in a single venture. They may enter or withdraw from the venture at any time, by buying or selling shares, leaving it to others to carry on.

The principal-agent problem

The legal cornerstone of business transactions is agency law.

An **agent** is a person empowered to act so as to legally bind another, the principal. An agent must be loyal to the principal, act with reasonable care, follow reasonable instructions, and make an appropriate accounting. So long as the agent acts with authority, the principal is bound to perform the obligations to third parties. The third parties are similarly liable to the

独资企业(Sole proprietorship):业主根据自身利益而独立经营的企业。

合伙制企业(Partnership):由独立合伙人组成的合伙企业。

有限合伙制企业(Limited partnership):由一个或多个投资合伙人和至少一个营运合伙人组成。投资者仅仅根据其出资额度对企业负责。

公司(Corporation):是一个独立的法人实体,它是将许多人组织起来使他们的人力和资本很好地在一项投资中组合的企业。

代理问题(The principal-agent problem):委托人与代理人由于目标不一致而产生利益冲突的情况。

代理人(Agent):由委托人授权,并在法律上与委托人紧密联系在一起的行为人。

principal. There are several possible solutions to the principal-agent problem: Each tries to align the interests of the agent with those of the owners.

• Ownership—sell part of the firm to the agent, or have the agent buy shares in the corporation, or grant the agent shares or options to buy shares.

• Incentive pay—include incentives in the agent's compensation package that reflect the principal's interest. However, there are several problems with stock-options as solutions to the principal-agent problem. First, the holdings of current shareholders are diluted since the firm issues more shares to fulfill a stock option plan. The existing shares will decline in value relative to what they would otherwise be. Second, when the market turns downward, many of the manager's call options are under the water—that is, way out-of-the-money and are practically worthless. Thus, their incentive effect is nearly nil. Under some conditions, the exercise price may be reset so as to restore managerial incentives, but this seems unfair to shareholders that have purchased their stock on the open market. At times, the shares have also been backdated to a lower exercise price to build in intrinsic profits. Third, when a manager has inside information, he/she may exercise early or book earnings for goods not delivered so as to cash in the options before the bad news hits the market. Fourth, managers have an incentive to book earnings early, to exaggerate them, or remove negative items from income statements in order to cash in their bonus or stock options. In short, stock options may distort incentives.

• Monitoring—but who will "monitor" the monitor? Many international accounting firms have been fined for signing off on obviously fraudulent earnings and income statements. Partly this is due to conflicts of interest when the auditing firm also seeks investments from the firm.

Financial distress and bankruptcy

Financial distress can be defined in several ways:
• Business failure (a business has terminated with a loss to creditors.)
• Legal bankruptcy (Firms or creditors bring petitions to a court for bankruptcy.)
• In Chapter 7, or liquidation, the debtor's property is sold off by a trustee to pay the debts owed to creditors. An individual debtor can keep a modest amount of household property or realty under federal or state exemptions. The states of Texas and Florida are famous for its bankrupt managers

and owners with multi-million dollar homes sheltered from the bankruptcy court due to "Homestead Laws. "

• In Chapter 11, or business reorganization, the business is continued by its management or a trustee while creditors' claims are frozen pending approval of a plan. With court approval, the plan can modify or forgive debts, recapitalize a corporation, provide for mergers or takeovers, or dispose of assets.

• In Chapter 13, or adjustment proceedings, individuals with a regular income who cannot pay their debts may elect adjustment proceedings instead of liquidation. In these cases, claims of creditors are frozen until the individual presents a plan to pay off the creditors from income that is approved by a trustee. With court and creditor approval, debts may be stretched out or compromised while the debtor still retains all property.

偿债能力 (Solvency) : 指的是公司按时偿还债务的能力。

• Technical insolvency occurs when a firm defaults on a legal obligation, for example, by not paying a bill. **Solvency** means the ability of the firm to pay its liabilities on time. The short-term solvency of a firm is measured two ways: the current solvency ratio (the ratio of its current assets to its current liabilities), and the quick solvency ratio (the ratio of its liquid assets to its current liabilities). Rules of thumb suggest a minimum current ratio of 2 to 1, and a minimum quick ratio of 1 to 1.

• Accounting insolvency occurs when the total book value of liabilities exceed the book value of total assets. Owner's equity, the difference between assets and liabilities, is negative.

The break-even point and the profit-maximizing point

In principle, the valuation of a firm requires only three things: a forecast of its profits or free-cash flow, an estimate of its terminal value when sold in say 5 years, and a weighted average cost of capital of the firm with which to discount free-cash flows and the terminal value. The exercise is part art, part science. When these three variables are estimated, the net present value of the firm is given by substitution into the standard NPV formula:

$$NPV = \pi_0 + \frac{\pi_1}{(1+i)} + \frac{\pi_2}{(1+i)^2} + \frac{\pi_3}{(1+i)^3}$$
$$+ \frac{\pi_4}{(1+i)^4} + \frac{\pi_5}{(1+i)^5} + \frac{T_5}{(1+i)^5} \qquad (5.15)$$

where π represents profits (or rather free-cash flow) in each year, T_5 the terminal value when the firm is sold in the fifth year, and i the weighted-average cost of capital. In the start-up year, costs typically exceed revenues, or $\pi_0 < 0$. For the NPV to be positive there must be positive cash flow in at least one of the future years. In each period, it is assumed that production is at the profit-maximizing level requiring that marginal revenue equal marginal costs (the slope of the revenue curve equals the slope of the cost curve, as depicted in Figure 5.8.)

Figure 5.8 Profit maximization by the firm

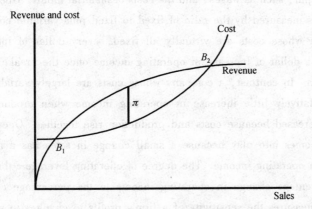

Note that a second-order condition requires that costs be rising faster than revenues, otherwise the marginal cost equals marginal revenue would imply a profit minimum. This can easily occur with economies of scale where average cost is declining.

Financial and operating leverage

A start-up business faces two serious questions—how much financial leverage and how much operating leverage it should take on? Higher financial leverage, as measured by the debt to debt plus equity ratio, benefits the owners greatly when the firm does well. Earnings per share are more responsive to a rise in earnings before interest, because the debt obligations—interest and principal payments to bondholders—are fixed. Shareholder dividends thus rise elastically with respect to earnings before interest. That is the positive side of financial leverage.

However, if the firm does poorly after getting started, the creditors are nevertheless legally entitled to interest and principal payments, but the shareholders can only hope for dividends. Earnings per share can easily be negative while the firm is making losses and yet paying creditors as its business is growing. However, it may be forced into bankruptcy after only a few months if it does not reach a break-even point quickly. New restaurants of-

ten do not stay in business for over a year, partly due to financial leverage,
as was the case of the *Azteca*, whose start-up was 100% debt financed.

The degree of operating leverage at start up is another critical decision that may jeopardize a firm's survival. Operating leverage is the extent to which a company's costs of operating are fixed—rent, insurance, and salaries—as opposed to variable—materials and direct labor—costs that vary with output, such as wages, and the costs of material inputs. Operating leverage is measured by the ratio of fixed to fixed plus variable costs. In a company whose costs are virtually all fixed, every dollar of increase in sales is a dollar of increase in operating income once the breakeven point has been. In contrast, a company whose costs are largely variable would show relatively little increase in operating income when production and sales increased because costs and production rise together. Operating leverage comes into play because a small change in sales has a magnified effect on operating income. The degree of operating leverage—the ratio of the percentage change in operating income to the percentage change in sales—measures the sensitivity of a firm's profits to changes in sales volume. A firm with a high degree of operating leverage has a breakeven point at a relatively high sales level.

An international business plan: the *Azteca Café*

This is all very well and good, but how is it put into practice, particularly abroad? Let's take the example of the *Azteca Café* whose revenues and costs are in Mexican pesos, its functional currency. As a start-up in 2001, its initial investment costs were N$500,000 for the oven and hood with fire extinguisher, grease trap, tables, chairs and dinnerware, plus renovation of the existing facility. The owner/manager, Juan Olive elected straight line depreciation of his investment over five years. His forecast of free cash flow in pesos in indicated in Table 5.13.

Table 5.13   Forecast of the Azteca's free cash flow in new Mexican pesos

	2001	2002	2003	2004	2005
Free cash flow in Mexican pesos	N$(332,683)	N$(108,046)	N$60,553	N$123,615	N$82,554

He had borrowed from a local bank the entire amount at 22% in pesos, which gives us the weighted average cost of capital (no equity was brought to the project). The *Azteca's* forecasted revenue and costs yielded a free cash flow projection for five years. In addition, a terminal value was predicted as a no-growth perpetuity of its fifth year's free cash flow. Unfortunately, the business plan was done at the end of the *Azteca's* first year of operations. Had it been done earlier, the project would not have taken place.

In the first year, Juan accumulated arrears in his rent, his loan and in payment of the 15% value-added tax in Mexico. His cash-flow was negative so he sought finance by running arrears. The business plan was prepared in May 2001 to value the restaurant in pesos. Naturally, the value of debt arrears had to be subtracted from the net present value of forecasted free-cash flow.

The business plan summary is presented in Table 5.14.

Table 5.14   Discounted free cash flow of the Azteca

Valuation of the Azteca café	2001	2002	2003	2004	2005	Terminal value 2005
Free cash flow in Mexican pesos	N$(332,683)	N$(108,046)	N$60,553	N$123,615	N$82,554	N$375,247
Present value in Mexican pesos	N$(272,691)	N$(72,592)	N$(33,347)	N$(55,799)	N$(30,545)	N$(138,841)
PV of free cash flow in Mexican pesos	N$(86,750)	22.0% WACC in N$				
Spot exchange rate (USD per peso)	$0.1098					
PV of free cash flow in US dollars	$(9,525)					

In addition, the landlord could padlock the restaurant door at any moment with a court order, and the lender could seize the oven and equipment on which he held the lien. The state was about to file criminal charges for tax evasion. *The Azteca Café* was clearly in serious financial distress. Could it be sold? The net present value of free cash flow was negative, but the restaurant was even worth less. Let's deduct debts from the net present of free cash flow in Table 5.15.

Table 5.15 Discounted free cash flow minus existing liabilities of the Azteca

Present value of free cash flow	N $ (86 ,750)
Rent arrears	N $ (225 ,000)
Loan arrears	N $ (50 ,000)
Value-added tax arrears	N $ (60 ,000)
Estimated NPV of the Azteca (in N $)	N $ (421 ,750)
Spot exchange rate(USD per peso)	$0. 1098
Estimated NPV of the Azteca café(in USD)	$ (46 ,308)

New equity financing was sought to recapitalize the restaurant and repay the loan and rent arrears. Meetings of potential investors took place, but the decision was taken that any more money put into the venture would be lost. In any case, ignoring the arrears, the net present value of cash flow was negative. The potential investors informed the restaurant's lawyer that they would not invest in the *Azteca Café*. The owner declared a liquidation bankruptcy in June 2001, turning in his keys to the landlord. The bank took the equipment and sold it in auction. It also required the owner, Juan, to sell his home and took its equity. Finally, it rescheduled the remaining balance of his loan, with penalties. Moral of the story: look before you leap! That is, do a reasoned business plan.

International financial management covers the international cost of capital, working capital balance management, offshore banking, international tax management, transfer pricing, mergers and acquisitions and currency forecasting and conversion. There are perfectly legal and reasoned ways of reducing tax liabilities, yet there may be the temptation to abuse some of these tools. Chapter 6 deals with some of the more abusive international financial deals that cross the line in terms of accounting, legal, and ethical standards.

Optimal investment analysis

市场风险（Market risk）:也称为系统风险，表示与整体经济状况相关的风险因素。

公司特定风险（Firm specific risk）:也称为可分散风险，表示可以通过分散投资消除的风险因素。

Market risk, also known as systematic risk, represents risk factors that are common to the whole economy. **Firm specific risk**, also known as diversifiable risk, represents risk factors that can be eliminated by diversification. The variance of security i, σ_i^2, can be written as the sum of the market risk and the firm specific risk:

$$\sigma_i^2 = \beta_i^2 \sigma_M^2 + \sigma_{e_i}^2 \qquad (5.16)$$

where

$$\beta_i^2 = \frac{\sigma_{iM}}{\sigma_M^2}$$

and σ_{iM} is the covariance between security i's return and the market return, and σ_M^2 is the variance of the market return. The *beta* (β) of an individual security measures the security's sensitivity to market movements and therefore is known as its market risk. For example, the *beta* of the Standard & Poor's 500 index share should be about one since it reflects a broad selection of market stocks. A riskier security would have a *beta* greater than one, and a less risky security would have a *beta* less than one.

Portfolio diversification

The level of market risk is dealt with by choosing the *betas* in the portfolio since the systematic risk is a weighted average of the individual security *betas*. Systematic variance equals $\beta_P^2 \sigma_m^2$, where β_P is the simple average of the individual security *betas*. By choosing β_P^2, we decide the systematic variance of the portfolio. A choice of domestic and international *betas* can reduce systematic risk relative to a choice of only domestic *betas*. In short, systematic risk is manipulated by choosing the average *beta* of the securities, but the number of securities does not matter.

Non-systematic risk is diversifiable by increasing the number of securities. By sufficiently diversifying, the investor can virtually eliminate firm-specific risk. By holding both domestic and international securities, portfolio diversification is more efficient since the universe of assets is the choice set. Figure 5.9 illustrates the reduction of portfolio risk as the number of securities in the portfolio increases.

资产投资组合分散风险（Portfolio Diversification）：非系统风险可以通过增加证券的数量得到分散。

Figure 5.9   Portfolio diversification and market risk

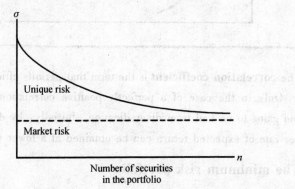

Unique risk

Market risk

Number of securities
in the portfolio

Asset allocation with one domestic and one foreign asset

Here we consider the allocation of the investment budget between two risky funds, a domestic fund and a foreign fund. If the proportion invested in the domestic fund is w_d, then the remainder is invested in the international (g for global) fund, $w_g = 1 - w_d$.

Some basic relationships hold:

$$r_P = w_d r_d + w_g r_g \qquad (5.17)$$

$$E(r_P) = w_d E(r_d) + w_g E(r_g) \qquad (5.18)$$

$$\sigma_P^2 = (w_d \sigma_d)^2 + (w_g \sigma_g)^2 + 2(w_d \sigma_d)(w_g \sigma_g)\rho_{dg} \qquad (5.19)$$

That is:

• The rate of return on the portfolio is a weighted average of the rates of return on the domestic and global funds.

• The expected rate of return on the portfolio is a weighted average of the expected rates of return on the domestic and global funds.

• The variance of the portfolio is the sum of the square of weighted volatilities plus a term involving the correlation coefficient, ρ_{dg}, between the domestic and the global funds. In general, the efficient investment portfolio has the shape depicted in Figure 5.10.

Figure 5.10   The efficient investment frontier

相关系数（Correlation coefficient）：该相关系数决定了风险分散的有效性。当完全正相关时，分散化并不会带来收益；只有当完全负相关时，分散化的潜在收益才达到最大。

The **correlation coefficient** is the term that permits efficient diversification. Only in the case of a perfectly positive correlation, $\rho_{dg} = 1$ are there no gains to be had from diversification. Initially, by diversification, a higher rate of expected return can be obtained at a lower volatility.

The minimum risk portfolio

The minimum risk portfolio is found by differentiating (5.19) with respect to the portfolio weights, setting the result equal to zero, and solving. The weight of global shares in the minimum variance portfolio is given by:

$$w_g^* = \frac{\sigma_d^2 - \sigma_g \sigma_d \rho_{dg}}{\sigma_d^2 + \sigma_g^2 - 2\sigma_g \sigma_d \rho_{dg}} \qquad (5.20)$$

The minimum risk portfolio, while a point on the efficient investment frontier, will not be chosen because higher expected reward can be achieved by a small increase in risk.

The efficient investment frontier

The efficient investment frontier is derived by maximizing the expected return, subject to a given risk. Alternatively, it can be derived by minimizing the risk for a given expected rate of return on the portfolio. For a given level of risk, $\bar{\sigma}_P^2$, the efficient weight of the global asset is given by:

有效投资前沿(The efficient investment frontier):在给定风险水平下最大化预期利润,或者在给定证券组合预期回报下最小化风险得到的投资组合。

$$w_g = \frac{E(r_g)\sigma_d^2 - E(r_d)\sigma_g \sigma_d \rho_{dg}}{E(r_g)(\sigma_d^2 - \sigma_g \sigma_d \rho_{dg}) + E(r_d)(\sigma_g^2 - \sigma_g \sigma_d \rho_{dg})} \qquad (5.21)$$

Note that this is the share of the global asset necessary to be on the efficient investment frontier, a purely technical condition. This share maximizes expected portfolio return for each level of risk. Our next step in the optimal efficient portfolio analysis is to maximize the Sharpe "reward to risk" ratio.

The asset allocation decision

Investors may be risk averse, demanding a higher rate of return—a risk premium—for holding risky assets. Risk may be reduced either by converting risky assets into safe assets such as money market assets or by constructing a risky portfolio efficiently, diversifying away unsystematic risk. Consider an investor holding a risky portfolio, P, along with a risk-free asset, T, such as US T-bills. The risky portfolio consists of some domestic and some foreign assets.

For example, a hypothetical portfolio might be as illustrated in Table 5.16.

Table 5.16 A hypothetical complete portfolio

Company	Assets	Complete portfolio weights	Risky portfolio weights
General Motors, US	$50	0.5	0.625
Tiger International	30	0.3	0.375
Portfolios			
(Portfolio P)	80	0.8	1.0
US T-bills (Portfolio T)	20	0.2	
Complete portfolio (Portfolio C)	100	1.0	

This investor is holding 62.5% of her risky portfolio in General Motors, U.S. and 37.5% of P in Tiger International. Let w represent the holdings in US securities and w^* indicate the holdings of international securities in the risky portfolio, so that $w + w^* = 1$. Thus, $w = 0.625$ and $w^* = 0.375$. The weight of the risky portfolio, P, in the complete portfolio, C, including risk-free investments is denoted by z. Thus the weight of the risk-free asset in the complete portfolio is $1 - z$. T-bills represent 20% of the complete portfolio, or $1 - z = 0.2$, and risky assets 80% of C, or $z = 0.8$. General Motors, US represents 50% of the complete portfolio and Tiger International 30%.

The investor is thus holding a risk-free asset and a bundle of risky assets which can be thought of as one risky asset. In this way, the investor can keep the relative shares of the two risky assets constant in the risky portfolio P, and at the same time reduce risk by selling them off proportionately to acquire more of the risk-free asset, Treasuries.

By changing the distribution of the risky asset relative to the risk-free asset, yet maintaining the mix of assets in the risky portfolio, the investor can reduce the risk of the complete portfolio yet remain on the efficient investment frontier. That is, z can be reduced in C while maintaining w and w^* fixed in P.

Portfolio expected return and risk

Notation:

r_P —Rate of return on the risky portfolio

r_f —Rate of return on the **risk-free asset**

$E(r_P)$ —Expected rate of return on the risky portfolio

σ_P —The standard deviation (*volatility*) of the risky portfolio

无风险资产（Risk-free asset）：通常是指短期政府债券。

$E(r_f) = r_f$—Expected rate of return on the risk-free asset

$E(r_c)$—Expected rate of return on the complete portfolio

Consequently, with a fraction z of risky assets in the portfolio and $1 - z$ of risk-free assets, the rate of return on the complete portfolio is:

$$r_C = zr_P + (1 - z)r_f \qquad (5.22)$$

Consequently, the expected rate of return on the complete portfolio is:

$$E(r_C) = zE(r_P) + (1 - z)r_f \qquad (5.23)$$

or equivalently,

$$E(r_C) = r_f + z[E(r_P) - r_f] \qquad (5.24)$$

Which has a perfectly natural interpretation: The complete portfolio has a base return equal the risk-free rate, r_f, plus an expected market risk premium, $[E(r_P) - r_f]$ on its exposure to risky assets, z. Risk-averse investors demand a positive market risk premium. The standard deviation of the complete portfolio is indicated by:

$$\sigma_C = z\sigma_P \qquad (5.25)$$

since the volatility of the risk free asset is zero. Substituting $z = \dfrac{\sigma_C}{\sigma_P}$ into (5.25), we have:

$$E(r_C) = r_f + \left[\frac{E(r_P) - r_f}{\sigma_P}\right]\sigma_C \qquad (5.26)$$

which is the **capital allocation line (CAL)**. Figure 5.11 plots the capital allocation line depicting the rise in expected portfolio return against the standard deviation of the risky asset. It is the investment opportunity set resulting from different values of z.

资本配置线（Capital allocation line）：该曲线反映了相对于风险资产的标准差，预期组合收益的上升。

Figure 5.11   Capital allocation

When $z = 0$, the CAL begins at r_f and $\sigma_C = 0$. When $z = 1$, the portfolio has only the risky asset and its standard deviation is σ_P and its expected rate of return $E(r_P)$.

The slope of the investment opportunity schedule is **the Sharpe "reward to risk" ratio**:

夏普回报—风险比率
（The Sharpe "reward to risk" ratio）：又称为回报—波动比率，它是市场风险溢价对风险证券组合标准差的比率。

$$\frac{E(r_P) - r_f}{\sigma_P} \tag{5.27}$$

The slope is also called the reward-to-volatility ratio since it is the ratio of the market risk premium to the standard deviation of the risky portfolio.

Financial leverage (purchases "on margin")

保证金（Margin）：在证券市场融资购买证券时，投资者所需缴纳的自备款。

By borrowing, an investor can invest on the CAL line to the right of point P, thereby levering her investment in the risky asset. Our investor has an investment budget of \$100 and borrows, for example, on margin an additional \$50 at the risk free rate, thereby investing \$150 in the risky asset. In this case, $z = 1.5$, reflecting a levered position in the risky asset, and $(1 - z) = -0.5$ reflecting a short or borrowed position in the risk-free asset.

Borrowing to invest in the risky asset requires a margin account with a broker. Purchases "on margin" may not exceed 50% of the purchase value. If the net worth of the margin account is \$100, the investor can borrow up to \$100, for a total investment of \$200. In this case, $z = 2$, assets in the account would equal \$200 and liabilities \$100. In practice, an investor can borrow from his or her credit card, deposit this with a broker, and lever the borrowed sum. In most instances, the leveraged borrower cannot borrow at the risk free rate, so therefore faces a lowered *CAL* line beyond P because she pays a higher interest rate to borrow. That is, there is a kink at the point P.

Risk aversion and asset allocation

Consider the following utility (happiness or choice) function:

$$U = E(r_C) - \frac{A\sigma_C^2}{2} \tag{5.28}$$

This investor enjoys higher expected return, $E(r_C)$, but dislikes higher risk, σ_C. The level of risk aversion is $A > 0$. The higher A, the more risk averse the investor.

Utility maximization: mathematically

The investor's objective is to maximize utility (utils!) by selecting the fraction, z, of the investment budget to be invested in the risky portfolio, P. The expected return and variance of the complete portfolio are $E(r_C) = r_f + z[E(r_P) - r_f]$ and $\sigma_C^2 = z^2 \sigma_P^2$ respectively. To choose the best allocation to the risky asset, we maximize utility, equation (5.28) with respect to z. That is, maximize the quadratic utility function by differentiating with respect to z and setting the result equal to zero:

$$U(z) = E(r_C) - \frac{A\sigma_C^2}{2} = r_f + z[E(r_P) - r_f] - \frac{Az^2\sigma_P^2}{2} \quad (5.29)$$

which yields z^* the optimal share of the risky portfolio in the complete portfolio:

$$z^* = \frac{E(r_P) - r_f}{A\sigma_P^2} \quad (5.30)$$

The optimal share of the risky asset:
- Rises with increases in the market risk premium, $E(r_P) - r_f$.
- Falls with increases in the degree of risk aversion, A.
- Falls with increases in market volatility, σ_P^2.

Notice that risk aversion, a negative sign attached to the variance of the portfolio, guarantees a maximum rather than a minimum utility.

最优的风险资产持有份额（The optimal share of the risky asset）：最优的风险资产持有份额拥有以下特点：随着市场风险溢价的上升而上升；随着风险厌恶程度的上升而下降；随着市场波动率的上升而下降。

Utility maximization: graphically

Figure 5.12 illustrates the optimal allocation of assets for a risk averse investor who chooses to hold approximately half the portfolio in the risky asset and half in the safe asset. This optimal allocation yields the highest level of utility (at point C, the tangency of the capital allocation line and the highest indifference curve).

Figure 5.12   The optimal complete and market portfolios

Figure 5.13 illustrates a levered portfolio where the investor has borrowed on margin of approximately 50%. In our example, if the net worth in the account is $100, margin purchases may be up to 50% of the purchase, so the investor can buy "on margin" an additional $100 of the risky asset. The investor would then have $200 on the asset side of the account and $100 on the liability side, yielding $z = 2$.

Figure 5.13   A leveraged complete portfolio

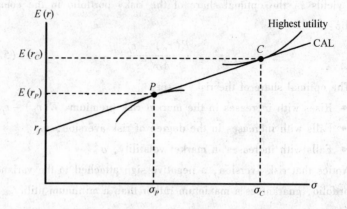

Naturally, a levered portfolio has a greater expected rate of return and a higher risk than an unlevered one.

The tangency of the capital asset line to the investment opportunity frontier at point P yields the highest expected reward-risk ratio. It is therefore the optimal risky portfolio. The optimal risky portfolio is found by the CAL with the steepest slope tangent to the efficient investment frontier at P. The optimal complete portfolio is found by allocating z percent of the portfolio to the risky asset composed of domestic and international assets. The remainder of the optimal complete portfolio, $(1 - z)$, is composed of US Treasury bills.

Let's consider an application of the theory of the optimal complete portfolio. The risk-averse investor has the following utility function:

$$U = E(r_c) - 0.5A\sigma_c^2 = E(r_c) - \sigma_c^2 \qquad (5.31)$$

Once again, $E(r_C) = r_f + z[E(r_P) - r_f]$. This investor has a degree of risk aversion, $A = 2$, since $0.5A = 1$. We are also given the following data: $E(r_P) = 0.15$, $r_f = 0.05$, $\sigma_P^2 = 0.10$. Consequently, the market risk premium is 10%, as is the variance of the market portfolio. We may directly substitute the data into the optimal share of the risky portfolio of the investor:

$$z^* = \frac{E(r_P) - r_f}{A\sigma_P^2} = \frac{0.15 - 0.05}{2 \times 0.10} = \frac{0.10}{0.20} = \frac{1}{2} \quad (5.32)$$

The optimal solution for this investor is to hold half her portfolio in the optimal risky asset and half in the risk-free asset. The expected return on the complete portfolio is $0.05 + \dfrac{0.10}{2} = 0.10$ or ten percent. The variance of the complete portfolio is $\left(\dfrac{1}{2}\right)^2 (0.10) = 0.025$. Its volatility is the square root of 0.025, or 0.158. Finally, the utility of the investor is $0.100 - 0.025 = 0.075$.

The separation property

Portfolio choice is separated into two separate parts: first, selection of the optimum risky portfolio at (P) which is a purely technical consideration and second, the personal investor choice of the best mix of the risky portfolio and the risk-free asset (C). Risk aversion plays no role in the first part; it enters into play in the second part of the portfolio choice. The optimum risky portfolio is the same for all investors, independent of their degree of risk aversion. It is point of tangency of the highest CAL line to the efficient investment portfolio. The second part, construction of the complete portfolio composed of US Treasury bills and the risky portfolio, depends on personal preference, that is, risk tolerance. This separation theorem is due to James Tobin (1958), the 1983 Nobel Laureate in Economics. Since the optimal investment portfolio comprised of domestic and global securities is the same for all investors, a passive index fund of domestic and global securities will usually yield better results than an actively managed fund since the latter have higher management and trading fees.

Determination of the market risk premium

The market portfolio of all assets in the universe, each held in proportion to its market value, represents an efficient fund of risky assets. This is known as the **mutual fund theorem**. A passive index fund holding both domestic and international assets may therefore be viewed by the rational investor as a close approximation to the optimal risky portfolio. In addition, a passive index fund saves management and transaction fees.

Net aggregate lending (borrowing) is zero, viewing Treasuries as the liabilities of the citizens who both issue and hold Treasuries. Some investors are net lenders $z_i < 1$ while others are net borrowers $z_j > 1$, but on ag-

分离性质（The separation property）：证券组合选择决策可以分离成为两个独立的部分：第一，在 P 点选择最优风险组合；第二，个人选择风险组合与无风险资产的最优组合 C。

市场风险溢价（Market risk premium）：市场平均收益与无风险资产收益之差。

共同基金定理（Mutual fund theorem）：由市场上全部证券所构成的证券组合，每一种都依据其市场价值的比例而持有，表示了风险资产的有效基金。

gregate, the average z must equal 1. Therefore, for the average global investor $z = 1$. Since the optimal portfolio of the individual investor with average risk aversion, A^*, is:

$$z^* = \frac{E(r_P) - r_f}{A^* \sigma_P^2} \qquad (5.33)$$

and the average investor has $z = 1$, the risk premium on the market portfolio is proportional to its risk and average risk aversion.

$$E(r_P) - r_f = A^* \sigma_P^2 \qquad (5.34)$$

Which states that the market risk premium depends on the average degree of risk aversion times the riskiness of the market portfolio, as measured by its volatility. The average investor's portfolio is thus the market portfolio having expected value $E(r_P)$ and volatility σ_P as illustrated in Figure 5.14.

Figure 5.14　The mutual fund theorem

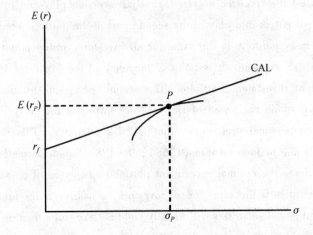

资本资产定价模型 (Capital asset pricing model) :资本资产定价模型是由美国学者威廉·夏普(William Sharpe) 等人在现代投资组合理论的基础上发展起来的,它是现代金融市场价格理论的支柱,被广泛应用于投资决策和公司理财领域。

The CAPM (Capital asset pricing model)

The individual contribution of an individual security to the standard deviation of the market portfolio is $\beta_i \sigma_P$. Furthermore, by definition, $\beta_P = 1$ for the market portfolio. The investor's trade-off between risk and return should be the same for the market portfolio and an individual security's per unit contribution to the market portfolio's risk:

$$\frac{E(r_P) - r_f}{\beta_P \sigma_P} = \frac{E(r_i) - r_f}{\beta_i \sigma_P} \qquad (5.35)$$

Noting that $\beta_P = 1$ and re-arranging (5.35), yields the *CAPM's expected return beta* relationship:

$$E(r_i) = r_f + \beta_i [E(r_P) - r_f] \tag{5.36}$$

Which states that the expected return on asset i equals the risk free rate plus the market risk premium times the market risk coefficient, β_i, of the individual security.

Exchange rate volatility in the reward to risk model

The rate of return on the global portfolio is the sum of the rate of appreciation of foreign currency, s, and the rate of return in foreign currency on the foreign asset, r_{g^*}, or:

$$r_g = s + r_{g^*} \tag{5.37}$$

ignoring cross product terms, sr_{g^*}, as small.

Consequently, the expected rate of return on the foreign asset in terms of home currency is the expected sum of the percentage appreciation of foreign currency and the rate of return in foreign currency on the foreign asset:

$$E(r_g) = E(s) + E(r_{g^*}) \tag{5.38}$$

Thus, the expected rate of return of the risky portfolio may be written:

$$E(r_p) = w_d E(r_d) + w_g [E(s) + E(r_{g^*})] \tag{5.39}$$

and the variance of the risky portfolio is:

$$\sigma_p^2 = w_d^2 \sigma_d^2 + w_g^2 [\sigma_s^2 + \sigma_{r_{g^*}}^2 + 2\text{Cov}(s, r_{g^*})] + 2 w_d w_g \text{Cov}(r_d, s + r_{g^*})$$

$$\tag{5.40}$$

Where

$$\text{Cov}(r_d, s + r_g) = E[(r_d - E(r_d))((s + r_{g^*}) - E(s + r_{g^*}))]$$

That is: the expected return on the risky portfolio includes a foreign exchange term as well as the returns in the different currencies. Due to interest rate parity, the expectation is that:

$$\text{Cov}(r_d, s + r_{g^*}) > 0$$

while

$$\text{Cov}(s, r_{g^*}) < 0$$

also due to IRP.

Our basic result in an international setting is therefore that the optimal share of domestic assets and foreign assets in the risky portfolio is given by:

$$z^* = \frac{E(r_p) - r_f}{A\sigma_p^2}$$

$$= \frac{w_d E(r_d) + w_g [E(s) + E(r_{g^*})] - r_f}{A\{w_d^2 \sigma_d^2 + w_g^2 [\sigma_s^2 + \sigma_{r_{g^*}}^2 + 2\text{Cov}(s, r_{g^*})] + 2 w_d w_g \text{Cov}(r_d, s + r_{g^*})\}}$$

$$\tag{5.41}$$

Changes in the exchange rate play a central role in optimum portfolio allocation. However, according to interest rate parity, the expected change in the exchange rate reflects interest rate differentials, or expected inflation rate differentials. That is:

$$E(s) = E(r_g) - E(r_{g^*})$$

Nevertheless, deviations in exchange rate movements from interest rate differentials or, equivalently, deviations in movements in the exchange rate relative to expected inflation rates raise the issue of currency risk. In reality, the real exchange rate frequently differs from relative purchasing power parity, so that returns on foreign assets converted into home currency can deviate significantly from returns expected from IRP.

Home bias

本国偏好(Home bias): 是指即使有相对较佳的海外投资机会,人们仍倾向于投资于本国。

Residents seem empirically to have a strong preference for home assets over foreign assets. For instance, an optimal risky portfolio for US residents might have 30% foreign assets, but US residents hold only 12.5%. This puzzle cannot be fully explained by the various reasons offered:

• Asymmetric information and search costs regarding the expected return and volatility of foreign assets.

• Conversion costs due to the bid-ask spread on foreign currencies.

• Hedging against risk from deviations in exchange rates from purchasing power and interest rate parity. Investors may be "short" home goods in their planned consumption baskets, so therefore hold domestic assets primarily as a hedge against unanticipated exchange rate depreciations of their foreign assets.

In the case of China, home bias is absolute since capital controls still exist on individual holdings of assets abroad. The SAFE (State Administered Foreign Exchange) system does not yet permit purchases of foreign exchange for individual investments in securities abroad. As capital controls are liberated, the Chinese investor will diversify some of her holdings of assets toward foreign securities so as to maximize its expected rate of return for a given level of risk, or, equivalently, to minimize its variance for a given expected rate of return. By the same token, world investors will beat a path to the Shanghai and Shenzhen exchanges to diversify their portfolios and take advantage of the high expected return in China. It is hard to predict if inflows will exceed outflows, but that is likely with high returns in China and low returns in Europe and America.

Conclusion

The Markowitz-Sharpe model of risk aversion is a powerful tool for application to the analysis of the optimal portfolio of a client, based upon her degree of risk aversion. It rests solidly on the idea of portfolio diversification, showing that portfolios offer higher returns for given risk than do individual securities, thereby revolutionizing the theory of investment finance. In 1990, Merton Miller, William Sharpe, and Harry Markowitz were jointly awarded the Nobel Prize in Economics for their contributions.

Questions and problems

5.1 The international weighted average cost of capital

Consider the data in of a European IBM subsidiary (in Euros). The borrowing rates represent those of the subsidiary in terms of Euros. The parent firm has its headquarters in New York.

Cost of debt	10
Cost of equity	15
Capital structure:	
Debt	30
Equity	70
Corporate tax rate:	
United States	35
Europe	45
Expected inflation:	
United States	3
Europe	2

a. Calculate the weighted average cost of capital (WACC) to IBM in euros.

b. Convert the WACC to US dollars.

5.2 Transfer pricing

Consider the Figure below indicating the marginal costs of production of an intermediate good as well as the marginal cost of marketing the final good. The intermediate good and the marketing are bundled as a joint product, one-to-one. The demand (average revenue) and the marginal revenue curves are drawn as well.

Answer the following:

a. What is the profit maximizing level of sales (units of production)?

b. What will your firm charge the final customer?

c. What is the optimal transfer price that the marketing division will pay for intermediate goods supplied to the marketing division?

5.3 Foreign currency conversion of free cash flows

Consider the data on the U.S. and the U.K. Assume the required real rates of return are the same.

U.S. and U.K. data (percent per annum)	
U.S. inflation rate	3
U.K. inflation rate	2
U.S. Treasury	5
U.K. Treasury	4
WACC$_\pounds$	15
WACC$_\$$	

a. If the WACC in US dollars is 15%, what is the WACC in pounds sterling, given the above data? Recall that the conversion rule for the WACC is:

$$\left(\frac{1 + \text{WACC}_\pounds}{1 + \text{WACC}_\$}\right) = \left(\frac{1 + r_{uk}}{1 + r_{us}}\right)$$

and the interest rate parity rule for forecasting the exchange rate is:

$$F = S\left[\frac{(1 + r_{us})}{(1 + r_{uk})}\right]^n$$

Now consider the estimated free cash flows in British pounds of a two-year project by a UK subsidiary.

Method A

• Discount foreign currency flows to the present at the foreign currency discount rate, then convert the NPV in FOREX to home currency at the spot rate.

Year	0	1	2
Free-cash flows(£)	−100	60	70
Present value of cash flow(£)	−100		
NPV(£)			
Spot exchange rate($/£)	1.77		
NPV($)			

Method B

- Convert foreign currency cash flows to home currency, and discount to the present at the home currency discount rate.

Year	0	1	2
Free-cash flows(£)	−100	60	70
Exchange rate forecast	1.77		
Free-cash flows($)	−177		
Present value of cash flow($)			
NPV($)			

b. On the basis of the inflation rate, interest rate and weighted average costs of capital (WACC$_\$$), should the US parent firm undertake this project? (i.e. compute the net present value (NPV) in dollars using the two methods.)

5.4 Trade finance

You intend to export 100 computers worth $2,000 each from Miami, FL to Cochabamba, Bolivia. This is the first shipment to a new client, and naturally, you hope to be paid in USD for the computers. Essentially, your options are cash-in-advance, an open account, or a letter of credit. List below the advantages and disadvantages of each, spelling out who bears the counterparty risk in each case.

a. Cash-in-advance

b. An open account

c. A letter of credit

5.5 Trade finance

You have received a confirmed standby letter of credit indicating that Citibank, Nassau will pay you $1,000,000 (one million dollars) every 30 days for one year beginning in 30 days.

a. If you need Bahamian dollars now for payments today, what can you do with the letter of credit immediately?

b. What proceeds in Bahamian dollars would you expect (the Bahamian dollar has since inception been rigidly pegged to the US dollar at one-to-one)?

5.6   International taxation

Headquarters of your computer company is located in Texas, but you have a branch for assembly and re-export to Europe that is located in Ireland where the corporate tax rate is 12.5% for foreign companies. Fill in the cells on international taxation in the table below. Explain your result.

Irish branch	
Irish income	$100
Irish taxes paid	$12.5
US taxes	
Net income	

Headquarters of your computer company is still located in Texas, but now you export computer parts for assembly to an Irish-incorporated subsidiary that re-invests its profits in Ireland. Fill in the cells below. Explain your result.

Irish branch	
Irish income	$100
Irish taxes paid	$12.5
US taxes	
Net income	

5.7   International taxation

As Treasurer of U.S. Exports, Inc. you have set up a Foreign Sales Corporation in the Bahamas for the export to Europe of your US manufactures, and are applying arm's length pricing of your goods "shipped" to the FSC. Your exempt foreign trade income from the sale or lease of export property is indicated by:

Foreign sales corporation (arm's length pricing)	
Foreign trade income	$100
Bahamian taxes paid	
US taxes	
Net income	

a. Fill in the blank cells, recalling that the portion of foreign trade income exempt from taxes is 34%, and the Bahamas has no income tax.

b. In the second case, your FSC is set up according to special administrative rules which exempt 17/23 of foreign trade income from U.S. taxation. Fill in the blank cells below and explain your answer.

Foreign sales corporation(administrative rules)

Foreign trade income	$100
Bahamian taxes paid	
US taxes	
Net income	

5.8 Mergers and acquisitions

Consider indicating the net present value of Firms A and B.

	Firm A	Firm B
Value	$20	$10
Shares outstanding	10	10

Answer the following questions:

a. What is the current value of the shares of each firm?

b. If Firm A acquires Firm B, and the value of the combined Firm A is $40, what is the value of synergy?

c. Suppose that Firm A offers cash of $15 to the shareholders of Firm B, what is the premium A is offering?

d. Do you think they will accept (2/3 majority required)?

e. If they do, what will be the new value of Firm A?

f. If Firm A were instead to offer shares in the new, combined Firm A, how many shares in the new firm would they have to offer to make a share offer equivalent to cash of $15?

g. Now suppose that Firm A offers $10 in cash and the rest in shares in the new Firm A. How many shares would it have to offer in order to make the equivalent of the cash offer of $15?

5.9 Mergers and acquisitions

Consider the data below indicating the standalone net present values of Firms A and B.

	Firm A	Firm B
Value	$40	$10
Shares outstanding	20	10

Firm A's due diligence indicates that it will have costs of integration the first year of $2, but a perpetual increase in profits of $1 per year beginning the first year. Its cost of capital is 10%.

Answer the following questions:

a. What is the current value of the shares of each firm?

b. What is the value of synergies, net of integration costs?

    c. Suppose that Firm A offers cash of $14 (or $14, including standa-lone value of $10 and $4 in synergy) to the each of shareholders of Firm B, what is the premium A is offering?

    d. Do you think they will accept (2/3 majority required)?

    e. If they do, what will be the new value of Firm A?

    f. If Firm A were instead to offer shares in the new, combined Firm A, how many shares in the new firm would they have to offer to make a share offer equivalent to cash of $14?

5.10 An international business plan

Consider whether or not to acquire a subsidiary that has the following cash flow in euros. There is no terminal value. You are given the basic data below, and the WACC in euros is 10%.

Year	0	1	2	3	4	5
Free-cash flows(€)	(50)	10	10.5	11.0	11.6	12.2
Present value(€)	(50.0)					
NPV(€)						
Spot exchange rate(£ / €)	0.71					
NPV(£)						

Discount foreign-currency cash flows to present at the euro discount rate, convert the NPV to the home currency, pounds sterling, at the spot exchange rate.

5.11 Offshore banking

You are the head of new accounts in Citybank, New York, when one fine afternoon Raúl, appears in your office with you bank's external re-lations officer in México. Raúl happens to have a big suitcase full of money, $100 million, and wishes to deposit the money in Citybank, NY, an Edge Act Bank.

    a. How much would Citybank stand to make annually on Raúl $100 million dollars transfer?

    b. Would you have to report the deposit? If so, to whom?

    c. Apart from reporting requirements, is it worth it to Citybank to take the deposit?

    d. Answer the above on the assumption that Raúl instead just wants to transfer the money to his account in Switzerland through Citybank, N.Y.

5.12　Optimal portfolio analysis

Consider the following utility function of an investor:

$$U = E(r_c) - \frac{A\sigma_c^2}{2} = E(r_c) - 2\sigma_c^2$$

Where $E(r_c)$ is the expected rate of return on her complete portfolio (composed of a risky asset and a risk-free asset), σ_c^2 is the variance (the squared standard deviation (volatility) of the complete portfolio), and A is the coefficient of risk aversion. Answer the following:

a. What is the coefficient of risk aversion, A, of this particular investor?

The expected return on the complete portfolio is given by:

$$E(r_c) = r_f + z(E(r_P) - r_f)$$
$$= 0.05 + z(0.15 - 0.05) = 0.05 + 0.1z$$

where z is the proportion of the complete portfolio held in the risky asset, which has an expected rate of return, $E(r_P)$, of 15%, while $(1 - z)$ is the percent held in the risk-free asset, US Treasuries. Treasuries bear a risk free rate, r_f, of 5%. Furthermore, the variance of the risky asset is given by $\sigma_P^2 = 0.1$ or ten percent.

b. Find the optimal proportion of assets held in the risky asset and the proportion held in the risk-free asset.

c. Compute the expected rate of return on the complete portfolio.

d. Compute the variance of the complete portfolio.

e. Compute the level of utility (happiness!) of this investor.

5.13　Optimal investment analysis

Consider the following data on a complete portfolio composed of 50% (that is $z = 0.5$) risky assets with $\sigma_P^2 = 0.4$ and $E(r_P) = 0.20$, The complete portfolio thus also has 50% risk free assets with certain return 5%, that is 0.05. Answer the following:

a. What is the expected rate of return on the complete portfolio?

b. What is the variance of the complete portfolio?

c. What is the standard deviation of the complete portfolio (its volatility)?

5.14　Double marginalization

A firm monopolizing a market would set marginal cost equal to marginal revenue to maximize its profits, as shown below.

Demonstrate the following proposition:

"If the firm sold instead to a downstream retailer at a transfer price above c, the retailer would charge a higher price, p_r, and sell a lower quantity, q_r, thereby reducing total profits."

This phenomenon is known as "double marginalization", providing an incentive for the upstream producer to acquire the downstream retailer, thereby maximizing profits. Coca-cola and Pepsi are both attempting to acquire their downstream bottlers.

5.15 Abusive transfer pricing

XYZ Hardware, Inc. New York incorporated a Foreign Sales Corporation (FSC) in Nassau, the Bahamas, a tax haven with no income taxes, to act as an invoicing center in its export operations. While the hammer is sent directly to Europe from New York, the FSC is billed for the export of the hammer, and it bills the European subsidiary for the import of the hammer. The invoice center has its own income statement from operations, and maintains working capital balances in Nassau.

XYZ, Inc. has a marginal cost of producing the hammer of $2, the price at which it "sells" it to the FSC. In turn, the FSC bills *XYZ, Europe* $5 for the hammer, the price at which it sells the hammer.

a. Indicate the profits, if any, booked by *XYZ, Inc.* at each of its locations:

    i. *XYZ, Inc. N.Y.*

    ii. *XYZ, Europe, S.A.*

    iii. *XYZ FSC*, Nassau

b. If the FSC repatriates the profits to the US and is in the 33.3% marginal income tax bracket, what is the amount of tax paid by *XYZ*, *Inc*, *N. Y.*?

c. If the FSC in Nassau keeps the profits there as working capital balances, what is the amount of tax paid by *XYZ*, *Inc*, *N. Y.*?

References and suggested reading

Abdallah, Wagdy (2004), *Critical Concerns in Transfer Pricing and Practice*, Westport, CN, Praeger.

Al-Eryani, Mohammed F., Pervaiz Alam, and Syed H. Akhter (1990), "Transfer Pricing Determinants of U. S. Multinationals," *Journal of International Business Studies*, 21(3): 409—425.

Adler, Michael (1974), "The Cost of Capital and Valuation of a Two-Country Firm," *Journal of Finance*, 29(1): 119—132.

Aliber, Robert Z. (1980), "The Integration of the Offshore and the Domestic Banking System," *Journal of Monetary Economics*, 6(4): 509—526.

Anderson, Ronald (2002), "Capital structure, firm liquidity, and growth," in *Firms' Investment and Finance Decision: Theory and Empirical Methodology*, Cheltenham, UK; Northhampton, MA: Edward Elgar.

Azzara, Thomas (2003), *Tax Havens of The World*, New Providence Press.

Bangs, David H. Jr. (1998), *The Business Plan*, Chicago: Upstart Publishing, Inc.

Barrett, M. Edgar (1977), "The Case of the Tangled Transfer Price," *Harvard Business Review*, 55(3): 20—36.

Bradshaw, Mark, Brian Bushee, and Gregory Miller (2004), "Accounting choice, home bias, and U. S. investment in non-U. S. firms," *Journal of Accounting Research*, 42(5): 795—841.

Cumming, Douglas (2005), "Capital Structure in Venture Finance," *Journal of Corporate Finance*, 11(3): 550—585.

Dixit, Avinash, Susan Skeath and David H. Reiley, Jr. (2009), *Games of Strategy*, 3rd edition, New York and London: W. W. Norton and Co.

Dye, Ronald and Sri Sridhar (2005), "Moral Hazard Severity and Contract Design," *RAND Journal of Economics*, 36(1): 78—92.

Eckbo, E. B. (1983), "Horizontal Mergers, Collusion and Stockholder Wealth," *Journal of Financial Economics*, 11(2): 241—276.

Eiteman, David K., Arthur I. Stonehill, and Michael H. Moffett (2000), "Principles of Multinational Taxation," in *Multinational Business Finance*, 10th ed., Reading MA: Addison-Wesley Publishing Company.

Emery, Douglas, R. , John D. Finnerty, and John D. Stove (1998), *Principles of Financial Management*, Upper Saddle River NJ: Prentice Hall.

Ganguin, Blaise (2005), *Fundamentals of Corporate Credit Analysis*, New York: McGraw-Hill.

Ghauri, Pervez and Peter Buckley (2003), "International Mergers and Acquisitions: Past, Present, and Future." in *Advances in Mergers and Acquisitions*, Volume 2, Amsterdam: Boston and Oxford Elsevier Science.

Grauer, Robert R. , and Nils Hakansson (1987), "Gains from International Diversification: 1968—1985 Returns on Portfolios of Stocks and Bonds," *Journal of Finance*, 42(3): 721—739.

Gup, Benton (2004), *Too Big to Fail: Policies and Practices in Government Bailouts*, Westport, CT: Praeger.

Harris, Milton and A. Raviv (1991), "The Theory of Capital Structure," *Journal of Finance*, 46 (1): 297—355.

Harvey, Campbell R. (1991), "The World Price of Covariance Risk," *Journal of Finance*, 66(1): 111—158.

Haugen, R. A. , and L. Senbet (1988), "Bankruptcy and Agency Costs: Their Significance to the Theory of Optimal Capital Structure," *Journal of Financial and Quantitative Analysis*, 2(3): 73—86.

Ioannou, Lori (1995), "Taxing Issues," *International Business*, 8(3): 44—45.

Isenbergh, Joseph (2002), *International Taxation: U. S. Taxation of Foreign persons and Foreign Income*, New York: Aspen Publishers.

Jensen, M. C. (1986), "Agency Costs of Free Cash Flow, Corporate Finance, and Takeovers," *American Economic Review*, 76(2):323—330.

Kane, Edward (1987), "Competitive Financial Re-regulations: An International Perspective," in *Threats to International Financial Stability*, R. Portes and A. Swoboda, eds. , London: Cambridge University Press.

Keen, Michael (2004), "Pareto-efficient international taxation." *American Economic Review*, 94(1): 259—275.

Levich, Richard M. (1990), "The Euromarkets After 1992," in *European Banking in the 1990s*, J. Dermine, ed. , Oxford: Basil Blackwell.

Lowengrub, Paul and Michael Melvin (2002), "Before and After International Cross-listing: an Intraday Examination of Volume and Volatility," *Journal of International Financial Markets, Institutions, and Money*, 12(2): 139—155.

Marino, Anthony and John Matsusaka, (2005), "Decision Processes, Agency Problems, and Information: An Economic Analysis of Capital Budgeting Procedures," *Review of Financial Studies*, 18(1): 301—325.

Markowitz, Harry (1952), "Portfolio Selection," *Journal of Finance*, 7 (1): 77—91.

Maroney, Neal, Naka Atsuyuki and Theresia Wansi (2004), "Changing Risk, Return, and Leverage: the 1997 Asian Financial Crisis," *Journal of Financial and Quantitative Analysis*, 39(1): 143—166.

Masson, Dubos, J. (1990), "Planning and Forecasting of Cash Flows for the Multinational Firm: International Cash Management," *Advances in Financial Planning and Forecasting*, 4(2): 195—222.

Meyers, S. C. (1976), "A Framework for Evaluating Mergers," in S. C. Meyers, ed., *Modern Developments in Financial Management*, New York: Praeger.

Miller, Merton (1977), "Debt and Taxes," *Journal of Finance*, 32(2): 261—275.

Modigliani, Franco, and Merton H. Miller (1958), "The Cost of Capital, Corporation Finance, and the Theory of Investment," *American Economic Review*, 48(3): 261—298.

Modigliani, Franco, and Merton H. Miller (1963), "Corporate Income Taxes and the Cost of Capital: A Correction," *American Economic Review*, 53 (3): 433—443.

Moffett, Michael H., and Arthur Stonehill (1989), "International Banking Facilities Revisited," *Journal of International Financial Management and Accounting*, 1(1): 88—103.

Mork, Randall, Andrei Schleifer, and Robert W. Vishney (1990), "Do Managerial Objectives Drive Bad Acquisitions," *Journal of Finance*, 45(1): 31—48.

OECD (2005), *E-commerce: Transfer Pricing and Business Profits Taxation*, Paris: Organization for Economic Cooperation & Development.

Ostro-Landau, Nilly (1995), "Avoiding the Global Tax Web," *International Business*, 8(9): 12.

Plasschaert, S. R. F. (1985), "Transfer Pricing Problems in Developing Countries," in *Multinationals and Transfer Pricing*, A. M. Rugman and L. Eden, eds., New York: St. Martins Press, 247—266.

Ross, Stephen A., Randolph W. Westerfield, and Jeffrey F. Jaffe (2005), *Corporate Finance*, 3rd ed. Irwin IL: McGraw-Hill, Chapters 15—16, 415—492.

Roll, Richard., and Stephen A. Ross (1984), "The Arbitrage Pricing Theory Approach to Strategic Portfolio Planning," *Financial Analysts Journal*, 40(3): 14—26.

Ross, Stephen A. (1974), "Return, Risk and Arbitrage," in Friend and

Bicksler, eds. , *Risk and Return in Finance*, New York: Heath Lexington.

Solnick Bruno, and B. Noetzlin (1982), " Optimal International Asset Allocation," *Journal of Portfolio Management*, 9(1):11—21.

Salvatore, Dominick (1996), *Managerial Economics in a Global Economy*, 3rd edition, New York: McGraw-Hill, Inc.

Sharpe, W. F. (1964), " Capital Asset Prices: A Theory of Market Equilibrium Under Risk," *Journal of Finance*, 19(3): 425—442.

Shirreff, David (2004), *Dealing with Financial Risk*, New York: Bloomberg Press.

Soenen, L. A. , and Raj Aggarwal (1987), " Corporate Foreign Exchange and Cash Management Practice," *Journal of Cash Management*, 7(2): 62—64.

Srinivsan, VenKat, and Yong H. Kim (1986), " Payments Netting in International Cash Management: A Network Optimization Approach," *Journal of International Business Studies*, 17(2): 1—20.

Stillman, R. (1983), " Examining Antitrust Policy toward Horizontal Mergers," *Journal of Financial Economics*, 11(2): 225—240.

Stultz, Rene M. (1995), "Globalization of Capital Markets and the Cost of Capital: the Case of Nestlé," *Journal of Applied Corporate Finance*, 8(3): 30—38.

Tobin, James (1958), " Liquidity Preference as Behavior Towards Risk," *Review of Economic Studies*, 26(1): 65—86.

Yunker, Penelope J. (1983), " A Survey of Subsidiary Autonomy, Performance Evaluation and Transfer Pricing in Multinational Corporations," *Columbia Journal of World Business*, 18(3): 51—64.

Yunker, Penelope J. (1982), *Transfer Pricing and Performance Evaluation in Multinational Corporations: A Survey Study*, New York: Praeger.

CHAPTER 6

International Financial Scams and Swindles

国际金融欺诈与骗局

Pyramids: an international perspective

Financial history is full of **Ponzi schemes**, where pyramids of investors invest in notes with no or scant underlying assets. The scheme Carlo Ponzi devised in 1919 is today called a "Ponzi Pyramid". In December, Mr. Ponzi initiated an investment scheme in Boston, establishing his business as The Security Exchange Company promising 50% interest in ninety days on his notes. The negotiable Ponzi note declared:

庞氏骗局（Ponzi schemes）：庞氏骗局将后一轮投资者的投资作为投资收益支付给前一轮的投资者，以此类推，使卷入的人和资金越来越多。当投资者和资金难以为继时，庞氏骗局便会骤然崩溃。

> **FYI**: The Ponzi Note
>
> The Securities Exchange Company, for and in consideration of the sum of exactly $1,000 of which receipt is hereby acknowledged, agrees to pay to the order of _____, upon presentation of this voucher at ninety days from date, the sum of exactly $1,500 at the company's office, 27 School Street, room 227, or at any bank. The Securities Exchange Company, Per Charles Ponzi.
>
> Source: Mark C. Knutson(1996).

Hundreds of initial investors purchased the Ponzi notes. At first, many were redeemed at maturity, some even before after 45 days, and many were rolled over. The word got out. New investors beat a path to his door, their cash permitting redemption of his first issues. He had a gimmick that attracted gullible investors, arguing that he could buy international postal reply coupons in Italy and then sell them to the US post office for five times what he paid. According to Ponzi, the arbitrage opportunity was due to misalignment of postal exchange rates. He claimed to cash in the stamps, thus profiting up to 400%. After fees, he could "plausibly" pay 50% quarterly yet keep about 200% in profits, so he said.

Indeed, he kept a few postal coupons on hand in his office to show to investors. With the money he collected from new "investors", he re-paid the first ones their principal plus the promised 50% return, a classic pyramid scheme with no underlying assets. Naturally, the first investors promoted the scheme by word of mouth. It rapidly mushroomed.

There is always one problem with Ponzi schemes: The last investors who are brought into the scheme ultimately find that there are not enough new investors since the flow of new investment must increase exponentially. The cash flow stops—leaving them holding worthless Ponzi notes. A run to redeem the notes takes place, forcing insolvency bankruptcy. Let's take a simple example of an initial investment in a 3 month Ponzi note of $1,000, which we will rollover in each period. The quarterly interest rate is 50%, equivalent to an annual rate of 406%. For the sake of argument, suppose we rollover the Ponzi note for two years, assuming the scheme has not collapsed by then. Table 6.1 illustrates the growth in the liabilities of the Ponzi scheme were the initial $1,000 rolled over every three months into new Ponzi notes.

Table 6.1   A Hypothetical Ponzi game with rollover at a quarterly rate of return of 50%

	Initial Investment $1,000	Principal	Interest
3 mos.	$1,500	$1,000	$500
6 mos.	$2,250	$1,500	$750
9 mos.	$3,375	$2,250	$1,125
12 mos.	$5,063	$3,375	$1,688
15 mos.	$7,594	$5,063	$2,531
18 mos.	$11,391	$7,594	$3,797
21 mos.	$17,086	$11,391	$5,695
24 mos.	$25,629	$17,086	$8,543

Within two years, Ponzi would be liable for $25,639 to repay both principal and interest on the initial $1000 investment. Since there is no underlying asset yielding a positive return, the rate of growth of new deposits would have to be over 400% a year, that is $[(1.5)^4 - 1]$, for Ponzi to be able to redeem his notes. New investments would have to more than quintuple yearly. For this reason, Ponzi schemes usually collapse within a year.

Bernie Madoff's Ponzi game lasted much longer—over 40 years—in part, because the promised rate of return was between 1 and 2 percent per month, between 12.7% and 26.8% per annum respectively. If the Madoff fund could grow at 25% per year, it could sustain such promised rates of return. His reputation grew over the years and he served as Chairman of the Board of the NASDAQ.

In the case of Carlo Ponzi, the cash flow was stopped after nine months by an investigation by the District Attorney of Boston, even though Ponzi had not defaulted on a single note. The scheme broke down in July 1920 when he was ordered not to take any new deposits, pending the results of the investigation. Consider a $1,000 Ponzi note investment bearing 50% in three months. If no more Ponzi investments were made, at the end of three months, Ponzi would pay $500 dollars in interest. At the end of six months, he would pay the remaining $500, thus being insolvent since he has no underlying investments. He would have to default on the initial note. Clearly, new investors are required at an increasing rate to pay interest and redemptions by previous investors.

In general, assuming a constant interest rate, r, **the no Ponzi game (NPG) condition** requires that debt not grow faster than the rate of interest on the debt, or:

$$\lim_{t \to \infty} D(t) e^{-rt} = 0 \qquad (6.1)$$

If debt is growing at a faster rate than the interest rate, interest is being paid by the new debt and the debt is not sustainable. If $D(t) = D_0 e^{gt}$, $\lim_{t \to \infty} D_0 e^{(g-r)t} = 0$ when $g < r$.

Why would so many people invest in a scheme that ultimately had to collapse? The reason seems to be that the early investors did see great returns on their money. Those in early on a speculative bubble gain by cashing out early. It was, however, the age-old pyramid scheme. Since investors had their notes redeemed until the investigation, not a single complaint had been filed.

On July 26, 1920, Ponzi's house of cards collapsed, The Boston District Attorney ordered Ponzi to suspend taking in new investments until an auditor examined his books. This was the death knoll to the Ponzi game since there were no underlying investments. The public continued to sup-

无 庞 氏 骗 局 条 件 (No Ponzi game (NPG) condition) :无庞氏骗局条件要求负债的增长率低于负债的利率。

port Ponzi until August 10, 1920, since he attempted to pay off an investor run from his cash deposits in banks. On August 10, the auditors, banks, and newspapers declared that Ponzi was bankrupt. A final audit of his books concluded that he had taken in enough funds to buy approximately 180,000,000 postal coupons, of which they could only confirm the purchase of two. On the witness stand in his trial, Ponzi discussed locations of various safety deposit boxes in the U.S., deposits overseas, and responded evasively to questions about his solvency. Miss Lucy Mell, his 18 year old assistant office manager, testified that she only had knowledge of transactions within the office, not of Ponzi's outside dealings. When asked if there were any postal reply coupons in the office, she replied "Yes, one or two for samples. " (http://www. mark-knutson. com) Ponzi's family reported that his attorneys were preparing a defense of "financial dementia. " At the trial, Charles Rittenhouse, an accountant employed by the receivers of Ponzi's estate, testified that $9,582,591 was invested in Ponzi's scheme reflecting notes with a face value of $14,374,755. When the business shut down, $4,263,652 of investments were outstanding, with a face value of $6,396,353.

Imposing a maximum five year sentence for a mail fraud count, Judge Hale added these words: "The defendant conceived a scheme which on his counsel's admission did defraud men and women. It will not do to have the public, the world, understand that such a scheme as his through the United States' instrumentality could be carried out without substantial punishment. " The same issue of "substantial punishment" arises in the cases of Enron, Parmalat, Vivendi, BCCI, Barings, WorldCom, and Tyco, to name some of more recent financial abuses. After three and a half years in prison, Ponzi was sentenced to an additional seven to nine years by Massachusetts's authorities. He was released on $14,000 bond pending an appeal. He turned up in Jacksonville, Florida under the assumed name of Charles Borelli and immediately launched a pyramid land scheme. He purchased land at $16 an acre, subdividing it into twenty-three lots, and sold each lot at $10 apiece. Ponzi promised investors that their initial $10 investment would translate into millions of dollars in just two years. Much of the land was underwater and worthless, marsh or swamp land. The land boom in Florida was petering out, too late to rescue Ponzi. In February 1926 the Duval County Grand Jury returned a four count indictment against Ponzi and his *Charpon*, *Florida Land Syndicate*. He was charged with violating Florida regulations for conducting business as a trust, offering securities for sale without filing a declaration of trust, selling units of indebtedness without a permit from the State Controller, and doing real-estate business without paying a $150 license fee. Once again, he jumped bail on June 3, 1926 and ran to Texas. He was captured on June 28th in a New Orleans and sent back to Boston to complete his jail term. After seven years, Ponzi was released on good behavior and deported to Italy on October 7, 1934. Back in Rome, Benito Mussolini offered him a position with Italy's new national airline. He served as the Rio de Janeiro branch manager from 1939—1942. The airline failed during WWII and Ponzi was unemployed. He passed away January 15, 1949 in a Rio de Janeiro charity ward at the age of 67. (Source: http://www. mark-knutson. com)

Parmalat(a multi-national Italian dairy and food corporation)

Parmalat, though having underlying assets and operations, ultimately sought Ponzi finance. As Gianfranco Tabasso of the EACT Payment Commission poignantly remarks: "In situations like Parmalat, it is evident how critically important they (treasurers and CFOs) are in detecting and perpetrating frauds. A serious corporate fraud cannot be carried out without the connivance of the treasurer and the CFO. Put another way, the treasurer and the CFO are more important than internal audit and accounting, in the detection of possible frauds, even when perpetrators are CEOs, board members, or other top brass. " (op. cit. , 25)

What really defines a Ponzi scheme? Gianfranco Tabasso of the EACT Payment Commission notes: "This is the second time in a hundred years that a Parmesan has cheated American investors. In the early 1920s, Carlo Ponzi did it in Boston with the ' postal coupon scheme' and became so famous that Ponzi Games and Ponzi Finance are in all university textbooks and Ponzi has his own dedicated web site http://www. mark-knutson. com. Carlo Ponzi's was a pure high-risk financial scheme with no underlying assets. Parmalat is a dairy and food company, with real assets, which produces and sells real goods, in a sector traditionally considered low risk. Carlo Ponzi operated his scheme alone from a central office of two rooms attended by twelve clerks. Parmalat is a multibillion dollar multinational listed on the Milan Stock Exchange which has over 250 companies around the world; its boss, Calisto Tanzi, has had lots of interested helpers, bankers, auditors, family, managers, tax and legal professionals, and consultants. Carlo Ponzi's swindle lasted nine months before it was discovered: Parmalat's went on for more than ten years, an unbelievable length of time in a world where listed companies are subject to corporate governance, reporting, anti-money laundering regulations, market abuse legislation, auditing, external regulations and rating companies. Banks place bonds on the market and earn commission, corporations collect the money and don't have to find new shareholders and answer embarrassing questions. Only investors, who lay out capital but remain far away from the game, are at risk." (*op. cit.*, pp. 21—22) But serious problems started right after the Parmalat stock listing, so Tonna (Parmalat's CFO who ran Parmalat Finanziaria, the holding company) created a network of financial companies, all based in fiscal paradises—tax havens. They would be used to issue bonds, channel funds back and forth, create firewalls and, last but not least, concoct fake balance sheets to shore up the consolidated balance sheet and sell nearly EUR 8 billion of new Parmalat bonds.

Parmalat started in 1962 when Calisto Tanzi inherited a small ham factory from his father near Parma. At 22, he opened a pasteurization plant selling milk for the first time in Tetrapack triangular cartons. The milk cartons were a success: sales grew rapidly from EUR 100,000 in 1962 to 50 million in 1970. It was declared insolvent in December 2003, with Enrico Bondi replacing Calisto Tanzi and later becoming official liquidator. There were: "Public attorneys pursuing various kinds of crimes and misdemeanors, from money laundering to collusion in fraud, false communication to markets, insider trading, market abuse, obstruction of justice etc. It appears almost all the money went to cover operating losses, particularly in South America, but ... some of it was diverted to the family's private businesses and to the personal accounts of family members, top managers and various professionals who were privy to and participated in the Parmalat fraud." (*op. cit.*, 23)

庞 氏 融 资 (Ponzi finance):在一个经营单位的利息支付超过其营业所得的现金流时,运用发行新债的办法来偿还旧债的一种金融活动。

"**Ponzi finance**" is defined by Charles Kindleberger (1989) "as a type of financial activity engaged in when interest charges of a business unit exceeds cash flows from operations ... with the repayment of debt with the issuance of new debt."

Clearly, an unintentionally unsuccessful operation could have negative cash flow and thus not be able to pay interest charges. To constitute the payment of old debt from the issue of new debt must be present. This was an aspect common to both the Ponzi game and the Parmalat fraud, though the latter had real operations. WorldCom executives were also involved in borrowing to repurchase stock, but were subject to margin calls they ultimately could not meet. Stocks in WorldCom were collateral for the debt, but triggered the margin calls when they lost value.

Lest we think that Ponzi schemes are a thing of the past, "Investors ... had allocated at least $115 million to Mr. Wright's hedge-fund firm, International Management Associates LLC. Over the prior seven years, which included the worst bear market since the Great Depression, Mr. Wright had reported average annual returns of more than 27%. ... The Securities and Exchange Commission and International Management investors filed separate lawsuits against Mr. Wright, accusing him of fraud. The SEC estimates that Mr. Wright, who handled International Management's investments, managed somewhere between $115 million and $185 million of client money. After more than two weeks of searching, the hedge fund's court-appointed receiver and the SEC have found only about $150,000 of it ... in two Ameritrade accounts." Kirk S. Wright, an African American, "... may have taken advantage of the city's black professionals," including "... successful black professionals from Atlanta, and former football players" from the Denver Broncos and the Tennessee Titans American football teams (*The Wall Street Journal*, March 9, 2006: A1, A12). Two Atlanta anesthesiologists turned hedge-fund partners claim they were also duped out of $1.5 million by Wright. They and others were recruited for the aggressive marketing of the hedge fund, which seems not to have had any underlying investments. "In 2004, it hired Thomas H. Birk, a Los Angeles-based salesman who had previously raised money for several major brokerage firms. Mr. Birk, who is white, would troll Western golf courses talking up Mr. Wright's investment record. ... Mr. Birk eventually raised more than $10 million." (*op. cit.*, A12) "Mr. Wright is missing," although his lawyer says that "he speaks to him regularly on the phone. ... Regulators believe that virtually all the assets of the funds have been dissipated. Mr. Wright's older brother ... has urged his brother to turn himself in." (*op. cit.*, A12) Carlo Ponzi must be smiling from his grave in Brazil.

The Bernie Madoff Ponzi Game

The Madoff Ponzi game is remarkable both in terms of its longevity and its shrewdness. The scheme began as *Bernard L. Madoff Investment Securities LLC*, founded in 1960, and came to a dramatic end during the 2008 financial crisis. Bernie Madoff reportedly told his sons on December

10, 2008 that he was struggling to meet $7 billion in redemption requests and that his hedge fund was "One big lie, a giant Ponzi game". Mark and Andrew turned their father in on December 11, 2008, when Bernie was arrested by the FBI. He is now serving a federal prison sentence of 150 years in North Carolina. Trustee Irving Picard, the lawyer in charge of recovering assets for Madoff's investors, is aggressively trying to "claw back" monies from those who exited early with profits or who served as "feeder" funds to the Madoff scheme. One of his sons, Mark, committed suicide in December 2010. Bernie Madoff's lavish lifestyle has come to a humbling end, leaving his family and reputation in tatters.

The Securities and Exchange Commission is, in principle, charged with uncovering securities fraud to protect investors. In 1999, Harry Markopolos, a financial analyst, was asked by a managing partner at *Rampart*, Dave Fraley, to design a financial product that would, like Madoff's, consistently deliver net returns of 1—2 percent a month. Markopolos later said that he knew within five minutes that Madoff's numbers didn't add up—always rising in a volatile market. It took him another four hours to prove that the reported returns could have only been obtained through fraud, in particular, a Ponzi game. In 1999, Harry Markopolos informed the U. S. Securities and Exchange Commission (SEC) that he believed it was legally and mathematically impossible to achieve the gains that Madoff claimed. He also filed a formal complaint with the Boston office of the SEC in the spring of 2000. Markopolos then sent a more detailed submission to the SEC a year later. Finally, Markopolos sent a 21-page memo in November 2005 to SEC regulators, entitled "The World's Largest Hedge Fund is a Fraud." It outlined 30 red flags that alleged Madoff's returns could not possibly be legitimate. Markopolos reported to the branch chief of the SEC's New York office, to whom he gave his 21-page report, claiming that Madoff was paying off old investors with money from new investors. However, the SEC's New York chief approved an internal memo in November, 2007 to close an SEC investigation of Madoff without bringing any claim. The SEC did nothing until Madoff turned himself in to the FBI, despite ten years of warnings by Markopolos. George Stigler, Nobel Laureate in 1982, was right: the regulators are "captured" by those they regulate!

Two back officers in Madoff's operation created false trading reports to support the returns claimed to each customer, including an initial false trade and the fictitious closing trade to fit the client's statement. Trades were backdated and account statements manipulated.

In his March 2009 guilty plea, Madoff admitted that his scheme was to deposit client money into a Chase account, rather than invest it. When clients wanted to redeem their money, "I used the money in the Chase Manhattan bank account ... to pay the requested funds." In the meantime, he purchased many homes, a boat, a watch collection and nice cars.

Size of loss to investors

About $36 billion was invested into the Madoff scam, returning $18 billion to investors, with $18 billion missing. Half of Madoff's investors earned more than their investment. The withdrawal amounts in the final six years were subject to "clawback" or return of money lawsuits filed by trustee Irving Picard. Of the total amount, Picard said that the total amounts owed to customers were $57 billion, of which $17.3 billion was actually invested by the customers, $7.6 billion has been recovered, but pending lawsuits, only $2.6 billion would be available to repay victims. If all the recovered funds are returned to those who lost, their net loss would be just under $10 billion. The US Internal Revenue Service ruled that investors' capital loss in this and other fraudulent investment schemes can be treated as a business loss for tax purposes. This will allow the victims to claim them as net operating losses, to reduce their tax liability if they have income tax liabilities otherwise.

Affinity fraud

Madoff was a prominent philanthropist, who served on boards of non-profit institutions—many of which entrusted his firm with their endowments. The collapse and freeze of his personal and business assets, and those of his firm pushed charitable foundations into bankruptcy, such as the *Chais Family Foundation*, the *Robert I. Lappin Charitable Foundation*, the *Picower Foundation*, and the *JEHT Foundation*. Sheryl Weinsteim, former chief financial officer of *Hadassah*, called Madoff a "beast" at his sentencing hearing.

According to the *New York Post*, Madoff "worked the so-called 'Jewish circuit' of well-heeled Jews he met at country clubs on Long Island and in Palm Beach." In this type of affinity fraud—taking advantage of your own ethnic, religious, or related group members—he also defrauded institutions such as *Yeshiva University*, *Kehilath Jeshurun Synagogue*, the *Maimonides School*, *Ramaz* and the *SAR Academy*.

同族诈骗（Affinity fraud）：同族诈骗往往针对具有相同种族、相同宗教信仰或其他相同背景的人。

Ponzi games are like mushrooms after the heavy rains, they just pop up miraculously. While the SEC has now begun to scrutinize them more vigorously, Ponzi games are part of the fabric of humankind, offering quick riches to aspiring "Madoffs" that prey upon gullible investors.

In his testimony to the U. S. congress, Markopoulus said: "My experiences with other SEC officials proved to be a systemic disappointment and led me to conclude that the SEC securities' lawyers, if only through their investigative ineptitude and financial illiteracy, colluded to maintain large frauds such as the one to which Madoff later confessed." Furthermore, "Government has coddled, accepted, and ignored White-collar crime for too long," he testified to congress. "It is time the nation woke up and realized that it's not the armed robbers or drug dealers who cause the most economic harm, it's the white collar criminals living in the most expensive homes who have the most impressive resumes who harm us the most. They steal our pensions, bankrupt our companies, and destroy thousands of jobs, ruining countless lives."

Madoff's scheme stands out in its longevity. At its inception, Madoff may have developed a trading platform that was developed further by the NASDAQ. Surely, by not promising exorbitant returns, the rate at which he needed to recruit new money was not nearly so high as in Carlo Ponzi's case. A one percent monthly rate of return would yield 12.8% per annum, one and one half percent an annual yield of 19.6%, while a two percent monthly rate yields 26.8% per annum. By keeping returns below 2% and increasing new investor's monies by 25% per year, Madoff could satisfy redemptions without any underlying investment. During the 2008 financial crisis, redemption requests rose significantly at all hedge funds, revealing Madoff's scheme and putting him into bankruptcy and jail.

Other Affinity Ponzi games

Affinity frauds can target any group of people who take pride in their shared characteristics, whether they are religious, ethnic, or professional.

The "gimmick": Ponzi games typically have a gimmick that tricks gullible investors who are unable or unwilling to do due diligence. Here are some stories they tell potential investors:

Ponzi supposedly arbitraged Italian international reply postage coupons, realizing over 400% profits since the exchange rate was misaligned.

Scott Rothstein, a Fort Lauderdale lawyer, sold fictitious structured legal settlements that promised the holder a stream of cash flow from the structured settlement. He is currently serving a 50-year prison sentence.

Neil Shapiro, Miami, fraudulently claimed to arbitrage food and commodities in bulk, buying low and selling high in different regions of the United States. He is currently serving a 20 year sentence.

The MMM corporation of Russia promised high returns on their investments, much like Ponzi, only to go bankrupt, leaving thousands of investors holding worthless notes.

Consolidated General, Inc. sent you beads to braid into jewelry which they would buy back if you didn't sell them at a good price.

A nationwide scheme primarily targeted African-American churches and raised at least $3 million from over 1,000 churches, believing they would receive large sums of money from the investments—between 7% and 30% annually, building projects in the US.

Corporate governance failures

Adam Smith made an interesting observation concerning **the principal-agent problem**:

委托—代理问题 (Principal-agent problem): 因为委托人和代理人的目标不一致和信息不对称而导致的委托人利益受损的情况。

Applying the Concept: Adam Smith on the principal-agent problem

---

The directors of such (joint stock) companies, however, being the managers rather of other people's money than of their own, it cannot well be expected that they should watch over it with the same anxious vigilance with which the partners in a private copartnery frequently watch over their own. Like the stewards of a rich man, they are apt to consider attention to small matters as not for their master's honour, and very easily give themselves a dispensation from having it. Negligence and profusion, therefore, must always prevail, more or less, in the management of the affairs of such a company.

Adam Smith (1776), *An Inquiry into the Nature and Causes of the Wealth of Nations*, Ch. 1, "Of the Expences of the Sovereign or Commonwealth": 107.

It is appropriate to begin discussion of corporate governance failures with Smith's perceptive observation.

United Air Lines

Unsecured creditors and executives at the United Airlines Corporation agreed to a deal in which 400 executives will be awarded 10 million shares, 8% of the number to be issued in total upon emergence from bankruptcy. UAL stakeholders, including employees have on the other hand been asked to make great sacrifices, for example to their pension plan. Elizabeth Warren, Professor at Harvard Law School said on January 12, 2005: "Chapter 11 was traditionally about sharing the pain, but now it is more a game of feast and famine—starving the shareholders and creditors while the management team grows fat on big salaries." Annual salaries for the top eight UAL executives will total $3.5 million when UAL exits bankruptcy, rounded up by target bonuses equal from 55 to 100 percent of salary, depending on the executive. There are also $1.39 million in retention bonuses earmarked for seven top executives. Ms. Warren continues: "The lawyers and management team are running the show. Shareholders are out of the picture and creditors are often unsure about the overall financial stability of the company. That is a perfect set of circumstances for the management to extract much higher compensation than they would get if other people were competing for those management jobs." As Ms. Morgenstern, the *New York Times* journalist put it: "Got your airsickness bag handy?" (Source: Gretchen Morgenstern, "Gee, Bankruptcy Never Looked so Good," *The New York Times*, January 15, 2006: sec. 3, 3—4.) Let's now look back on corporate scandals. Keep your airsickness bag handy.

Enron

安然公司（Enron）于 2001 年 12 月 2 日正式破产,这是美国当时最大的一宗商业破产案。

Enron filed for bankruptcy on December 2, 2001. Its accountant, Arthur Andersen, LLP, went bankrupt. Enron is a story of one of the largest business failures of its time in the United States. To call it a failure of governance would be an understatement. The story has many facets:

1. Fraudulent accounting which escaped taxes, booked loans as profits and estimates of future profits as current income from deals, and moved losses off the books, recording them as operational profits.

2. The creation of the Raptors, four private investment partners, was managed by Andrew Fastow, the CFO of Enron, a clear conflict of interest. These partnerships drained profits from Enron and moved losses off the Enron books. The partnerships were an accounting trick to appear to book

profits as a hedge. However, they were funded by Enron shares, so did not provide the insurance of a hedge.

3. The large scale shredding and forging of documents, and deletion of e-mails that might compromise Enron in a SEC investigation.

4. Insider trading with the early selling of shares for "estate planning" by CEO Jeffrey K. Skilling, who was indeed found guilty of insider trading.

5. The misleading of employees and investors as to the true financial condition of Enron.

6. The "locking in" or freezing of the employees' right to sell Enron shares from their pensions in an effort to keep its price from falling further.

7. The payments of large bonuses to executives based on improper accounting reports of earnings.

In May 2006, Kenneth Lay, Enron Chairman, was found guilty of one count of conspiracy, two counts of wire fraud, and three counts of securities fraud. CEO Jeffrey Skilling was found guilty of one count of conspiracy, twelve counts of securities fraud, five counts of falsifying business records, and one count of insider trading. Appeals are in process.

Accounting and legal firms knowingly approved illegal accounting and business practices, including conflict of interest partnerships, the Raptors in particular. David D. Duncan, head of the Andersen audit team went along with the deals provided that Enron's board of directors approve them. (Source: "Concerns Grow Amid Conflicts Officials Seek to Limit Probe, Fallout of Deals" by Peter Behr and April Witt , *Washington Post*, July 30, 2002: A01.)

In 2000, Enron was burning cash at a rate of $700 million a year. It is difficult to sustain negative cash flow at this rate. It declared bankruptcy in December 2001. In the end, "Lay was never able to clearly explain how the (Raptor) partnerships worked or why anyone shouldn't assume the worst, namely that they were set up to hide Enron's problems, inflate earnings, and personally benefit the executives who managed them." (*Business Week*) When the Raptor's losses and accounting errors (for example a $1.2 billion equity loss) came to light, Enron's shares sank. In a Hyatt ballroom filled with several thousand Enron employees, Kenneth Lay is quoted: "Let me say right up front, I am absolutely heartbroken about what's happened. Many of you were a lot wealthier six to nine months ago, are now concerned about the college education for your kids, maybe the mortgage on your house, maybe your retirement, and for that I am incredibly sorry. But we are going to get it back. " (Source: "Losses, Conflicts Threaten Survival CFO Fastow Ousted in Probe of Profits", by April Witt and Peter Behr, *Washington Post*, July 31, 2002: A01.) The same day, Lay is reported to have taken a $4 million cash advance from the company. Over the next three days, he withdrew an additional $19 million. He immediately repaid $6 million of the amount by transferring his Enron stock to the company. That allowed him to sell stock but avoid an immediate reporting requirement. (*The Washington Post*, *op. cit.*)

In a last ditch effort to save Enron, Lay attempted to sell the company to Dynergy, Inc. , a smaller Houston based company. Enron misled Dynegy before their proposed merger, saying that its European trading operations had a $53 million operating profit in the previous quarter. In its disclosure, Enron reported that its European operations had actually incurred a $21 million loss. Chuck Watson, the founder and CEO of Dynergy was surprised by the debt disclosure, which he called a " $690 million bullet in the head," killing the merger deal.

Ex-Enron Chairman and CEO Kenneth Lay surrendered to FBI authorities July 8, 2004 after being indicted in the government's crackdown on corporate scandals. On May 25, 2006 a federal jury found Lay and Skilling guilty of conspiracy, wire and securities fraud, and Skilling one count of insider trading in connection with Enron's 2001 collapse. (*The Washington Post*, May 25, 2006) Lay has since passed away, not serving any time in jail. Skilling is serving time, but appealing his guilty verdict.

Enron's Chapter 11 business re-organization plan received court approval in 2004. The July 15, 2004 Enron press release stated: "At the conclusion of the claims reconciliation process, the allowable claims against the company are expected to be approximately $63 billion, Cooper (Stephen F. Cooper, Enron's acting CEO and chief restructuring officer) said. The cash and equity assets available for ultimate distribution are expected to be around $12 billion, he added, not including recoveries from litigation. " (Source: www. enron. com) Enron was just the first chapter in what was to prove to be a series of corporate scandals of huge proportions.

WorldCom

In July 2005, Bernard J. Ebbers, former CEO of the telecommunications company, WorldCom, was sentenced to 25 years in prison for conspiracy to commit securities fraud, and false filing of 10Q and 10K income statements with the SEC. In the 31 page indictment, US Attorney David

N. Kelley charged: "Rather than disclose WorldCom's true operating performance and financial condition, in or about April 2002, Ebbers and Sullivan instructed subordinates, in substance and in part, to falsely and fraudulently book certain entries in WorldCom's general ledger, which were designed to increase artificially WorldCom's reported revenue and to decrease artificially WorldCom's reported expenses, resulting in, among other things, artificially inflated figures for WorldCom's EPS, EBITDA, and revenue growth rate. These adjustments included (a) the improper capitalization of line cost expenses, and (b) increases to revenue, which in light of their departure from prior revenue recognition policies, and in light of their aggregate amount, made WorldCom's reported revenue materially misleading. Ebbers and Sullivan instructed others to make these adjustments solely in an effort to report results that would satisfy analysts' expectations, even though Ebbers and Sullivan knew that WorldCom's true results in fact failed to meet those expectations." (US Attorney David N. Kelley, UNITED STATES DISTRICT COURT NY, USA v. BERNARD J. EBBERS, Defendant. INDICTMENT S3 02 Cr. 1144: 15.)

WorldCom's CFO, Scott Sullivan received a 5 year sentence, significantly lighter for providing evidence and testifying against Bernard Ebbers. The jury found that Ebbers and Sullivan intentionally defrauded shareholders that owned the company, resulting in the biggest bankruptcy in American history, much larger than the Enron bankruptcy. Accounting fraud was at the center of the stage in the WorldCom bankruptcy, fraudulently reporting high revenues and low costs. Their favorite technique seemed to be moving operation expenses to capital expenditures so as not to be reflected as operating costs, but rather as capital investments.

Adelphia

Adelphia's founder, John Rigas, and his son Timothy, the cable company's former CFO, got 15 years and 20 years in prison sentences, respectively, for their role in fraud that led to the collapse of the US's largest cable companies. Prosecutors accused them of conspiring to hide $2.3 billion in Adelphia debt, stealing $100 million, and lying to investors about the company's financial condition.

Tyco International, Inc. , a Bermuda company

In September 2002, the SEC indicted former Tyco International, Ltd. , executives CEO Dennis Kozlowski, CFO Mark Schwartz, and General Counsel Mark Belnick on charges of civil fraud, theft, tax evasion, and not filing insider sales of the company's stock, as required by the SEC. (www.tycofraudinfocenter.com) They are accused of giving themselves interest-free or low interest loans for personal purchases of property, jewelry, and other items, which were neither approved by directors nor repaid to the company. Loan forgiveness of $37.5 million did not appear on Kozlowski's or Schwartz's income returns for 1999. Kozlowski and Schwartz are also accused of issuing bonuses to themselves and others without the approval of Tyco's board of directors. It is alleged that these bonuses acted as de facto loan forgiveness for employees who had borrowed company money. They are also being indicted on charges of selling company stock without reporting their insider sales, fraud, and making fraudulent statements. All in all, Kozlowski and Schwartz were accused by the SEC of "looting" Tyco of $600 million. Both Kozlowski and Schwartz were found guilty in June 2005. On September 19, 2005, New York Justice Obus ordered Mr. Kozlowski to repay $97 million to Tyco International, Inc., and an additional $70 million in fines. Mr. Swartz was ordered to pay $38 million to Tyco, and $35 million in fines. In addition, they have been sentenced to serve between 7 to 25 years in prison. Under New York State law, each will have to serve at least six years, 11 months and nine days before being eligible for parole. Both plan to appeal. (*Wall Street Journal*, September 20, 2005: C1.) They are also liable for civil suits.

Hollinger International

A special committee of the publishing company, Hollinger International Inc., concluded in a report that Sir Conrad M. Black and F. David Radler ran a "corporate kleptocracy," diverting to themselves the company's entire earnings of $400 million over seven years. It also ordered certain directors, particularly Richard N. Perle, to return $5.4 million in pay for "putting his own interests above those of Hollinger's shareholders." It criticizes the payment of $226 million to Ravelston for management fees from 1996 to 2003—a company controlled by Sir Black that, in turn, essentially owned 68% of the voting shares of Hollinger. Mr. Perle is singled out for "flagrant abdication of duty" in signing bonuses and loans to Sir Black at the expense of shareholders. He is also said to have earned a bonus of $3.1 million from Hollinger Digital, his project, even though it lost $49 million. In the report's terms "It is hard to imagine a more flagrant abdication of duty than a director rubberstamping transactions that directly benefit a controlling shareholder without any thought, comprehension, or analysis. In fact, many of the consents that Perle signed as an executive committee member approved related-party transactions that unfairly benefited Black ... and cost Hollinger millions ...." (*New York Times*, September 1, 2004: C6).

Countrywide Financial

Angelo Mozilo, former chief executive of subprime lender Countrywide Financial Corp., paid $67.5 million in 2010 to settle civil fraud charges filed by the SEC. He didn't admit or deny wrongdoing. Countrywide was purchased by Bank of America Corp. in July 2008. Since then, BOA has been subjected to costly litigation on claims of fraudulent lending by Countrywide Financial. BOA's share, ticker symbol BAC, are worth $5.27 on December 28, 2011, while it was worth $33.61 at the close July 30, 2008, representing an 83% fall since the purchase of Countrywide. In a program at Countrywide known internally as "Friends of Angelo," mortgage loans were purportedly made on favorable terms to politicians and congressmen who could influence legislation and regulation in Countrywide's favor.

Olympus, Japan

The Olympus accounting practice known as "tobashi," was used for "hiding bad loans" or "selling or divesting unwanted stocks." By selling loss-making assets or loans to dummy companies in a *tobashi deal*, losses can be shifted off Olympus financial statements. In 2008, Olympus bought Gyrus for $1.9 billion. Under the transaction, a financial adviser based in the Cayman Islands received a payout of $687 million—more than a third of the purchase price. Olympus also bought three small Japanese companies for a total of ¥73.49 billion ($940.1 million) from 2006 to 2008 that had little or no operational revenue. A year later, the company wrote down their value by nearly $700 million. Olympus admits to hiding losses. (*Wall Street Journal*, November 8, 2011)

The Sarbanes-Oxley Act of 2002

The recent scandals in corporate governance spawned new legislation—the U.S. Sarbanes-Oxley Act of 2002. Many companies are com-

2002 年《萨班斯-奥克斯利法案》(The Sarbanes-Oxley Act of 2002): 根据安然(Enron)、世界通讯(Worldcom)等财务欺诈事件所暴露出的公司和证券监管问题,美国立法机构于 2002 年制定了《萨班斯-奥克斯利法案》作为监管法规。

plaining about the higher than expected cost of compliance with "SOX" or "Sarbox", as the Act is commonly known. The Act addresses most major issues in corporate governance and disclosure, and has the following main titles:

Title I: Public Company Accounting Oversight Board which establishes an independent accounting oversight board with whom public accounting firms, including foreign ones that prepare audits, must register for inspection.

Title II: Auditor Independence prohibits a public accounting firm from providing non-audit services to its client, in particular:

(1) bookkeeping or other services related to the accounting records or financial statements of the audit client;

(2) financial information systems design and implementation;

(3) appraisal or valuation services, fairness opinions, or contribution-in-kind reports;

(4) actuarial services;

(5) internal audit outsourcing services;

(6) management functions or human resources;

(7) broker or dealer, investment adviser, or investment banking services;

(8) legal services and expert services unrelated to the audit; and

(9) any other service that the Board determines, by regulation, is impermissible.

(H. R. 3763-28 Sarbanes-Oxley Act of 2002, Sec. 201)

Title III: Corporate Responsibility requires that CEOs and CFOs certify in annual or quarterly reports that:

(1) the signing officer has reviewed the report;

(2) based on the officer's knowledge, the report does not contain any untrue statement of a material fact or omit to state a material fact . . .

(3) based on such officer's knowledge, the financial statements, and other financial information included in the report, fairly represents in all material respects the financial condition and results of operations of the issuer as of, and for, the periods represented in the report;"

(H. R. 3763-28 Sarbanes-Oxley Act of 2002, Sec. 302)

It also provides for forfeiture of bonuses and profits as a result of misreporting (Sec. 304), prohibits insider trades during pension fund blackout periods when the firm suspends the right of more than a majority of participants of pension plans from selling their shares in the company (Sec.

306), and provides for "disgorgement" or fair funds for investors whose rights are violated (Sec. 308).

Title IV: Enhanced Financial Disclosures requiring accurate compliance with GAAP principles (Sec. 401), disclosure of material off-balance sheet transactions, arrangements and obligations (Sec. 401), prohibits personal loans to executives (Sec. 402), requires greater disclosure of equity transactions involving management and principal stockholders (Sec. 403), establishes a code of ethics for senior financial officers (Sec. 406), and requires real time issuer disclosures of material changes in the financial condition or operations of the issuer (Sec. 409).

Title V: Analyst Conflicts of Interest requiring disclosure of:

(1) the extent to which the securities analyst has debt or equity investments in the issuer that is the subject of the appearance or research report;

(2) whether any compensation has been received by the registered broker or dealer .. from the issuer that is the subject of the appearance of research report ...

(3) whether an issuer, the securities of which are recommended in the appearance or research report is, or during the 1-year period preceding the date of appearance or date of distribution of the report has been, a client of the registered broker or dealer, and if so, stating the types of services provided to the issuer.

(H.R.3763-28 Sarbanes-Oxley Act of 2002, Sec.15D)

Title VI: Commission Resources and Authority which appropriates monies for the Commission and its activities.

Title VII: Studies and Reports commissions the study of public accounting firms with the view of increasing competition by studying the factors that have led to industry consolidation (Sec. 701), the study of the role and function of the credit rating agencies in the evaluation of issuers of securities with a view to identifying conflicts of interest (Sec. 702), a report on the number of securities professions who have violated securities laws, which laws were violated, and what punishments, if any, were meted out (Sec. 703). Sec. 704 mandates a report on enforcement actions, while Sec. 705 requires a study "... on whether investment banks and financial advisers assisted public companies in manipulating their earnings and obfuscating their true financial condition."

Title VIII: Corporate and Criminal Fraud Accountability provides for criminal penalties for the destruction, alteration, or falsification of records in Federal investigations and bankruptcy (Par. 1519) and extends the statute of limitations for securities fraud from 2 to 5 years after the violation (Sec. 804).

Title IX: White-Collar Crime Penalty Enhancements raises from 5 to 20 years the possible punishments for mail and wire fraud (Sec. 903) and raises the monetary penalties from $5,000 to $100,000 in one case, and from $100,000 to $500,000 in another, and criminal penalties from one year to ten years for violations of the employee retirement income security act of 1974 (Sec. 904). Sec. 906 establishes corporate responsibility for financial reports, providing criminal penalties of up to $1,000,000 or 10 years in prison or both, for certifying a fraudulent report, and up to $5,000,000 or 20 years in prison or both for a corporate officer who "willfully certifies" a fraudulent statement that misrepresents the financial conditions and result of operations of the issuer (Par. 1350).

Title X: Corporate Tax Returns requires that the Federal income tax return of a corporation be signed by the chief executive officer.

Title XI: Corporate Fraud and Accountability proscribes the tampering with the records or impedes the carrying out of an investigation (Sec. 1102), increases criminal penalties of the SEC act of 1934 substantially, up to 10 or 20 years, as well as up to $5 million or $25 million, depending on the violation (Sec. 1106). Finally, it provides for criminal penalties up to 10 years and similar fines for retaliating against an employee who provides information on the company to any law enforcement officer (Sec. 1107). It is appropriately entitled "Retaliation Against Informants."

To sum up, the Sarbanes-Oxley Act of 2002 means business and severe penalties for knowingly committing securities fraud or false accounting. It also means significantly increased costs of compliance. One prominent accountant gave insight on remedies to fraud and SOX. "If you devote attention to safeguards for minimizing the immense risks of fraud that have happened all too frequently in the last five years especially, my sense of the key preventatives are:

1. The risks of financial ruin and long jail terms to perpetrators such as Ebbers. (If justice were quicker and harder, we wouldn't have needed SOX, though CEO certifications required by SOX are a positive reminder of the CEO's responsibilities.)

2. Independent, competent boards such as SOX supports.

3. A strong SEC-type body, perhaps international in scope, to regulate public companies.

4. More standardizing accounting rules for the various industries, enabling apples-to-apples comparisons.

5. More principles-based accounting; today there are in the US too many rules and not enough judgment, even on such issues as revenue recognition.

6. SOX rules on auditor independence, including a cooling off period for hiring top level people from the audit firm, are a big step in the right direction." (David Lieberman, CFO, University of Miami)

Other financial abuses

Retention bonuses are payments that a firm may pay to retain an employee. In principle, the firm should determine the unusually high or unique qualifications of the employee that makes it essential to retain an employee. Clearly, retention bonuses may have the opposite effect. For instance, if an employee is to be awarded a million dollars at the end of the year for staying on one year, he or she has an incentive to seek another job while remaining at his or her post for one year. In many cases, the firm is in financial distress, so the current management might award itself retention bonuses to manage its downfall or cash out its remaining assets. For the same reason, management may make itself personal loans, knowing that the company is headed for bankruptcy. This practice is now prohibited under SOX, but K-Mart managers cashed out a great deal before its bankruptcy through bonuses and personal loans. Retention bonuses are often abused—after all, the managers that took the firm into the ground should be considered for dismissal, let alone be awarded a bonus for poor performance. Days before Enron Corp. declared bankruptcy on December 2, 2001, it announced that it would not abide by severance payments to its employees. At the same time, the company gave executives retention bonuses totaling more than $55 million. The generous executive payouts, many of which were made on November 30, were approved by the new Enron management team—Jeff McMahon, Enron president, and Ray Bowen, the CFO. McMahon received a bonus of $1.5 million and Bowen got $750,000. Enron's practices seemed not to change: handsome rewards to executives days before reneging on its employee severance commitments. Enron's planned severance package—subsequently scrapped—cost $120 million and would have provided an average payment to employees of approximately $30,000. That plan was discarded. Instead, at least $105 million was distributed in executive bonuses. To add insult to injury, the

留职奖金(Retention bonuses):公司支付给员工以留住他的一笔报酬。

Enron blackout of sales of Enron stock by employees, two thirds of their pension assets, was reported to have been accompanied by unreported insider sales by management. (*Washington Post*, *op. cit.*) Once again, this practice would be illegal under SOX, if discovered. Indeed, former CEO Jeffrey Skilling has been found guilty of one count of insider trading.

AMR

Shortly after two of its three unions had ratified $1.8 billion in annual wage and other concessions April 14, 2003. AMR (parent of American Airlines) filed its annual 10K report with the SEC revealing a retention bonus plan for the company's top seven executives of about $5 million each for another year of service and a bulletproof $41 million pension trust fund designed to protect executives' retirement monies from possible bankruptcy. AMR stood by its pension trust fund, but then AMR CEO Donald J. Carty and six other senior AMR executives gave up the retention bonuses on April 18. The remaining stewards union ratified the restructuring plan, despite the considerable anger provoked among union members. Neither plan was disclosed to shareholders, AMR's labor unions, or the SEC until the April 15, 2003 SEC filing. ("'Timely disclosure' at center of AA flap," *Dallas Business Journal*, April 28, 2003.) In the end, the unions had no better alternative than to approve the restructuring plan. Carty has since been replaced as CEO of American Airlines.

Insider trading

内 幕 交 易 (Insider trading):内幕交易行为是指知悉证券交易内幕信息的人员利用所知悉的内幕信息,自己进行证券交易或者泄露该信息或者建议他人进行证券交易的行为。

The term "insider trading" can mean the perfectly legal buying and selling of stock by a company's corporate insiders who comply by reporting their trading in advance. Insider trading is legal when these corporate insiders trade stock of their own company, but report in advance these trades to the U.S. Securities and Exchange Commission (SEC) and their income statements contain all information relevant to the financial standing of the firm. The SEC discloses the intention to sell on the EDGAR (Electronic Data Gathering and Retrieval) database. That way, the insider trading is disclosed and anyone can speculate about the corporate insider's opinion of the fortunes of his or her company. In the past, there have been loopholes that have allowed executives to skirt the disclosure rules, but SOX attempts to close them.

Insider trading is illegal when a person bases their trade of stocks in a publicly listed company on information that is not shared with the public.

It is also illegal to give someone a tip, so they can trade on the inside information. In Europe, the possibility of insider trading in EADS, the Airbus consortium is being investigated by the French Finance Commission. Noël Forgeard, co-President of EADS, his three children and other French and German directors sold their shares in EADS in March 2006, three months before announcing further, lengthy delays in the delivery of the jumbo Airbus 380 jet which triggered a sharp fall in the value EADS shares. Mr. Forgeard claims it was not insider trading, that he had no idea that there would be further delays. Innocent until proven guilty, of course, but the Airbus workers were apparently aware that they were far behind schedule due to extreme "customizing" for each customer. The French press are having a heyday with the affair, saying that Forgeard was either a liar, incompetent, or both!

In the News: U.S. Congressional insider trading

"Several academic studies show that the investment portfolios of congressmen and senators consistently outperform stock indices like the Dow and the S&P 500, as well as the portfolios of virtually all professional investors. Congressmen do better to an extent that is statistically significant, according to studies including a 2004 article about "abnormal" Senate returns by Alan J. Ziobrowski, Ping Cheng, James W. Boyd and Brigitte J. Ziobrowski in the *Journal of Financial and Qualitative Analysis*. Democrats' portfolios outperform the market by a whopping 9%. Republicans do well, though not quite as well. And the trading is widespread, although a higher percentage of senators than representatives trade—which is not surprising because senators outperform the market by an astonishing 12% on an annual basis. These results are not due to luck or the financial acumen of elected officials. They can be explained only by insider trading based on the nonpublic information that politicians obtain in the course of their official duties."

Source: "Congress's Phony Insider-Trading Reform", *Wall Street Journal*, December 13, 2011.

The punishment for illegal insider trading depends on the situation. The person can be fined, banned from sitting on the executive or board of directors of a public company and even jailed. The Securities Exchange Act of 1934 in the United States allows the Securities and Exchange Commission to give a person a reward—"a bounty"—to someone who gives the Commission information that results in a fine of insider trading. SOX 2002 makes it illegal to retaliate against whistle-blowers. Yet, it would be wise to think twice before blowing a whistle. The government may not be able to save your job. "Other reasons" might suffice, and you would have to pay lawyers to fight your company, not a pleasant thought.

In the News: Expert networks

Raj Rajaratnam's, a billionaire and founder of Galleon, a hedge fund, was sentenced to 11 years in prison, the longest-ever term imposed in an insider-trading case. Expert networks are independent research networks that pay so-called experts for information on public companies. In fact, many of the experts were employed in the very same firm whose information they provided to Galleon on which to trade. In a revealing text message, Ray was told: Don't buy Polycom's stock "till I get guidance; want to make sure guidance OK," wrote Roomy Khan, a former Intel Corp. employee who had been suspected of providing inside information to sources. In another case, The U. S. accused Mr. Rajat Gupta, former director at Goldman Sachs Group, Inc. of passing along nonpublic information to Raj Rajaratnam, namely that Warren Buffet was buying shares in Goldman. Mr. Gupta and Mr. Rajaratnam, were good friends whose regular discussions of business included the illegal tips, according to authorities. The insider-trading investigation that has so far focused primarily on those who profited directly from stock tips, but is now examining a culture where prosecutors say secrets are swapped freely among powerful business figures. "There is a lot of insider trading—and some of that goes to high places," according to Charles Munger, vice chairman of Berkshire Hathaway Inc., whose investment in Goldman during the heat of the financial crisis in 2008 was one of Mr. Gupta's alleged leaks. While some expert networks may be legitimate, one of the biggest challenges they face is legal compliance with respect to information passed on from the expert to the hedge fund. In the absence of insider trading on private information, it is hard to see how some hedge funds that use experts are able to consistently rack up higher than market returns.

Source: *The Wall Street Journal*, October 14, 2001: A14.

滥用税收机制(Abusive tax schemes):通过利用外国税收管辖权,便可以达到避税的目的。有一些避税行为是合法的,另一些则不然。

Abusive tax schemes

Taxes may be evaded by using a foreign jurisdiction. Evasion can be as simple as depositing unreported cash or checks into a bank account in a tax haven. Others methods are more elaborate involving domestic and foreign trusts and partnerships. Some are perfectly legal. Others are not.

A U. S. resident receives checks from customers, the checks are sent for deposit in the resident's International Business Corporation (IBC) of an offshore bank. The foreign bank uses its correspondent bank account to process the checks. When the check clears, the taxpayer's IBC account is credited for the payments. The customer who receives the canceled check does not know that the payment was made offshore. However, the U. S. taxpayer has transferred the unreported income to an offshore tax haven. Interest income goes untaxed in the tax free jurisdiction. Some Florida dentists went afoul of the law when they were discovered using credit cards issued by the foreign bank in Nassau in order to transfer the monies back to the US. U. K. tax expatriates move to the Bahamas to live from the income transferred or earned there. Or they incorporate in the Bahamas or Bermuda, but avoid staying more than 180 days in the US over a three year period to avoid residency issues for the business. False billing scams abroad can also be used to evade taxation.

Undisclosed executive compensation

The SEC requires that income statements now expense beginning January 2006 the value of options granted to executives in order to "improve the value of the firm." The generosity of deferred compensation, bonuses, and options has sometimes only been revealed to shareholders as a result of accidental claims due to divorce proceedings. A former Chairman of General Electric is retained as a consultant at $86,000 a year after his retirement in 2001, including "lifetime access to company facilities and services comparable to those which are currently made available to him by the company." These benefits are "unconditional and irrevocable" according to a General Electric 2001 proxy statement. The former executive also has an $80,000 per month Manhattan apartment owned by the company, in addition to other perks of significant value, such as use of the company airplane. In this particular case, the executive probably deserves such a "golden parachute," but the shareholders should be informed of the package.

Many managers "manage" to protect their pensions and health benefits, while defaulting on those of their employees. Some have the company pay their income taxes, unbeknown to the shareholders. Christopher Cox, the head of the US Securities and Exchange Commission won unanimous support from SEC commissioners to overhaul proxy-statement disclosure of

高管的秘密薪酬（Undisclosed executive compensation）：公司高管的薪酬、奖金以及期权有时并不会向股东披露。

top executives in the following ways:

1. Require companies to provide a total compensation figure for executives.

2. Include a dollar value of stock options in the summary compensation table.

3. Disclose any executive perks that are more than $10,000 in value.

4. Provide an actual amount to specify what payments executives would receive should there be a change in control or change in responsibilities.

5. Create a new disclosure table that would cover the details of retirement plans, including what the executive would receive in potential annual payments and benefits.

6. Create a new director compensation table similar to the executive summary compensation table that would disclose payments received by directors in a given year.

(*Wall Street Journal*, January 10, 2006: A1-2)

At least this is a step in the right direction, although Cox himself was totally unaware that Markopolous had persistently informed the SEC that Bernie Madoff was operating a Ponzi game. It is easier to pass regulations than to enforce them.

The shareholders should know what executive compensation is, and perhaps have an advisory say on it. Adam Smith hit the nail on the head, once again. As Professor Lucian A. Bebchuk, Director, Corporate Governance Program, Harvard University aptly put it: "The positive effect will be that on the margin—and it is an important margin—there will be a new so-called outrage constraint. The caveat is that even though there is an outrage constraint, shareholders have very limited power to do anything about it." (Stephen Labaton, "S. E. C. to Tighten Reporting Rules for Executive Pay." *New York Times*, January 18, 2006: C2.) In the meantime, average chief executive pay of CEOs of Fortune 500 companies has risen from $2.82 million in 2004 in 1990 to $11.8 million in 2004. Professor Bebchuk also found that in the S&P 500 companies, those with pension plans the median actuarial value given to chief executives is about $15 million (*op. cit.*, C2).

Many of these abusive financial practices are subject to a "Wells letter". The SEC Wells notification letters are mandated under Exchange Rules 17.1 and 17.2, which provide that prior "to submitting its report [to the Business Conduct Committee], the staff shall notify the person(s) who is the subject of the report . . . of the general nature of the allegations" in violations of exchange rules, such as conduct inconsistent with just and equitable principles of trade, failure to provide requested information and the like. This is to notify the person of the initiation of an investigation into possible exchange violations and to give that person the opportunity to respond to allegations within one year.

Derivative scandals and rogue traders

Barings Bank

Britain's oldest merchant bank had financed the Napoleonic wars, but was brought down by a single, rogue trader, Nick Leeson, then 28 years old, in February 1995. His losses were so great that Barings was unable to meet a SIMEX (Singapore International Monetary Exchange) margin call and was declared insolvent. In British Parliament, the Chancellor of the Exchequer announced somberly: "*With permission, Madam Speaker, I would like to make a statement about the insolvency of the merchant bank Barings. The Bank of England announced late last night, ahead of the opening of the Far East financial markets, that Barings was unable to continue trading...*" (February 27, 1995). At the time of the announcement, Leeson was on the run from the Singapore Branch of Barings where he was chief trader and settlements officer. Arrested in Frankfurt, Germany on March 3, 1995, he was returned to Singapore where he served 4 years of a 6 and one half-year sentence for fraud and forgery. Barings was sold to ING, a Dutch bank, for a symbolic £1 the same day of his arrest. ING assumed the liabilities of Barings.

Many have raised the twin questions: How did this happen and what are the lessons to be learned? There are two basic versions on how this happened, Nick Leeson's and Barings, but only one set of lessons that everyone seems to agree upon. Let's begin with the problems that led to the debacle with a view of drawing lessons.

First, Nick Leeson was both chief trader and settlements officer, a conflict of interest that left his activity essentially unsupervised. "An internal memo dated in 1993 had warned the London headquarters about allowing Leeson to be both trader and settlement officer, 'We are in danger of setting up a system that will prove disastrous. '" ("Crime Case Closed", *BBC*)

Secondly, the absence of checks and balances allowed Leeson to set

衍生工具丑闻(Derivative scandals):衍生工具的交易员在缺乏有效监管的情形下,为了牟取个人利益而采取赌博式交易策略,从而给公司带来巨大的损失。

up an error account 88888 which started with £ 20,000 losses from one of the traders he recruited, but was transferred losses of £ 827 million, or $1.4 billion in the end. This was done by trading at a loss to other Barings accounts which profited, showering bonuses on Leeson and his associates.

Thirdly, unauthorized trading for the account of Barings took place. Leeson and his traders were authorized to trade futures and options orders for clients or for other firms within the Barings organization, and were allowed to arbitrage price differences between Nikkei futures traded on the SIMEX and Japan's Osaka exchange. Neither of these activities would risk the assets of Barings, if conducted as authorized. Trading the futures and options for clients only risked the client's monies and margins, while arbitraging according to the law of one prices is riskless. Not realizing that Leeson was taking speculative positions, booking his losses in error account 88888, and his profits in other Barings accounts, the management in London did not fully realize the potential danger of his dual role—trader and settler.

Fourthly, doubling his positions when they moved against him. Leeson had the bad habit of doubling his losing position in the hopes of recovering his losses when the market moved in his favor, in this instance, a rise in the Nikkei Index. His long bet might have worked had not the January 17, 1995 Kobe earthquake rocked Japan and the Tokyo Exchange. In the words of authors Stephen J. Brown of the Stern School of Business, New York University and Onno W. Steenbeekb of the Erasmus School of Finance, Rotterdam: "The empirical evidence suggests that Leeson followed a doubling strategy: he continuously doubled his position as prices were falling." Indeed, Leeson confirms that he followed this strategy. "I felt no elation at this success. I was determined to win back the losses. And as the spring wore on, I traded harder and harder, risking more and more. I was well down, but increasingly sure that my doubling up and doubling up would pay off ... I redoubled my exposure. The risk was that the market could crumble down, but on this occasion it carried on upwards ... As the market soared in July (1993) my position translated from a £6 million loss back into glorious profit. I was so happy that night I didn't think I'd ever go through that kind of tension again. I'd pulled back a large position simply by holding my nerve ... but first thing on Monday morning I found that I had to use the 88888 account again ... it became an addiction." (Leeson, 1996: 63—64). Doubling is disastrous when the market moves systematically against the trader. Yet, there is a temptation to win the money back by doing so. Ironically, 10 years later on the SIMEX, China Aviation Oil Corporation's (CAOC) Jiulin Chen, the 43-year-old CEO of Singapore-listed CAOC kept doubling his bet that oil prices would fall, which they never did while he was trading. This resulted in another SIMEX scandal. Both Leeson and Chen made margin deposits and margin calls until they could no longer do so. Both tend to fault SIMEX, but the exchange was just practicing prudent collateral requirements for a clearing-house.

Fifthly, trading on margin affords a great deal of leverage, which can be your best friend if prices move in your direction, but your worst enemy when they move against you. Consider an asset which you borrow from a broker to sell forward at $100 with a margin deposit of $5. If the market price of the forward falls 5% your margin is wiped out and you will get a call for "margin maintenance" from your broker. If you cannot be reached within 24 hours or fail to restore margin, the broker will liquidate your position at a loss. The more leveraged you are, the smaller is the price movement against you that triggers a margin call. Leeson had plenty of these from SIMEX, and had to get the cash for margins from London. He argued that large transactions were needed to make small arbitrage profits and that both the SIMEX and Tokyo Exchanges required margin. Also, due to time differences he stated that there would be intra-day "advance margin calls" that Barings would have to meet due to time differences of location of the ultimate client. In other cases, he simply traded from account 88888. Leverage was also to play a big role in the downfall of China Aviation Oil Company and Long Term Capital Management.

Sixthly, Leeson was a good liar. In his ten year on article in *The Observer*, he notes: "Barings people had begun to ask some serious questions at last about the huge amounts of cash that had been disappearing in Singapore. Tony Railton, a senior bank official, had found a hole in the balance sheet—not the sort you plug by putting your finger in the dyke, more like one that threatens to wash the whole dam away. His colleague Tony Hawes, a London-based director, was on a tour of southeast Asia looking at funding requirements, and was due to be in Singapore on my birthday— 25 February. But still they allowed me to fob them off with flimsy excuses for my cash-guzzling operation. I believe that they were all so desperate to believe in my success for personal reasons; their bonuses depended on it and there were only a few days before these were due to be signed off . . .

By 23 February it all became too much. That day, which will be imprinted on my mind forever, my then-wife Lisa and I packed a couple of small suitcases and made our way to the airport. " Since Leeson fled on February 23, leaving his letter of apology and tendering his resignation, it is clear he did not meet with Tony Hawkes when both realized the jig was up.

Seventhly, Leeson's trades were inherently risky. A short straddle on the Nikkei index is fine if there is low volatility in the Tokyo Exchange, but not when the volatility is high. A short straddle is a combination of a short call and a short put with the same exercise price. Thus the seller of both a call and a put on the Nikkei Index, Leeson was betting there would be little movement. In the event, the city of Kobe had a major earthquake and he had to honor the put he had sold. Leveraged long positions in the Nikkei Index ate margin cash when the index fell. Matters became much worse when Leeson doubled his long positions in the Nikkei. Many broker-age houses have stop-loss rules requiring the trader to take the losses, pre-venting them from growing larger. Options trading is inherently risky since you lose 100% of your investment, the option premium, when it expires out of the money.

Eighthly, Leeson was, in his own words, "eager to please, eager to succeed. " (*The Observer*) He seemed to have a big ego, anxious to be a star for Barings. So anxious to succeed, he falsified documents and trades to generate profits which would generate everyone, including himself, large bonuses. He told a pack of lies. It is also disingenuous to claim, as he does in *The Observer*: "The Bank of England, which a decade ago this weekend was sitting on a powder-keg with a burning fuse, was surely right not to have bailed Barings out. It was a comparatively small bank, poorly run, and an accident waiting to happen. " Although it is certainly true, as he states: "Open-outcry trading pits are virtually a thing of the past and have been largely replaced with automated systems. Many of the anomalies that existed on the trading floor in my day, often bordering on the illegal, have been removed, and that can only be advantageous in promoting fair and accessible markets for everyone. "

He is quick to note, however, that the China Aviation Oil Company scandal involving the same type of rogue trading and doubling of losing po-sitions to recover losses happened again in 2005 on the SIMEX. Nick Lee-son now lives in Galway, Ireland and is a motivational speaker. In April 2005, Mr. Leeson was appointed commercial director of the Galway Foot-ball Club.

China Aviation Oil Company

A Singapore-listed company, China Aviation Oil Company (CAOC) controlled by a Chinese state-owned enterprise, lost $550 million in 2004 from short sales of oil derivatives on SIMEX. (*New York Times*, December 2, 2004; *Wall Street Journal*, December 3, 2004; and the *Wall Street Journal*, December 6, 2004.) Jiulin Chen, the then 43-year-old CEO of China Aviation Oil Company, Singapore, was taken into custody for investigation of Singapore's worst financial scandal in nearly a decade since Nick Leeson took down Barings in 1995 in unauthorized trading. Mr. Chen appears to have pursed the same dogged policy of doubling his short sales of oil futures in the hopes that oil prices would fall. For example, In April 2004, Chen decided to extend the maturity of the futures sales held by CAOC, as well as dramatically increase the size of their short position. Clearly, he and his risk management team felt that oil prices would fall. In the event, oil price rose continuously to record highs.

As oil prices kept rising, the margin requirement on CAOC's futures trading also surged, draining its cash flow. On October 10, 2004, CAOC's books showed losses of US $180 million, and it did not have the $80 million necessary to make the margin calls. On October 21, 2004, CAOHC, knowing that its Singapore affiliate was in financial distress, sold 15% of CAOC's shares to a few fund management companies without revealing its desperate financial condition, in violation of insider-trading regulations. The parent CAOHC immediately lent the $108 million in cash from the sale to CAOC in the hope of rescuing it.

Chen stated that he had no idea CAOC would be required to pay huge amounts in margin calls as a result of its trading. By engaging in speculative trading, Chen had violated strict prohibitions by Chinese regulators. His authorized trading purpose was to hedge fuel needs for Chinese aviation companies. In one example of a money-losing trade, CAOC entered into a derivative agreement on September 1, 2004 that involved 100,000 barrels of jet fuel. CAOC sold a call that the average monthly spot price for Singapore-traded jet fuel oil would not rise above $37 a barrel during October. Fuel prices rose to an average price of $61.25. CAO suffered a loss of $24.25 per barrel, or $2.4 million in total, having to honor the short call that was deep into the money.

CAOC filed for bankruptcy on November 30, 2004 citing losses of some US $550 million from oil derivatives trading. Jiulin Chen and CAOC management lost money by doggedly gambling against rising oil prices, increasing the amounts of oil futures it sold. CAOC's short position increased losses from an initial US $5.8 million to a staggering US $550 million.

Time and again, Chen extended the maturity date of most of the short futures contracts CAOC held to 2005 and 2006, essentially doubling his position. CAOC's trading volume ballooned and oil prices kept rising. By engaging in speculative trading, Chen had violated strict prohibitions by Chinese regulators and was accordingly jailed for fraud and the violation of security laws.

Some critics suspected that CAOC had no risk-control mechanism in place. But the mechanism did exist. The company's risk-control manuals were developed by the consulting firm Ernst & Young, and were similar to those of other international oil companies. In addition, CAOC had a seven-member risk-control committee, staffed by Singaporean employees. The company also had internal rules that any trader losing more than US $200,000 must report the losses to the committee. Losses above US $375,000 are to be reported also to the CEO personally. The rules also stipulate mandatory stop-loss sales of the position when they reach US $500,000. Chen claims: "The US $500,000 must refer to actual losses—all our losses were book-value losses at the time, which didn't count," he told *Caijing* on December 7, 2004. In China, airlines were expressing concern that the rescue operation will lead to surging fuel costs, since CAOHC was the country's sole importer of aviation fuel. Chen, the center of the scandal, did not lose confidence: "If I can get just another US $250 million, I am sure I will turn things around." he said in a mobile phone message to a *Caijing* reporter on December 9, after he was freed on bail. Chen also believed that the Chinese government had a responsibility to bail CAOC out, saying "CAOC represents a standard of Chinese enterprises overseas."

The Chinese State-owned Asset Supervision and Administration Commission (SASAC) was briefly supportive of a rescue plan. It asked for foreign currency quotas for hundreds of millions of US dollars from the State Administration of Foreign Exchange (SAFE), the exchange control body. The SASAC, however, changed its mind. It ruled instead that the state would not go against its own principles against rescuing an insolvent company. It recommended that senior management of the company be punished.

In the end, we have a Leeson-like story: Unauthorized trading, doubling of losing positions, and not informing the parent company until the subsidiary could not make its margin calls. In the case of Leeson, he doubled bets that the Nikkei Index would rise. In the case of Chen, he doubled bets that the oil price would fall. In both cases, they could no longer make margin calls and their firms went bankrupt.

UBS AG

A Swiss Bank, UBS, said a rogue trader, London employee Kweku Adoboli, incurred $2 billion in losses using the firm's own money. Apparently, the losses were from unauthorized derivatives-trading. The bank said no client positions were affected, but top resignations and curtailing of proprietary trading at UBS resulted. ("UBS: Rogue Trader Hit Firm," *Wall Street Journal*, September 16, 2011)

Société Générale

Jérôme Kerviel, a trader at Société Générale, was sentenced to five years in jail, two of them suspended. He was also ordered to pay damages of €4.9 billion. The judge ruled that he had fraudulently manipulated his reported trades, concealing his losing trades from his colleagues with off-setting transactions. "Plus ça change, plus c'est la même chose" or "The more things change, the more they remain the same." (*Der Spiegel*, November 16, 2010) It is clear that the world's largest banks have increasingly greater difficulty monitoring their traders' activity. Electronic trading takes less than a second.

Long Term Capital Management

Long Term Capital Management (LTCM), a hedge fund, was founded in 1994 by John Meriwether. Nobel laureates Myron Scholes of Stanford University and Robert Merton of Harvard University were co-principals. LTCM's reputation afforded them greater leverage than other hedge funds: they reportedly were able to leverage $4.8 billion of investor and principal money into $100 billion of positions. In the end, this leverage was to prove their worst enemy.

In 1996 and 1997, LTCM had paid its investors high yields, nearly 40% annually. However, during 1998, the hedge firm engaged in a variety of leveraged bets on the convergence of corporate and sovereign bond yields, but they diverged. Apparently, they also expected sovereign credit

长 期 资 本 管 理 公 司 (Long Term Capital Management):长期资本管理公司是一家对冲基金公司,它于 1994 年成立。和其他的对冲基金相比,长期资本管理公司的声誉给了他们很大的杠杆能力:据说他们可以用 48 亿美元对高达 1000 亿美元的头寸进行杠杆操作。

spreads to decrease, but once again the spreads increased. LTCM bought Russian short-term sovereign GKOs and sold Japanese bonds. The hedge fund was wrong about the direction of Japanese yields and worse yet, Russia defaulted (Wilmott, 2000).

On August 21, 1998 LTCM is reported to have lost $550 million. It was felt that a LTCM bankruptcy was too risky on the grounds of its "systemic" impact on US financial markets. Alan Greenspan, then Governor of the Federal Reserve System, organized a recapitalization of $3.6 billion by 12 investment banks in return for a 90% stake in LTCM. In the event, LTCM recovered in the subsequent years, yielding a good return on investment to the banks.

This is a different story than the previous ones, although there are some similarities. The investors were hedge fund participants risking their own and investor's monies, there was far too much leverage in hindsight—apparently over 20 to 1, and the Russian default left many holding worthless securities. No one claims there was any fraud in LTCM, only high leverage and risky bets that went bad.

Backdating of options grants

期权授予回溯(Backdating of options grants): 管理者的期权授予日期总是被回溯到一个股票价格低点,从而使得管理者能够获得更大的收益。

In a blockbuster article March 18, 2006, "The Perfect Payday," the *Wall Street Journal* exposed the dating of options grants to executives at or near the lowest share price of the year, which is extremely unlikely. The options are then exercised at or near the high price when vested, or upon leaving the company. Consider the case of Affiliated Computer Services, Inc. 's former CEO: "It was the same through much of Mr. Rich's tenure: In a striking pattern, all six of his stock-option grants from 1995 to 2002 were dated just before a rise in the stock price, often at the bottom of a steep drop ... Just lucky? A *Wall Street Journal* analysis suggests the odds of this happening by chance are extraordinarily remote—around one in 300 billion ... The Securities and Exchange Commission is examining whether some option grants carry favorable grant dates for a different reason: They were backdated. "

How can this be? Let's say Mr. Back Dater, CEO of XYZ Corp. is awarded one million call option grants on July 5, 2005 when the share price is $50 at 4:00pm of that or the previous day. They vest or can be exercised in one year. On July 5, 2006 Mr. Back Dater is eligible to buy at $50 and sell say at $60, the share price that day, earning $10 million. Fair enough. However, in cahoots with the compensation committee or some board members, the options are backdated to May 5, 2005 when the stock was at its low point, $20 a share. Bingo, he has hit the jackpot: $40 million in the exercise of the options. Where does the extra $30 million come from? It comes from the shareholders, of course.

The *Wall Street Journal* reports other possible malfeasance: "On Oct. 13, 1999, William W. McGuire, CEO of giant insurer UnitedHealth Group Inc., got an enormous grant in three parts that ... came to $14.6 million in options. So far, he has exercised about 5% of them, for a profit of about $39 million. As of late February (2006) he had 13.87 million unexercised options left from the October 1999 tranche. His profit on those, if he exercised them today, would be about $717 million more. The 1999 grant was dated the very day UnitedHealth stock hit its low for the year. ... At Mercury Interactive Corp., a Mountain View, Calif., software maker, the chief executive and two others resigned late last year. Mercury said an internal probe found 49 cases where the reported date of options grants differed from the date when the options appeared to have been awarded. The company said it will have to restate financial results ... Another company, Comverse Technology Inc., said ... that its board had started a review of its past stock-option practices, including "the accuracy of the stated dates of options grants". Shares of Vitesse Semiconductor Corp. ... now rest at about the level of a decade ago. But Louis R. Tomasetta, chief executive of the Camarillo, Calif., chip maker, reaped tens of millions of dollars from stock options. In eight of Mr. Tomasetta's nine option grants from 1994 to 2001, the grants were dated just before double-digit price surges in the next 20 trading days. The odds of such a pattern occurring by chance are about one in 26 billion." Following the *Wall Street Journal* story, there have been waves of resignations of top executives, some cashing out to boot, as well as an avalanche of new SEC investigations into possible backdating.

There are several obvious problems with the backdating of options: firstly, it is illegal to forge or backdate options grants, secondly, the shareholders are usually not informed, thirdly, it mocks the supposed link of options grants to the incentives of executives to raise the profitability of the firm, and finally, it steals wealth from shareholders. While the practice also violates Sarbanes-Oxley's prompt disclosure rules, many corporate executives in the U.S. are apparently doing so with impunity, at least so far.

Money laundering

The list of financial *peccadillos* would be incomplete without the mention of money laundering. An interesting case has been under investigation for some years now, and is finally going to court in Germany.

In the News : **Five Indicted in German Money-Laundering Case**

"German prosecutors indicted five men, including four German banking executives, on charges of laundering $150 million for a former Russian telecommunications minister in one of the highest-level criminal probes of a Russian official outside Russia. The indictments follow a six-year investigation into allegations that four current or former Commerzbank AG executives and a Danish lawyer, Jeffrey Galmond, assisted former Russian telecommunications minister Leonid Reiman in selling telecommunications assets he allegedly secretly controlled in offshore companies, while concealing who the true owner was. The prosecutors allege that Mr. Reimen had surreptitiously converted telecom businesses from state ownership to that of a number of foreign companies that he allegedly set up and controlled after the collapse of communism in the early 1990s. "

Source: David Crawford, *Wall Street Journal*, December 13, 2011.

Lessons learned

Many of the financial mishaps and schemes reviewed here resulted from under-estimating the risks of leverage. Borrowing to sell short can trigger margin calls as the asset rises in price. Stop losses rather than rolling over losing positions by doubling up are recommended by most internal risk management procedures. When there is too much leverage, a small move in the price of the asset in the wrong direction can initiate large losses and margin calls. That seems to be one lesson from Barings, LTCM, and CAOC.

Illegal insider trading, falsification of earnings to ensure gains in options and bonuses, moving losing positions off balance sheets, and other conscious corporate frauds that apparently took place at Enron and World-Com would seem to merit greater punishments, in addition to the restoration of investor funds or worker pensions. Poor governance and the failure of checks and balances within the firm bring with them the risk of bankruptcy. Monitoring trading activities of rogue traders that set up offsetting positions and accounts that conceal their losses is a challenge to the banks.

Backdating of options grants is outright fraud, direct theft from the shareholders and should be prosecuted. Retention bonuses may retain talented officers, such as at Apple Computer following the tragic loss of Steve Jobs, but they often seem to be the last refuge of corporate scoundrels to finance a year of job-seeking in a troubled company. Debt forgiveness on personal loans to executives, now prohibited by SOX, is also a bad practice. Money laundering will always be an issue with illegal activities, as well as the transfer of funds to support terrorism.

Conclusion

Adam Smith was right in 1776. Managers will often put their own interest ahead of the interest of the shareholders. The so-called efforts to align the interest of the managers with those of the owners through stock options and grants, bonuses and other "incentive pay" linked to reported earnings has reaped a harvest of falsified earnings and backdated options grants. Poorly performing firms are rewarding their CEOs at record levels. Indeed, there seems to be little relationship between performance and executive reward. Shareholders are not always informed of executive compensation nor are they consulted, as they would surely balk. The Cox ruling attempts to remedy this, but it is unclear what shareholders can do about the issue. Accountants will say what they are told to say in many circumstances, though SOX will punish them severely if they are caught. SOX attempts to eliminate some of the conflicts of interest in auditing firms. There is an ethical crisis in management. At the same time, there will always be pyramid schemes that attract those seeking high short term gains. Leverage always compounds the risk, and margin calls can rise rapidly when a bad leveraged bet is doubled. It is difficult to foresee much change, despite the heavy penalties that are now being meted out. There are always other scandals about to happen.

> ## In the News: Trolling for outperforming hedge funds
>
> "In 2009, the SEC began developing a computer-powered system that now analyzes monthly returns from thousands of hedge funds. Officials won't say exactly how it works or how much it cost to build, but the agency has announced four civil-fraud lawsuits filed as a result of what it calls the 'aberrational performance initiative.' ... The hedge funds have one thing in common: Their performance seems too good to be true, with some trouncing the overall market and others churning out modest results without ever suffering a down month. Some funds on the list stumble but still always outperform rival hedge funds ... In 2008, ThinkStrategy reported a 4.6% return on its Capital Fund-A hedge fund. It was the sixth year in a row that Chetan Kapur, a 36-year-old New Yorker, seemed to have a Midas touch. In contrast, the average hedge fund fell roughly 19% in 2008, with losses in eight of the year's 12 months, according to data from Hedge Fund Research Inc. The SEC alleged in its civil-fraud suit against Mr. Kapur that the 4.6% return figure was faked. The hedge fund actually had a 90% loss in 2008, according to the SEC's lawsuit."
>
> Source: "SEC Ups Its Game to Identify Rogue Firms," by Jean Eaglesham and Steve Eder, *The Wall Street Journal*, December 27, 2011.

Questions and problems

6.1 Pyramid investments

Pyramid investments of Fort Lauderdale, in business for two years, has promised to pay 3% per month on notes redeemable in one year. It has redeemed any notes presented for redemption so far.

a. Indicate the annual rate of return that is promised on these notes.

b. Why might there not have been any default on the notes to date?

c. Do you think that this investment is sustainable?

6.2 Insider trading

Some argue that insider trading "helps in price discovery" of a firm's true value since the inside traders have information material to the financial situation of the firm. Besides, even if they buy low and sell high, it is not to the same shareholder, so it does not matter. Do you agree or disagree with this argument? Explain why.

6.3   Doubling down

Rogue traders often seem to have a strategy of "doubling down" on their initial bet in the same, wrong direction, even though the price has moved in the opposite one. Explain why this strategy is highly unlikely to succeed in terms of movements in the future price of the asset.

6.4   Sarbanes-Oxley and Dodd-Frank

In your view, would these two Acts of Congress survive an economic cost-benefit analysis? Think like an economist, not a regulator.

6.5   Backdating of options grants

There are various problems involved with the backdating of options grants.

a. What are the legal ones?

b. What are the ethical ones?

c. Who gains and who loses financially in a backdating episode? Explain.

References and suggested reading

Brown, Stephen J. and O. W. Steenbeek (2001), "Doubling: Nick Leeson's Trading Strategy," *Pacific-Basin Finance Journal*, 9(2): 83—99.

Forelle, Charles and James Bander (March 18, 2006), "The Perfect Payday: Some CEOs reap millions by landing stock options when they are most valuable. Luck—or something else?" *The Wall Street Journal*.

Hoffman, William (April 25, 2003), "Timely disclosure at center of AA flap," *Dallas Business Journal*.

Jarvis, Christopher (2000), "The Rise and Fall of Albania's Pyramid Schemes," *Finance and Development*, 37(1): 46—49.

Jorion, Philippe (1995), *Big Bets Gone Bad: Derivatives and Bankruptcy in Orange County*, San Diego, Academic Press.

Leeson, N. (1996), *Rogue Trader*, London: Little, Brown and Co.

Kindleberger, Charles (1989), *Manias, Panics and Crashes: A History of Financial Crises*," 2nd ed. New York: Basic Books.

Nimalendran, M., Ritter R. Jay, and Donghang Zhang (2004), "Are trading commissions a factor in IPO allocation?" Working paper, University of Florida.

Niskanen, William (2005), *After Enron: Lessons for Public Policy*, Lanham, MD: Rowman and Littlefield Publishers.

O'Hara, Philip (2001), "Insider trading in financial markets: liquidity, ethics, efficiency," *International Journal of Social Economics*, 28 (12):

1046—1062.

Prystay, Chris (June 10, 2005), "Five are charged in case involving CAO Singapore," *The Wall Street Journal*: A6.

Prystay, Chris (May 31, 2005), "Singapore exchange to bolster listing rules," *The Wall Street Journal*.

ERisk. com (2004), Barings Case Study, http://www. erisk. com/ Learning/CaseStudies/ref_case_barings. asp.

Quing, Hao (2004), "Laddering in Initial Public Offerings," Working paper, University of Florida, Gainesville, FL.

RiskGlossary. com (1996), "Nick Leeson and Barings Bank".

Searsey, Dionne and Li Yuan (June 21, 2005), "Adelphia's John Rigas gets 15 years," *The Wall Street Journal*: A3.

Western, David (2004), *Booms, Bubbles, and Busts in the U. S. Stock Market*, London & New York: Routledge.

Stigler, George (Spring 1971), "The Theory of Economic Regulation," *The Bell Journal of Economics and Management*, 2(1): 3—21.

Wilmott, Paul (2000), *Paul Wilmott on Quantitative Finance*, New York: John Wiley and Sons.

www. caijing. com. cn

Tabasso, Gianfranco (2004), "A Modern Replica of Ponzi Finance: The Painful Lessons of the Parmalat Affair," *Treasury Management International*, 126:21—25.

Zuckoff, Mitchell (2005), *Ponzi's Scheme: the True Story of a Financial Legend*, New York: Random House.

7 CHAPTER

Financial Leverage, Moral Hazard and Counterparty Risk: The Financial Crisis of 2007—2009

金融杠杆、道德风险和对手风险:2007—2009 年的金融危机

When housing prices and share prices fall, households suffer a loss in wealth. In particular, U. S. household net wealth fell $11 trillion in 2008, 77% of 2008 GDP. This loss in wealth curbed consumer spending. Households raised their savings rates to restore their wealth, pensions and savings. At the same time, falling asset prices bankrupted leveraged borrowers who were put in financial distress, default, or foreclosure. Leveraged banks, especially investment banks were also put on the brink of insolvency and negative equity. Bankruptcies raised the specter of counterparty risk, and credit, even interbank credit, came to a halt. The ultimate consequence of these developments led to the recession of 2008—2009 in the United States. It is useful to simplify the dénouement of the financial crisis and its economic effects in a simple drawing, Figure 7.1.

Figure 7.1 The financial crisis of 2008—2009

Financial leverage

Financial leverage is the best friend of an investor when asset prices rise, but her worst enemy if asset prices fall. This is because the multiplied effect on equity depends on the degree of financial leverage. U. S. publicly-listed firms are required to file **balance sheets** quarterly, known as the 10Q, and at the end of their fiscal year, the 10K. The balance sheet of a firm measures the "probable" value of a firm's assets, A, and its liabilities or debt, D, defining stockholders equity, E, as the difference between its assets and its liabilities:

$$\text{Assets}(A) = \text{Liabilities }(D) + \text{Stockholders' Equity }(E)$$

Assets are defined as:

probable future economic benefits obtained or controlled by a particular entity as a result of past transactions or events (Statement of Financial Accounting Standards (SFAC 6, paragraph 25) of the Federal Accounting Standards Board (FASB) of the United States), while liabilities are:

probable future sacrifices of economic benefits arising from present obligations of a particular entity to transfer assets or provide services to other en-

资产负债表（**Balance sheet**）:表示企业在一定日期的财务状况的主要会计报表。

资产 = 负债 + 所有者权益

tities in the future as a result of past transactions or events (SFAC 6, paragraph 35).

Stockholder's equity is thus:

The residual interest in the net assets of an entity that remains after deducting its liabilities (SFAC 6, paragraph 49).

The *International Accounting Standards Board* (IASB) was established in 1973 to harmonize global accounting standards adopted similar definitions.

Market and impairment rules may require "markdowns" to the value of assets and liabilities, particularly in the accounting for investments in securities. Thus financial institutions are required to "mark to market" much of their assets to recognize probable losses. Marking to market has a multiplied effect on the equity held, and may result in negative equity or bankruptcy.

We have:

$$\text{Assets} \equiv \text{Liabilities} + \text{Equity} \equiv A \equiv D + E \qquad (7.1)$$

Three definitions of financial leverage

1. For financial institutions in particular, the financial leverage ratio is often defined by the ratio of assets to equity:

资产/权益 = A/E

$$\frac{\text{Assets}}{\text{Equity}} = \frac{A}{E} \qquad (7.2)$$

2. For firms, the debt to equity ratio is often used:

负债/权益 = D/E

$$\frac{\text{Liabilities}}{\text{Equity}} = \frac{D}{E} \qquad (7.3)$$

Clearly, from the definition $A = D + E$ the relationship between these two measures of financial leverage is simply:

$$\frac{A}{E} = \frac{D}{E} + 1$$

Consequently, when liabilities are constant:

$$\frac{\Delta A}{A} = \frac{\Delta E}{A}$$

or

$$\frac{\Delta A}{A} = \left(\frac{E}{A} \right) \frac{\Delta E}{E}$$

Thus

$$\frac{\Delta E}{E} = \left(\frac{A}{E} \right) \frac{\Delta A}{A} \qquad (7.4)$$

权益的变化百分比等于杠杆率与资产变化百分比的乘积。此公式表明,杠杆率放大了由资产变化而引起的权益变化。

Consequently, when debt is constant, the percentage change in the value of equity equals the degree of financial leverage times the percentage change in the value of assets. For instance, at purchase, a mortgage borrower that makes a 20% down payment has a financial leverage ratio of $A/E = 5$, or $D/E = 4$, since $\frac{\Delta E}{E} = \left(\frac{D}{E} + 1\right)\frac{\Delta A}{A}$. As a result, a change in the value of a home of 10% causes a 50% change in the borrower's home equity, as indicated in Figure 7.2. Financial leverage is a good friend when asset prices rise, but a poor one when they fall.

Figure 7.2 The magnification effect of financial leverage on gains and losses

如图 7.2 所示，由于杠杆率为 5，因此资产变化 10% 导致权益变化 50%

负债/资产 = D/A = D/(D + E)

3. A third index of financial leverage is defined by debt to assets, or

$$\frac{\text{Debt}}{\text{Assets}} = \frac{D}{A} = \frac{D}{D + E} \tag{7.5}$$

This is also given by the ratio of the first two measures of financial leverage since $\frac{D/E}{A/E} = \frac{D}{A} = \frac{D}{D + E}$. The third definition, $[D/(D + E)]$, has the merit of ranging from zero for the unlevered firm, to 1 for the bankrupt firm with zero equity.

A simple application of the leverage concept is to determine what percentage decline in the value of assets will make equity zero. In this case, with debt constant:

$$\Delta A = - E$$

or

$$\frac{\Delta A}{A} = - \frac{E}{A} = - \frac{1}{A/E}$$

That is, if the value of assets falls by the reciprocal of the financial average ratio, equity will be wiped out. For instance, an investment bank with a 30 to 1 degree of financial leverage would only be able to sustain a 1/30th fall in the ·value of its assets before becoming bankrupt, that is a 3.3% fall.

财务杠杆的一个简单应
用是决定多大的资产变
动比率会使权益变为零。
具体地说,当资产的下降
比率为财务杠杆的倒数
时,权益变为零。例如,
如果财务杠杆为 30/1,
那么资产下降 1/30 便会
导致破产。

Securitization

Securitization stands for the bundling of contracts to future cash flows into a security that can be traded for the present value of its expected cash flow. Any asset that yields a future expected cash flow can, in principle, be bundled with other assets, either similar or unlike, that then are sold as a single security. The securitization of mortgage backed assets of different credit worthiness, including sub-prime or risky mortgages, was not a problem so long as housing prices kept rising. A typical MBA would be composed of say 20% prime mortgages, 40% Alt A, of slightly less credit quality, then 40% sub-prime loans which have a higher risk of default.

资产证券化(Securitiza-
tion):以特定的资产组
合或特定现金流为支持,
发行可交易证券的一种
融资形式。

The present value of the cash flow thus depends largely upon the likelihood of payment of principal and interest on the mortgages. With rising housing prices, the likelihood of default is small, thus the value of the MBA is great. The moment housing prices fell, this led to defaults by highly leveraged sub-prime borrowers, and thus a rapid fall in the value of mortgage backed assets. Indeed, MBAs became illiquid, in part due to the difficulty of evaluating their fundamental value, so the MBA market froze following the precipitous fall in their value. The FED ultimately purchased over a trillion dollars of MBAs in the open market to avert a collapse of the investment and commercial banks that held them. A **collateralized debt obligation** is also a security backed by a bundle of other assets. A synthetic CDO is one that holds no underlying assets, so that a spot buyer is betting that the price will rise, while a spot seller is expecting the price to fall. If a synthetic CDO is bought for future delivery, it is a long position, while a sale for future delivery is a short position. It is said that Goldman Sachs shorted MBAs that it had structured and sold to investors, expecting to benefit from a fall in their price. In any case, GS settled with the Justice department for having possibly misled investors and betting against their position. In principle, there is nothing wrong with securitization. However, it played a major role in passing on the risk to ultimate investors. For instance, the mortgage originator makes a loan to someone

债务担保证券(collater-
alized debt obligation,
CDO):以抵押债务信用
为基础,基于各种资产证
券化技术,对债券、贷款
等资产进行结构重组,重
新分割投资回报和风险,
以满足不同投资者的需
要的创新性衍生金融产
品。

who does not otherwise qualify, but sells it immediately to Fannie Mae, Freddie Mac, or a Wall Street investment bank who bundles the mortgage with others to sell them to investors.

The mortgage lender has no credit risk, so there is said to be "moral hazard" in his or her mortgage origination. The original lender has "no skin in the game": That is, cannot lose if the borrower defaults. This insurance against loss does not provide the right incentives for the original lender to verify the credit worthiness of the borrower. The main incentive is to make the loan to collect the fees, then immediately sell it. The credit rating institutions typically scored the MBAs as AAA, the highest notation, which is fine while the market is rising. A triple A rating is necessary to be able to sell MBAs to some pension funds, such as CALPERS in California. There is thus said to be "moral hazard." Everyone gains while housing prices continue to rise, but they do fall!

Reduced mortgage leverage in China

在中国，首套住房的首付款比例（down payments）已经提高到30%，第二套住房的首付款比例已经提高到50%。

In China, down payments have been increased to 30% for the first property and 50% for the second. This means that the financial leverage ratios are 3.33 and 2 respectively. Thus, at loan origination, it would take a 30% and 50% fall in the market value of the home before being "under the water" or in negative equity territory. This has the advantage of making strategic default less likely, but the disadvantage of raising the "cost of carry" of real estate.

Such stabilization measures, along with increased mortgage rates, should effectively reduce the rate of housing price rises. Economic growth in China has been fueled by construction, so the policy of slowing investment in housing must be done with extreme care. However, when the inflation rate rises relative to the nominal interest rate, the real cost of carry falls.

Financial leverage of some selected firms

Here are some measures of financial leverage reported in Table 7.1 for U.S. tech companies drawn from www.sec.gov, 10K and 10Q forms.

Table 7.1. Financial leverage of some US tech firms

Microsoft Corp, Sept. 30,2010		Apple Inc. , Sept. 25,2010		IBM Corp. , Sept. 30, 2010	
Assets*	91,540	Assets	75,183	Assets	107,174
Stockholders' Equity	46,942	Stockholders' Equity	47,791	Stockholders' Equity	22,359
A/E	1.95	A/E	1.57	A/E	4.8
D/E	0.95	D/E	0.57	D/E	3.8
D/(D+E) or D/A	49%	D/A	36%	D/A	79%

* millions of USD.

and some manufacturing firms in Table 7.2:

Table 7.2   Financial leverage of some industrial manufacturing firms

General Motors, Sept. 30,2010		Boeing Aircraft, Sept. 30,2010	
Assets*	137,238	Assets	65,222
Stockholders' Equity	23,718	Stockholders' Equity	4,552
A/E	5.8	A/E	14.3
D/E	4.8	D/E	13.3
D/A	83%	D/A	93%

* millions of USD.

as well as some financial firms in Table 7.3:

Table 7.3   Financial leverage of some financial institutions

Countrywide Financial, June 30, 2008		Merrill Lynch, Sept. 30, 2010	
Assets*	172,076	Assets	502,915
Stockholders' Equity	10,420	Stockholders' Equity	43,479
A/E	16.5	A/E	11.6
D/E	15.5	D/E	10.6
D/A	94%	D/A	91%

* milions of USD.

In general, tech firms have lower leverage than financial firms, but leverage varies in manufacturing.

Leveraged households

During the housing boom, mortgage loans were made at 20% down, 10% down, and in some cases zero down payment, implying financial leverage of 5, 10, and infinity respectively. Many of these mortgages were sold directly to Fannie Mae and Freddie Mac, who guaranteed them against default, bundled some and sold them as mortgage backed assets as well as holding them. Other mortgages were sold to Wall Street institutions who similarly bundled them, selling them to investors as mortgage backed assets or collateralized debt obligations. In most cases, the mortgage lender passed on the credit risk as did the investment banks. However, both Fannie Mae and Freddie Mac kept many MBAs as security investments, thus holding the credit risk.

The role of the government: Fannie Mae and Freddie Mac

房利美（Fannie Mae）：
即联邦国民抵押贷款协
会，是最大的美国政府赞
助企业，主要业务是在美
国房屋抵押贷款二级市
场中收购贷款，并通过向
投资者发行机构债券或
证券化的抵押债券，以低
成本集资，赚取利差。

房地美（Freddie Mac）：
即联邦住宅抵押公司，是
第二大的美国政府赞助
企业，商业规模仅次于房
利美。

"Fannie Mae has expanded home ownership for millions of families in the 1990's by reducing down payment requirements," said Franklin D. Raines, Fannie Mae's (then) chairman and chief executive. "Yet there remain too many borrowers whose credit is just a notch below what our underwriting has required who have been relegated to paying significantly higher mortgage rates in the so-called sub-prime market." Fannie Mae, the nation's largest underwriter of home mortgages does not lend money directly to consumers, instead it purchase loans that banks make on what is called the secondary market. By expanding the type of loans that it will buy, Fannie Mae is hoping to spur banks to make more loans to people with less than-stellar credit ratings." (Steven Holmes, "Fannie Mae Eases Credit to Aid Mortgage Lending," *New York Times*, September 20, 1999)

A prescient remark was made by Peter Wallison of the American Enterprise Institute at the time: "From the perspective of many people, including me, this is another thrift industry growing up around us ... If they fail the government will have to step up and bail them out the way it stepped up and bailed out the thrift industry."

Indeed, this is a prime example of moral hazard: mortgage lending institutions such as Countrywide Financial made sub-prime loans on stated income with little likelihood of repayment if home prices did not rise, and sold the mortgages to Fannie Mae and Freddie Mac, thereby passing on the credit risk to the US taxpayer ultimately. Similarly, these loans could be sold to an eager Wall Street who bundled them as Mortgage Backed Assets (MBAs), passing on the default risk to investors who purchased them.

The investment banks also were burned holding MBAs, especially Lehman Bros. and Citibank. As of 2011, the Federal rescue of Fannie Mae and Freddie Mac has cost the taxpayer over $120 billion, nor has any meaningful reform of these now state owned institutions been implemented, including in the Dodd-Frank Act of 2010.

Rising and falling home equity

When housing prices are expected to rise forever as they did in the recent past, this is good news for the homeowner whose equity in the home rises. Even the NINJA borrower (no income, no job, and no assets) enjoys rising equity. Here is an example of a fixed interest rate mortgage of 6% that is serviced by the lender for one year. In light of rising prices, the amount of equity increases in Table 7.4, depending on the increase in the market value of the home, and the degree of financial leverage.

资产价格上升时,权益也随之增长。但权益的增长不仅由资产价格上升所决定,还取决于杠杆率的大小。

Table 7.4 Rising equity with rising home prices

Loan origination(8-15-08,6% fixed rate, 30 years)

Value of house	Down payment	Value of Mortgage	Equity
100	0	100	0
100	10	90	10
100	20	80	20
100	30	70	30

1 year later(9-15-09,market rates remain at 6%)

Value of house	Down payment	Value of Mortgage	Equity
110	0	98.77	11.23
110	10	88.89	21.11
110	20	79.02	30.98
110	30	69.07	40.93

1 year later(9-15-09,market rates remain at 6%)

Value of house	Down payment	Value of Mortgage	Equity
120	0	98.77	21.23
120	10	88.89	31.11
120	20	79.02	40.98
120	30	69.07	50.93

1 year later(9-15-09,market rates remain at 6%)

Value of house	Down payment	Value of Mortgage	Equity
130	0	98.77	31.23
130	10	88.89	41.11
130	20	79.02	50.98
130	30	69.07	60.93

			(Continued)

1 year later(9-15-09 , market rates remain at 6%)

Value of house	Down payment	Value of Mortgage	Equity
140	0	98.77	41.23
140	10	88.89	51.11
140	20	79.02	60.98
140	30	69.07	70.93

However, when the market price of the home falls, the mortgage goes "under the water", exhibiting negative equity sooner, the greater the financial leverage and the greater the fall in the market price of the home. A striking example of the boom in housing prices took place in Miami, Florida as reported in Table 7.5. Home prices nearly tripled from January 2000 to December 2006, then plummeted in half by February 2011.

Table 7.5   The boom and the bust in Miami's home prices

Miami, Florida

January 2000	100	% change
December 2006	281	181%
February 2011	138	− 51%

Source: The Standard and Poor's/Case-Shiller Home Price Index.

This represents a compound annual rate of appreciation of 19% per year during the housing boom and a fall of 16% per year during the bust. For the United States 20 city index, prices doubled from January 2000 to July 2006 to a level of 206, then fell to 138 in February 2011. The boom increased household wealth through increasing equity values, then destroyed most of the wealth during the bust. Further, the bust gave rise to the problem of negative equity. Table 7.6 indicates the problem of falling equity when home prices decline.

Table 7.6   Falling equity with falling home prices

Loan origination(8-15-08 ,6% fixed rate, 30 years)

Value of house	Down payment	Value of Mortgage	Equity
100	0	100	0
100	10	90	10
100	20	80	20
100	30	70	30

(Continued)

1 year later(9-15-09, market rates remain at 6%)

Value of house	Down payment	Value of Mortgage	Equity
90	0	98. 77	- 8. 77
90	10	88. 89	1. 11
90	20	79. 02	10. 98
90	30	69. 07	20. 93

.1 year later(9-15-09, market rates remain at 6%)

Value of house	Down payment	Value of Mortgage	Equity
80	0	98. 77	- 18. 77
80	10	88. 89	- 8. 89
80	20	79. 02	0. 98
80	30	69. 07	10. 93

1 year later(9-15-09, market rates remain at 6%)

Value of house	Down payment	Value of Mortgage	Equity
70	0	98. 77	- 28. 77
70	10	88. 89	- 18. 89
70	20	79. 02	- 9. 02
70	30	69. 07	0. 93

1 year later(9-15-09, market rates remain at 6%)

Value of house	Down payment	Value of Mortgage	Equity
60	0	98. 77	- 38. 77
60	10	88. 89	- 28. 89
60	20	79. 02	- 19. 02
60	30	69. 07	- 9. 07

The positive and negative effects on mortgage holder equity can be vividly seen in the Home Price Index in Figure 7.3. From 1996 to 2007, a ten year period, housing prices rose at a near accelerating rate, topping out at 20% in 2005. In 2007, housing prices began falling and are still falling in May 2012.

The fall in housing prices of 2006—2007 were both dramatic and unanticipated. Once unsold inventories of existing and new houses reach ten or eleven months supply, and prices are cut, the drop was sharp and steep. As a fraction of GDP, residential construction fell from 6.2% in 2005 and 5.8% in 2006 to 4.2% in 2007. In terms of USD, that represents a decline in residential investment of 127 billion USD, as reported in Table 7.11. Due to the stock-flow nature of the housing cycle, the downturn is by no means over. "There is very little, if any, good news about housing. Prices continue to weaken, trends in sales and construction are

Figure 7.3   The change in housing prices in the US

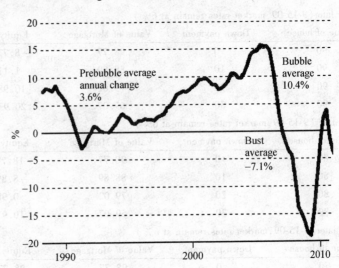

Source: The Standard and Poor's Case/Shiller Home Price Index and *the Wall Street Journal*.

disappointing." says David M. Blitzer, Chairman of the Index Committee at S&P Indices. ... Recent data on existing-home sales, housing starts, foreclosure activity and employment confirm that we are still in a slow recovery. Existing home sales and housing starts rose in March, but remain close to recent lows. Foreclosure activity showed decreases in mortgage delinquencies in the fourth quarter of 2010, but are still close to historic highs." (April 26, 2011, S&P Indices accessed May 8, 2011, www. standardandpoors)

In the News: China's Real Estate Sector

China's real estate sector showed a slowdown of the rise in real estate prices during 2008, then a brief fall in early 2009, before rising again at high annual rates, as shown in Figure 7.4.

Figure 7.4   China: Sales price index of residential and commercial buildings in 70 large and medium size cities (percentage change from a year earlier)

Source: Chinese National Bureau of Statistics, *the Wall Street Journal*.

Floor space sold was at reduced rates during almost all of 2008, reflecting the fall in demand relative to a year earlier, consistent with the fall in prices in early 2009. Once again, the rise in sales of floor space resumed in 2009, but slowed somewhat in 2010, as shown in Figure 7.5.

Figure 7.5   China: Real estate floor space sold (percentage change in square meters from a year earlier)

Source: Chinese National Bureau of Statistics, *the Wall Street Journal*.

> **In the News**: China's policies to slow real estate lending and inflation
>
> ---
>
> Table 7.7 reports China's policies to slow the rise in housing prices.
>
> **Table 7.7** China's policies to slow the rise in housing prices
>
> | APRIL 15, 2010 | MAY 6 | SEPT. 29 | OCT. —NOV. | OCT. 20 | DEC. 25 | JAN. 26, 2011 | JAN. 28 | FEB. 8 |
> |---|---|---|---|---|---|---|---|---|
> | The State Council raises minimum down payments for second-home purchases to 50% from 40% | Shenzhen restricts apartment purchases by foreigners and Hong Kong and Macau residents to one each until the end of the year | New rules require a 30% down payment on putchases of primary residences. Banks are ordered to stop lending for third-home purchases. | Several local govemments introduce limits on home purchases. | The central bank raises interest rates by a quarter percentage point. | The central bank raises interest rates by a quarter percentage point. | The State Council raises down-payment requirements for second-home purchases to 60% from 50%. | Shanghai and Chongqing start trials of an annual property tax. | The central bank raises interest rates by a quarter percentage point. |
>
> Note: Most recent figure is from December 2010; includes residential and commercial property.
>
> Source: National Bureau of Statistics (property price); WSJ reporting (timeline).

Strategic default

Falling housing prices often imply mortgage holders have negative equity, giving them an incentive to "walk away" from their mortgages. High leverage entailed in low down payments mean that small housing price declines may trigger a strategic default choice.

Default and foreclosure, by the same token, add to the momentum for housing prices to fall. A vicious cycle of falling housing prices, rising default rates and further falling prices as the foreclosed homes come onto the market is a key feature of the slowdown in real estate construction.

A potential buyer who has deposited $50,000 in earnest money to purchase a condominium under construction is under no obligation to buy the unit when it is finished. If the market price of the condominium has fallen $50,000 below its sales price, the potential buyer has the option to forfeit, leaving the $50,000 with the builder. Or she can recover some or all of the deposit by claiming that the contract conditions were not satisfied.

The importance of residential construction in investment has led to slowdowns in the major economies of the world from the problem of default in sub-prime mortgages, negative equity, and strategic forfeit of contracts. Figure 7.6 illustrates an optimal strategic default when equity is sufficiently negative to warrant the costs of default.

Figure 7.6　Optimal strategic default with negative equity

Source: Yong Chen, Michael Connolly, Wenjin Tang, and Tie Su(2009).

Applying the Concept: Foreclosure

Foreclosure is a process that allows a lender to recover some of the amount owed on a defaulted loan by selling or taking ownership (repossession) of the property securing the loan. The foreclosure process begins when a borrower/owner defaults on loan payments (usually mortgage payments) and the lender files a public default notice, called a Notice of Default or Lis Pendens. The foreclosure process can end one of four ways:

1. The borrower/owner reinstates the loan by paying off the default amount during a grace period determined by state law. This grace period is also known as pre-foreclosure.

2. The borrower/owner sells the property to a third party during the pre-foreclosure period. The sale allows the borrower/owner to pay off the loan and avoid having a foreclosure on his or her credit history.

3. A third party buys the property at a public auction at the end of the pre-foreclosure period.

4. The lender takes ownership of the property, usually with the intent to re-sell it on the open market. The lender can take ownership either through an agreement with the borrower/owner during pre-foreclosure or by

取消抵押品赎回权(Foreclosure):允许债权人通过出售或获得所有权的方式,对违约贷款的损失进行一定程度的弥补的过程。

In Colorado in 2009, the rate of foreclosure per 100 mortgages was
15.3%, 17.5% in Nevada, 11.3% in California, 11% in Michigan,
and 8% in Florida (Source: *RealtyTrac.*)

The loan to value ratio

Home mortgages typically require a down payment. For instance, the
benchmark down payment in the United States is 20%, while it is 30% in
China on the first home. The *loan to value* (LTV) ratio in these two instances is 80% and 70% respectively. The LTV ratio represents the mortgage loan to the assessed value of the asset, the home in this instance, or
$\frac{D}{A}$. Note that:

$$1 - LTV = \frac{A}{A} - \frac{D}{A} = \frac{E}{A}$$

Consequently, financial leverage equals:

$$\frac{A}{E} = \frac{1}{1 - LTV}$$

We can thus in Table 7.8 have a simple relationship between LTV,
the percentage down payment, and financial leverage at loan origination:

Table 7.8　Loan to value and financial leverage

Loan to Value	Down payment	Financial leverage
0.99	0.01	100.0
0.95	0.05	20.0
0.90	0.10	10.0
0.85	0.15	6.7
0.80	0.20	5.0
0.75	0.25	4.0
0.70	0.30	3.3
0.65	0.35	2.9
0.60	0.40	2.5
0.55	0.45	2.2
0.50	0.50	2.0

Of course, a NINJA loan, no income, no job, no assets and a LTV
= 1 would have infinite leverage!

Pre-construction "earnest money"

A good time to buy a real estate investment is during the pre-construction finance phase. A builder must pre-sell from 60% to 70% of his/her units to qualify for construction finance. In order to buy during this phase, a deposit of 10% of the sales prices is made. The "earnest money" is then deposited in a third-party escrow account until the development is completed and the closing can take place. In the meantime, the builder can obtain a "bridge" loan or mezzanine finance while the construction loan is pending.

This pre-construction finance period is thus critical to launch the development. If the builder fails to pre-sell sufficient units, the project is off and the deposits returned. What happens when a buyer purchases the unit early at a fairly good market price, the market price rises, then suddenly falls? This describes many condominium and apartment developments in US cities. The potential buyer, not having closed yet, is in a unique position of holding a call option to buy the unit at a sales or strike price determined in advance. If the market price is below the sales prices less the earnest monies, the buyer has the business option to forfeit.

Following the developer's filing of official condominium documents, the most the buyer can lose by failing to close is the initial deposit. This is a contractual forfeit. Say the buyer purchases the unit for delivery in one year for $500,000, depositing $50,000 in "earnest" or good faith money in the escrow account. In one year, if the unit appreciates 10%, the buyer will close, earning potential profits of $50,000. However, should the market price fall 10% or more, the buyer has the legal option to forfeit on the contract, forfeiting to the builder the initial $50,000 deposit. Some recovery of the initial deposit may also be possible.

保证金（Earnest money）：房产购买者付给开发商以确保未来购房的担保金。

Applying the Concept: Credit Default Swap

The buyer of a credit swap pays premia for credit protection against the default of a bond or firm, whereas the seller of the swap guarantees the credit worthiness of the product. The risk of default is transferred from the holder of the security to the seller of the swap. For example, the buyer of a credit swap will be entitled to the par value of the bond by the seller of the swap, should the bond default—fail to make its coupon payments.

信用违约互换（Credit Default Swap）：互换的购买者向互换的出售者支付一定费用，从而将违约风险转移到互换的出售方。

Figure 7.7 illustrates the cash flows between the protection buyer and seller when there is no default.

如图所示,互换的购买者持有债券,他因为持有债券而面临信用违约风险。因此,他向互换出售者购买互换,并支付一定金额的费用,当债券发行人违约时,债券持有人(即互换的购买者)并不会损失惨重,因为互换的出售者会把债券的面值支付给互换的购买者。

Figure 7.7 A credit default swap with no default

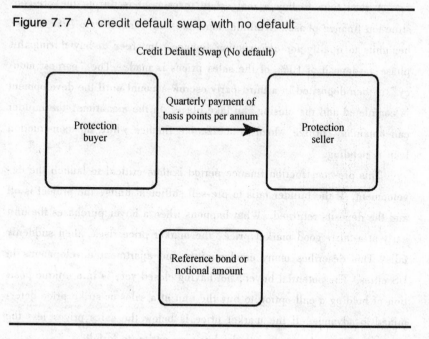

Credit Default Swap (No default)

When a default occurs, the seller of the credit default insurance pays the protection buyer, as illustrated in Figure 7.8.

Figure 7.8 A credit default swap with a default

Credit Default Swap (Default)

The difference between a credit default swap and an insurance policy against default is that anyone can purchase the insurance, even those who have no direct interest in the loan. This type of investor is commonly referred to as a speculator, while the one holding the bond is referred to as a hedger. If the borrower defaults on the loan, not only does the lender receive payment by the insurance company, the speculator receives money as well. Speculation proved key to the massive losses by AIG when Lehman Brothers defaulted since AIG had sold credit default swaps against LB and other defaults. A significant portion of the AIG bailout monies of up to $173 billion were paid to investment banks that had purchased Credit Default swaps from AIG. Credit default swaps are not traded on an exchange and there is no required reporting of transactions to a government agency. This may be changed by the Dodd Frank regulation bill, but that remains to be seen. A graphical representation of the major purchases of credit default insurance against the default of mortgage backed assets, including those of Lehman Brothers, is provided in Figure 7.9.

Figure 7.9 AIG's default swap insurance to five major Wall Street Banks

The payouts ranged from 3.3 billion dollars to UBS to 11 billion dollars to the Société Générale, as illustrated in Figure 7.10. AIG, originally headquartered in Shanghai, received a TARP loan of $85 billion, most of which has been converted to preferred shares in AIG.

Figure 7.10 AIG's payments of default swap insurance sold to five major Wall Street Banks

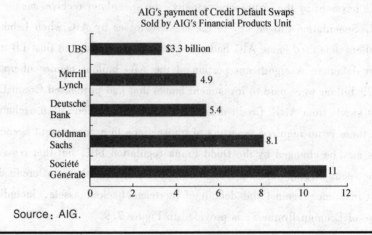

AIG's payment of Credit Default Swaps Sold by AIG's Financial Products Unit

Source: AIG.

Counter-party risk

High leverage and securitization of assets compounds counter-party risk—the risk that default of a counter-party in a contract, loan or impairment of a security inflicting loss on the investor holding the counterpart, the lender, or the holder of the security. The securitization of mortgages and collateralization of debt obligations spreads leveraged counterparty risk throughout the financial system. At the height of the financial bubble, leveraged mortgage backed assets and collateralized debt obligations were held by Fannie Mae (FNMA), Freddie Mac (FM) and the Federal Home Loan Mortgage Corporation (FHLMC), known as Freddie Mac, as well as investment banks and insurance companies. Fannie Mae and Freddie Mac were previously Government Sponsored Enterprises but were put under the conservatorship of the Federal Housing Finance Agency (FHFA) September 2008 after its stock fell to 50 cents and was delisted in June. Wall Street banks issued notes and shares rated investment grade to other investors and financial institutions worldwide. When the consumer defaults on the initial loan, the default spreads throughout the financial system, impairing the mortgage back assets and collateralized debt obligations on which they reside, as in Figure 7.9 elaborated by Wachovia Research in 1994.

Figure 7.11　Counterparty Risk

如图所示,交易对手风险在金融系统中传递。

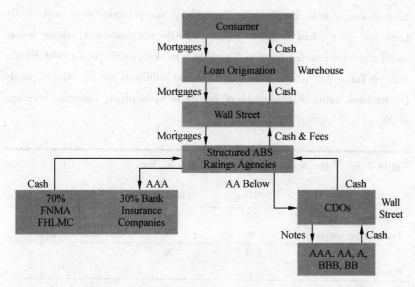

Source: Wachovia Research, 1994.

(FNMA) Federal National Mortgage Association, commonly known as Fannie Mae.

(FHLMC) Federal Home Loan Mortgage Corporation, known as Freddie Mac.

(ABS) Asset Backed Securities.

(CDOs) Collateralized Debt Obligations.

(Ratings Agencies) Standard and Poor's, Moodys, Fitch.

Defaults on such levered assets sends counterparty fear through the financial system, giving rise to the term "toxic" assets that ceased to be traded as financial markets froze, leaving investors holding illiquid assets of dubious value. Indeed, since trading in many markets came to a halt, it was difficult to value many assets. Thus, "marking to market" was not possible since there was no mechanism for price discovery. The US Treasury and the Federal Reserve Bank intervened by purchasing many of these assets and lending to the insolvent banks, thus providing a market for the assets and liquidity for the banks. Nowhere was the impact more important than on commercial and investment banks, as well as insurance companies holding these assets.

Leveraged financial institutions

Both commercial and investment banks were highly leveraged prior to the financial crisis. During the housing boom, this meant rising bank prof-its. Of course, during the bust in housing prices and the value of mortgage backed assets held by them as securities, many banks were technically bankrupt, i. e. had negative equity. While not insolvent, these banks could not continue for long as "zombie" banks. Consider *Levered Bank, Inc.* in Table 7.9 whose assets are 100 and liabilities are 95. Consequent-ly, its book value or shareholders' equity is 5, implying financial leverage of 20.

Table 7.9 Bank leverage (Levered Bank, Inc.)

	Assets	Liabilities	
Reserves	10	95	Debt
Loans & securities	90	5	Shareholders' equity
	100	100	
Financial leverage			
Assets/Equity	20		
Debt/Equity	19		

Now suppose that the value of its loans and securities fall by 10%, and are "marked to market" at 91. Note: if the bank's assets are availa-ble-for-sale or traded securities, the balance sheet carrying value is the market value. If they are classified as held-to-maturity assets, they may be carried at cost. The hypothetical balance sheet in Table 7.10 would have negative shareholders' equity, that is, it would be bankrupt from an ac-counting point of view. Its book value would be negative.

Table 7.10 Bank leverage and accounting bankruptcy (Levered Bank, Inc.)

	Assets	Liabilities	
Reserves	10	95	Debt
Loans & securities	81	−4	Shareholders' equity
	91	91	

联邦存款保险公司(Fed-eral Deposit Insurance Corporation, FDIC):是美国国会建立的独立的联邦政府机构,通过为存款提供保险、检查和监督金融机构以及接管金融机构,来维持美国金融体系的稳定性和公众信心。

If this were a single bank in isolation, the **Federal Deposit Insur-ance Corporation (FDIC)** could take over the operation of the bank, re-capitalize it, and sell it when it has a healthier balance sheet. Or, it could liquidate the bank entirely.

However, when it is virtually all banks, the monetary and fiscal authorities may decide that it is a "systemic crisis," a crisis of the financial system that has dire consequences for the economy as a whole. Then authorities may put in place an emergency Troubled Asset Relief Program (TARP) as in the United States to make loans to financial institutions and take ownership stakes in them, such as preferred or common shares. In the UK, Ireland, and Europe, some banks became state enterprises. The authorities may also attempt to merge weaker banks with stronger banks.

The harbinger of the crisis: Bear Stearns

Bear Stearns, a global investment bank headquartered in N.Y., engaged in securities trading and brokerage, until its collapse and distress sale at $10 a share to JPMorgan Chase in 2008, brokered by the FED. Bear Stearns held asset-backed securities which had lost significant value. In March 2008, the Federal Reserve Bank of New York provided an emergency loan to avert a sudden collapse of the company. However, on March 28, 2008, it was sold to JPMorgan Chase for ten dollars per share, financed by a loan from the FED, far below the 52-week high of $133.20 per share before the crisis. This was, however, an improvement on the two dollars per share originally agreed upon by Bear Stearns and JP Morgan Chase. The FED guaranteed against further losses by JPMorgan Chase in the risky loan to JPMorgan. At the same time, the FED launched its Primary Dealer Credit Facility to make loans to *primary dealers* —those that trade with the FED in its open market operations, including investment banks. The latter thus became eligible for emergency loans even though not being member commercial banks in the Federal Reserve System. Figure 7.12 reports losses in 2007 of global financial institutions.

贝尔斯登公司(Bears Stearns):成立于1923年,曾是美国第五大投资银行,在2008年的美国金融风暴中因亏损严重而被收购。

Among the top eleven losers in Figure 7.12, there are seven American financial institutions.

The bankruptcy of Lehman Brothers

Lehman Bros., a N.Y. investment bank, borrowed significant amounts to fund its investments in the years leading to its bankruptcy in 2008. Much of its investing was in mortgage backed assets, making it vulnerable to a housing downturn. Its leverage ratio—assets to owner's equity, increased from approximately 24:1 in 2003 to 31:1 by 2007. The Fed and the Treasury attempted a sale of Lehman Bros. to Bank of America,

雷曼兄弟公司(Lehman Brothers):成立于1850年,曾为美国第四大投资银行,于2008年9月15日宣布申请破产保护。

but BOA's due diligence forecast only negative equity and future operating losses. An offer by Barclays was rejected by the British monetary authorities, leading to the bankruptcy filing of September 15, 2008. The Lehman Bros. bankruptcy shook the financial world, raising the specter of counterparty risk and ushering in a flight to safety and cash.

Figure 7.12   Losses to financial institutions in 2007, billions of USD (as of February 19, 2008)

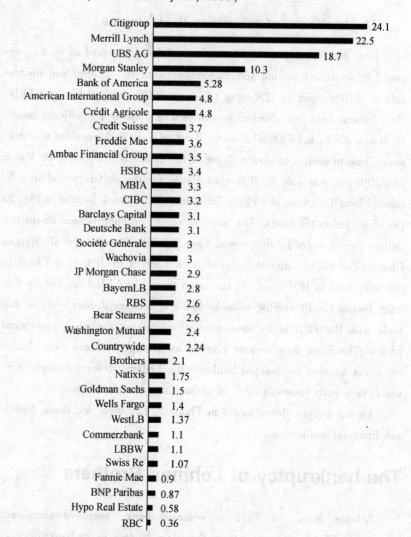

Citigroup	24.1
Merrill Lynch	22.5
UBS AG	18.7
Morgan Stanley	10.3
Bank of America	5.28
American International Group	4.8
Crédit Agricole	4.8
Credit Suisse	3.7
Freddie Mac	3.6
Ambac Financial Group	3.5
HSBC	3.4
MBIA	3.3
CIBC	3.2
Barclays Capital	3.1
Deutsche Bank	3.1
Société Générale	3
Wachovia	3
JP Morgan Chase	2.9
BayernLB	2.8
RBS	2.6
Bear Stearns	2.6
Washington Mutual	2.4
Countrywide	2.24
Brothers	2.1
Natixis	1.75
Goldman Sachs	1.5
Wells Fargo	1.4
WestLB	1.37
Commerzbank	1.1
LBBW	1.1
Swiss Re	1.07
Fannie Mae	0.9
BNP Paribas	0.87
Hypo Real Estate	0.58
RBC	0.36

Source: *RealtyTrac*, February 19, 2008.

While generating tremendous profits during the boom, Lehman Bros. leveraged position meant that just a 3.2% decline in the value of its assets would entirely eliminate its book value or equity. According to the bankruptcy court examiner's report: "On January 29, 2008, Lehman Brothers Holdings Inc. (LBHI) reported record revenues of nearly $60 billion and record earnings in excess of $4 billion for its fiscal year ending November 30, 2007. During January 2008, Lehman's stock traded as high as $65.73 per share and averaged in the high to mid-fifties implying a market capitalization of over $30 billion. Less than eight months later, on September 12, 2008, Lehman's stock closed under $4, a decline of nearly 95% from its January 2008 value. On September 15, 2008, LBHI sought Chapter 11 protection, in the largest bankruptcy proceeding ever filed. There are many reasons Lehman failed, and the responsibility is shared. Lehman was more the consequence than the cause of a deteriorating economic climate.

Lehman's financial plight, and the consequences to Lehman's creditors and shareholders, was exacerbated by Lehman executives, whose conduct ranged from serious but non-culpable errors of business judgment to actionable balance sheet manipulation; by the investment bank business model, which rewarded excessive risk taking and leverage; and by Government agencies, who by their own admission might better have anticipated or mitigated the outcome. "

Accounting shenanigans at Lehman Bros.

"Lehman did not disclose, however, that it had been using an accounting device (known within Lehman as "Repo 105") to manage its balance sheet—by temporarily removing approximately $50 billion of assets from the balance sheet at the end of the first and second quarters of 2008. In an ordinary repo, Lehman raised cash by selling assets with a simultaneous obligation to repurchase them the next day or several days later; such transactions were accounted for as financings, and the assets remained on Lehman's balance sheet. In a Repo 105 transaction, Lehman did exactly the same thing, but because the assets were 105% or more of the cash received, accounting rules permitted the transactions to be treated as sales rather than financings, so that the assets could be removed from the balance sheet. With Repo 105 transactions, Lehman's reported net leverage was 12.1 at the end of the second quarter of 2008; but if Lehman had used ordinary repos, net leverage would have to have been reported at 13.9. Contemporaneous Lehman e-mails describe the "function called repo 105 whereby you can repo a position for a week and it is regarded as a

雷曼兄弟公司的破产,一方面是因为其有着高杠杆率,另一方面,雷曼兄弟公司还利用"Repo 105"("回购 105")隐瞒其杠杆率。

true sale to get rid of net balance sheet. " Lehman used Repo 105 for no articulated business purpose except "to reduce balance sheet at the quarter-end. " Rather than sell assets at a loss, "[a] Repo 105 increase would help avoid this without negatively impacting our leverage ratios. " Lehman's Global Financial Controller confirmed that "the only purpose or motive for [Repo 105] transactions was reduction in the balance sheet" and that "there was *no substance* to the transactions. " (Report of Anton R. Valukas, Examiner, *op. cit.*)

Lehman reported that it had been in talks with Bank of America and Barclays for the company's possible sale. Bank of America declined, and Barclays ended its bid to purchase all or part of Lehman when the UK monetary authorities rejected the deal. Lehman Brothers filed for Chapter 11 bankruptcy protection on September 15, 2008. The Dow Jones closed down over 500 points, −4.4%, on September 15, 2008, a drop subsequently exceeded by a −7.0% plunge on September 29, 2008.

The resultant credit squeeze due to counterparty risk— *Cash is king*!

Due to counterparty risk, bank lending virtually came to a halt, even interbank lending. Commercial banks built up their excess reserves, as illustrated in Figure 7.13, following the bankruptcy of Lehman Bros.

Figure 7.13   Excess Reserves Held by U.S. Depository Institutions (USD billions)

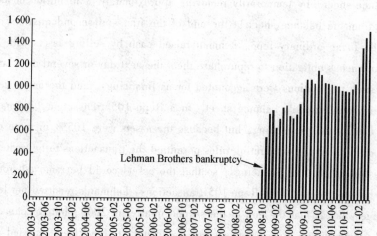

Source: Federal Reserve Board 2011.

As a result of the freezing of markets, the Federal Reserve Bank stepped in to prevent failure of the major investment banks, AIG, provided a *Term Asset-backed Security Loan Facility* (TALF) for the purchase of illiquid assets, holding up to 1.5 trillion dollars of MBAs as well as 400 billion dollars of commercial paper. Governor Bernanke had broadly interpreted the emergency powers of the FED to purchase assets from non-member banks, including investment banks, as well as commercial paper from firms. At the time of the crisis, this provided the necessary liquidity and equity to prevent systemic bank failure.

Figure 7.14　Total borrowings from the Federal Reserve System (USD millions)

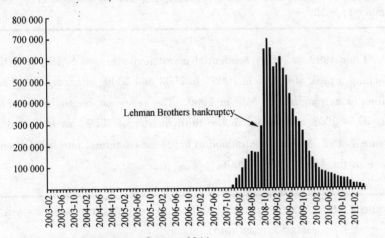

Source: Federal Reserve System 2011.

The Bank of China

"Bank of China saw its Hong Kong stock price fall by as much as 8.1 percent Friday as investors sold shares in reaction to the bank's report it holds US $9.65 billion (7.2 billion) in subprime asset-backed securities and collateralized debt obligations, or CDOs. That's 3.8 percent of its total securities investments." ("Bank of China reports heavy exposure to subprime crisis", The Associated Press, August 24, 2007.) Further, "Bank of China said Tuesday that third-quarter profit rose 22 percent, posting the slowest earnings growth among the country's largest lenders after a $322 million loss on U.S. subprime mortgage investments." ("Bank of China profit hamstrung by mortgage losses," Luo Jun, *Bloomberg News*, October 31, 2007.)

The macro-economic impact of the financial crisis

Residential construction, a spark-plug during the housing boom, sputtered during the bust, as recorded in Table 7.11.

Table 7.11 Residential investment as a share of GDP in the United States: 1999—2009

(Billions of Dollars)	1999	2000	2001	2002	2003	2004	2005	2006	2007	2008	2009
RI	426	449	472	509	578	681	775	762	629	472	352
GDP	9,354	9,952	10,286	10,642	11,142	11,868	12,638	13,399	14,062	14,369	14,119
RI as % of GDP	4.6%	4.5%	4.6%	4.8%	5.2%	5.7%	6.1%	5.7%	4.5%	3.3%	2.5%

Source: Bureau of Economic Analysis, Department of Commerce, September 1, 2010.

From 1999 to 2007, residential investment averaged 5.1% of GDP, reaching a peak of 6.1% in 2005. In 2008 and 2009, it averaged 2.9%, falling to a trough of 2.5% in 2009. The recession began in the third quarter of 2008 and ended in the third quarter of 2009, as indicated in Figure 7.15. A sharp contraction of 8.9% at an annual rate in GDP took place in the 4th quarter of 2008.

Figure 7.15 US GDP growth (percentage change at a seasonally adjusted annual rate)

Source: Bureau of Economic Analysis, Department of Commerce.

In the fourth quarter of 2008, the main negative forces are investment and consumption spending, as shown in Figure 7.16.

Figure 7. 16   The contributions of consumption and investment expenditure to growth in real GDP(Annual rate, seasonally adjusted)

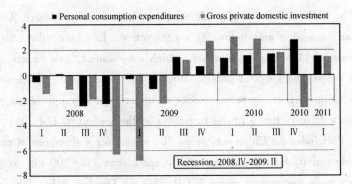

Source: Bureau of Economic Analysis, Department of Commerce.

New "mark to model" rules for assets whose price discovery is difficult were put in place by the FASB (Federal Accounting Standards Board). This makes markdowns of "legacy" assets less severe, but will make price discovery more difficult and the banks less likely to sell the assets at a larger discount. The danger is that it could lead to "zombie" banks. Due to counterparty risk, liquidity risk, and increasing collateral requirements, interbank lending has frozen significantly. Efforts by the FED to increase liquidity to promote increased credit have not yet succeeded. The commercial banks hold the new liquidity created by the Fed—"cash is king", credit is risky.

In Europe, the recession was deep and recovery is slowing as seen in Figure 7. 17 and has become negative in 2012.

当金融市场的流动性极低时,"mark to market"(逐日盯市)的定价方法便无法实现,因此,FASB(联邦会计准则委员会)允许金融机构运用"mark to model"(参照模型)方法来为难以估值的资产进行定价。通常来说,参照模型方法的估值会高于逐日盯市方法的估值。

Figure 7. 17   Annualized quarterly change in GDP for the euro area

Source: *Wall Street Journal*, November 7, 2011.

Europe's sovereign debt troubles have worsened since the recession.

Greek debt is over 150% of GDP, Italian 120%, Irish 112%, Portugueuse 102%, and Germany's 82%.

China's Purchaser's Manufacturing Index

The PMI is an index of manufacturing sector activity. Above 50 suggests an expansion and below 50 a contraction. In China, the index is composed of 11 sector sub-indices, which are: output, new orders, new export orders, backlogs of orders, stocks of finished goods, purchases of inputs, input prices, imports, stocks of major inputs, employment, and supplier's delivery time. In the beginning of the second half of 2011, the HSBC PMI index for China was below 50, suggesting a slowdown of manufacturing activity for the first time in recent history, the 100 city average property price per square meter fell 0.25% in October 2011. (Source: *Wall Street Journal*, October 1, 2011.)

The Troubled Asset Relief Program (TARP)

不良资产救助计划 (Troubled Asset Relief Program)：为了应对 2008 年的次贷危机，美国政府通过收购金融机构的不良资产以稳定金融市场的计划。该计划于 2008 年 10 月 3 日由美国前总统乔治·W.布什签署生效。

The TARP was signed into law by U.S. President George W. Bush on October 3, 2008. It allows the United States Treasury to purchase or insure up to $700 Billion of "troubled assets", defined as "(A) residential or commercial mortgages and any securities, obligations, or other instruments that are based on or related to such mortgages, that in each case was originated or issued on or before March 14, 2008, the purchase of which the Secretary determines promotes financial market stability; and (B) any other financial instrument that the Secretary, after consultation with the Chairman of the Board of Governors of the Federal Reserve System, determines the purchase of which is necessary to promote financial market stability, but only upon transmittal of such determination, in writing, to the appropriate committees of Congress."

The TARP allows the Treasury to purchase illiquid, difficult-to-value assets from banks and other financial institutions. The targeted assets can be mortgage backed asset and collateralized debt obligations, which were sold in a booming market until 2007 when they were hit by widespread foreclosures on the underlying loans. TARP was intended to improve the liquidity of these assets by purchasing them using secondary market mechanisms, thus allowing participating institutions to stabilize their balance sheets and avoid further losses. Table 7.12 indicates the initial levels of support that financial and automotive firms received from the TARP.

Table 7.12   TARP loans to financial and automobile companies

Company	Preferred stock purchased (millions USD)
Citigroup	$45,000
Bank of America	$45,000
AIG(American International Group)	$40,000
JPMorgan Chase	$25,000
Wells Fargo	$25,000
GMAC Financial Services(Ally)	$17,300
General Motors	$13,400
Goldman Sachs	$10,000
Morgan Stanley	$10,000
PNC Financial Services Group	$7,579
U.S. Bancorp	$6,600
Chrysler	$4,000
Capital One Financial	$3,555
Regions Financial Corporation	$3,500
American Express	$3,389
Bank of New York Mellon Corp	$2,000 to $3,000
State Street Corporation	$2,000 to $3,000
Discover Financial	$1,230

Source: U.S. Treasury.

Indeed, under the Term Asset-Backed Securities Loan Facility program, the FED has purchased commercial paper along with mortgage backed assets to the tune of $400 billion and $1.2 trillion respectively. Under the TARP program, many banks and financial institutions avoided bankruptcy and have mostly repaid their loans with interest. In the cases of AIG, the insurance company, and Citicorp, the Treasury has become a majority shareholder, and may not receive repayment in full. Loans to the automobile maker and the purchase of shares in General Motors (GM), will also not result in full repayment unless the common stock price rises substantially from its current $20.11, December 29, 2011. It would probably need to triple in price.

Citigroup converted $25 billion of preferred shares to common shares, AIG has repaid most of its TARP funds, while GMAC, now Ally, General Motors and Chrysler have not. Most financial institutions, with the exception of Citi and AIG, have repurchased their preferred shares, both due to financial recovery and a desire not to be subject to TARP governance regarding executive pay.

The Volcker Rule

沃克尔法则（Volcker Rule）：要求吸收存款的银行必须剥离其衍生产品业务。

保罗·沃克尔（Paul Volcker）：美国经济学家，他曾在里根和卡特总统时期出任美联储主席，结束了美国20世纪70年代到80年代初的高通胀，受到广泛的赞誉。30年后，沃克尔以83岁高龄再度出山，担任经济复苏顾问委员会主席，帮助奥巴马推进经济复苏政策。

Paul Volcker served as governor of the Federal Reserve System from 1979 to 1987, putting a stop to the inflation of the late 1970s. As a person of great integrity, he also served as the Chairman of the Swiss Bank report on the holdings of assets of those that had died and lost them in World War II. Volcker challenges the conventional wisdom that financial innovations have contributed anything to economic growth, suggesting instead that they have created moral hazard and contributed to the financial crisis.

At the *Future of Finance Initiative* in January 2009, major questions about the future role of finance were raised. Volcker challenges the conventional wisdom in his answers.

In the News: Does financial innovation contribute to economic growth?

You concluded with financial-services executives showing cultural sensitivity and responsible leadership. Well, I have been around the financial markets for 60 years, and how many responsible financial leaders have we heard speaking against the huge compensation practices?

Every day I hear financial leaders saying that they are necessary and desirable, they are wonderful and they are God's work. Has there been one financial leader to stand out and say that maybe this is excessive and that maybe we should get together privately to think about some restraint?

I hear about these wonderful innovations in the financial markets, and they sure as hell need a lot of innovation. I can tell you of two—credit-default swaps and collateralized debt obligations—which took us right to the brink of disaster. Were they wonderful innovations that we want to create more of?

You want boards of directors to be informed about all of these innovative new products and to understand them, but I do not know what boards of directors you are talking about. I have been on boards of directors, and the chance that they are going to understand these products that you are dishing out, or that you are going to want to explain it to them, quite frankly, is nil.

I mean: Wake up, gentlemen. I can only say that your response is inadequate. I wish that somebody would give me some shred of neutral evidence about the relationship between financial innovation recently and the growth of the economy, just one shred of information.

Do Innovations Do Much Good?

A few years ago I happened to be at a conference of business people, not financial people, and I was making a presentation. The conference was being addressed by a very vigorous young investment banker from London who was explaining to all these older executives how their companies would be dust if they did not realize the joys of financial innovation and financial engineering, and that they had better get with it.

I was listening to this, and I found myself sitting next to one of the inventors of financial engineering. I didn't know him, but I knew who he was and that he had won a Nobel Prize, and I nudged him and asked what all the financial engineering does for the economy and what it does for productivity.

Much to my surprise, he leaned over and whispered in my ear that it does nothing—and this was from a leader in the world of financial engineering. I asked him what it did do, and he said that it moves around the rents in the financial system—and besides, it's a lot of intellectual fun. Now, I have no doubts that it moves around the rents in the financial system, but not only this, as it seems to have vastly increased them.

How do I respond to a congressman who asks if the financial sector in the United States is so important that it generates 40% of all the profits in the country, 40%, after all of the bonuses and pay? Is it really a true reflection of the financial sector that it rose from $2\frac{1}{2}\%$ of value added according to GNP numbers to $6\frac{1}{2}\%$ in the last decade all of a sudden? Is that a reflection of all your financial innovation, or is it just a reflection of how much you pay? What about the effect of incentives on all our best young talent, particularly of a numerical kind, in the United States?

In Britain, I was just talking to a high-tech company about the immense attraction to go into finance when both Britain and the United States are suffering from a basic inability to produce things competitively, to keep up with the new economy. Is this a result of financial innovation that we should be really worried about?

Let us think about what structural changes are necessary to produce what is the heart of the problem, about too big to fail, moral hazard and the rest. As I say, I agree with many of your individual suggestions, but there were no suggestions in the area of moral hazard. It was suggested to improve regulation, and that may help, but having gone that far, it is better that you talk about some more serious structural changes.

I made a wiseacre remark that the most important financial innovation that I have seen the past 20 years is the automatic teller machine. That really helps people and prevents visits to the bank and is a real convenience.

What is the role of commercial banks?

Commercial banks are still at the heart of the system. In a crisis, everybody runs back to the commercial banks. They, after all, run the payment system. We cannot have this global economy without commercial banks operating an efficient payment system globally as well as nationally. They provide a depository outlet for individuals and businesses, and they are still big credit providers for small and medium-size businesses, but they backstop most of the big borrowers as well. The commercial-paper market is totally dependent on the commercial banking market. They are an essential financial institution that has historically been protected. It has been protected on one side and regulated on the other side.

I think that fundamental is going to remain. People are going to think it is important, it is important, it needs regulation and in extremis it needs protection—deposit insurance, lender of last resort and so forth.

I think that it is extraneous to that function that they do hedge funds, equity funds and that they trade in commodities and securities, and a lot of other stuff, which is secondary in terms of direct responsibilities for lenders, borrowers, depositors and all the rest.

There is nothing wrong with any of those activities, but let you nonbank people do it and you can provide fluidity in markets and flexibility. If you fail, you're going to fail, and I am not going to help you, and your stockholders are going to be gone, and your creditors will be at risk, and that is the way that it should be.

How can I be so blithe about making that statement? We need a new institutional arrangement which I believe has a lot of support. We need a resolution facility. What can that resolution facility do? If one of you fails and has systemic risk, then it steps in, takes you over and either liquidates or merges you, but it does not save you. That ought to be a kind of iron cross. How many other innovations can you tell me that have been as important to the individual as the automatic teller machine, which is in fact more of a mechanical innovation than a financial one?"

Source: Paul Volcker's remarks, excerpted from the *Journal Report*, Alan Murray, the *Wall Street Journal*, December 14, 2009.

These thoughts gave rise to the Volcker Rule, where commercial banks making commercial loans are entitled to Federal Deposit Insurance and Federal Savings and Loan Insurance Corporation (FSLIC), but investment banks who risk their investors money in proprietary trading are not.

Thus, while investment banks were encouraged to take over and establish commercial banks to be entitled to TARP monies during the crisis, they are now urged to either do commercial and investment banking or investment banking with proprietary trading desks, but not both. In particular, Goldman Sachs has shed itself of its proprietary trading branch to remain qualified as a commercial bank.

The Dodd-Frank Regulatory Bill

To remedy the moral hazard problem, the Dodd-Frank financial regulation bill of 2010 attempted to address the "**too big to fail**" problem. Partly, through the Volcker rule, the attempt is to restrain risk taking by commercial banks whose deposits are guaranteed by the FDIC. Investment banks who risk their investors' and their own money would, in principle, be allowed to fail. In practice, moral hazard is alive and well—large banks will probably never be allowed to fail, surely not *en masse*. The Lehman Bros. bankruptcy put the financial system at risk of systemic failure. As with the Sarbanes-Oxley Bill of 2002, the fear is that regulatory costs will exceed the benefits of any regulation. Worse yet, a new Consumer Protection Agency will make consumer credit more costly and reduce credit to the consumer. The US regulatory environment for financial institutions is becoming less friendly, discouraging business in the US, encouraging it to take place elsewhere.

"大而不倒"（"too big to fail"）：指当一些规模极大或在产业中具有关键性重要地位的企业濒临破产时，政府不能等闲视之，甚至要不惜投入公帑相救，以避免那些企业倒闭后所掀起的巨大连锁反应造成社会整体更严重的伤害，这种情况即称为"大而不倒"。

There were sufficient SEC regulations in place to stop the Madoff Ponzi game and sufficient warnings to the SEC to warrant a serious investigation of Madoff. However, as Stigler reminds us, regulators are typically "captured" by those they regulate. It is not clear how regulators will enforce the "5% skin in the game rule" for mortgage origination.

Conclusion

The financial crisis still lingers on in the United States. Housing prices are still falling in November 2011, and foreclosures rising. Some banks still have underperforming assets that are not marked down on their balance sheet. The unemployment rate was above 9% till November 2011, when it fell to 8.4% as a result of workers exiting the labor force. New hiring is not progressing at a rate that would permit a strong economic recovery. **Milton Friedman** once likened a business contraction to pulling

米尔顿·弗里德曼（Milton Friedman）：美国经济学家，1976 年被授予诺贝尔经济学奖，以表彰他在消费分析、货币供应理论及历史和稳定政策复杂性等范畴的贡献。

down on a rubber band, with recovery snapping back. Most recoveries have been of the rubber band variety. This one is not.

Despite record liquidity, low Fed Fund and Treasury rates, businesses and banks have not yet regained enough confidence in the future to invest and lend at a greater stride. Consumer wealth in the form of stock market equities has recovered, but their wealth in home equity has not, indeed it has fallen further. The consumer confidence level is still low and consumer spending slowing, though recovering a bit at the end of 2011. Businesses, banks, and consumers have been de-leveraging, which makes recovery difficult since it curtails private spending. New business and financial regulations as well as rapidly rising U. S. debt signals higher future taxes for businesses, banks, and households.

Government spending in the US has not followed a golden rule that deficits only be financed for public investment spending. On the contrary, the Economic Stimulus Bill of January 2009 focused, as did most state and local spending, on government **consumption** spending: That is, on consumption smoothing during the recession. This does not lay a strong foundation of renewed infrastructure for long term economic recovery. The *Boston Globe* summarized the economic stimulus plan succinctly, pointing out that only a small portion of the bill was specifically devoted to infrastructure. "Five weeks before becoming president, Barack Obama urged passage of a massive economic stimulus package, vowing that it would 'create millions of jobs by making the single largest new investment in our national infrastructure since the creation of the federal highway system in the 1950s.' But the bill passed by the House yesterday dedicates only about 5 percent of the $819 billion measure to highway, mass transit, and rail projects." (Source: "Only 5 percent of $819b plan would go toward infrastructure: Critics say transportation is shortchanged," Michael Kranish, *The Boston Globe*, January 29, 2009.) Indeed, it would appear from Figure 7.18 that the economic stimulus program is a misnomer: it was instead a consumption smoothing scheme.

Figure 7.18 The economic spending plan of January 2009, a consumption smoothing program

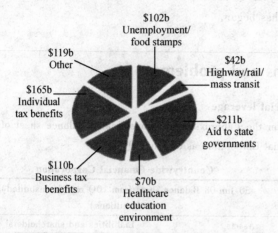

Source: Michael Kranish, Globe Staff, January 29, 2009.

如图所示,经济刺激计划中,仅有约 5% 的资金投入了基础设施建设。

Indeed, **Robert Barro**(1990) finds that increased government consumption spending significantly reduces real economic growth in a sample of 98 countries:

> For the 98 countries for which g^c/y (government consumption as a fraction of GDP) was measured (Barro 1990, table 1), a regression of the average annual growth rate of real per capita GDP from 1960 to 1985 on a set of explanatory variables yielded an estimated coefficient on g^c/y of −0.12 (standard error =0.03). Thus there is an indication that an increase in resources devoted to non-productive (but possibly utility-enhancing) government services is associated with lower per capita growth. (Barro, *op. cit.*, S124.)

罗伯特·巴罗(Robert Barro):哈佛大学经济学教授,美国著名古典宏观经济学家。他在 1990 年的研究中发现,在一个包含 98 个国家的样本中,政府支出的增长显著地减缓了真实经济增长。

Policymakers have fooled themselves into believing in the Keynesian government spending multiplier. When households and businesses are taxed more in the present and the future to finance government consumption spending it is likely that the multiplier will be zero (**Ricardian Equivalence**), or negative if the deficit money is not well spent—i. e. on government consumption and wars around the globe.

李嘉图等价(Ricardian Equivalence):在某些条件下,政府无论用债券还是税收筹资,其效果都是相同的或者等价的。

The U. S. now seems hampered by stagnating growth, rapidly growing sovereign debt, and a depreciating dollar. Europe's sovereign debt crisis has given a temporary respite to the exhausted dollar. The US benefits greatly from the dollar being the world's reserve and settlement currency.

However, no growth policy is in sight. Ultimately, inflation will come. More regulation and taxation are not growth policies. It will take years for the Chinese yuan to become a world reserve and settlement currency, but the process has begun.

Questions and problems

7.1　Financial leverage

Consider the (approximated) consolidated balance sheet of Countrwide Financial Corporation as of June 30, 2008.

Countrywide Financial Corporation

30-Jun-08 Balance sheet from 10Q report(unaudited)
(USD billions)

Assets	Liabilities and shareholders' equity
200	190 Liabilities
	10 Shareholders' equity
200 Total Assets	200 Liabilities plus shareholders' equity

Answer the following questions:

a. Compute three measures of financial leverage of Countrywide Financial.
   1.
   2.
   3.
b. What percent must the value of Countrywide Financial's assets be marked down (fall) in order for it to have zero equity?
c. Discuss the following statement: "For a given level of debt, a 10% rise (or fall) in asset values implies a multiplied rise (or fall) in equity as a percent (of itself), depending upon the degree of financial leverage."

7.2　The economic stimulus and Ricardian equivalence

Consider an economic stimulus where every citizen receives a $1,000 lump-sum check from the Treasury, but government expenditure and current taxes remain constant. Thus, each payment must be financed by a $1,000 new issue of government bonds. Would you expect this economic stimulus package to have a large effect on spending? Why or why not?

References and suggested reading

Barro, Robert J. (1990), "Government Spending in a Simple Model of

Endogeneous Growth," *The Journal of Political Economy*, 98 (5), Part 2: S103—S125.

Chen, Yong, Michael Connolly, Wenjin Tang and Tie Su (2009), "The Value of Mortgage Prepayment and Default Options," *The Journal of Futures Markets*, 29(9): 840—861.

Mankiw, N. Gregory and Laurence M. Ball (2011), *Macroeconomics and the Financial System*, New York: Worth Publishers, 537—574.

附录

货币的时间价值

Appendix

The Time Value of Money

利息 (Interest) :利息是时间偏好的结果。消费者总是偏好即期消费,而不是未来消费。因此,他们要求获得利息收入才会储蓄。

Interest is the result of time preference: consumption now is preferred to consumption in the future. To renounce consumption, households require interest in order to save. In a closed economy, savings finances investment and therefore economic growth. The same is true for open economies: excess national savings translates into a current account surplus which finances other countries savings deficiency, a current account deficit.

There are several truisms regarding interest:

1. Higher expected inflation causes nominal interest rates to rise by the same amount to compensate savers for the expected loss in principal: the decline in purchasing power of the savings put aside. This is known as the Fisher equation.

2. The risk of default causes nominal interest rates to rise according, paying a risk premium to the saver willing to take the risk of default.

3. The nominal interest rate must be above the expected rate of inflation plus the default risk premium, so that the real rate of interest on savings is positive.

This yields the risk-augmented Fisher equation where:

$$1 + r = (1 + R)(1 + \pi)(1 + \rho) \tag{A.1}$$

where

r = the nominal rate of interest

R = the real rate of interest

π = the expected rate of inflation

ρ = the default risk premium

When there is no risk of default, say for the moment on US Treasuries, $\rho = 0$. Thus we have for default free assets:

$$1 + r = (1 + R)(1 + \pi) \tag{A.2}$$

The expected real rate of interest is:

$$R = \frac{r - \pi}{1 + \pi} \tag{A.3}$$

which is always positive in a free capital market. However, if the actual inflation exceeds the expected inflation sufficiently, the realized real rate R^* may be negative:

当真实的通货膨胀率大大超过预期通货膨胀率时,真实的利率可能为负。

$$R^* = \frac{r - \pi^*}{1 + \pi^*} \qquad (A.4)$$

Indeed, the worst rate of realized return is -100%. When π^* is very large, R^* approaches minus one. That is, the entire investment is lost:

$$\lim_{\pi^* \to \infty} = \frac{r - \pi^*}{1 + \pi^*} = -1 = -100\% \qquad (A.5)$$

When a default occurs, the real rate of return can also be negative. In the case of full default on interest and principal, the real rate of return is once again -100%. The interest rate is a truly important price. It is the price of present consumption in terms of future consumption.

Notation:

t = time in years

m = frequency of interest payment per year (number of conversion periods per year)

r = nominal rate of interest rate per annum

i = interest rate of the conversion period

P = present value

A = accumulated value

r_e = effective rate of interest per annum

For example, if the original principal is P dollars and the interest is compounded per period at the rate of i, then at the end of the first period, the new principal, or accumulated amount, will be the sum of principal plus interest on principal.

$$A_1 = P + iP = P(1 + i)$$

The interest earned at the end of the second period is computed on A_1, so at the end of the second period, the accumulated amount will be:

$$A_2 = A_1 + iA_1 = (1 + i)A_1 = (1 + i)(1 + i)P = (1 + i)^2 P$$

Similarly at the end of the $n'th$ period, the accumulated amount will be:

$$A_n = P(1 + i)^n \qquad (A.6)$$

To convert the annual nominal rate of interest, r, to a periodic interest rate, we divide r by m, so that $i = \dfrac{r}{m}$ where m is the number of payment or conversion periods per year. Consequently, $n = mt$. We substitute these in (A.6) to derive the equation that indicates the accumulated value of a present sum P yielding annual interest of r paid m times per annum:

$$A = P \left(1 + \frac{r}{m}\right)^{mt} \qquad (A.7)$$

If interest earned is added to the principal and thereafter earns interest itself at the same rate, it is called **compound interest**. For example, in Table A.1 a sum of $1,000 principal paid now will accumulate into the following amounts after three years, $t = 3$, with payments of 5% interest m times a year:

Table A. 1   Accumulated interest after three years depending on the frequency of interest payments per year

t	m	r	P	$A(3\ \text{years})$
3	1	0.05	$1,000	$1,157.63
	2			$1,159.69
	4			$1,160.75
	12			$1,161.47

Notice that monthly interest payments, $m = 12$, yield a slightly higher accumulated sum than quarterly, $m = 4$, semi-annual, $m = 2$, or annual, $m = 1$, payments. In general, the more frequent the interest payment the greater the accumulated value.

Present value

Thus, the present value of the initial investment to be set aside at an annual rate of interest r with m conversion periods per year is indicated by (A.8). In Table A.2, the present value of one thousand dollars to be received in three years is calculated as a function of the number of conversion periods per year.

$$P = A \left(1 + \frac{r}{m}\right)^{-mt} \qquad (A.8)$$

Table A.2 calculates the present value of a sum to be paid depending on the number of conversion periods.

Table A.2   The present value of 1,000 dollars paid in year 3 using a discount rate of 5%, depending on the number of conversion periods paying r on P

t	m	r	$A(3\text{ years})$	P
3	1	0.05	$1,000	$863.84
	2			$862.30
	4			$861.51
	12			$860.98

The interpretation of this result is that you only need to make an initial investment of $860.98 to accumulate one thousand dollars in three years if the 5% interest on $860.99 is paid monthly, $m=12$. However, if the 5% interest is paid only quarterly, $m=4$, you must set aside today a slightly higher amount, $861.51 dollars to accumulate one thousand dollars in three years.

The effective rate of interest per annum is simply:

$$r_e = \left(1 + \frac{r}{m}\right)^m - 1 \quad \text{since} \quad t = 1 \qquad (A.9)$$

You are promised a 2% monthly rate of return, say by Bernie Madoff. The effective rate of interest per annum, if you indeed receive 2% a month, is:

$$r_e = \left(1 + \frac{0.02 \times 12}{12}\right)^{12} - 1 = 26.8\%$$

Similarly, when you are paid 2% quarterly, this represents an effective rate of 8.24% per annum:

$$r_e = \left(1 + \frac{0.02 \times 4}{4}\right)^4 - 1 = 8.24\%$$

The simple rates of interest are $2 \times 12 = 24\%$ and $2 \times 4 = 8\%$ respectively.

When this rate of interest is promised, *caveat emptor*!

Table A.3 indicates the effective rate of interest, depending on the number of conversion payments.

Table A.3 The effective rate of interest depending on the number of conversion payments

r	m	r_e
5%	1	5%
	2	5.06%
	4	5.095%
	12	5.116%

Continuously compounded interest

连续复利（Continuously compounded interest）：连续复利是在期数趋于无穷大的极限情况下得到的利率，此时不同期之间的间隔很短，可以看作是无穷小量。

Let $x = \dfrac{m}{r}$. Then in (A.7) we have

$$A = P \left(1 + \frac{1}{x} \right)^{xrt} = P \left[\left(1 + \frac{1}{x} \right)^x \right]^{rt} \qquad (A.10)$$

In the limit as t approaches infinity:

$$\lim_{x \to \infty} A = P \left[\lim_{x \to \infty} \left(1 + \frac{1}{x} \right)^x \right]^{rt}$$

but

$$\lim_{x \to \infty} \left(1 + \frac{1}{x} \right)^x = e$$

Therefore

$$\lim_{m \to \infty} P \left[\left(1 + \frac{r}{m} \right)^m \right]^{rt} = Pe^{rt} \qquad (A.11)$$

This yields the accumulated value continuously compounded:

$$A = Pe^{rt} \qquad (A.12)$$

There is little difference between daily compounding and continuous compounding, as seen in Table A.4: Table A.4 indicates the accumulated value of discrete and continuous compound interest payments on an initial investment of \$1,000, depending on the number of conversion payments.

Table A.4   Accumulated values of an initial payment of $1,000 with continuous versus discrete conversion payments of interest r percent per year paid on P

m	r	P	A 1 year	A 2 years	A 3 years	A 4 years	A 5 years
1	0.05	$1,000	$1,050.00	$1,102.50	$1,157.63	$1,215.51	$1,276.28
2			$1,050.63	$1,103.81	$1,159.69	$1,218.40	$1,280.08
4			$1,050.95	$1,104.49	$1,160.75	$1,219.89	$1,282.04
12			$1,051.16	$1,104.94	$1,161.47	$1,220.90	$1,283.36
360			$1,051.27	$1,105.16	$1,161.82	$1,221.39	$1,284.00
Continuous			$1,051.27	$1,105.17	$1,161.83	$1,221.40	$1,284.03

The corresponding present value is indicated by equation (A.13) and shown in Table A.5.

$$P = Ae^{-rt} \qquad (A.13)$$

Table A.5   Present values of $1000 paid in each year

m	r	P	P year 1	P year 2	P year 3	P year 4	P year 5	P every year*
1	0.05	$1,000	$952.38	$907.03	$863.84	$822.70	$783.53	$4,329.48
2			$951.81	$905.95	$862.30	$820.75	$781.20	$4,322.01
4			$951.52	$905.40	$861.51	$819.75	$780.01	$4,318.19
12			$951.33	$905.03	$860.98	$819.07	$779.21	$4,315.61
360			$951.23	$904.84	$860.72	$818.74	$778.81	$4,314.35
Continuous			$951.23	$904.84	$860.71	$818.73	$778.80	$4,314.31

* If the cash flow of $1,000 is received every year.

Once again, the present values are the amounts that must be set aside now at interest rate r with m conversion periods per year to yield $1,000 in the year indicated.

In general, if a project or firms is expected to generate "free cash flow" of $1,000 a year for five years, we then add the corresponding present values. For simplicity, consider only annually compounded interest at 5%. A firm generating free cash flow of $1,000 a year for five years would have an equity value today of $4,329.48, as shown in Table A.6.

Table A.6   Present values of free cash flow of $1,000 per year every year for 5 years

m	r	Free cash flow every year	P year 1	P year 2	P year 3	P year 4	P year 5	Sum of Ps Net Present value(equity value)
1	0.05	$1,000	$952.38	$907.03	$863.84	$822.70	$783.53	$4,329.48

The general formula for the net present value of an investment yielding free cash flow or a coupon payment of Π_i in period i for n periods is given by:

$$P = \Pi_0 + \frac{\Pi_1}{(1+r)} + \frac{\Pi_2}{(1+r)^2} + \frac{\Pi_3}{(1+r)^3} + \cdots + \frac{\Pi_n}{(1+r)^n}$$

$$(A.14)$$

This is perhaps the most important formula in finance for the valuation of assets, securities and firms.

A related formula is the **return on investment (ROI)** which is that rate of discount, δ, which makes the present value equal to zero, or:

$$0 = \Pi_0 + \frac{\Pi_1}{(1+\delta)} + \frac{\Pi_2}{(1+\delta)^2} + \frac{\Pi_3}{(1+\delta)^3} + \cdots + \frac{\Pi_n}{(1+\delta)^n}$$

$$(A.15)$$

which is a polynomial equation often yielding multiple solutions.

An example might be as illustrated in Table A.7.

Table A.7   The internal rate of return

	$(6,666.67)	$1,000.00	$1,000.00	$1,000.00	$1,000.00	$7,666.67
IRR	15%					

投资回报率(**Return on investment, ROI**):投资回报率是使投资的现值为零的折现率。

式(A.14)中给出的净现值公式在资产、证券和企业的估值中具有十分重要的用途。

Ranking investments or securities is better done by their net present value, particularly when the discount rate includes an appropriate risk and inflation premium. A special but important case is that of perpetuities that pay a sum in perpetuity.

Perpetuities

永续年金(**Perpetuities**):永续年金是指无限期支付的年金,它可以被视为普通年金的特殊形式,即期限趋于无穷的普通年金。式(A.16)给出了永续年金的现值公式,式(A.17)给出了增长率为 g 的永续年金的现值。

Let K be the dividend or sum paid in perpetuity. A no-growth perpetuity of K dollars has a present value:

$$P = \frac{K}{r} \qquad (\text{A.16})$$

A perpetuity of K dollars growing at the rate g has a present value:

$$P = \frac{K}{r - g} \qquad (\text{A.17})$$

These two formulas can be derived in different ways.

• **Continuous discounting**: \$1 growing at the continuous rate g in perpetuity discounted at the rate r yields a present value of:

$$\int_0^\infty e^{-(r-g)t}dt = \frac{1}{r - g} \qquad (\text{A.18})$$

found by taking the integral and evaluating in the limit as t approaches infinity and at $t = 0$ provided that $r > g$. If r were less than g, the perpetuity value would be unbounded, i. e. infinite.

• **Discrete discounting**: A perpetuity of \$1 growing at the rate g per period forever discounted at the rate r per period yields a present value of:

$$\frac{1}{r - g} \qquad (\text{A.19})$$

Let Z the present value of a one dollar perpetuity growing at g per period:

$$Z = \frac{1}{1 + r} + \frac{1 + g}{(1 + r)^2} + \frac{(1 + g)^2}{(1 + r)^3} + \cdots + \frac{(1 + g)^{n-1}}{(1 + r)^n}$$

Multiply both sides by $\frac{1+g}{1+r}$ and subtract the result, yielding:

$$Z - \left(\frac{1 + g}{1 + r}\right)Z = \frac{1}{1 + r} - \frac{(1 + g)^n}{(1 + r)^{n+1}}$$

or

$$Z\left[\frac{1 + r}{1 + r} - \left(\frac{1 + g}{1 + r}\right)\right] = \frac{1}{1 + r} - \frac{(1 + g)^n}{(1 + r)^{n+1}}$$

or

$$Z\left(\frac{r - g}{1 + r}\right) = \frac{1}{1 + r} - \frac{(1 + g)^n}{(1 + r)^{n+1}}$$

or

$$Z = \frac{1}{r - g} - \left(\frac{1}{r - g}\right)\frac{(1 + g)^n}{(1 + r)^n} = \frac{1}{r - g} - \left(\frac{1}{r - g}\right)\left(\frac{(1 + g)}{(1 + r)}\right)^n$$

When $0 < g < r$, in the limit as n approaches infinity, the right hand term approaches zero, so:

$$Z = \frac{1}{r - g} \qquad (\text{A.20})$$

Remarks:

• A level perpetuity: When a one dollar perpetuity does not grow, its discounted value is simply:

$$\frac{1}{r} \tag{A.21}$$

Applications:

1. Terminal values

When $g > r$, the perpetuity has infinite value, $i.\,e.$ is unbounded from above. Consequently, as g approaches r, the terminal value of a business approaches infinity. Terminal values of a business are useful in discounting free cash flow. The first three years of free cash flow can be forecast, then the third year free cash flow can be assumed to be constant thereafter to infinity. Consequently the net present value of the firm is estimated as:

$$P = \Pi_0 + \frac{\Pi_1}{(1+r)} + \frac{\Pi_2}{(1+r)^2} + \frac{\Pi_3}{(1+r)^3} + \frac{T_3}{(1+r)^3} \tag{A.22}$$

where

$$T_3 = \frac{\Pi_3}{r} \tag{A.23}$$

If the last year's free cash flow grows forever at the rate g, the terminal value is indicated by:

$$T_3 = \frac{\Pi_3}{r - g} \tag{A.24}$$

As a practical matter, the assumption of a high growth rate in free cash flow relative to a low weighted average cost of capital implies a high terminal value even when discounted at 3 or 5 years, over-estimating the value of the business. That is, the lion's share of the present value of the business is its terminal value, which may not be credible. In Table A.8, an example of equity valuation might be:

> 终值（Terminal value）：
> 如果第三年到未来的现金流可以被认为恒定，那么终值公式可以用式（A.23）表示；如果从第三年起未来的现金流以增长率 g 增长，那么终值公式可以用式（A.24）表示。
>
> 当永续年金的增长率大于贴现率时，永续年金的价值为无穷大。

Table A.8 The net present value of free cash flow plus terminal value

	year 1	year 2	year 3	year 4	year 5	Sum of NPVs
Free cash flow	$1,000	$1,000	$1,000	$1,000	$7,666.67	(equity value)
NPV at 15%	$869.57	$756.14	$657.52	$571.75	$3,811.69	$6,666.67

In year 5, the free cash flow is $1,000 plus $1,000 divided by 0.15—the value of the firm as a perpetuity beginning in year 6—or $6,666.67.

2. A coupon bond

A bond with a fixed coupon of C payable annually for n years, at which time a face value of F_n is also paid, is worth today:

$$P = \frac{C_1}{(1+r)} + \frac{C_2}{(1+r)^2} + \frac{C_3}{(1+r)^3} + \cdots + \frac{F_n + C_n}{(1+r)^n} \quad (A.25)$$

where r is the per annum market rate of interest. The coupon payments can be split from the face payment, so that the discounted coupon flow when it is paid annually is worth:

$$P = \frac{C_1}{(1+r)} + \frac{C_2}{(1+r)^2} + \frac{C_3}{(1+r)^3} + \cdots + \frac{C_n}{(1+r)^n} \quad (A.26)$$

while the face payment is treated as a **zero coupon bond** with maturity n. Consequently, its value is:

$$P = \frac{F_n}{(1+r)^n} \quad (A.27)$$

零息债券（Zero coupon bond）:零息债券是指以贴现方式发行,不附息票,而于到期日时按面值一次性支付本利的债券。

If the same bond pays the coupon semiannually, twice a year, it is worth:

$$P = \frac{C_1}{\left(1+\frac{r}{2}\right)^{2\times0.5}} + \frac{C_2}{\left(1+\frac{r}{2}\right)^{2\times1}} + \frac{C_3}{\left(1+\frac{r}{2}\right)^{2\times1.5}}$$
$$+ \frac{C_3}{\left(1+\frac{r}{2}\right)^{2\times2}} + \cdots + \frac{(F_n + C_n)}{\left(1+\frac{r}{2}\right)^{2n}} \quad (A.28)$$

For example, Table A.9 values a 2 year coupon bond with interest paid every six months.

Table A.9 The net present value of a semi-annually paid 5% coupon bond with face value of $1000

r	m	t	A	P	Coupon	Face	Coupon + Face
0.05	2	0.5	$50	$48.78	$48.78		
		1	$50	$47.59	$47.59		
		1.5	$50	$46.43	$46.43		
		2	$1,050	$951.25	$45.30	$905.95	
				$1,094.05	$188.10	$905.95	$1,094.05

3. China versus the United States in real GDP: an arithmetic calculation

If income per capita in the US grows at the rate γ_{us} and income per capita in China grows at the rate γ_c, we have: $y^{us} = y_0^{us} e^{\gamma_{us}t}$ and $y^c = y_0^c e^{\gamma_c t}$.

China's income per capita overtakes that of the US when:

$$y_0^c e^{\gamma_c t} = y_0^{us} e^{\gamma_{us} t}$$

or

$$\frac{y_0^{us}}{y_0^c} = e^{(\gamma_c - \gamma_{us})t}$$

That is:

$$\ln\left[\frac{y_0^{us}}{y_0^c}\right] = (\gamma_c - \gamma_{us})t$$

or

$$\hat{t} = \frac{\ln\left[\dfrac{y_0^{us}}{y_0^c}\right]}{(\gamma_c - \gamma_{us})} \qquad (\text{A.29})$$

If China grows 7% faster than the U. S., China's income per capita in purchasing power parity terms (Source: www. cia. org/worldfactbook, June 2011) overtakes that of the US in 26.5 years.

$$\hat{t} = \frac{\ln\left[\dfrac{47,400}{7,400}\right]}{0.07} = \frac{\ln[6.4]}{0.07} = \frac{1.86}{0.07} = 26.5$$

In terms of absolute levels of income in purchasing power of billions of US dollars, China's real GDP overtakes that of the United States in 5.7 years.

$$\hat{t} = \frac{\ln\left[\dfrac{14,720}{9,872}\right]}{0.07} = \frac{\ln[1.491]}{0.07} = \frac{0.3995}{0.07} = 5.7$$

(Source: www. cia. org/worldfactbook, June 2011.)

4. Ricardian equivalence

李嘉图等价（Ricardian equivalence）：在某些条件下,政府无论通过债券还是税收筹资,其效果都是相同的或者等价的。

In his "Essay on the Funding System" (1820) David Ricardo studied whether it makes a difference to finance a war with the £ 20 million in current taxes or to issue government bonds with infinite maturity and annual interest payment of £ 1 million in all following years financed by future taxes. At the assumed interest rate of 5%, Ricardo concluded that ...

"In point of economy there is no real difference in either of the modes, for 20 millions in one payment, 1 million per annum for ever ... are precisely of the same value."

That is:

$$P = \frac{K}{r} = \frac{1}{0.05} = 20$$

When households and businesses are taxed more in the present and the future to finance current government consumption spending, it is likely that the spending multiplier will be zero (Ricardian Equivalence), or even negative if the deficit money is not well spent.

5. Sovereign debt

The primary fiscal deficit is written:

$$G_t + V_t - T_t$$

Where G_t is governmental spending on goods and services, V_t is governmental transfer payments (from Jane to Paul), T_t is governmental revenues from taxes, The total fiscal deficit includes interest payments at r on the Treasury's debt D_t.

Consequently, the total deficit may be written:

$$G_t + rD_{t-1} + V_t - T_t \qquad (A.30)$$

It is often useful to express the total deficit as a percentage of GDP, Y_t.

$$\frac{G_t + rD_{t-1} + V_t - T_t}{Y_t} \qquad (A.31)$$

Several countries have had total deficits that are a high fraction of GDP, such as Ireland, 32%, and Greece, 14%, in the recent past.

Consequently, debt this year is indicated by last year's debt, plus the interest payments on the debt, plus this year's primary deficit.

$$D_t \equiv (1 + r)D_{t-1} + G_t + V_t - T_t \qquad (A.32)$$

As a fraction of GDP, the debt to GDP ratio is indicated by:

$$\frac{D_t}{Y_t} \equiv (1 + r)\frac{D_{t-1}}{Y_t} + \frac{G_t + V_t - T_t}{Y_t} \qquad (A.33)$$

As a rule of thumb, when debt to income rises above 100%, a risk premium emerges. Greece's debt to income ratio is currently 1.5 for instance.

The financing of a deficit is necessary, so that:

$$G_t + rD_{t-1} + V_t - T_t \equiv \Delta H_t + \Delta D_t \qquad (A.34)$$

Where ΔH_t is newly printed high-powered, base money (i.e. Federal Reserve Bank purchases of US Treasury bonds), also known as "the printing press", and ΔD_t is the sale of new Treasury bonds to the public, domestic and foreign (approximately 52% of Treasuries are sold to US investors and banks, and 48% to foreign investors and banks, including Central Banks).

The increase in total Treasury debt, ΔB_t, is the sum of Treasuries sold to the FED and those sold to domestic and foreign individuals, firms, and banks, that is:

$$\Delta B_t = \Delta H_t + \Delta D_t \qquad (A.35)$$

The **no Ponzi game (NPG) condition** is written, with constant interest rate r, in the continuous case for convenience:

$$\lim_{t \to \infty}\left[D(t)e^{-rt}\right] = 0. \qquad (A.36)$$

That is, debt cannot increase faster asymptotically than the interest

总财政赤字 (Total fiscal deficit)：总的财政赤字在主要财政赤字的基础上，还包括了国债的利息支出。

财政赤字的融资 (Financing of deficit)：财政赤字的融资主要有两种方式：一是发行高能的基础货币，也即政府开动"印钞机器"；二是通过新发债券融资。

无庞氏骗局条件 (No Ponzi Game condition)：政府债务的增长速度不能大于利率的增长速度，否则就会产生违约风险，也即产生所谓的"庞氏骗局"。

rate. This gives an inter-temporal budget constraint for the government. In the case of most European governments and the US government in 2011, the inter-temporal budgets constraint does not seem to be satisfied. Should that continue, we can expect many sovereign defaults, including that of the US Treasury, either by explicit default by missing a payment or implicit default by unanticipated inflation.

6. Interest and default risk

违约风险（Default risk）：违约风险由信用风险溢价度量。信用风险溢价是由无风险利率折现的资产现值与资产实际价值的差值。

Default or credit risk is measured by the percentage discount of the market value of an asset relative to the present value of its payments at a risk-free interest rate (say a AAA US Treasury rate, held till August 4, 2011). In the Figure A.1, the present value of sovereign bonds as a fraction of GDP is indicated along the horizontal axis, discounted by the risk-free rate. If there is no default risk, the market value of the bonds plotted on the vertical axis would be the same, as plotted along the 45-degree line from the origin. When there is default risk, the market value falls below the risk-free value indicated along the 45-degree line. As indebtedness increases relative to income, holding other things such as income constant, it becomes more difficult to service the debt, so a discount emerges. It is entirely conceivable that additional debt might reduce the expected present value of repayment—more debt would have in fact less market value. In that case, the market value curve slopes downward. In the previous example of a risky coupon bond with a present value of 100% of GDP at the risk-free rate, the present value of expected repayment is only 75% in one year. The default-risk premium is 25/75 = 35.33%.

Figure A.1   Measuring default risk

6. The rule of 70

How long does it take for a variable to double, such as GDP per capita, if the growth rate is g percent? If y is growing at the rate γ percent, we have:

$$y = y_0 e^{\gamma t}$$

To double, the variable must be $2y$ or:

$$y_0 e^{\gamma t} = 2y_0$$

Or

$$e^{\gamma t} = 2$$

Taking natural logarithms, and solving:

$$\gamma t = \ln(2) = 0.693147 \approx 0.7$$

or

$$t \approx \frac{0.7}{\gamma} \qquad (\text{A.}37)$$

In words, anything that grows at 7% will double every ten years. If y grows at 3.5%, it will double every twenty years, while if it grows at 14%, it will double in 5 years. Compound growth takes place more rapidly than simple growth. Just divide 70 by the rate of growth to get the number of years it takes for something to double.

7. A Ponzi Game

When interest promised on an investment is "too good to be true" it is usually *not* true. Suppose that you are offered two percent a month compounded on an investment that is to be redeemed in one year, but not before. The compounded annual rate of return on this investment is:

$$r_e = (1 + r_{12})^{12} - 1 = (1.02)^{12} - 1 = 26.8\%$$

Unless this investment scheme can manage to gain new investors, there are few, if any, investments that can *ex ante* yield 26.8%, so there is a high possibility of default—that this is a Ponzi Game. *Ex post*, there are many realized returns exceeding 27%, the problem is identifying them beforehand.

8. Interest rate parity

When two assets are default risk free, the interest rate differential on the two assets reflects the expected percentage currency rate change between them. Interest rate parity says:

$$\frac{F_{\$/£}}{S_{\$/£}} = \frac{(1 + r_{us})}{(1 + r_{uk})} \qquad (\text{A.}38)$$

Subtracting unity from each side of (A.38) and simplifying, we have:

$$\frac{F_{\$/£}}{S_{\$/£}} - 1 \equiv E(s)$$

70 法则（The rule of 70）：用 70 除以增长百分比即可以得到价值翻倍所需的时间。例如，如果某一资产价值以 7% 的年增长率增长，则需要 70/7 = 10 年的时间使资产价值翻倍。

$$= \frac{(1 + r_{us})}{(1 + r_{uk})} - 1 = \frac{(1 + r_{us})}{(1 + r_{uk})} - \frac{(1 + r_{uk})}{(1 + r_{uk})} = \left(\frac{r_{us} - r_{uk}}{1 + r_{uk}} \right) \quad (A.39)$$

Note that the expected percentage increase in the dollar price of the pound, indicated by $E(s)$, is indicated by:

$$E(s) = \frac{r_{us} - r_{uk}}{1 + r_{uk}} \cong r_{us} - r_{uk} \qquad (A.40)$$

Thus, the expected dollar depreciation—or pound appreciation—is equal the percentage difference in interest rates. If the interest rate on US Treasuries is two percent greater than on UK Treasuries, the dollar price of the pound is expected to rise by approximately 2%. That is, the dollar is expected to depreciation 2% or the pound to appreciate 2%. In the Fisher equation, this reflects typically a higher expected rate of inflation in the US compared to the UK.

9. Synergy

AT&T offered Deutsche Telecom $39 billion for its USA T-Mobile network. AT&T's due diligence estimated (approximately) costs of integration of $1 billion a year for two years, then synergies of $3 billion forever thereafter. Consequently, if AT&T's cost of borrowing is say 5%, the acquisition would add value to AT&T, about $11 billion, as shown in Table A.10.

Table A.10 The net present value of estimated synergies and integration costs

	year	year	forever	Total synergy
Borrowing cost	1	2	In perpetuity	
5%	$(1.00)	$(1.00)	$3.00	
			$60	
NPV	$(0.95)	$(0.91)	$51.83	$49.97

However, the ROI is only 8%, so that higher borrowing costs would not make the acquisition worthwhile, as shown in Table A.11.

Table A. 11 The internal rate of return on AT&T's offer to Deutsche Telecom

	$(39.00)	$(0.95)	$(0.91)	$51.83
IRR	8%			

The due diligence agreement with T-Mobile was that AT&T would pay between $3 billion and $6 billion in broadband spectrum should the deal fall through for any reason. Due to regulatory opposition by the US Justice Department, the FCC, and a suit by Sprint, AT&T has withdrawn its offer. It paid a penalty fee of 4 billion USD.

Conclusion

The payment of interest on securities reflects the fact that money today is worth more than money tomorrow. Put differently, putting aside money today will bring money plus interest tomorrow. This appendix reviews the mechanics of compound interest and uses it for discounting future cash flows; receipts and payments. The analysis applies to business planning, terminal values, Ricardian Equivalence, coupon bonds, credit risk, and the inter-temporal budget constraint. The power of saving in building wealth is amplified by compound interest. Saving in secure assets that pay compound interest is often a more sure way of building wealth than counting on asset appreciation. Indeed, growth models focus upon saving and investment along with technological change as the source of growth in income and the capital stock. In this context, saving is income that is not consumed.

Solutions to Problems

1.1 Yes, due to different jurisdictions having different regulations, tax rates, accounting procedures, forms of business organization, and bankruptcy laws.

1.2 The purpose of the SEC is to provide transparency to investors through timely disclosure of income statements, the balance sheet, and information material to the financial condition of the firm. The idea is to level the playing field to combat illegal insider trading and abuses. Documents can be falsified, but now under Sarbanes-Oxley of 2002 require the signature of the Chief Executive Officer (CEO) and Chief Financial Officer (CFO) attesting to their veracity to the best of their knowledge.

2.1 The cost of mining, refining, and minting metallic monies is a natural brake to the overproduction of metallic money. The mint profits—value as money less cost of production—are significantly less than with paper money. Robert Mundell put it succinctly, "You cannot print gold, and you cannot melt paper." If inflation takes place, the commodity value of the coin is greater than its face value as money, so it gets melted. Thus, growth in the hard money supply stops.

2.2 a. Cross rates determine the fixed parity of two monies fixed to gold. That is:

$$\frac{\$/G}{\pounds/G} = \$/\pounds = 2$$

b. Yes, because an arbitrage profit can be made.

c. Ignoring transaction costs, a "round trip" beginning and ending in pounds would involve the following steps:

1. Sell one pound for \$2.01 on the foreign exchange market.
2. Buy an ounce of gold from the Bank of the United States for \$2, profiting by 1 cent.
3. Sell an ounce of gold to the Bank of England for one pound.
4. Keep one cent profit in USD, or

5. Convert to ½ cent profit in pounds, to finish the round trip.

d. The money supply of England goes up by one pound, while the money supply in the United States falls by two dollars. In other words, the Bank of England buys one ounce of gold from the public, while the Bank of the United States sells one ounce of gold to the public.

e. Yes, the Bank of the United States could buy $2 worth of bonds from the public, while the Bank of England could sell one pound of bonds to the public. The monetary effects of the gold flows would be neutralized.

3.1 a. The net present value of and rate of return on the flow of payments and receipts in pounds is given by using the $= NPV(values : rate)$ less initial cost and $= IRR(values, guess)$ formulas in Excel:

Net present value and rate of return

Interest rate	10%
Initial investment	$-£100$
Year 1 income	£50
Year 2 income	£50
Year 3 income	£50
Net present value (NPV)	£24
Internal rate of return (IRR)	23.4%

Alternatively, the NPV and ROI can be calculated manually from the formulas:

$$NPV = -100 + \frac{50}{1.1} + \frac{50}{(1.1)^2} + \frac{50}{(1.1)^3}$$

and

$$100 = \frac{50}{1 + \delta} + \frac{50}{(1 + \delta)^2} + \frac{50}{(1 + \delta)^3}$$

b. If you were to sell this investment worth £24 at 1.76 dollars per pound, it would be worth £24.34 × 1.76 = $42.84

3.2 a. Setting the quantity supplied equal to the quantity demanded in the foreign exchange market and solving for S yields an equilibrium exchange rate of 20 pesos per dollar. That is:

$$90 - 2S = -10 + 3S \quad \text{yields} \quad 5S = 100 \quad \text{or} \quad S = \frac{100}{5} = 20$$

b. If the Central Bank maintained a fixed exchange rate of 15 pesos per dollar, there would be an excess demand for dollars equal to $25. That is:

$$Q_D - Q_S = 90 - 2(15) + 10 - 3(15) = 100 - 75 = 25$$

c. If the Central Bank had only $15 million left in foreign reserves, it could devalue to 20 to reach equilibrium without selling reserves, or partially devalue and sell some reserves. It could borrow additional reserves and sell them on the exchange market. To maintain its reserves for a rainy day, it could float the currency, letting supply and demand equilibrate at 20. The imposition of exchange controls would only create a parallel market, an implicitly floating exchange rate.

d. If the Central Bank instead wanted to add $10 million to its holdings of foreign reserves, it could depreciate the exchange rate to 22 pesos per dollar. Adding 10 to the demand curve, and solve for S by setting supply equal to demand. That is:

$$100 - 2S = -10 + 3S \quad \text{yields} \quad 5S = 110 \quad \text{or} \quad S = \frac{110}{5} = 22.$$

3.3   a. With a floating exchange rate, the equilibium rate is determined by the supply equals demand equilibrium. By inspect of Figure 3.2 the equilibrium exchange rate would be 1.2 pesos per dollar.

b. To maintain a one-to-one exchange rate the central bank must supply an additional 10 million USD to the foreign exchange market, just enough to satisfy total demand at that price. Essentially, the Central Bank adds horizontally 10 million USD to the supply curve, shifting total supply to the right by that amount.

c. The sale of dollars by the central bank to the foreign exchange market reduces the money supply held by commercial banks and the public. As the money market in Argentina becomes less liquid, interest rates in pesos rises and the rate of inflation falls. This reduces the demand for dollars and simultaneously increases its supply in the foreign exchange market. The graphic illustrates the flows of funds from foreign exchange market purchases and sales of foreign exchange.

3.4   a. The bid-ask spreads are indicated in the table below. Recall the rule that 1/bid in one quotation equals the ask in the other. Similarly, 1/ask in one quotation equals the bid in the other.

	European Quotations (£/$)		American Quotations ($/£)	
	Bid	Ask	Bid	Ask
Spot	0.56577086	0.56596299	1.7669	1.7675
Spread	0.00019212		0.0006	
Mid-point	0.56586692		1.7672	

b. The spreads are simply the difference between the ask and the bid.

c. The mid-point equals the sum of the bid and the ask divided by two.

d. In both cases, the bid-ask spread as a percent of the mid-point is 0.033592, or about 3%.

3.5 a. Recalling the rule that 1/bid in one quotation equals the ask in the other and 1/ask in one quotations equals the bid in the other, we have:

	European Quotations (£/$)		American Quotations ($/£)	
	Bid	Ask	Bid	Ask
Spot	0.5658	0.5660	1.7668	1.7675
Spread	0.0002		0.0007	
Mid-point	0.5659		1.7671	
Spread/Mid-point(%)	0.0004		0.0004	

b. The bid-ask spread is 0.0002 in pounds and 0.0007 in dollars.

c. The mid-points are 0.5659 pounds per dollar and 1.7671 dollars per pound respectively

d. The bid-ask spread is 0.04 percent in terms of each quotation.

3.6 Since the points quotation is lower than the offer, add 0.0214 to the one month spot outright bid and 0.0220 to the outright offer. Similarly, add the points of the two and three month divided by 10,000 to obtain the two and three month forward outright quotations.

	European Quotations (£/$)	
	Bid	Ask
Spot	1.7669	1.7675
Points	Bid	Ask
1 month	214	220
2 months	283	298
3 months	388	416
	American ($/£)	
	Bid	Ask
1 month	1.7883	1.7889
2 months	1.7952	1.7967
3 months	1.8057	1.8085

3.7 a. By inspection, the forward premium on the pound is 2%, while US Treasuries are 1% higher than UK Treasuries at point Z. Consequently, the gain on forward cover in selling the pound will more than offset the loss on investing in UK Treasuries.

b. Ignoring transactions costs, the steps taken in this riskless arbitrage opportunity are:

1. Sell US Treasuries (r_{us} rises)
2. Buy pounds spot (sell dollars spot) (S rises)
3. Buy US Treasuries (r_{uk} falls)

4. Sell pounds forward (buy dollars forward) (F falls)

The net gain for the individual arbitrageur would be 1%, a 2% gain on forward cover and a 1% loss on the interest rate differential. As a result of many arbitrageurs taking advantage of this profit opportunity $\left(\dfrac{F-S}{S}\right)$, the premium on the pound falls, and ($r_{us} - r_{uk}$), the interest rate difference in favor of US Treasuries, rises.

3.8   a. The absolute version of purchasing power parity predicts that the exchange rate will reflect the different costs of purchasing the same bundle of goods (the inverse of the absolute purchasing power of each currency in terms of goods). Consequently, the PPP rates are indicated in the table:

	Cost of Basket	Purchasing Power Parity Rates
U.S.	$60	1.666667 dollars per pound
England	£36	0.6 pounds per dollar
Mexico	N$540	9 pesos per dollar

b. No, because the market exchange rates do not accurately predict the true purchasing powers of different currencies. Those countries with relatively cheap labor-intensive goods such as haircuts, a non-traded good, will find that the equilibrium rate does not fully reflect the purchasing power of the currency. There is little arbitrage in non-traded goods such as haircuts.

c. Therefore it is not a surprise to find that the PPP prediction for the pound is fairly accurate, but the equilibrium rate of 11 persos per dollar "over-values" the dollar in terms of the purchasing power parity rate of 9 pesos per dollar.

d. Taking the current equilibrium rates as given, the purchasing power parity predictions are:

Initial equilibrium rates	Relative PPP	PPP forecast
0.566	1.5	0.849 pounds per dollar
11	1.5	16.5 pesos per dollar

Essentially, take the initial equilibrium rates as the base rates for the forecast, then multiply by 3/2, the expected inflation differential relative to the United States. While the absolute PPP forecast may be significantly off, the relative PPP is still the best forecast of the movement in future exchange rates. It is embodied in the nominal interest rate on risk free Treasuries, which do not exist in Mexico due to previous default. For this reason, the relative PPP forecast may be the most accurate.

e. Mexico and England are both net oil exporters, while the US is a net oil importer. A rise in the price of oil would appreciate the pound and the peso relative to the PPP forecast. It would cause a real appreciation of the pound and the peso. However, a rise in the price of wheat would be likely to cause a real appreciation of the dollar.

4.1 a. "I never hedge, since it reduces my bottom line!"

This CFO has reckoned the costs of hedging foreign exchange risk against the benefits, and concluded that the costs exceed the benefits. This is likely to be a firm that does not face significant losses due to being exposed to foreign exchange risks in operations and contracts. This firms has a low probability of bankruptcy costs. As a result, it does not perceive any benefits in lowered borrowing costs due to risks of financial distress from foreign exchange losses. The cost of the hedges clearly outweighs the benefits in lowered risk of financial distress. Put simply, the foreign exchange exposure of this firm may be minimal.

b. "I always hedge, since I cannot take the risk of exchange rate losses bankrupting my firm."

This firm is likely to have significant foreign exchange exposure, so that its value at risk from unanticipated changes in the exchange rate is high. Higher earnings in foreign exchange must be volatile and/or the exchange rate volatile. The high risk of financial distress from going unhedged would significantly increase its borrowing costs. Investing in the hedges provides the benefit of significantly lowering the chances of financial distress and bankruptcy costs. In this situation, the CFO chooses to hedge. It may even increase the net present value of the firm due to lowered borrowing costs. Put simply, the foreign exchange exposure of this firm is large.

4.2 a. It's yield to maturity, r, is solved for by:

$$\$80 = \frac{\$100}{1+r} \quad \text{or} \quad r = \frac{\$100}{\$80} - 1 = 0.25 = 25\%$$

b. Its risk premium, ρ, is approximately $25\% - 5\%$, or 20%. More precisely, it is solved by:

$$(1.05)(1+\rho) = 1.25 \quad \text{or} \quad \rho = \frac{1.25}{1.05} - 1 = 19.05\%$$

4.3 a. Your options expire today out of the money. You would never buy at £80 when the spot price is £50. Consequently, your total annual compensation is £12,000.

b. Zero percent since they are out of the money.

If today's share price is instead £100.

a. Your options are now in the money—profitable if exercised. Since you buy at £80 and sell at £100 you make £20 in profits on each share. Buying 1,000 shares at £80 and selling them at £100 earns you £20,000 today. Your total compensation is thus £32,000.

b. Consequently, the percent of your total compensation in the form of stock options is $\dfrac{20,000}{32,000} - 1 = 62.5\%$.

4.4 a. She made 2 cents per option upon exercise, but paid 1 cent for each one. Her profit per option was 1 penny. She thus made only $1 in net profits.

b.

1. The put was in the money—the buyer bought at $1.20 and sold at $1.25, making 5 cents per option.

2. Tomas lost 4.5 cents per option or $40.50 in total. His gain from the sale of the option of half a cent was outweighed by losses of 5 cents per option.

3. Yes, the writer or seller of the option is contractually obligated to honor the option if it is presented for exercise. Otherwise, he is in default. If it expires out of the money, the writer keeps the premium.

4.5 i. Martha might sell £100 thousand for delivery in 90 days. She would lock in the bid price of the pound now, $1.78, for settlement in 90 days. This would be a forward market hedge.

ii. She might purchase a put option to sell pounds sterling at a strike price of $1.78 and a cost per option of $.0028 per £, or $280 for a notional amount of £100,000. This would be an options hedge.

iii. She might borrow £100/1.02 = £98.04 thousand today for 3 months, sell the pounds spot, having no further pound exposure. With the proceeds from accounts receivable, she would pay the principal, £98.04, and interest, £1.96, in pounds, exactly equaling her expected receipts in pounds. This would be a money market hedge.

iv. She invoices British Baking Imports in US dollars to shift the exchange rate exposure to the importer. She thus invoices $178 thousand dollars deliverable in 90 days.

v. British Baking can similarly buy dollars forward, purchase an option to buy dollars at a strike price, or make today a money market loan in USD that matures in 90 days with principal and interest of $178 thousand.

4.6 a. The translation of these assets into US dollars on the consolidated balance sheet of the US parent firm would have a favorable effect on this portion of the balance sheet:

Assets	Original value	New Value
€ 200	$200	$240

b. Some alternative balance sheet hedges would be:

1. Acquire short term debt, an equal liability, of 200 euros.

2. Sell the 200 euros spot (i. e. buy dollars spot) , thus removing the exposure from the balance sheet.

3. Acquire accounts payable of 200 euros.

4.7 a. As a French company, I am exposed to operating exposure next year. If the dollar falls below 0.8 euros, I will lose, while if it rises above 0.8 euros, I will gain. My exposure equals $10 × 110 = $1,100.

b. Operating exposure can be hedged in a number of ways: some involve financing others involve operations. Firstly, I can borrow in dollars so that my revenues from the sale of widgets in dollars are offset by payments of interest and principal on a matching basis. If my comparative advantage is borrowing in euros, I could do so then swap the euro loan for a dollar loan. These would be a financial hedge. In terms of operations, I could move production from France to the United States, thereby acquiring a "natural hedge" involving payroll, rent and other expenses in US dollars. These are just two techniques for hedging my operating exposure. A risk-sharing currency contingency clause or invoicing in euros would also be techniques for managing exchange rate exposure. All these techniques of hedging involve some costs.

4.8 a. If the exchange rate unexpectedly changes to $0.25 per peso, "operating losses" due to not hedging would equal 25 cents per peso, or $2,500.

b. Since this is ongoing operating exposure, Tiny Tots could seek a loan in pesos and use the earnings from accounts receivables in pesos to service the loan. Any loss on the peso would be offset by an equal gain on its peso loan. To obtain the loan on favorable terms, Tiny Tots could borrow in USD, its currency of comparative advantage, then swap the USD loan for an Argentine peso loan. Indirect financing could also be done by back-to-back parallel loans whereby Tiny Tots makes a dollar loan to an Argentine subsidiary in the U.S., and Argentine headquarters makes a similar loan to Tiny Tots in pesos. Relocating production to Argentina would also give Tiny Tots a "natural hedge"— matching expenditures in pesos.

c. If Tiny Tots relocates production to Argentina and expects second quarter costs of production and distribution to be 5,000 pesos, the net exposure would only be 5,000 pesos. Only that amount would need to be hedge to be "perfectly" hedged.

d. Theoretically, profitability could go either way. The costs of the hedges might be offset by lowered borrowing costs. In this case the NPV of Tiny Tots would rise. The more likely case is that the cost of the hedges would reduce the NPV of the firm.

4.9 a. Headquarters gains because euro denominated assets are 400, while liabilities are 300. There is a net 100 long position in euros on the balance sheet.

b. The gains of $0.10 \times 100 = \$10$ would be added to the cumulative translation adjustment line in the balance sheet.

c. Some alternative ways of acquiring a perfect balance sheet hedge would be to pay off 100 euros of in accounts payable or debt in advance, sell the 100 euros in cash for dollars, or increase short term debt in euros by 100.

5.1 a. The weighted average cost of capital in euros would be, using a European marginal income tax rate of 45% :

$$WACC = 0.3[10(1 - 0.45)] + 0.7(15) = 12.15\% \text{ in euros}$$

If IBM is able to apply the higher tax as credits against other income, it would imply an effective marginal income tax rate of 35%. In this case, the WACC in euros would be:

$$WACC = 0.3[10(1 - 0.35)] + 0.7(15) = 12.45\% \text{ in euros}$$

b. In terms of USD, the weighted average cost of capital would be:

$$1.1245 \left(\frac{1.03}{1.02}\right) - 1 = 0.13552 = 13.552\% \text{ in USD}$$

using the US marginal income tax rate.

5.2 a. The profit maximizing level of sales is 100 since the marginal cost of the bundled product equals its marginal revenue at that level of output.

b. The firm will charge the final customer $7.00 per unit, found by the demand for that quantity of output (its average revenue).

c. To guarantee that the production unit provides exactly the optimum amount to the marketing division, the latter will pay the production unit a transfer price of $3.00. The production unit in turn maximizes its profits by setting marginal production cost equal to the fixed transfer price.

5.3 The WACC in pounds sterling is indicated below as 13.9% :

	U.S. & U.K. data (percent per annum)
U.S. inflation rate	3
U.K. inflation rate	2
U.S. Treasury	5
U.K. Treasury	4
$WACC_\$$	15
$WACC_\pounds$	13.9

which is solved for either by using PPP or IRP, that is:

$$WACC_\pounds = (1.15)\left(\frac{1.02}{1.03}\right) - 1 = 0.139 = 13.9\%$$

or

$$WACC_{£} = (1.15)\left(\frac{1.04}{1.03}\right) - 1 = 0.139 = 13.9\%$$

b. The NPV in USD differs only by rounding done by both methods:

Method A

Discount foreign currency flows to the present at the foreign currency discount rate, then convert the NPV in forex to home currency at the spot rate.

	Year		
	0	1	2
Free cash flows (£)	−100	60	70
Present value of cash flow (£)	−100	52.68	53.96
NPV (£)	6.64		
Spot exchange rate ($/£)	1.77		
NPV ($)	11.74		

Method B

Convert foreign currency cash flows to home currency, discount to the present at the home currency discount rate.

	Year		
	0	1	2
Free cash flows (£)	−100	60	70
Exchange rate forecast	1.77	1.787	1.8042
Free cash flows ($)	−177	107.22	126.29
Present value of cash flow ($)	−177	93.24	95.50
NPV ($)	11.73		

5.4 Your shipment of 100 computers worth $2,000 each amounts to $200,000 in export revenues. Here are some of the international means of payment and who bears the counterparty risk:

a. Cash in advance guarantees the exporter of payment, but does not guarantee the importer of shipment. The importer bears the counterparty risk.

b. An open account into which the importer pays upon delivery of the shipment puts the counterparty risk on the exporter. The exporter could ship coincidentally with the payment, the bank invoicing the importer, receiving the funds at the same time the exporter delivers the bill of lading to the bank.

c. A documentary letter of credit is a guaranteed means of payment for goods which, when confirmed, substitutes the bank's credit for that of the importer. The bank bears the counterparty risk. In return, it collects fees for issuing the letter of credit.

5.5 a. If you need Bahamian dollars today, you can sell (discount) the letter of credit today since it is confirmed and irrevocable. The L/C is a negotiable instrument.

b. The L/C is virtually riskless, so you might use the Bahamian Treasury rate of 6% per annum, representing nearly a half a percent per month (0.486755 percent per month). The discounted value of the L/C would therefore be worth 11,628,800 Bahamian dollars at a compound monthly rate of 0.49 percent and 11,618,932 at a simple monthly rate of 0.5 percent.

	1	2	3	4	5	6	7	8	9	10	11	12
	1,000,000	1,000,000	1,000,000	1,000,000	1,000,000	1,000,000	1,000,000	1,000,000	1,000,000	1,000,000	1,000,000	1,000,000
PV at 0.487%	995,156	990,336	985,538	980,764	976,014	971,286	966,581	961,899	957,239	952,603	947,988	943,396
Sum of PV	11,628,800											

	1	2	3	4	5	6	7	8	9	10	11	12
	1,000,000	1,000,000	1,000,000	1,000,000	1,000,000	1,000,000	1,000,000	1,000,000	1,000,000	1,000,000	1,000,000	1,000,000
PV at 0.5%	995,025	990,075	985,149	980,248	975,371	970,518	965,690	960,885	956,105	951,348	946,615	941,905
Sum of PV	11,618,932											

5.6 In the first case, repatriation of earnings gets the firm a tax credit of 12.5%, but 22.5% is added to make the effective corporate tax rate on Texas headquarters of 35%.

a. Thus we have $65 in net income:

Irish branch

Irish income	100 USD
Irish taxes paid	12.5 USD
US taxes	22.5 USD
Net income	65.00 USD

b. In the second case, the earnings are not repatriated but instead re-invested in Ireland. Consequently, the firm has $87.5 in net earnings, or:

Irish branch

Irish income	100 USD
Irish taxes paid	12.5 USD
US taxes	0
Net income	87.5 USD

5.7 a. The portion of foreign trade income exempt from taxes is 34%, meaning taxable income from the FSC in the Bahamas is $66. Applying a corporate income tax rate of 35% to taxable income yields taxes of $23.10, leaving $76.90 as net income under arm's length pricing.

Foreign Sales Corp. (arm's length pricing)

Foreign trade income	100 USD
Bahamian taxes paid	0
US taxes	23.1
Net income	76.9

c. In the second case of an FSC set up according to special administrative rules exempting 17/23 of foreign income taxation, the result would be:

Foreign Sales Corp. (special administrative rules)

Foreign trade income	100 USD
Bahamian taxes paid	0
US taxes	9.13
Net income	90.87

since only $26.08 is taxable at the 35% rate.

5.8 a. By inspection, the value of Firm A is $20 and of Firm B is $10.

b. If the value of the consolidated firm is $40, synergy is $10 since the separate firms only have a combined value of $30.

c. If Firm A offers cash of $15 a share to the owners of Firm B, they are offering a premium of 50%, that is, a premium of $5 per share.

d. It is likely that 2/3 of the shareholders will accept the premium, unless management of Firm B activate an extremely effective poison pill defense or the shareholders want to hold out for another bidder or an improvement in the initial bid.

e. Firm A would be worth $25 if it offers $15 in cash for Firm B: That is, $40— $15.

f. Using the formula $\alpha = 15/40$, and solving

$$n_w = \frac{\alpha n}{(1 - \alpha)} = \frac{\frac{15}{40}(10)}{\left(1 - \frac{15}{40}\right)} = 6 \text{ shares.}$$

g. If Firm A offered $10 in cash and the rest in shares, it would have to offer:

$$n_w = \frac{\alpha n}{(1 - \alpha)} = \frac{\frac{5}{30}(10)}{\left(1 - \frac{5}{30}\right)} = 2 \text{ shares.}$$

This is because after the $10 cash offer, Firm A would be worth $30 and the new shares would have to be 5/30th or 1/6th of the new firm's value.

5.9

a. Firm A's shares are worth $2.00 and Firm B's $1.00.

b. The value of synergies, net of integration costs, is $10 – $2 = $8.

c. A 40% premium.

d. Probably, unless the shareholders want to hold out for a better offer.

e. With the cash offer, the new value of Firm A will be $58 – $14 = $44. There are still only 20 shareholders, so the share price is now $2.20.

f. $n_w = \left[\,(14/58)\times 20\,\right]/(1-14/58)\,\right] = 6.36364$ shares. Then Firm A's share is worth: $\$58/26.36364 = \$2.20$. This is the same value as with the cash offer.

5.10 At a 10% cost of borrowing in euros, this investment would have a negative net present value. It should not be undertaken.

	Year					
	0	1	2	3	4	5
Free cash flows(€)	(€50.0)	€10.0	€10.5	€11.0	€11.6	€12.2
Present value (€)	(€50.0)	€9.1	€8.7	€8.3	€7.9	€7.5
NPV(€)	(€8.5)					
Spot exchange rate(£ / €)	0.71					
NPV(£)	− £6.00					

5.11 a. If fees are about 1% , Citybank would stand to earn annually about $10,00, hardly worth the money laundering.

b. Yes the cash deposit is over $10,000 so would have to be reported to the U.S. Treasury.

c. The transfer would also constitute money laundering and thus be in violation of anti-money laundering laws and conventions. The fees are certainly not worth the reputational risk.

5.12 a. The coefficient of risk aversion is 4 , since $A/2 = 2$, $A = 4$.

b. The optimal fraction of the complete portfolio held in the form of risky assets is given by: $z = \dfrac{E(r_P) - r_f}{A\sigma_P^2} = \dfrac{0.15 - 0.05}{4(0.1)} = \dfrac{0.1}{0.4} = 25\%$. Consequently, 75% is held in the risk-free asset.

c. The expected rate of return on the complete portfolio is given by:
$$E(r_c) = 0.05 + 0.25(0.15 - 0.05) = 0.075 = 7.5\%$$

d. The variance of the complete portfolio is:
$$\sigma_c^2 = z^2\sigma_P^2 = (0.25)^2 \times 0.1 = 0.00625$$

e. The level of utility of this investor is indicated by:
$$U = E(r_c) - 2\sigma_c^2 = 0.075 - 2(0.0065) = 0.0625$$

5.13 a. The expected rate of return on the complete portfolio is a weighted average of returns on the risky and the risk free assets:
$$E(r_c) = 0.5(0.20) + 0.5(0.05) = 0.125 = 12.5\%$$

b. The variance of the complete portfolio is:
$$(0.5)^2 0.4 = 0.1 = 10\%$$

c. The standard deviation or volatility of the complete portfolio is the square root of its variance, or:
$$\sqrt{0.10} = 0.3162 \text{ or about } 32\%$$

5.14 At a transfer price of q_r, the downstream retailer would maximize profits by charging p_r, selling q_r units. Profits would thus be the dashed rectangle above marginal revenue, rather than the solid rectangle. Profits to the upstream manufacturer would be the small dashed rectangle below marginal revenue.

5.15

a.

i. *XYZ, Inc. N.Y.* makes $0 profits.

ii. *XYZ, Europe, S.A.* makes $0 profits.

iii. *XYZ FSC, Nassau* makes $3 profits.

b. If the profits are repatriated, the tax paid is $1.

c. If the profits are not repatriated, the taxes are $0 because there are no income taxes in Nassau.

6.1 A Ponzi scheme is an investment that relies upon new debt paying interest, dividends, and redemptions from old debt. Usually there is no underlying asset, proving ultimately unsustainable.

a. It is unlikely that there is an underlying asset that bears 50% per annum, *ex ante*. Such high rates of return indicate high credit risk and likelihood of default.

b. Because the sellers of the investment are initially able to pay the first investors with money from new investors.

c. No, because past performance is not a good indicator of future performance, and additionally, they are unlikely to rise at this rate.

6.2 Insider trading involves trading on inside information on the potential future financial performance of a firm. As such, some investors benefit from unshared information at the expense of others. The SEC views insider

trading as a form of theft. Firms are required to disclose all information material to their financial health and performance. Insider trading is thus both illegal
and unethical. Its price discovery role is too late for the uninformed investor.

6.3 The doubling strategy is tempting since the investor can recover initial losses if the price of the asset moves in the right direction. However, there
is a great risk of increased leverage, particularly since the asset has already
moved out of the money. The likelihood that doubling up will work is increasingly remote.

6.4 On the one hand, the benefit of SOX and Dodd-Frank is to deline-
ate what is appropriate and what is inappropriate financial behavior. SOX also
increased penalties to meaningful ones, and prohibited some previously common practices, such as lending to CEOs. On the other hand, compliance with
SOX and Dodd-Frank is costly, prohibitively so for small firms. Regulators are
usually not vigilant and enjoy being "captured." On balance, these Acts probably have costs that outweigh their benefits.

6.5 a. Forgery and perjury are illegal. Stating a false issue date for
grants of shares or options for illicit gains is against the law.

b. Fraudulently taking money from a firm is unethical. The managers' are
supposed to be loyal to the owners, the shareholders.

c. The undetected back dater gains financially at the expense of the shareholders. If the fraud is detected, the back dater loses financially, but the
shareholders do not gain.

7.1 a.

1. $\dfrac{\text{Assets}}{\text{Equity}} = \dfrac{A}{E} = \dfrac{200}{10} = 20$

2. $\dfrac{\text{Liabilities}}{\text{Equity}} = \dfrac{D}{E} = \dfrac{190}{10} = 19$

3. $\dfrac{\text{Debt}}{\text{Debt + Equity}} = \dfrac{D}{A} = \dfrac{190}{200} = 0.95$

b. For a given level of debt, $\Delta A = -E$ implies

$$\frac{\Delta A}{A} = -\frac{E}{A} = -\frac{1}{A/E} = -\frac{1}{20} = -5\%$$

c. When debt is constant, we have:

$$\frac{\Delta E}{E} = \left(\frac{A}{E}\right)\frac{\Delta A}{A}$$

That is, the percentage change in equity equals the degree of financial leverage, a multiple of the percentage change in the value of assets.

7.2 Ricardian equivalence states that the present value of new taxes to
be levied in the future will exactly equal $1,000 per citizen. Therefore, if full

Ricardian equivalence held, consumers and investors know that the present value of their wealth is unchanged. Consequently, they will not change their expenditures. On the other hand, older generations know they will escape some of the new taxes, so if they do not have a strong bequest motive, they will increase their spending. In general, a lump sum check from the Treasury financed by a new bond issue will have a limited effect on spending because permanent income is unchanged.

索引　Index

Amsterdam, Bank of　阿姆斯特丹银行　25

Anti-corruption Agreement (OECD)　《反腐败协议》
　　(OECD)　181

Arbitrage　套利：
　　covered interest　抛补套利交易　79—81
　　forward price and cost of carry　远期合约价格和
　　　持仓成本　75
　　in gold　黄金套利　17
　　"law of one price"　一价定律　86
　　spot and future rates　即期和远期套利　78
　　triangular, and cross rates　三角套利和交叉套利
　　　84—85

American depositary receipts　美国存款凭证　170

Argentina currency board crisis　阿根廷货币危机
　　(2001)　28

"Arm's length" pricing rules　公平交易定价规则：
　　re-invoicing centers　再开票中心　138—139
　　transfer pricing　转移价格　171

Asia, silver standard　亚洲的银本位　17

Asset allocation　资产配置：
　　decision　资产配置决策　199
　　one domestic and one foreign asset　国内和国外
　　　资产的资产配置　198
　　and risk aversion　资产配置与风险厌恶　202

Aztec Café and international business planning　阿兹
　　特克咖啡馆与国际商业计划　194

Back-to-back (parallel) loans and diversification　背
　　对背(平行)贷款和分散化管理　141—142

Banco Santander Central Hispano (BSCH) of Madrid
　　西班牙国际银行(BSCH),马德里　5,188

Bank of China　中国银行　287

Bank of England　英格兰银行：
　　establishment/history　建立和历史　25—26
　　and gold windows　黄金窗口　17

Bank for International Settlements (BIS)　国际清算
　　银行：
　　and foreign exchange market　国际清算银行与外
　　　汇交易市场　42
　　history　历史　29

Bankruptcy and financial distress　破产和财务困境
　　191

Bankruptcy Code United States　美国破产法　117

Banks and banking history　银行与银行业历史
　　25—26

Banque de France and gold windows　法兰西银行和
　　黄金窗口　17

Barings Bank derivative scandals　巴林银行衍生工
　　具丑闻　247--251

Barro, Robert　罗伯特·巴罗　297

Bear Stearns　贝尔斯登　283

Bebchuk, Lucian　A. 卢西恩·贝查克　246

Belnick, Mark　马克·贝尔尼克　236

Bid-ask spread　买卖价差：
　　diagram　图示　44
　　foreign currency swaps　外汇互换　141
　　foreign exchange market　外汇市场　42
　　transaction costs　交易成本　81
　　covered interest arbitrage　抛补套利　79

Big Macs arbitraging　巨无霸汉堡套利　64

Bilbao Viscaya (of Barcelona)　比尔巴鄂比斯凯国
　　有银行(巴塞罗那)　5

Bills of exchange　汇票　23

Birk, Thomas H.　托马斯·伯克　227

Black, Fischer　费雪·布莱克　96

Black, Sir Conrad M.　康纳德·布莱克　236

Blacklisted countries, Offshore banking　离岸银行业务列入黑名单国家，190

Borelli, Charles（Carlo Ponzi）　查尔斯·博雷利（卡罗·庞齐）　224

Break-even point　收支平衡点　192

Bretton Woods Conference, New Hampshire（1944）　布雷顿森林会议，新罕布什尔州（1944）　24

Bretton Woods system（1944）　布雷顿森林体系（1944）　24

Bribery　贿赂　4

Budget deficits: convergence　一致性条款中的财政预算赤字　56

Business failure　企业经营失败　191

Business plans, international　国际商业计划：

  Azteca Café　阿兹特克咖啡馆　194—196

  bankruptcy, and financial distress　破产和财务困境　191

  break-even point, and profit-maximizing point　收支平衡点和利润最大化点　192—193

  financial and operating leverage　金融和经营杠杆　193—194

  forms of business organization　企业组织形式　190

  principal-agent problem　代理问题　190

Business reorganization　公司重组　192

Business Software Alliance, and Intellectual Property Rights　商业软件联盟知识产权　11

CAC 40 Index　券商公会40种股票指数　31

Call options（FOREX）　外汇看涨期权：

  Hedging　套期保值　131

  payoff from　看涨期权的收益　99—100

Capital asset pricing model（CAPM）　资本资产定价模型（CAPM）　206

Capital structure　资本结构：

  international　国际资本结构　169

  international financial management　国际金融管理　167—170

Cargill（Minnesota）　卡吉尔（明林苏达）14

Carry, cost of and forward arbitrage price　持仓成本和远期套利价格　75

Carty, Donald J.　唐纳德·卡迪　242

cash-in-advance and trade finance　预付现金和贸易融资　144

Cassell, Gustav　古斯塔夫·卡塞尔　109

Cayman Islands　开曼群岛　188

Ceiling price and fixed exchange rate system　价格上限和固定汇率制度　46

Central banks　中央银行：

  balance sheets　资产负债表　48

  BIS as bank of　国家清算银行　41

  foreign reserves holdings of　中央银行持有的外汇储备　47

  intervention in foreign exchange market　外汇市场的干预　45

  neutralization by　冲销　49

  purchase of dollars by　买进美元　45

  sale of dollars by　卖出美元　46

  Treasury, independence from central bank　中央银行独立于财政部　16

Charles I（King）　查尔斯一世（国王）　25

Chen, Jiulin　陈久霖　249, 251, 252

China　中国：

  history of monies　货币历史　17

  yuan　人民币　57—61

  China Aviation Oil Corporation（CAOC）　中航油　251—253

  CHIPS clearing system　纽约银行同业清算系统　61

  Zhou Dynasty（China）　中国周朝　17

Clearing House Interbank Payments System（CHIPS）　纽约银行同业清算系统　61

Coinsurance principle, mergers and acquisitions　并购和共同保险原则　187

Collars as hedges　领子期权　131—133, 153—154

Collections and trade finance　托收与贸易融资　144

Commodities　商品：

  cost of carry and forward arbitrage price　持仓成本和远期套利价格　75

  forwards and futures in　商品远期和商品期货　74—78

speculative positions (forward contracts) 远期合约的投机性头寸 74

Common Law 共同法体系 3

Compensation, undisclosed 秘密薪酬 245

Compound interest 复利 302

Convention Against Bribery of Foreign Public Officials in International Business (OECD) 《反对在国际商务活动中贿赂外国官员公约》（OECD） 4

Convention Against Corruption (UNCAC) 《联合国反腐败公约》(UNCAC) 4

Cook Islands, removal from NCCTs list (2005) 2005 年 FATF 将库克群岛从非合作国家和地区的名单中除去 189

Corporate governance failures 公司治理失灵：

    Adelphia 阿德菲亚 235

    Enron 安然 232—234

    Hollinger International 霍林格国际公司 236

    Tyco International Inc. (Bermuda) 泰科国际公司（百慕大） 235—236

    United Airlines 联合航空公司 232

    WorldCom 世界通讯公司 234—235

Corporate Taxes: a worldwide summary 《公司所得税：世界范围内的总结》 6

Corporations: defined 公司的定义 30

Correlation coefficient, asset allocation 相关系数，资产配置 198

Corruption 腐败 4—5, 12

Counterparty risk 交易对手风险 280

Covered interest arbitrage 抛补套利 79:

    differential 抛补套利差别 81

    example 抛补套利实例 82

    parity 抛补的利率平价 81

    transaction cost 交易成本 81

    uncovered interest arbitrage 非抛补套利 78

Credit ratings 信用评级 116

Credit default swaps 信用违约互换 277

Crockett, A. 克罗基特 29

Cross rates 交叉汇率：

    triangular arbitrage 三角套利 84—85

Crosslisting on foreign stock exchanges 在国外证券交易所交叉上市 170

Cumulative translation adjustment 累积转换调整 143

Currencies 货币：

    comparative advantage in currency markets 货币市场的比较优势 140

    features of international finance 国际金融的特点 1

    foreign currency options 外汇期权 95

    foreign currency swaps 外汇互换 140

    hard 硬币 13

    soft 软币 103

    strong and fast food 强势货币和快餐 41—42

Currency contingency clauses 通过货币或有条款分散风险 133

Currency invoicing 选择计价货币 133

Currency payments, leads and lags in 货币提前或延期支付 138

Davies, Glyn 格林·戴维斯 18

Decimalization (UK) 分割性(英国) 16

Default risk, and credit ratings 违约风险和信用评级：

    graph 图示 122

    premium 违约风险溢价 121

Derivative scandals 衍生工具丑闻：

    Barings Bank 巴林银行 247—251

    CAOC 中航油 251—253

    LTCM 长期资本管理公司 253

Diversification 分散化：

    operating exposure 经营风险 135

    accounting exposure 会计风险 142

    back-to-back (parallel) loans 背对背(平行)贷款 141—142

    currency contingency clauses, risk sharing by 通过货币或有条款分散风险 133

    currency invoicing, risk-shifting by 通过选择计价货币分散风险 133

    FASB52 142

    financing, diversifying 分散融资 139

    foreign currency swaps 外汇互换 141

    hedge accounting 对冲会计法 143

    leads and lags in currency payments 提前或延期支付 138

natural hedges 自然套期保值 139

　　of production, sourcing and sales 生产、原料供应与销售的国际分散化 137

　　re-invoicing centers 再开票中心 138—139

　　trade finance 贸易融资 144

Documentation in trade finance 跟单,贸易融资 145

Dodd-Frank Act 《多德—弗兰科法案》 295

Dollars 美元:

　　covered interest arbitrage 抛补套利 78

　　free-cash flows in 美元自由现金流 192

　　greenback 绿底美元 22, 26

　　purchase of by central bank 央行买进美元 45

　　sale of, by central bank 央行卖出美元 46

Dornbusch, Rudiger 鲁迪格·多恩布什 62

Double coincidence of wants and back-to-back loans 需求的双重巧合与背对背贷款 141—142

Dow Jones Industrial Average (DJIA) 道琼斯工业平均指数 30

Duncan, David D. 大卫·邓肯 233

Dynergy Inc. 戴纳基公司 234

"Earnest money" 保证金 277

EADS (Airbus consortium) 空中客车公司 243

Ebbers, Bernard J. 伯纳德·埃伯斯 234

Economic Stimulus Act 美国《经济刺激法案》 296

Ecuador, dollarization (2000) 厄瓜多尔,美元化 (2000) 15

EDGAR (Electronic Data Gathering and Retrieval) database EDGAR(电子数据收集、分析及检索)系统 8, 242

...ective rate of interest 有效利率 31

...ective trade weights, and RER 有效贸易权重, ...RER 指数 71

...nt investment frontier 有效投资前沿 199

...corporate governance failure 安然,公司治...失灵 232—234

... 欧元 16, 37

...t 欧洲交易所 31

...ge rate forecasting 汇率预测 87

...ge Rates 汇率:

...on Woods system 布雷顿森林体系 24

fixed see fixed exchange rate system 固定汇率 45—52

floating 浮动汇率,见"浮动汇率制度" 42—44

forecasting 汇率预测 87

long-run movement 汇率长期变动 61

manipulation 汇率操纵 58

and money 汇率与货币 16

pegged 盯住汇率 17, 24, 27, 32

Executive compensation, undisclosed 高管的秘密薪酬 245—247

Fannie Mae 房利美 268

FASB 52: accounting requirements 美国财务会计准则委员会52:

　　accounting rules 会计准则 2

　　and diversification 分散经营 137

Fast food 快餐:

　　Big Macs, arbitraging 巨无霸汉堡套利 64

　　strong currencies 强势货币 64

Fastow, Andrew 安德鲁·法斯托 232

Features of international finance 国际金融的特点:

　　accounting rules 会计准则 2

　　currencies 货币 1

　　institutional framework 制度框架 4

　　intellectual property rights 知识产权 11

　　language 语言 5

　　legal framework 法律框架 3

　　political risk 政治风险 10

　　regulatory framework 监管体系 7

　　stakeholders 利益相关者 3

　　taxation 税收 6

Federal Deposit Insurance Corporation 联邦存款保险公司 26

Federal Reserve System (FED) 联邦储备体系 26—27

Federal Savings and Loan Insurance Corporation 联邦存贷款保险公司 26

Fiat money 不兑现货币 16

Filings, corporate 公司文档:

　　EDGAR database EDGAR 系统 8, 242

Finance and international finance contrasted 金融学与国际金融学的比较 1

Financial abuses 金融丑闻:

AMR 242

backdating of options grants 期权授予的回溯 254

executive compensation, undisclosed 高管的秘密薪酬 245—247

insider trading 内幕交易 242—244

retention bonuses 留职奖金 241—242

tax schemes 税收机制 244—245

Financial Accounting Standards Board (FASB) 美国财务会计准则委员会(FASB):

and US GAAP 和美国通用会计准则体系 2; see also FASB 142

Financial Action Task Force (FATF) 金融特别行动组 189

Financial leverage 金融杠杆 202, 261—265

Financial Times 金融时报 87

Fisher equation 费雪方程 300

Fixed exchange rate system 固定汇率制度 45—53

ceiling price 价格上限 45

convergence issues 一致性问题 36

diagram 图表 46

floor price 价格下限 45

irrevocably fixed rates 不可避免的固定汇率制度 53

"monetary anchor" role of rate 固定汇率的"货币锚"作用 49

and money supply 固定汇率制度和货币供给 47—49

neutralization policy 冲销政策 49

purchase of dollars, by central bank 央行买进美元 45

sale of dollars, by central bank 央行卖出美元 46

Floating exchange rate system 浮动汇率制度 42—44:

diagram 图示 42

foreign exchange 外汇 42—44

floor price 价格下限 45

Footsie 100 Index 富士 100 指数 31

Forecasting, exchange rates 预测汇率 87

Foreclosure 丧失抵押品赎回权 275

Foreign Corrupt Practices Act (FCPA) 1977, United States 1977 年美国《反海外腐败法》 3, 4

Foreign currency swaps 货币互换 140

currency markets, comparative advantage 货币市场的比较优势 140—141

FOREX swap, interest savings from 货币互换交易节省的利息 141—142

foreign exchange 外汇 42—44

American and European quotations 美式标价法和欧式标价法 42—44

bid-ask spread 买卖价差 141

central bank intervention 央行干预 45

CHIPS clearing system 纽约银行同业清算系统 61

day trading in 冲销 43

free-cash flow 自由现金流 192

futures 期货 71, see futures contracts

history 外汇交易历史 16—17

IMF 国际货币基金组织 44—45

London FOREX market 伦敦外汇市场 24—25, see FOREX market

long-run movement of exchange rates 汇率长期变动 61

Foreign investor relief facility (FIEF) 外国投资者救助措施(FIEF) 27

Foreign sales corporations (FSCs) 外国销售公司 175

FOREX market 外汇市场:

American and European quotations 美式报价法和欧式报价法 42—44

call options, payoff from 看涨期权的收益曲线 99—100

and euro, launching of 欧元启动 54

foreign currency swaps, interest savings 货币互换交易节省的利息 141—142

history 历史 16—17

London, as leading center 伦敦,世界最大的外汇交易中心 24—25

option Greeks 外汇期权敏感系数 103

options valuation 期权定价 96

put options, profit from 看跌期权的

100—102

transactions costs　外汇市场交易成本　81—82

FOREX transactions exposure（hedging）　外汇交易风险（套期保值）：

accounts payable　应付账款　127, 131, 132, 133

accounts receivable　应收账款　123—127, 132

call option　看涨期权　131

forward market hedge　远期市场套期保值　130

forward market sale　远期市场出售　125—126

long position　多头头寸　124—125

money market hedge　货币市场套利　126—127, 130—131

remaining unhedged　不进行套期保值　128—129

short position　空头头寸　127, 132

Forms of business organization　商业组织形式　190

Forward contracts　远期合约：

arbitrage price and carry, cost of　套利价格和持有成本　75

commodities, futures in　商品期货　74

futures　期货　71

speculative positions　投机头寸　74

forward market hedges　125—126

Frankfurt Stock Exchange　法兰克福股票交易所　33

Freddie Mac　房地美　266

Free-cash flows　自由现金流：

in dollars　美元自由现金流　1

foreign exchange　外汇自由现金流　88

Friedman, Milton　米尔顿·弗里德曼　17, 60

Futures contracts　期货合约：

arbitrage determination　期货合约的套利决定机制　78—87

definition of futures　期货的定义　71

Forward contracts　期货与远期合约　71—72

initial margin　初始保证金　48

Boris　鲍里斯·费奥多　5

Agreement on Tariffs and Trade（GATT）　关税总协定（GATT）　175：

political risk　政治风险　10—11

General Electric　通用电气　176

Generally accepted accounting principles（GAAP）, United States　美国通用会计准则体系（GAAP）　2

Giddy, Ian　伊安·基蒂　114, 115

Gold　黄金：

arbitrage in　黄金套利　17

as hedge against inflation　黄金作为通货膨胀时期的保值手段　78

hedged forward position in　黄金期货对冲组合　77

long position in　持有黄金多头　75

gold points　黄金输送点　17

goldsmith bankers　金匠银行家　25

gold sovereign　金磅　19

gold standard　金本位制　17, 53, 104

gold windows　黄金窗口　17

Graham, Lindsey　林赛·格雷厄姆　58

Great Depression（1929—1937）, United States　美国大萧条（1929—1937）　8, 17

Greenback dollar　绿底美元　22, 26

Greenspan, Alan　艾伦·格林斯潘　254

Gresham's Law　格雷欣法则　23

Hamburg, Bank of　汉堡银行　25

harmonic index, defined　调和指数的定义　70

Hawkes, Tony　托尼·霍克斯　250

Hedge accounting　对冲会计法　143

Hedging　套期保值：

collars as hedges　领子期权套期保值　131—133

credit ratings　信用评级　116—119

currency contingency clauses, risk-sharing by　通过货币或有条款分散风险　133

currency invoicing, risk shifting　通过选择计价货币转换风险　133

definition　套期保值的定义　113

gold, and inflation　黄金和通货膨胀　78

natural hedges　自然套期保值　139

net worth of firm　公司净值　114

operating exposure　经营风险　135

"perfect" hedges　完全套期保值　113

Henry VII　亨利七世　19

Highly leveraged institutions（HLIs）　高杠杆交易机

构（HLIs） 29

Hollinger International, corporate governance failure
霍林格国际公司,公司治理失灵 236

Home equity　房屋权益 269

"Homestead Laws"　"家园法律" 192

Hunter, Duncan　邓肯·亨特 58

Hunter-Ryan China Currency Act　亨特-瑞安人民
币法案 60

Incentive pay　激励性报酬 191, 257

Independent Internal Evaluation unit（IMF）　内部独
立评估部门（IMF） 28

Indonesia, removal from NCCTs list（2005） 2005
年 FATF 将印度尼西亚从非合作国家和地区
的名单中去除 189

Inflation　通货膨胀:

functions of money　货币的职能 14

gold as hedge against　黄金作为通货膨胀时期的
保值手段 78

and taels, use of 白银在通货膨胀时期的使用
19

Treasury, independence of central bank from　中
央银行独立于财政部 16

ING（Dutch bank）　荷兰国际集团（荷兰银行）
247

Insider trading　内幕交易 242—244

Insolvency　破产:

technical/accounting　技术/会计 192

institutional framework　制度框架 4

features of international finance　国际金融的特点
1

intellectual property rights　知识产权 11

Interbank credit　银行间信贷 261

Internal rate of return（IRR）　内部回报率（IRR）
89, 121, 306, 314

Internal Revenue Act（1962）　《国内税收法》
（1962） 189

International financial management　国际金融管理:

American depositary receipts　美国存托凭证
170

break-even point　均衡点 192

capital structure　资本结构 167

crosslisting on foreign stock exchanges　在国外证
券交易所交叉上市 170

financial and operating leverage　财务和经营杠
杆 193—194

foreign sales corporation　外国销售公司 175

liquidity, and market integration　流动性和市场
一体化 171

Mergers and acquisitions　并购 182

offshore banking　离岸银行 187—190

optimal investment analysis　最优投资分析 196

taxation　税收 175

transfer pricing　转移价格 171

working capital management　营运资本管理
178

International Financial Statistics, publication　《国际
金融统计》,出版物 70, 71

International account standards（IAS）　国际会计准
则（IAS） 2

International Monetary Fund（IMF）　国际货币基金
组织:

corruption　腐败 4—5

establishment（1944）　建立（1944 年） 27

Magnification effect of leverage　杠杆的巨大作用
264

Monetary institutions　货币机构 29

"Moral hazard"　"道德风险" 27

Real effective exchange rates　真实有效汇率
70—71

International monetary institutions　国际货币机构
29

Intervention points in fixed exchange rate system　固
定汇率制度下的干预点 46, 47

International taxation　国际税收 175

Investment analysis　投资分析:

optimal asset allocation　最优资产配置 203

financial leverage　财务杠杆 202

market risk premium　市场风险溢价 205

market and unique risk　市场和单一 风险
196—197

minimum risk portfolio　最低风险组合
199

portfolio diversification　投资组合分散化

197—198

portfolio expected return and risk 组合的预期收益和风险 200—201

risk aversion and asset allocation 风险厌恶和资产配置 202

separation property 分离性质 205

utility maximization 效用最大化 202—205

Japan: FOREX transactions 日本外汇交易市场 25:

and USA 与美国 25

Jiaozi(paper money) 交子 19

Joint ventures and acquisition alternatives 合资,收购之外的办法 187

Jonathan's Coffee House (London Stock Exchange) 乔纳森咖啡馆(伦敦证券交易所) 31

Keynes, John Maynard 约翰·梅纳德·凯恩斯 61

Kindleberger, Charles 查尔斯·金德尔伯格 226

Kozlowski, Dennis 丹尼斯·克斯洛维斯基 235

Language 语言 5

Large and complex financial institutions (LCFIs) 大型综合金融机构 29

Latin America 拉丁美洲:

Peso 比索 15

Law of one price 一价定律 86

Lay, Kenneth 肯尼思·莱 233

leads and lags in currency payments 提前或延期支付货币 138

Leeson, Nick 尼克·里森 247—251

legal framework 法律框架 3—4

MATIF (futures exchange) Le MATIF(期货交易所) 31

ers of credit and bills of exchange 信用证与汇票:

finance 贸易融资 144

Brothers 雷曼兄弟 283

ge, financial and capital structure 财务杠杆资本结构 167

ged financial institutions 杠杆融资的金融机构 281

ged households 杠杆融资的家庭 267

Licensing agreements 专利使用权转让协议 187

Limited partnerships 有限合伙制企业 190

Lines-of-credit, and IMF 信贷额度与国际货币基金组织 27

Liquidity and market integration 流动性与市场一体化 171

Loan to value ratio 贷款价值比率 276

London, as FOREX center 伦敦,世界最为重要的外汇交易中心 24—25

London Stock Exchange 伦敦证券交易所 31

Long-run exchange rate movements 长期汇率波动 61

absolute purchasing power parity 绝对购买力平价 62

one price, strict law of 一价定律 65

relative purchasing power parity 相对购买力平价 65

Long Term Capital Management (LTCM) 长期资本管理公司(LTCM) 29

Lydian coinage 利迪亚货币 18

Macro-economic impact of the financial crisis 金融危机的宏观经济影响 288

Maastricht Treaty (1992) 《马斯特里赫特条约》(1992年) 22

Managed float and central bank intervention 有管理的浮动与央行干预 45

Marginal efficiency of investment (MEI) 边际投资效率 171

"Mark to model" 参照模型定价 289

Market risk 市场风险:

optimal investment analysis 最优投资分析 196

premium 市场溢价 205

Markowitz, Harry 哈里·马科维茨 167

Markowitz-Sharpe risk aversion model 马科维茨-夏普风险厌恶模型 209

Mell, Lucy 露西·梅尔 224

Mergers and acquisitions 并购:

international 国际并购 180

alternatives to acquisition 收购之外的办法 187

synergy 协同效应 184—187

的收益 100—102

intrinsic and time value 内在价值和时间价值 97

valuation 价值 96—98

Options grants, backdating 期权授予的回溯 254

OECD (Organization for Economic Cooperation and Development) 经济合作和发展组织:

Anticorruption Agreement 《反腐败协议》 181

Convention Against Bribery of Foreign Public Officials in International Business 《反对在国际商务活动中贿赂外国官员公约》 4

Ownership, and agency law 所有权,代理法 190

Paper money 纸币 16

Parallel (back-to-back) loans 平行(背对背)贷款 141—142

Paris Bourse 巴黎证券交易所 31

Parmalat pyramid 帕拉马特,金字塔计划 225—227

Paterson, William 威廉·派特森 26

People's Bank of China 中国人民银行 49

Perle, Richard N. 理查德·波尔 236

Perpetuities 年金 306

Philippines, removal from NCCTs list (2005) 2005年 FATF 将菲律宾从非合作国家和地区的名单中除去 189

Pieces of eight 八片币的定义 21

Points quotations 点数报价法 72—74

Political risk 政治风险 10—11

Ponzi, Carlo 卡罗·庞齐 221—227

Ponzi finance 庞齐融资 225, 226

Ponzi Pyramid 庞齐金字塔 221

Ponzi schemes 庞齐骗局 221

Portfolio diversification, optimal investment analysis 分散投资,最优投资分析 196

Portfolio expected return and risk 组合的预期收益风险 200—202

Principal-agent problem 代理问题:

business plans 商业计划 133—134

corporate governance failures 公司治理失灵 235—236

profit-maximizing point 利润最大化点 192—193

Purchasing Power Parity (PPP) 购买力平价:

long-run exchange rate movement 长期汇率走势 61

theory 理论 61

Purchasers manufacturing index 制造业购买指数 290

Purchases "on margin" 购买保证金 202

Put options (FOREX) 外汇看跌期权:

at-the-money 平值期权 102

profit from 外汇看跌期权的利润 100—102

Pyramids 金字塔:

Parmalat 帕拉马特 225—227

Ponzi schemes 庞齐骗局 221

Qing Dynasty (China) 中国清朝 22

Quasi-coins 准货币 18

Radler, F. David 大卫·雷德勒 236

Railton, Tony 托尼·雷尔顿 249

Raines, Franklin D. 弗兰克林·雷尼斯 268

Random investing, and foreign exchange 随机投资和外汇 89—91

Real effective exchange rate index (RER) 真实有效汇率指数 70—71

Real exchange and fictitious exchange 真实交易,虚拟交易 23

Real interest rate 真实利率 300

Regulatory framework 管理框架 7

Re-invoicing centers 再开票中心 138—139

Relative purchasing power parity 相对购买力平价 61, 65

Retention bonuses 留职奖金 241—242

Ricardian Equivalence 李嘉图等价 310

Rigas, John 约翰·里加斯 235

Risk aversion, and asset allocation 风险厌恶和资产分配 202

Reward-risk ratio 回报—风险比率 199

Risk-sharing by currency contingency clauses 通过货币或有条款分散风险 133

Risk-shifting by currency invoicing 通过选择计价货币转移风险 133

Rittenhouse, Charles 查尔斯·利特豪斯 224

Romans, metal monies made by 罗马,制造金属货币 19

Rule of 70 70 法则 313

的收益 100—102

intrinsic and time value 内在价值和时间价值 97

valuation 价值 96—98

Options grants, backdating 期权授予的回溯 254

OECD (Organization for Economic Cooperation and Development) 经济合作和发展组织:

Anticorruption Agreement 《反腐败协议》 181

Convention Against Bribery of Foreign Public Officials in International Business 《反对在国际商务活动中贿赂外国官员公约》 4

Ownership, and agency law 所有权,代理法 190

Paper money 纸币 16

Parallel (back-to-back) loans 平行(背对背)贷款 141—142

Paris Bourse 巴黎证券交易所 31

Parmalat pyramid 帕拉马特,金字塔计划 225—227

Paterson, William 威廉·派特森 26

People's Bank of China 中国人民银行 49

Perle, Richard N. 理查德·波尔 236

Perpetuities 年金 306

Philippines, removal from NCCTs list (2005) 2005年 FATF 将菲律宾从非合作国家和地区的名单中除去 189

Pieces of eight 八片币的定义 21

Points quotations 点数报价法 72—74

Political risk 政治风险 10—11

Ponzi, Carlo 卡罗·庞齐 221—227

Ponzi finance 庞齐融资 225, 226

Ponzi Pyramid 庞齐金字塔 221

Ponzi schemes 庞齐骗局 221

Portfolio diversification, optimal investment analysis 分散投资,最优投资分析 196

expected return and risk 组合的预期收益风险 200—202

agent problem 代理问题:

business plans 商业计划 133—134

corporate governance failures 公司治理失灵 —236

profit maximizing point 利润最大化点 192—193

Purchasing Power Parity (PPP) 购买力平价:

long-run exchange rate movement 长期汇率走势 61

theory 理论 61

Purchasers manufacturing index 制造业购买指数 290

Purchases "on margin" 购买保证金 202

Put options (FOREX) 外汇看跌期权:

at-the-money 平值期权 102

profit from 外汇看跌期权的利润 100—102

Pyramids 金字塔:

Parmalat 帕拉马特 225—227

Ponzi schemes 庞齐骗局 221

Qing Dynasty (China) 中国清朝 22

Quasi-coins 准货币 18

Radler, F. David 大卫·雷德勒 236

Railton, Tony 托尼·雷尔顿 249

Raines, Franklin D. 弗兰克林·雷尼斯 268

Random investing, and foreign exchange 随机投资和外汇 89—91

Real effective exchange rate index (RER) 真实有效汇率指数 70—71

Real exchange and fictitious exchange 真实交易,虚拟交易 23

Real interest rate 真实利率 300

Regulatory framework 管理框架 7

Re-invoicing centers 再开票中心 138—139

Relative purchasing power parity 相对购买力平价 61, 65

Retention bonuses 留职奖金 241—242

Ricardian Equivalence 李嘉图等价 310

Rigas, John 约翰·里加斯 235

Risk aversion, and asset allocation 风险厌恶和资产分配 202

Reward-risk ratio 回报—风险比率 199

Risk-sharing by currency contingency clauses 通过货币或有条款分散风险 133

Risk-shifting by currency invoicing 通过选择计价货币转移风险 133

Rittenhouse, Charles 查尔斯·利特豪斯 224

Romans, metal monies made by 罗马,制造金属货币 19

Rule of 70 70 法则 313

Ryan, Tim　蒂姆·瑞安　58

Sarbanes-Oxley Act, US (2002)　《萨班斯-奥克斯利法案》　237

analyst conflicts of interest　分析师的利益冲突　239

auditor independence　审计独立性　238

commission resources and authority　SEC 的资源和权限　239

corporate and criminal fraud accountability　公司和刑事欺诈责任　239—240

corporate fraud and accountability　公司和刑事欺诈责任　240

corporate responsibility　公司的责任　238

corporate tax returns　公司纳税申报表　240

enhanced financial disclosure　强化财务信息的披露　239

public company accounting oversight board　上市公司会计监察委员会　238

studies and reports　研究及报告　239

white-collar crime penalty enhancements　加重白领犯罪处罚　240

Scams and swindles 欺诈行为　221—260

Scholes, Myron　迈伦·斯科尔斯　253

Schumer, Charles　查尔斯·舒默　58

Schwartz, Mark　马克·施瓦茨　235

Securities Exchange Act (1934) (USA)　美国证券交易法 (1934)　243

Securities and Exchange Commission (SEC), United States　美国证券和交易委员会　7, 242, 243

Securities and Investments Board (UK)　英国证券和投资委员会　26

Securitization　证券化　265

Mortgage backed assets (MBAs)　住房抵押贷款资产　265

Collateralized debt obligations (CDOs)　债务抵押债券　265

Security Exchange Company and Ponzi schemes　证券交易公司,庞氏骗局　221

Seigniorage　铸币税　15:

paper money　纸币　16

Shanghai Stock Exchange (SSE)　上海证券交易所　31

Sharpe, William　威廉·夏普　206

Sharpe "reward to risk" ratio　夏普的回报风险比率　199

Shilling (UK)　英国先令　16

Silver penny　银质便士　19

Silver Purchase Act (1934), United States　美国《购银法案》　17

Silver standard (Asian countries)　银本位制(亚洲国家)　17

SIMEX (Singapore International Monetary Exchange)　新加坡国际货币交易所　247, 248, 249, 251

Smith, Adam　亚当·斯密　29, 231

Society for Worldwide Interbank Financial Telecommunications (SWIFT) clearing system　纽约清算所银行同业支付系统　60

Sole proprietorship　独资企业　190

Song dynasty (China)　中国宋朝　19

South East Asia crisis (1990s)　20 世纪 90 年代东南亚金融危机　24

Southwest Airlines　美国西南航空　137

Sovereign debt　主权债务　310

Speculative motive, working capital management　投机动机,营运资本管理　179

Speculative positions in forward contracts　远期合约的投机性头寸　74—75

Spot rates　即期价格　88

Stakeholders　利益相关者　3

Standard & Poor's, credit rating　标准普尔,信用评级　116

S&P 500 Index　标普 500 指数　30

Stand-by-loans and IMF　备用贷款与国际货币金组织　27

State Administration of Foreign Exchange (SAF), China　中国国家外汇管理总局(SAFE)

State Asset Supervision and Administration Co sion (SASAC), China　中国国有资产理委员会(SASAC)　252

Steenbeek, Onno W.　奥诺·斯丁比克　24

Sterilization policy　平衡政策　52

Sterling silver standard　"标准纯银"本位

Stock Exchange Automated Quotations (SEA tem　股票市场自动报价系统(SEAQ)

Stock exchanges　股票交易所:

　examples　实例　30—32

　foreign crosslisting　在外国证券交易所交叉上市
　　170

　"Open-outcry" trading　"公开喊价"交易　250

Stock market crash（1929）　股灾（1929）　8

Strategic default　策略违约　274

Structural adjustment loans（SALs）　结构调整贷款
　　（SALs）　28

Sullivan, Scott　斯科特·萨利芬　235

Sweden, Bank of　瑞典银行　18

SWIFT clearing system and CHIPS　SWIFT 清算系
　　统与 CHIPS 清算系统　61

Synergy　协同作用　182

Tabasso, Gianfranco　吉恩弗朗克·塔巴索　225

Taels（silver ingots）　银两（银锭）　19

Tanzi, Calisto　卡里斯托·坦兹　225

Taxation　税收:

　international operations　跨国经营　175—178

　international finance　国际金融　6—7

　foreign sales corporations　国际销售公司　175

　international　国际税收　175

　US, of foreign-source income　国外收入　175

Tax avoidance and transfer pricing　规避税收和转
　　移定价　174

Tax Reform Act（1984）　《税收改革法》　189

Tax schemes, abusive　滥用的税收机制　244—
　　245

Taylor, Francesca　弗朗西斯卡·泰勒　71

emporary employment　临时职业　180

rminal values　终值　308

ory of optimum currency areas　最优货币区理论
　　111

value of money　货币的时间价值　300

Stock Exchange　东京股票交易所　31

Fausto　唐纳·浮士多　226

f London, banking activities　伦敦塔, 银行
活动　25

ions motive, working capital management
易动机, 营运资本管理　179

pricing　转移价格:

external sales or purchases　外部买卖　172

imperfectly competitive market for the intermediate
　　good　中间产品的不完全竞争市场　172—
　　173

　optimal　最优转移价格　171—172

　and tax avoidance　规避税收　174

Translation exposure　转换风险　143

Treasury, independence from central bank　财政部,
　　独立于中央银行　16

Treasury Bills（T-Bills）　国库券　79

Triangular arbitrage equilibrium　三角套利均衡
　　84—85

Troubled Asset Relief Program（TARP）　不良资产
　　救助计划（TARP）　290

Tyco International Inc.（Bermuda）　泰科国际公司
　　（百慕大）　235

Unique risk　个别风险　196—197

United Airlines Corporation（UAL）　美国联合航空
　　公司　232

United Nations, Convention Against Corruption（UN-
　　CAC）　《联合国反腐败公约》　4

United States　美国:

　Bankruptcy Code　破产法　117

　capital gains tax　资本利得税　5

　CHIPS clearing system　清算系统　61

　Civil War（1861—1865）　美国内战（1861—
　　1865）　22

　Constitution　美国宪法　56

　Edge Act　埃奇法案银行　188

　FCPA 1977　1977 年《反海外腐败法》　3, 4

　foreign sales corporation　国外销售公司　175

　GAAP　美国通用会计准则体系　2

　Great Depression（1929—1933）　美国大萧条
　　（1929—1933）　8, 17

　SEC　美国证券交易委员会　7, 242

Utility maximization　效用最大化: 202—203

　graph　图形　203—204

Vault cash（cash on hand）　库存现金（现有现金）
　　49

Volcker rule　沃克尔法则　292

Wall Street Journal　《华尔街日报》　87

Wampum money　贝壳串珠作为货币　22

Washington Post　《华盛顿邮报》　233

Watson, Chuek 查克·沃森 234

Weighted average cost of capital（WACC） 资本的加权平均成本 167

Wells letter 威尔斯信函 246

William the Conqueror 征服者威廉 19

Working capital management 营运资本管理 178

World Bank and IMF 世界银行和国际货币基金组织 27—28

WorldCom 世界通讯公司 224，226，227，234—235

World Trade Organization（WTO）and GATT 世界贸易组织与关贸总协定 175

Wright, Kirk S. 科克·赖特 227

Yuan, and China 中国与人民币 57—61

Zero premium collar 零期权费领子期权 131—132

教师反馈及教辅申请表

  北京大学出版社以"教材优先、学术为本、创建一流"为目标,主要为广大高等院校师生服务。为更有针对性地为广大教师服务,提升教学质量,在您确认将本书作为指定教材后,请您填好以下表格并经系主任签字盖章后寄回,我们将免费向您提供相应教辅资料。

书号/书名/作者			
您的姓名			
校/院/系			
您所讲授的课程名称			
每学期学生人数	_____ 人	_____ 年级	学时	
您准备何时用此书授课			
您的联系地址			
邮政编码		联系电话 (必填)	
E-mail(必填)		QQ	
您对本书的建议:			系主任签字 盖章

我们的联系方式:

北京大学出版社经济与管理图书事业部

北京市海淀区成府路 205 号,100871

联系人: 徐 冰

电 话: 010-62767312 / 62757146

传 真: 010-62556201

邮 件: em@pup.cn   xubingjn@yahoo.com.cn

网 址: http://www.pup.cn

微 博: 北大出版社经管图书,http://weibo.com/pupem

acquisition by cash 现金收购 182—183

coinsurance principle 共同保险原则 187

acquisition by stock 股票收购 183—184

acquisition by stock and cash 股票和现金收购 184

Meriwether, John 约翰·梅里韦瑟 253

Merton, Robert 罗伯特·默顿 253

Mill, John Stuart 约翰·斯图尔特·穆勒 53

Miller, Merton 默顿·米勒 209

Minimum risk portfolio 最小风险组合 198—189

Mint profits 铸币利润 15

Monetary policy, expansionary 扩张性货币政策 49

Money 货币：

and exchange rates 与汇率 16—17

functions in economy 经济功能 14—15

prerequisites of good money 良币的先决条件 15—16

history 历史 17—23

medium of exchange 交换媒介 14

Money-changers 货币兑换者 23

Money market hedges 货币市场套期保值 126—127, 130—131

Money supply and fixed exchange rate system 货币供给与固定汇率制度 47—49

Monetary history 货币史 17—23

Moral hazard and IMF lending 道德风险与国际货币基金组织贷款 27

Mortgage leverage in China 中国的住房抵押贷款杠杆率 266

Multilateral Investment Guarantee Agency (MIGA) 多边投资担保代理公司 11

Mundell, Robert A. 罗伯特·蒙代尔 53

Mussolini, Benito 贝尼托·墨索里尼 225

Myanmar, as blacklisted country 缅甸,被列入黑名单国家 190

Napoleonic Law 拿破仑法律体系 3

NASDAQ (National Association of Securities Dealers Automated Quotations) 纳斯达克(全国证券商协会自动报价系统) 31

National Banking Act (1863), United States 美国《国家银行法》(1863年) 26

Nauru, as blacklisted country 瑙鲁,被列入黑名单国家 190

Net present value (NPV) 净现值 135, 157, 183, 195

Neutralization policy 冲销政策 49

New York Stock Exchange (NYSE) 纽约证券交易所(NYSE) 30, 31

Nigeria, as blacklisted country 尼日利亚,被列入黑名单国家 190

Nikkei futures 日经指数期货 248

Nikkei Index 日经指数 248, 250, 253

Nixon, Richard 理查德·尼克松 24

Non-Cooperative Countries and Territories (NCCTs) 不合作国家和恐怖分子 189

Non-deliverable futures (NDFs) 非现金交割远期外汇交易(NDFs) 24

Offshore banking 离岸银行 187—190:

blacklisted countries 列入黑名单国家 189—190

international financial centers 国际金融中心 132

special regimes 特殊制度 189

offshore financial centers (OFCs) 离岸金融中心 189

One price law of 一价定律：

arbitrage determination 套利决定机制 78

foreign exchange history 外汇历史 16—17

long-run exchange rate movements 长期汇率波动 61

Open accounts and trade finance 赊销与贸易融资 144

"Open-outcry" trading "公开喊价"交易 250

Operating exposure 经营风险 135

Operating leverage 经营杠杆 193—194

Opportunity cost of intermediate input, and transfer pricing 中间产品的机会成本与转移定价 172—173

Options, foreign currency 外汇期权 95—10

FOREX call options, payoff from 外汇看涨的收益 99—100

FOREX option Greeks 外汇期权敏感系数

FOREX put options, profit from 外汇看跌